Communication Complexity

Communication complexity is the mathematical study of scenarios where several parties need to communicate to achieve a common goal, a situation that naturally appears during computation. This introduction presents the most recent developments in an accessible form, providing the language to unify several disjointed research subareas. Written as a guide for a graduate course on communication complexity, it will interest a broad audience in computer science, from advanced undergraduates to researchers in areas ranging from theory to algorithm design to distributed computing.

Part I presents basic theory in a clear and illustrative way, offering beginners an entry into the field. Part II describes applications, including circuit complexity, proof complexity, streaming algorithms, extension complexity of polytopes, and distributed computing. Proofs throughout the text use ideas from a wide range of mathematics, including geometry, algebra, and probability. Each chapter contains numerous examples, figures, and exercises to aid understanding.

ANUP RAO is an associate professor at the School of Computer Science, University of Washington. He received his PhD in Computer Science from the University of Texas at Austin and was a researcher at the Institute for Advanced Study, Princeton. His research interests are primarily in theoretical computer science.

AMIR YEHUDAYOFF is Associate Professor of Mathematics at Technion – Israel Institute of Technology. He is interested in mathematical questions that are motivated by theoretical computer science and machine learning. He was a member of the Institute for Advanced Study in Princeton and served as the secretary of the Israel Mathematical Union. He has won several prizes, including the Cooper Prize and the Krill Prize for excellence in scientific research, and the Kurt Mahler Prize for excellence in mathematics.

Communication Complexity and Applications

Anup Rao
University of Washington

Amir Yehudayoff
Technion – Israel Institute of Technology

CAMBRIDGE
UNIVERSITY PRESS

CAMBRIDGE
UNIVERSITY PRESS

University Printing House, Cambridge CB2 8BS, United Kingdom

One Liberty Plaza, 20th Floor, New York, NY 10006, USA

477 Williamstown Road, Port Melbourne, VIC 3207, Australia

314–321, 3rd Floor, Plot 3, Splendor Forum, Jasola District Centre,
New Delhi – 110025, India

79 Anson Road, #06–04/06, Singapore 079906

Cambridge University Press is part of the University of Cambridge.

It furthers the University's mission by disseminating knowledge in the pursuit of
education, learning, and research at the highest international levels of excellence.

www.cambridge.org
Information on this title: www.cambridge.org/9781108497985
DOI: 10.1017/9781108671644

First published 2020

Printed in the United Kingdom by TJ International Ltd., Padstow Cornwall

A catalogue record for this publication is available from the British Library.

Library of Congress Cataloging-in-Publication Data
Names: Rao, Anup, 1980– author. | Yehudayoff, Amir, author.
Title: Communication complexity and applications / Anup Rao, Amir Yehudayoff.
Description: Cambridge ; New York, NY : Cambridge University Press, 2020. |
Includes bibliographical references and index.
Identifiers: LCCN 2019038156 (print) | LCCN 2019038157 (ebook) |
ISBN 9781108497985 (hardback) | ISBN 9781108671644 (epub)
Subjects: LCSH: Computational complexity.
Classification: LCC QA267.7 .R37 2020 (print) | LCC QA267.7 (ebook) |
DDC 511.3/52–dc23
LC record available at https://lccn.loc.gov/2019038156
LC ebook record available at https://lccn.loc.gov/2019038157

ISBN 978-1-108-49798-5 Hardback

Dedicated to our families.

Contents

Preface

COMMUNICATION IS AN ESSENTIAL part of our lives and plays a central role in our technology. Communication complexity is a mathematical theory that addresses a basic question:

> If two or more parties want to compute something about the information they jointly possess, how long does their conversation need to be?

It provides a systematic framework for measuring, discussing, and understanding communication.

The fundamental nature of communication complexity leads to many deep connections with the study of *computation* in general. This is not surprising – it is hard to imagine a computing machine that does not include communicating components. Moreover, the costs associated with communication are often the most significant costs involved in carrying out the computation. For example, in the human brain, most of the mass consists of *white matter* rather than *gray matter*. It is the white matter that facilitates communication between different regions of the brain.

In the years following the basic definitions by Yao,[1] communication complexity has become a standard tool for identifying the limitations of computation. The theory is general enough that it captures something important about many computational processes, yet simple and elegant enough that beautiful ideas from a wide range of mathematical disciplines can be used to understand it. In this book, we guide the reader through the theory along a path that includes many exquisite highlights of mathematics – including from geometry, probability theory, matrix analysis, algebra, and combinatorics. We will apply the theory to discover basic truths about Boolean circuits, proofs, data structures, linear programs, distributed systems, and streaming algorithms. Communication complexity is simultaneously beautiful and widely applicable.

The main protagonist of our story is the *disjointness* problem. Here Alice and Bob each have access to their own set and want to figure out whether or not these sets are disjoint. For example, imagine that Alice and Bob want to know if there is a movie that they would both enjoy. Alice knows the collection of movies that she would like to see, and Bob knows the movies he would like to see. How long does their conversation need to be? Set disjointness appears in many applications

[1] Yao, 1979.

Two sets are disjoint if they have no common elements.

of communication complexity, and it helps to illustrate many techniques applicable to understanding communication.

Our exposition is in two parts. The first part, entitled *Communication*, focuses on communication complexity per se. Here communication protocols are rigorously defined and the foundations of the theory are built. The second part, entitled *Applications*, uses the theory to derive conclusions about a variety of different models of computation. In the first part, disjointness serves as a litmus test to see how the ideas we develop are progressing. In the second part, results about disjointness help to determine the limits of other models of computation.

We intend to present the key ideas in the field in the most elegant form possible. This is a textbook of basic concepts, and not a survey of the latest research results. The reader is encouraged to discover the wider body of work that forms the theory of communication complexity by following the many references that are cited in the book.

Like this.

Each page of the book has a large margin, where one can find references to the relevant literature, diagrams, and additional explanations of arguments in the main text.

Acknowledgments

THANKS TO Noga Alon, Anil Ananthaswamy, Arkadev Chattopadhyay, Morgan Dixon, Yaniv Elchayani, Yuval Filmus, Abe Friesen, Mika Göös, Jeff Heer, Pavel Hrubeš, Weston Karnes, Guy Kindler, Vincent Liew, Venkatesh Medabalimi, Or Meir, Shay Moran, Aram Odeh, Rotem Oshman, Sebastian Pokutta, Kayur Patel, Sivaramakrishnan Natarajan Ramamoorthy, Cyrus Rashtchian, Thomas Rothvoß, Makrand Sinha, and Avi Wigderson for many contributions to this book.

We thank the National Science Foundation, the Israel Science Foundation, the Simons Institute for the Theory of Computing, the Technion-IIT, and the University of Washington for their support.

Conventions and Preliminaries

In this section, we set up notation and recall some standard facts that are used throughout the book.

We mostly use standard notation. The reader is advised to only skim through this section, and come back to it when necessary.

Sets, Numbers, and Functions

$[a, b]$ denotes the set of real numbers x in the interval $a \leq x \leq b$. For a positive integer n, we use $[n]$ to denote the set $\{1, 2, \ldots, n\}$. Following the convention in computer science, we often refer to the numbers 0 and 1 as bits. All logarithms in this book are computed in base 2, unless otherwise specified.

bit = binary digit.

There is a natural identification between the subsets of $[n]$ and binary strings $\{0, 1\}^n$. Every set $X \subseteq [n]$ corresponds to its indicator vector $x \in \{0, 1\}^n$, defined by $x_i = 1$ if and only if $i \in X$ for all $i \in [n]$.

Given a vector $x = (x_1, x_2, \ldots, x_n)$, we write $x_{\leq i}$ to denote $(x_1, \ldots, x_i)$. We define $x_{<i}$ similarly. We write x_S to denote the projection of x to the coordinates specified by the set $S \subseteq [n]$.

A *function* $f : D \to R$ is an object that maps every element x in the set D to a unique element $f(x)$ of the set R. A Boolean function is a function that evaluates to a bit, namely $R = \{0, 1\}$.

D is the domain and R is the range of the function.

Given two functions f, g that map natural numbers to real numbers, we write $f(n) \leq O(g(n))$ if there are numbers $n_0, c > 0$, such that if $n > n_0$ then $f(n) \leq cg(n)$. We write $g(n) \geq \Omega(f(n))$ when $f(n) \leq O(g(n))$. We write $f(n) \leq o(g(n))$ if $\lim_{n \to \infty} \frac{f(n)}{g(n)} = 0$.

Graphs

A graph is a pair $G = (V, E)$, where V is a set and E is a collection of subsets of V of size 2. The elements of V are called vertices and the elements of E are called edges. The size of the graph G is the number of vertices in it. A clique $C \subseteq V$ in the graph is a subset of the vertices such that every subset of C of size 2 is an edge of the graph. An independent set $I \subseteq V$ in the graph is a set that does not contain any edges. A *path* in the graph is a sequence of vertices $v_1, \ldots, v_n$ such that $\{v_i, v_{i+1}\}$ is an edge for each i. A *cycle* is a path whose first and last vertices are the same. A cycle is called *simple* if all of its edges are distinct. A graph is said to be *connected* if there is a path between every two distinct vertices in the graph. A graph is called a *tree* if it is connected and has no simple cycles. The *degree* of a vertex in a graph is the number of edges it is contained in. A *leaf* in a tree is a vertex of degree one. Every tree has at least one leaf. It follows by induction on n that every tree of size n has exactly $n - 1$ edges.

Probability

Throughout this book, we consider only finite probability spaces, or uniform distributions on compact sets of real numbers.

Let p be a probability distribution on a finite set Ω. That is, p is a function $p : \Omega \rightarrow [0, 1]$ and $\sum_{a \in \Omega} p(a) = 1$. Let A be a random variable chosen according to p. That is, for each $a \in \Omega$, we have $\Pr[A = a] = \Pr_p[A = a] = p(a)$. We use the notation $p(a)$ to denote both the distribution of the variable A and the number $\Pr[A = a]$. The meaning is clear from the context. For example, if $\Omega = \{0, 1\}^2$ and A is uniformly distributed in Ω, then $p(a)$ denotes the uniform distribution on Ω. However if $a = (0, 0)$, then $p(a)$ denotes the number $1/4$. Random variables are denoted by capital letters (like A) and values they attain are denoted by lowercase letters (like a). An event $\mathcal{E}$ is a subset of Ω. The probability of the event $\mathcal{E}$ is $\Pr[\mathcal{E}] = \sum_{a \in \mathcal{E}} p(a)$. Events are denoted by calligraphic letters.

> This notation is similar to how $f(x)$ is often used to refer to the function f, when x is a variable, and a fixed value when x is fixed. This notation makes many equations more succinct. We shall encounter complicated scenarios where there are several random variables with a complicated conditioning structure. In those cases, it is helpful to use as succinct a notation as possible.

Given a distribution on 4-tuples $p(a, b, c, d)$, we write $p(a, b, c)$ to denote the marginal distribution on the variables a, b, c (or the corresponding probability). We often write $p(ab)$ instead of $p(a, b)$, for conciseness of notation. We also write $p(a|b)$ to denote either the distribution of A conditioned on the event $B = b$, or the number $\Pr[A = a|B = b]$. In the preceding example, if $B = A_1 + A_2$, and $b = 1$, then $p(a|b)$ denotes the uniform distribution on $\{(0, 1), (1, 0)\}$ when a is a free variable. When $a = (0, 1)$ then $p(a|b) = 1/2$.

Given $g : \Omega \rightarrow \mathbb{R}$, we write $\mathbb{E}_{p(a)}[g(a)]$ to denote the expected value of $g(a)$ with respect to p. So, $\mathbb{E}_{p(a)}[g(a)] = \sum_{a \in \Omega} p(a)g(a)$.

The *statistical distance*, also known as *total variational distance*, between two probability distributions $p(a)$ and $q(a)$ is defined to be

> The proof of the second equality is a good exercise.

$$|p - q| = \frac{1}{2} \sum_a |p(a) - q(a)| = \max_{\mathcal{E}} p(\mathcal{E}) - q(\mathcal{E}),$$

where the maximum is taken over all events $\mathcal{E}$. For example, if p is uniform on $\Omega = \{0, 1\}^2$ and q is uniform on $\{(0, 1), (1, 0)\} \subset \Omega$, then when a is a free variable $|p(a) - q(a)|$ denotes the statistical distance between the distributions, which is $1/2$, and when $a = (0, 0)$, we have $|p(a) - q(a)| = 1/4$.

We sometimes write $p(x) \overset{\epsilon}{\approx} q(x)$ to indicate that $|p(x) - q(x)| \leq \epsilon$. Suppose A, B are two random variables in a probability space p. For ease of notation, we write $p(a|b) \overset{\epsilon}{\approx} p(a)$ *for average b* to mean that

$$\mathbb{E}_{p(b)}\left[|p(a|b) - p(a)|\right] \leq \epsilon.$$

Some Useful Inequalities

Markov

Suppose X is a nonnegative random variable, and $\gamma > 0$ is a number. Markov's inequality bounds the probability that X exceeds γ in terms of the expected value of X:

$$\mathbb{E}[X] > p(X > \gamma) \cdot \gamma \;\Rightarrow\; p(X > \gamma) < \frac{\mathbb{E}[X]}{\gamma}.$$

Concentration

A sum of independently distributed bits concentrates around its expectation. Namely, the value of the sum is close to its expected value with high probability. The Chernoff-Hoeffding bound controls this concentration. Suppose $X_1, \ldots, X_n$ are independent identically distributed bits. Let $\mu = \mathbb{E}\left[\sum_{i=1}^{n} X_i\right]$. The bound says that for any $0 < \delta < 1$,

$$\Pr\left[\left|\sum_{i=1}^{n} X_i - \mu\right| > \delta\mu\right] \le e^{-\delta^2\mu/3}.$$

When $\delta \ge 1$, the following bound applies

$$\Pr\left[\sum_{i=1}^{n} X_i > (1+\delta)\mu\right] \le e^{-\delta\mu/3}.$$

> The *binomial coefficient* $\binom{n}{k}$ is the number of subsets of $[n]$ of size k.

These bounds give estimates on binomial coefficients. The idea is to consider $X_1, \ldots, X_n$ that are uniformly distributed and independent random bits. For a number $0 \le a \le n/2$, we have

$$\sum_{k \in [n]:\,|k-n/2|>a} \binom{n}{k} \le 2^n \cdot e^{-\frac{2a^2}{3n}}.$$

The following upper bounds on binomial coefficients is also useful: for all $k \in [n]$,

$$\binom{n}{k} \le \frac{2^{n+1}}{\sqrt{\pi n}}.$$

Approximations

We will often need to approximate linear functions with exponentials. The following inequalities are useful: $e^{-x} \ge 1 - x$ for all real x, and $1 - x \ge 2^{-2x}$ when $0 \le x \le 1/2$.

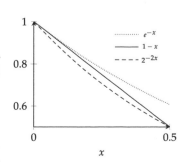

Cauchy-Schwartz Inequality

The Cauchy-Schwartz inequality says that for two vectors $x, y \in \mathbb{R}^n$, their inner product is at most the products of their norms.

$$\left| \sum_{i=1}^{n} x_i y_i \right| = |\langle x, y \rangle| \leq \|x\| \cdot \|y\| = \sqrt{\sum_{i=1}^{n} x_i^2} \cdot \sqrt{\sum_{i=1}^{n} y_i^2}.$$

Convexity

A function $f : [a, b] \to \mathbb{R}$ is said to be *convex* if

$$\frac{f(x) + f(y)}{2} \geq f\left(\frac{x + y}{2}\right),$$

for all x, y in the domain. It is said to be concave if

$$\frac{f(x) + f(y)}{2} \leq f\left(\frac{x + y}{2}\right).$$

Some convex functions: $x^2, e^x, x \log x$. Some concave functions: $\log x$, $\sqrt{x}$. Note that f is convex if and only if $-f$ is concave.

Jensen's inequality says if a function f is convex, then

$$\mathbb{E}\left[f(X)\right] \geq f(\mathbb{E}\left[X\right]),$$

for any random variable $X \in [a, b]$. Similarly, if f is concave, then

$$\mathbb{E}\left[f(X)\right] \leq f(\mathbb{E}\left[X\right]).$$

In this book, we often say that an inequality follows *by convexity* when we mean that it can be derived by applying Jensen's inequality to a convex or concave function.

A consequence of Jensen's inequality is the Arithmetic-Mean Geometric-Mean inequality:

$$\frac{\sum_{i=1}^{n} a_i}{n} \geq \left(\prod_{i=1}^{n} a_i\right)^{1/n},$$

which can be proved using the concavity of the log function:

$$\log\left(\frac{\sum_{i=1}^{n} a_i}{n}\right) \geq \frac{\sum_{i=1}^{n} \log a_i}{n} = \log\left(\prod_{i=1}^{n} a_i^{1/n}\right).$$

One can often prove that a function is convex by showing that its second derivative is nonnegative on the domain.

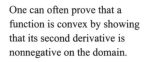

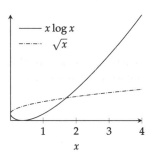

Try to prove the Cauchy-Schwartz inequality using convexity.

Basic Facts from Algebra

A few places in this book require knowledge about polynomials and finite fields. We cannot give a comprehensive introduction to these topics here, but we state some basic facts that are relevant to this book.

A *field* $\mathbb{F}$ is a set containing 0 and 1 that is endowed with the operations of addition, multiplication, subtraction, and division. If $a, b \in \mathbb{F}$, then $a + b, ab, a - b$ must also be elements of $\mathbb{F}$, and a/b is an element of $\mathbb{F}$ as long as $b \neq 0$. We require that $a - a = 0$ for all $a \in \mathbb{F}$, and

$a/a = 1$ for all $a \neq 0$. Several other requirements should be met, like commutativity and distributivity.

The simplest example of a field is the field of *rational numbers*. In applications, however, it is often useful to consider fields that have a finite number of elements. The simplest example of a finite field is a prime field. For a prime number p, there is a unique field $\mathbb{F}_p$ containing the p elements $0, 1, 2, \ldots, p - 1$. These numbers can be added, subtracted, and multiplied modulo p to get the corresponding field operations. One can define division as well, using the property that p is prime. See Figure 1 for an example.

+	0	1	2	3	4
0	0	1	2	3	4
1	1	2	3	4	0
2	2	3	4	0	1
3	3	4	0	1	2
4	4	0	1	2	3

×	0	1	2	3	4
0	0	0	0	0	0
1	0	1	2	3	4
2	0	2	4	1	3
3	0	3	1	4	2
4	0	4	3	2	1

/	1	2	3	4
0	0	0	0	0
1	1	3	2	4
2	2	1	4	3
3	3	4	1	2
4	4	2	3	1

Figure 1 The addition, multiplication, and division tables of $\mathbb{F}_5$.

Vector Spaces

Given a field $\mathbb{F}$, the set $\mathbb{F}^n$ can be viewed as a vector space over $\mathbb{F}$. The elements of $\mathbb{F}^n$ are called vectors. Addition of vectors is defined coordinate-wise, so $(v + w)_i = v_i + w_i$, for all i, and multiplication by a scalar $c \in \mathbb{F}$ is defined as $c \cdot (v_1, v_2, \ldots, v_n) = (cv_1, cv_2, \ldots, cv_n)$, for $c \in \mathbb{F}$.

Linear combinations of vectors are taken using scalar coefficients from the field $\mathbb{F}$. The usual notions of dimension, linear dependence, and linear independence make sense here. A subspace V of $\mathbb{F}^n$ is a set that is closed under additions and multiplications by scalars. Given a subspace $V \subseteq \mathbb{F}$, we define its dual subspace

$$V^\perp = \left\{ w \in \mathbb{F}^n : \sum_{i=1}^{n} v_i w_i = 0 \text{ for all } v \in V \right\}.$$

The following fact is useful: If $V \subseteq \mathbb{F}^n$ is a subspace, the sum of the dimensions of V and $V^\perp$ is always exactly n.

Polynomials

A *polynomial* over the variables $X_1, X_2, \ldots, X_n$ is an expression of the form

$$aX_1 X_2 X_3^2 + bX_3 X_7^3 X_5 - cX_1 X_4^4.$$

It is a linear combination of monomials, where the coefficients a, b, c are elements of a field. Every polynomial corresponds to a function that can be computed by evaluation, and every function $f : \mathbb{F}^n \to \mathbb{F}$ can be described by a polynomial.

A polynomial is called *multilinear* if every monomial is a product of distinct variables. For example: the polynomial

$$X_1 X_2 X_3 + 3X_3 X_7 X_5 - 2X_1 X_4$$

is multilinear, and the polynomial X_1^2 is not. A useful fact is that every function $f : \{0, 1\}^n \to \mathbb{F}$ can be *uniquely* represented as multilinear polynomial of n variables with coefficients from $\mathbb{F}$.

Introduction

THE CONCEPT OF A CONVERSATION is universal. In this book, we develop methods to determine the most efficient conversations for specific tasks. We start by exploring some examples that illustrate how such conversations arise, and why they are worthy of study.

We begin the story with one of the earliest applications of communication complexity: proving lower bounds on the area required for digital chips.[1] A chip design specifies how to compute a function $f(x_1, \ldots, x_n)$ by laying out the components of the chip on a flat grid, as in Figure I.1. Each component either stores one of the inputs to the function, or performs some computation on the values coming from adjacent components. It is vital to minimize the area used in the design because this affects the cost, power consumption, reliability, and speed of the chip.

[1] Thompson, 1979.

Because there are n inputs, we need area of at least n to compute functions that depend on all of their inputs. Can we always find chip designs with area proportional to n? The framework of communication complexity can be used to show that many functions require area proportional to n^2, *no matter what chip design is used*!

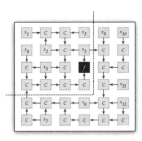

Figure I.1 Any chip can be broken into two pieces while cutting few wires.

The crucial insight is that the layout of the chip yields a conversation whose outcome is the value of f. If a chip design has area A, one can argue that there must be a way to cut the chip into two parts, each containing a similar number of the inputs, so that only $\approx \sqrt{A}$ wires are cut. Imagine that each part of the chip represents a person. The chip design describes how f can be computed by two people, each of whom knows roughly half of the input to f, with a conversation whose length is proportional to the number of wires that were cut. So, if we can show that computing f requires a conversation of length t, we can conclude that area A must be at least $\approx t^2$, no matter how the components of the chip are laid out. In this book, we will develop a wide variety of tools for proving that functions require conversations whose length is proportional to n. The area of any chip for such a function must be proportional to n^2.

A second example comes from a classical result about *Turing machines*. Turing machines are widely regarded as a universal model of computation – the extended Church-Turing thesis says that anything that is efficiently computable is efficiently computable by a Turing machine. A Turing machine can be thought of as a program written for a computer that has access to one or more *tapes*. Each tape has a *head* that points at a location on the tape. In each step of computation, the machine can read or write a single symbol at the location corresponding to a head, or move the head to an adjacent location. A Turing machine with more tapes is more powerful than a Turing machine with fewer tapes, but how much more powerful?

[2] Hartmanis and Stearns, 1965.

A classic result[2] shows that one can simulate a Turing machine that has access to two tapes with a Turing machine that has access to just one tape. However, the simulation may increase the number of steps of the computation by a factor of t, where t is the running-time of the machine. One can use communication complexity to show that this loss is unavoidable.[3]

Strictly speaking, the simulation increases by a factor of $\max\{n, t\}$, where n is the length of the input. However, for any computation that depends on the whole input, this maximum is t.

[3] Hennie, 1965.

To see why this is the case, we use the communication complexity of the *disjointness* function. Imagine that Alice knows a set $X \subseteq [n]$, and Bob knows a set $Y \subseteq [n]$. Their common goal is to compute whether or not the sets are disjoint – namely whether or not there is an element that is in both sets (see Figure I.2). Later in the book, we prove that Alice and Bob must communicate $\Omega(n)$ bits in order to achieve this goal.

Now, a Turing machine with access to two tapes can compute disjointness in $O(n)$ steps. If the sets are represented by their indicator vectors $x, y \in \{0, 1\}^n$, then the machine can copy y to the second tape and scan both x and y, searching for an index i with $x_i = 1 = y_i$. All of these operations can be carried out in $O(n)$ steps.

Figure I.2 looks very similar to the famous Sierpinski gasket, which is a well-known fractal in the plane. The gasket's area is zero, and its Hausdorff dimension is ≈ 1.585. The properties of disjointness we establish in this text imply analogous statements for the Sierpinski gasket.

However, one can use communication complexity to prove that a Turing machine with one tape must take at least $\Omega(n^2)$ steps to compute disjointness. The idea is that a machine that computes disjointness in T steps can be used by Alice and Bob to compute disjointness using $\approx \frac{T}{n}$ bits of communication. Intuitively, Alice and Bob can write down the input (x, y) on the single tape of the machine and try to simulate the execution of the machine. Neither of them knows the contents of the whole tape, but they can still simulate the execution of the machine with a small amount of communication. Every time the machine transitions from Alice's part of the tape to Bob's part, she sends him a short message to indicate the line of code that should be executed next. Bob then continues the execution. One can show that this simulation can be carried out in such a way that each message sent between Alice and Bob corresponds to $\Omega(n)$ steps of the Turing machine. So, if we start with a one-tape machine that runs in time $\ll n^2$, we end up with a protocol of length $\ll n$ bits that computes disjointness. This is impossible.

The two examples we have discussed give some feel for communication problems and why we are interested in studying them. Next, we continue this informal introduction with several other interesting examples of communication problems and protocols.

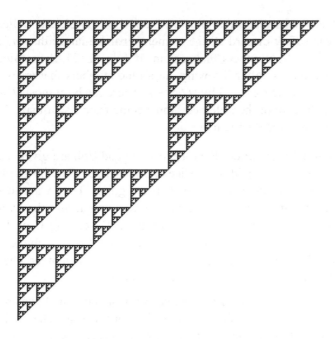

Figure I.2 Disjointness when $n = 8$. Each row corresponds to a set $X \subseteq [8]$, and each column corresponds to a set $Y \subseteq [8]$. The X, Y entry is black if and only if X and Y are disjoint.

Some Protocols

A *communication protocol* specifies a way for a set of people to have a conversation. Each person has access to a different source of information, which is modeled as an *input* to the protocol. The protocol itself is assumed to be known to all the people that are involved in executing it. Their goal is to learn some feature of all the information that they collectively know.

Equality Suppose Alice and Bob are given two n-bit strings. Alice is given x and Bob is given y, and they want to know if $x = y$. There is a trivial solution: Alice can send her input x to Bob, and Bob can let her know if $x = y$. This is a *deterministic* protocol that takes $n + 1$ bits of communication. Interestingly, we shall prove that no deterministic protocol is more efficient. On the other hand, for every number k, there is a *randomized* protocol that uses only $k + 1$ bits of communication and errs with probability at most 2^{-k} – the parties can use randomness to hash their inputs and compare the hashes. More on this in Chapter 3.

The terms *deterministic* and *randomized* will be formally defined later in the book.

See Chapter 3.

Median Suppose Alice is given a list of numbers from $[n]$ and Bob is given a different list of numbers from $[n]$. They want to compute the median element of the list that is obtained by combining these lists. If t is the total number of elements in their lists, this is the $\lceil t/2 \rceil$th element after the lists are combined and sorted. There is a simple protocol that takes $O(\log n \cdot \log t)$ bits of communication. In the first step, Alice and Bob each announce the number of their elements that are at most $n/2$. This takes $O(\log t)$ bits of communication. If there

For example, the median of $(1, 2, 3)$ and $(2, 3, 4)$ is 2, the third element in the list $(1, 2, 2, 3, 3, 4)$.

are k elements that are at most $n/2$ and $k \geq \lceil t/2 \rceil$, then Alice and Bob can safely discard all the elements that are larger than $n/2$ and recurse on the numbers that remain. If $k < \lceil t/2 \rceil$, then Alice and Bob can recurse after throwing out all the numbers that are at most $n/2$, and replacing $\lceil t/2 \rceil$ by $\lceil t/2 \rceil - k$. There can be at most $O(\log n)$ steps before all of their elements must come from a set of size 1. This single number is the median.

Cliques and Independent Sets Here Alice and Bob are given a graph G on n vertices. In addition, Alice knows a clique C in the graph, and Bob knows an independent set I in the graph. They want to know whether C and I share a common vertex or not, and they want to determine this using a short conversation. Describing C or I takes about n bits, because in general the graph may have 2^n cliques or 2^n independent sets. So, if Alice and Bob try to tell each other what C or I is, that will lead to a very long conversation.

A clique is a set of vertices that are all connected to each other. An independent set is a set of vertices that contains no edges. The degree of a vertex is the number of its neighbors.

Here we discuss a clever interactive protocol allowing Alice and Bob to have an extremely short conversation for this task. They will send at most $O(\log^2 n)$ bits. If C contains a vertex v with degree less than $n/2$, Alice sends Bob the name of v. This takes just $O(\log n)$ bits of communication. See Figure I.3 for an illustration. Now, either $v \in I$, or Alice and Bob can safely discard all the nonneighbors of v because these cannot be a part of C. This eliminates at least $n/2$ vertices from the graph. Similarly, if I contains a vertex v of degree at least $n/2$, Bob sends Alice the name of v. Again, either $v \in C$, or Alice and Bob can safely delete all the neighbors of v from the graph, which eliminates about $n/2$ vertices. If all the vertices in C have degree more than $n/2$, and all the vertices in I have degree less than $n/2$, then C and I do not share a vertex. The conversation can safely terminate. So, in each round of communication, either the parties know that $C \cap I = \emptyset$, or the number of vertices is reduced by a factor of 2. After k rounds, the number of vertices is at most $n/2^k$. If k exceeds $\log n$, the number of vertices left will be less than 1, and Alice and Bob will know if C and I share a vertex or not. This means that at most $\log n$ vertices can be announced before the protocol ends, proving that at most $O(\log^2 n)$ bits will be exchanged before Alice and Bob learn what they wanted to know.

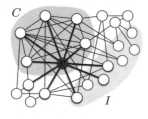

Figure I.3 The vertices that are not neighbors of v cannot be involved in any intersection between C and I.

One can show that if the conversation involves only one message from each party, then at least $\Omega(n)$ bits must be revealed for the parties to discover what they want to know. So, interaction is vital to bringing down the length of the conversation.

Disjointness with Sets of Size k Alice and Bob are given two sets $A, B \subseteq [n]$, each of size $k \ll n$, and want to know if the sets share a common element. Alice can send her set to Bob, which takes $\log \binom{n}{k} \approx k \log(n/k)$ bits of communication. There is a randomized

See Chapter 2.

protocol that uses only $O(k)$ bits of communication. Alice and Bob sample a random sequence of sets in the universe and Alice announces the name of the first set that contains A. If A and B are disjoint, this eliminates half of B. In Chapter 3, we prove that repeating this procedure gives a protocol with $O(k)$ bits of communication.

Disjointness with k Parties The input is k sets $A_1, \ldots, A_k \subseteq [n]$, and there are k parties. The ith party knows all the sets *except for* the ith one. The parties want to know if there is a common element in all sets. We know of a clever deterministic protocol with $O(n/2^k)$ bits of communication, and we know that $\Omega(n/4^k)$ bits of communication are required. We do not know of any randomized protocol with communication better than the deterministic protocol discussed earlier, but we do know every randomized protocol must have communication at least $\Omega(\sqrt{n}/2^k)$.

See Chapters 4 and 5. In Chapter 4, we prove that when $k > \log n$, it is enough for each party to announce the number of elements in $[n]$ that are in i of the sets visible to her for $i = 0, 1, \ldots, k$.

Summing Three Numbers The input is three numbers $x, y, z \in [n]$. Alice knows (x, y), Bob knows (y, z), and Charlie knows (x, z). The parties want to know whether or not $x + y + z = n$. Alice can tell Bob x, which would allow Bob to announce the answer. This takes $O(\log n)$ bits of communication. There is a clever deterministic protocol that communicates $\sqrt{\log n}$ bits, and one can show that the length of any deterministic conversation must increase with n. In contrast, there is a randomized protocol that solves the problem with a conversation whose length is a constant.

See Chapter 4.

Pointer Chasing The input consists of two functions $f, g : [n] \rightarrow [n]$, where Alice knows f and Bob knows g. Let $a_0, a_1, \ldots, a_k \in [n]$ be defined by setting $a_0 = 1$, and $a_i = f(g(a_{i-1}))$. The goal is to compute a_k. There is a simple k round protocol with communication $O(k \log n)$ that solves this problem, but any protocol with fewer than k rounds requires $\Omega(n)$ bits of communication.

See Chapter 6.

Part I

Communication

1

Deterministic Protocols

WE START OUR FORMAL DISCUSSION by defining exactly what we mean by a deterministic communication protocol. The definition is meant to capture a conversation between two parties. To be useful, the definition must be fairly general. It should capture settings where the parties have access to different information and want to use that information to generate meaningful messages. The conversations may be interactive – messages should be allowed to depend on earlier messages.

Suppose Alice's input is an element from a set $\mathcal{X}$ and Bob's input is an element from a set $\mathcal{Y}$. A communication protocol (see Figure 1.1) is an algorithm to generate a conversation between Alice and Bob. A *protocol* π is specified by a rooted binary tree. Every internal vertex v has two children. Every internal vertex v is *owned* by either Alice or Bob – we denote the owner by $\mathsf{owner}(v)$. The vertex v is also associated with a function f_v that maps an input of $\mathsf{owner}(v)$ to $\{0, 1\}$. For example, if $\mathsf{owner}(v)$ is Alice, then $f_v : \mathcal{X} \to \{0, 1\}$. We interpret the output bit of f_v as one of the children of v in the binary tree by associating 0 with the left child and 1 with the right child.

The outcome of the protocol π on input $(x, y) \in \mathcal{X} \times \mathcal{Y}$ is a leaf in the protocol tree, computed as follows. The parties begin by setting the *current* vertex to be the root of the tree. If $\mathsf{owner}(v)$ is Alice, she announces the bit $f_v(x)$. Similarly, if $\mathsf{owner}(v)$ is Bob, he announces the bit $f_v(y)$. Both parties set the new current vertex to be the child of v indicated by the announced value of f_v. This process is repeated until the current vertex is a leaf, and this leaf is the outcome of the protocol.

The input (x, y) induces a path from the root of the protocol tree to the leaf $\pi(x, y)$. This path corresponds to the conversation between the parties. A protocol, however, is *not* a conversation as we usually think of it. A protocol encodes *all* possible messages that *may* be sent by the parties during any potential conversation. It produces a conversation only when it is executed using a particular input.

The point of the definition above is to firmly focus on the number of bits communicated. We do not account for the methods used to generate the messages sent, nor the time it takes to compute them. We allow the protocol designer to pick the best possible message to send *ahead of time*. This choice leads to a versatile and clean model. It also allows

Although there are many other reasonable ways to define a communication protocol, they are all captured by the definitions we give here, up to some small change in the length of the communication.

The setup is analogous for k party protocols. Let $\mathcal{X}_1, \mathcal{X}_2, \ldots, \mathcal{X}_k$ be k sets. A k-party communication protocol defines a way for k parties to communicate information about their inputs, where the ith party gets an input from the set $\mathcal{X}_i$. Every vertex v is associated with a party i and a function $f_v : \mathcal{X}_i \to \{0, 1\}$.

Figure 1.1 An execution of a protocol.

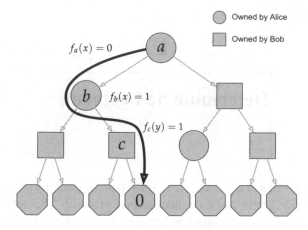

The length is the longest path from root to leaf in the tree.

If round(x, y) denotes the number of edges (v, u) on the path from the root of the tree to the leaf $\pi(x, y)$ so that owner$(v) \neq$ owner(u), then the number of rounds is 1 plus the maximum value of round(x, y) over all inputs x and y. For example, suppose Alice sends 2 bits, then Bob sends 3 bits, and then Alice sends 1 bit to end the protocol. The length is 6 and the number of rounds is 3.

We could have chosen a different definition of when the protocol computes a function – we might require only that any party that knows the messages of the protocol and one of the inputs can deduce $g(x, y)$. This distinction is sometimes important, but for Boolean functions it is not important because any party that knows the value of $g(x, y)$ can announce it with one more bit of communication.

us to bring many tools from mathematics to bear on understanding the model.

The *length* of the protocol π, denoted $\|\pi\|$, is the depth of the protocol tree. It is the length of the longest possible conversation that may occur when the protocol is executed. The *number of rounds* of the protocol is the maximum number of alternations between Alice and Bob during any execution.

In some practical applications – for example protocols that run between computers on the internet – conversations consist of only a few rounds of interaction, so it makes sense to limit the discussion to bounded round protocols. In other applications – like algorithms that exchange information between two parts of the same chip – it is not very expensive to have many rounds of interaction.

Let us make some basic observations that follow from the definitions:

Fact 1.1 *The number of rounds in π is always at most $\|\pi\|$.*

Because the number of leaves in a rooted binary tree of depth d is at most 2^d, we have:

Fact 1.2 *The number of leaves in the protocol tree of π is at most $2^{\|\pi\|}$.*

We are primarily interested in protocols that compute something using the inputs x, y. Given a function $g : \mathcal{X} \times \mathcal{Y} \to \mathcal{Z}$, we say that π computes g if $\pi(x, y)$ determines $g(x, y)$ for every input $(x, y) \in \mathcal{X} \times \mathcal{Y}$. Namely, we say π computes g if there is a map h from the leaves of the protocol tree to $\mathcal{Z}$ so that $h(\pi(x, y)) = g(x, y)$ for all x, y.

The *communication complexity* of a function g is the minimum length achieved by a protocol that computes g. In other words, the communication complexity is c if there is a protocol of length c that computes g, but no protocol can compute g with less than c bits of communication.

Now that we have a concrete mathematical model for communication, we can start to investigate the structure of this model. In the rest of this chapter, we discuss the basic properties of protocols, show

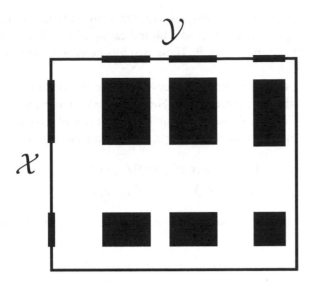

Figure 1.2 A combinatorial rectangle.

some natural operations on them, and describe several methods for proving lower bound on the communication complexity of specific functions.

Rectangles

TO UNDERSTAND A COMPUTATIONAL MODEL, it is often help-ful to identify simple building blocks that make the model. *Combinatorial rectangles* are the building blocks of communication protocols.

For brevity, we often say *rectangles*, instead of combinatorial rectangles.

The inputs to a communication problem come from a Cartesian product of the form $\mathcal{X} \times \mathcal{Y}$. A *rectangle* is a subset of this space of the form

$$R = A \times B \subseteq \mathcal{X} \times \mathcal{Y}.$$

See Figure 1.2. The following lemma provides an equivalent way to view rectangles that is useful.

For k party protocols, a rectangle is a cartesian product of k sets.

Lemma 1.3 *A set $R \subseteq \mathcal{X} \times \mathcal{Y}$ is a rectangle if and only if whenever $(x, y), (x', y') \in R$, we have $(x', y), (x, y') \in R$.*

Proof If $R = A \times B$ is a rectangle, then $(x, y), (x', y') \in R$ means that $x, x' \in A$ and $y, y' \in B$. Thus $(x, y'), (x', y) \in A \times B$. On the other hand, if R is an arbitrary set with the given property, if R is empty, it is a rectangle. If R is not empty, choose $(x, y) \in R$. Define $A = \{x' : (x', y) \in R\}$ and $B = \{y' : (x, y') \in R\}$. Then by the promised property of R, we have $A \times B \subseteq R$, and for every element $(x', y') \in R$, we have $x' \in A, y' \in B$, so $R \subseteq A \times B$. Thus $R = A \times B$. $\square$

If a function $f(x, y)$ is determined by whether or not (x, y) belongs to a rectangle $A \times B$, then it certainly has a very simple communication

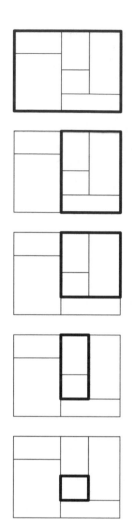

Figure 1.3 The evolution of the rectangle corresponding to the current vertex of the protocol tree as the protocol executes. The leaves define a partition into rectangles, which is shown in all steps.

protocol. Indeed, if Alice and Bob want to know if their inputs belong to the rectangle, Alice can send a bit indicating if $x \in A$, and Bob can send a bit indicating if $y \in B$. These two bits determine whether or not $(x, y) \in A \times B$.

The importance of rectangles stems from the fact that *every* protocol can be described using rectangles. For every vertex v in a protocol π, let $R_v \subseteq \mathcal{X} \times \mathcal{Y}$ denote the set of inputs (x, y) that would lead the protocol to pass through the vertex v during the execution, and let

$$\mathcal{X}_v = \{x \in \mathcal{X} : \exists y \in \mathcal{Y} \ (x, y) \in R_v\},$$
$$\mathcal{Y}_v = \{y \in \mathcal{Y} : \exists x \in \mathcal{X} \ (x, y) \in R_v\}.$$

As we prove next, these sets are rectangles in the space of inputs. See Figure 1.3.

Lemma 1.4 *For every vertex v in the protocol tree, the set R_v is a rectangle with $R_v = \mathcal{X}_v \times \mathcal{Y}_v$. Moreover, the rectangles given by all the leaves of the protocol tree form a partition of $\mathcal{X} \times \mathcal{Y}$.*

Proof The lemma follows by induction. For the root vertex r, we see that $R_r = \mathcal{X} \times \mathcal{Y}$, so indeed the lemma holds. Now consider an arbitrary vertex v such that $R_v = \mathcal{X}_v \times \mathcal{Y}_v$. Let u, w be the children of v in the protocol tree. Suppose the first party is associated with v, and u is the vertex that the parties move to when $f_v(x) = 0$. Define:

$$\mathcal{X}_u = \{x \in \mathcal{X}_v : f_v(x) = 0\},$$
$$\mathcal{X}_w = \{x \in \mathcal{X}_v : f_v(x) = 1\}.$$

We see that $\mathcal{X}_u$ and $\mathcal{X}_w$ form a partition of $\mathcal{X}_v$, and $R_u = \mathcal{X}_u \times \mathcal{Y}_u$ and $R_w = \mathcal{X}_w \times \mathcal{Y}_w$ form a partition of R_v. In this way, we see that the leaves in the protocol tree induce a partition of the entire space of inputs into rectangles.   □

When the purpose of a protocol is to compute a Boolean function $g : \mathcal{X} \times \mathcal{Y} \to \{0, 1\}$, it is useful to understand the concept of a *monochromatic* rectangle. We say that a rectangle $R \subset \mathcal{X} \times \mathcal{Y}$ is *monochromatic* with respect to g if g is constant on R. See Figure 1.4. We say that the rectangle is *1-monochromatic* if g only takes the value 1 on the rectangle, and *0-monochromatic* if g only takes the value 0 on R.

Fact 1.5 *If a protocol π computes a function $g : \mathcal{X} \times \mathcal{Y} \to \{0, 1\}$, and v is a leaf in π, then R_v is a monochromatic rectangle with respect to g.*

Combining this fact with Lemmas 1.2 and 1.4 gives:

Theorem 1.6 *If the communication complexity of $g : \mathcal{X} \times \mathcal{Y} \to \{0, 1\}$ is c, then $\mathcal{X} \times \mathcal{Y}$ can be partitioned into at most 2^c monochromatic rectangles with respect to g.*

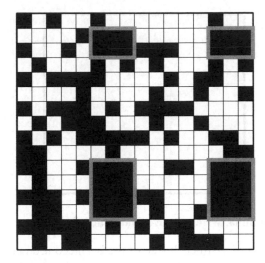

Figure 1.4 A Boolean function *g* represented as a matrix. The black entries are 1s and the white entries are 0s. A monochromatic rectangle is highlighted in gray.

This theorem is very useful for proving lower bounds on communication complexity: to prove that the communication complexity of *g* is high, it suffices to show that $\mathcal{X} \times \mathcal{Y}$ cannot be covered by few monochromatic rectangles.

Balancing Protocols

DOES IT EVER MAKE SENSE to have a protocol tree that has large depth but relatively few vertices? In other words, does it make sense to have a protocol tree that is not *balanced*? It turns out that one can always balance a protocol while approximately preserving the size of the tree, as in Figure 1.5. The following theorem captures this:

Theorem 1.7 *If π is a protocol with ℓ leaves, then there is a protocol that computes the outcome $\pi(x, y)$ with length at most $\lceil 2 \log_{3/2} \ell \rceil$.*

To prove the theorem, we need a well-known lemma about trees – every tree has a vertex that accounts for a significant fraction of the leaves, while excluding a significant fraction of the leaves, as in Figure 1.6.

Lemma 1.8 *In every protocol tree with $\ell > 1$ leaves, there is a vertex v such that the subtree rooted at v contains r leaves, and $\ell/3 \le r < 2\ell/3$.*

Proof Consider the sequence of vertices $v_1, v_2, \ldots$ defined as follows. The vertex v_1 is the root of the tree, which is not a leaf by the assumption on ℓ. For each $i > 0$, the vertex v_{i+1} is the child of v_i that has the most leaves under it, breaking ties arbitrarily. Let ℓ_i denote the number of leaves in the subtree rooted at v_i. Then, $\ell_{i+1} \ge \ell_i/2$, and $\ell_{i+1} < \ell_i$. Because $\ell_1 = \ell$, and the sequence is decreasing until it hits 1, there must be some i for which $\ell/3 \le \ell_i < 2\ell/3$. $\qquad\square$

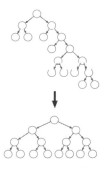

Figure 1.5 Balancing a protocol.

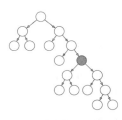

Figure 1.6 Every rooted binary tree must contain a vertex that accounts for at least 1/3rd fraction, but no more than a 2/3rd fraction of all the leaves.

Figure 1.7 A partition into rectangles that cannot be realized by any protocol.

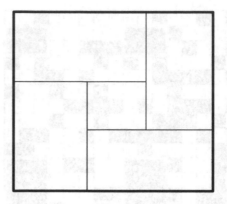

Given the lemma, we can prove Theorem 1.7:

Proof of Theorem 1.7 In each step of the balanced protocol, the parties pick a vertex v as promised by Lemma 1.8 and decide whether $(x, y) \in R_v$ using two bits of communication. That is, Alice sends a bit indicating if $x \in \mathcal{X}_v$ and Bob sends a bit indicating if $y \in \mathcal{Y}_v$. If $x \in \mathcal{X}_v$ and $y \in \mathcal{Y}_v$, then the parties repeat the procedure at the subtree rooted at v. Otherwise, the parties delete the vertex v and its subtree from the protocol tree and continue the simulation. In each step, the number of leaves of the protocol tree is reduced by a factor of at least $\frac{2}{3}$, so there can be at most $\log_{3/2} \ell$ such steps.   □

From Rectangles to Protocols

DOES EVERY PARTITION INTO RECTANGLES correspond to a protocol? Given that protocols correspond to partitions by rectangles, as in Theorem 1.6, one might wonder if there is a converse to the theorem. We cannot hope to show that every partition corresponds to a protocol – see Figure 1.7 for a counterexample. Nevertheless, we can show that small partitions yield efficient protocols.[1]

[1] Aho et al., 1983; and Yannakakis, 1991.

Theorem 1.9 *Let $\mathcal{R}$ be a collection of 2^c rectangles that form a partition of $\mathcal{X} \times \mathcal{Y}$. For $(x, y) \in \mathcal{X} \times \mathcal{Y}$, let $R_{x,y}$ be the unique rectangle in $\mathcal{R}$ that contains (x, y). Then there is a protocol of length $O(c^2)$ that on input (x, y) computes $R_{x,y}$.*

See Chapter 8 for more details.

Recent work[2] has shown that Theorem 1.9 is tight. There is a Boolean function g under which the inputs can be partitioned into 2^c monochromatic rectangles, yet no protocol can compute g using $o(c^2)$ bits of communication.

[2] Göös et al., 2015; and Ambainis et al., 2016.

The probabilistic method shows that there is a function that has a monochromatic rectangle *cover* of size 2^c, but communication complexity $\Omega(c^2)$. We discuss this at the end of this chapter.

Proof of Theorem 1.9 The parties are given inputs (x, y) and know a collection of rectangles $\mathcal{R}$ that partition the set of inputs. The aim of the protocol is to find the unique rectangle containing (x, y). In each round of the protocol, one of the parties announces the name of a rectangle in $\mathcal{R}$. We shall ensure that each such announcement allows the parties to discard at least half of the remaining rectangles.

A key concept we need is that of rectangles intersecting *horizontally* and *vertically*. We say that two rectangles $R = A \times B$ and $R' = A' \times B'$ intersect horizontally if A intersects A', and intersect vertically if B intersects B'. The basic observation is that if $x \in A \cap A'$ and $y \in B \cap B'$, then $(x, y) \in A \times B$ and $(x, y) \in A' \times B'$. This proves:

Fact 1.10 *Two disjoint rectangles cannot intersect both horizontally and vertically.*

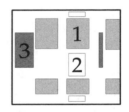

Figure 1.8 Rectangles 1 and 2 intersect vertically, while rectangles 1 and 3 intersect horizontally.

So, given any rectangle from our collection, every other rectangle can intersect it horizontally, or vertically, but not in both ways. This suggests an approach to reduce the space of potential rectangles that could cover (x, y). Consider this definition, illustrated in Figure 1.8:

Definition 1.11 Say that a rectangle $R = (A \times B) \in \mathcal{R}$ is *horizontally good* if $x \in A$, and R horizontally intersects at most $|\mathcal{R}|/2$ rectangles in $\mathcal{R}$. Say that R is *vertically good* if $y \in B$, and R vertically intersects at most $|\mathcal{R}|/2$ rectangles in $\mathcal{R}$. Say that R is *good* if it is either horizontally good or vertically good.

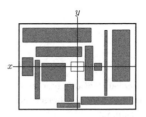

Figure 1.9 Either there is a rectangle consistent with x that intersects at most half of the other rectangles horizontally, or there is a rectangle consistent with y that intersects at most half of the other rectangles vertically.

Good rectangles can be used to reduce the number of rectangles under consideration. If Alice can find a rectangle R that is horizontally good, then announcing the name of this rectangle eliminates at least half of the rectangles from consideration. A similar thing happens if Bob can announce a rectangle that is vertically good. Moreover, we claim that there is always at least one good rectangle:

Claim 1.12 $R_{x,y}$ *is good.*

Recall that $R_{x,y}$ is the unique rectangle containing (x, y).

Proof Fact 1.10 implies that every rectangle in $\mathcal{R}$ does not intersect $R_{x,y}$ both horizontally and vertically. Thus either at most half of the rectangles in $\mathcal{R}$ intersect $R_{x,y}$ horizontally, or at most half of them intersect $R_{x,y}$ vertically. See Figure 1.9. □

In each step of the protocol, one of the parties announces the name of a good rectangle R, which must exist, because $R_{x,y}$ is good. This takes at most $c + 1$ bits of communication. The announcement leads to at least half of the rectangles in $\mathcal{R}$ being discarded. If R is horizontally good, then the parties can discard all the rectangles that do not intersect R horizontally. Otherwise they discard all the rectangles that do not intersect R vertically.

When only one rectangle remains, the protocol achieves its goal. Because $\mathcal{R}$ can survive at most c such discards, the communication complexity of the protocol is at most $O(c^2)$. □

Lower Bounds

ONE OF THE MAJOR CHALLENGES of theoretical computer science is to prove good lower bounds on the computational complexity of reasonable computational models. Communication complexity is a clean enough model that many interesting lower bounds can be proved. It is also extremely basic – this allows us to translate these lower bounds to other computational models.

Counting Arguments

Counting arguments are a standard way to establish the existence of hard functions in a given computational model. In a nutshell, a counting argument shows that almost all functions have very large complexity by establishing that there are a huge number of functions, but relatively few efficient algorithms.

Suppose we wish to compute $f : \{0, 1\}^n \times \{0, 1\}^n \to \{0, 1\}$. The communication complexity of every such function is at most $n + 1$. Alice can just send her input to Bob, and Bob replies with the value of f. Surprisingly, we can use counting to show that this trivial protocol is the best one can hope to do, for almost all functions f. We shall prove that almost all functions require $n - 1$ bits of communication.

There are 2^{2n} different inputs, and two possible choices for each input.

There are $2^{2^{2n}}$ possible functions $f : \{0, 1\}^n \times \{0, 1\}^n \to \{0, 1\}$. Now, suppose we are interested in functions that can be computed using c bits of communication. We wish to find an upper bound on the number of such functions. To do so, we need to estimate the number of deterministic protocols of length c. A protocol tree of depth c has at most 2^c leaves, and at most

In general, $(x - 1) \cdot (1 + x + x^2 + \cdots + x^r) = x^{r+1} - 1$.

$$1 + 2 + 4 + \cdots + 2^{c-1} = 2^c - 1 \le 2^c$$

nonleaf vertices. Each node in the tree is owned by either Alice or Bob and is associated with a function describing how they compute the next bit that they transmit. The number of choices for each node is at most $2 \cdot 2^{2^n} = 2^{2^n+1} \le 2^{2^{n+1}}$. This gives at most

$$\left(2^{2^{n+1}}\right)^{2^c} = 2^{2^{n+c+1}}$$

protocols of length c.

Now every protocol with 2^c leaves can compute at most 2^{2^c} Boolean functions because there are 2^{2^c} different ways to map the leaves to outputs of the function. So, the total number of functions with communication complexity c is at most

$$2^{2^{n+c+1}} \cdot 2^{2^c} = 2^{2^c + 2^{n+c+1}}.$$

We see that the fraction of such functions among all functions is

$$\frac{2^{2^c + 2^{n+c+1}}}{2^{2^{2n}}} = 2^{2^c + 2^{n+c+1} - 2^{2n}},$$

which is extremely small whenever $c < n - 1$. In other words, the vast majority of functions have almost full communication complexity.

Lower Bounds for Explicit Functions

The real difficulty with proving lower bounds arises when we try to prove lower bounds for specific problems of interest, rather than showing that there are *some* functions that have high complexity. Our ability to prove lower bounds for explicit functions hinges on our understanding of the underlying computational model.

The characterization provided by Theorem 1.6 is strong enough that it allows us to prove sharp lower bounds for many specific functions. For a given function of interest, if we show that the input space cannot be partitioned into 2^c monochromatic rectangles, then there is no protocol computing the function with c bits of communication.

Size of Monochromatic Rectangles

The simplest way to show that the input space cannot be partitioned into a few monochromatic rectangles is to show that there are no large monochromatic rectangles. If all monochromatic rectangles are small, then many of them are needed to cover the inputs.

Disjointness We start with one of the most important functions in communication complexity, our running example, the disjointness function $\mathsf{Disj} : 2^{[n]} \times 2^{[n]} \to \{0, 1\}$. See Figure 1.3. The function is defined by

$$\mathsf{Disj}(X, Y) = \begin{cases} 1 & \text{if } X \cap Y = \emptyset, \\ 0 & \text{otherwise.} \end{cases} \tag{1.1}$$

As always, Alice can send her whole set X to Bob, which gives a protocol with communication $n + 1$. Is this the best that they can do? Is there a nontrivial protocol?

A first attempt for proving a lower bound might to show that there is no large monochromatic rectangle. However, the Disj function *does* have large monochromatic rectangles. The rectangle $R = \{(X, Y) : 1 \in X, 1 \in Y\}$ has density $\frac{1}{4}$ and is 0-monochromatic. The solution is to show that there is no large 1-monochromatic rectangle.

Claim 1.13 *Every 1-monochromatic rectangle of* Disj *has size at most* 2^n.

Proof Indeed, suppose $R = A \times B$ is a 1-monochromatic rectangle. Let $X' = \cup_{X \in A} X$ be the union in all the sets of A and $Y' = \cup_{Y \in B} Y$. Then X' and Y' must be disjoint, so $|X'| + |Y'| \leq n$. On the other hand, $|A| \leq 2^{|X'|}, |B| \leq 2^{|Y'|}$, so $|R| = |A||B| \leq 2^{|X'|+|Y'|} \leq 2^n$. $\quad\square$

In addition, the number of 1 inputs of Disj is exactly 3^n. This is because for every element of the universe, there are three possibilities.

The element is only in X, or only in Y, or in neither. Overall, at least $3^n / 2^n = 2^{(\log 3 - 1)n}$ monochromatic rectangles are needed to cover the 1s of Disj.

Theorem 1.14 *The deterministic communication complexity of* Disj *is more than* $(\log 3 - 1)n$.

This gives a lower bound that is sharp up to a constant factor, but we did not prove that $n + 1$ bits of communication are required. We now discuss two examples where this method yields optimal lower bounds.

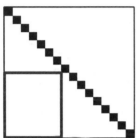

Figure 1.10 The equality function does have large monochromatic rectangles.

Equality Consider the equality function EQ : $\{0, 1\}^n \times \{0, 1\}^n \to \{0, 1\}$ defined as:

$$\text{EQ}(x, y) = \begin{cases} 1 & \text{if } x = y, \\ 0 & \text{otherwise.} \end{cases} \tag{1.2}$$

Again, the trivial protocol has length $n + 1$. Can we do better? As with disjointness, the equality function *does* have large monochromatic rectangles. The rectangle (see Figure 1.10) $R = \{(x, y) : x_1 = 0, y_1 = 1\}$ has density $\frac{1}{4}$ and is 0-monochromatic. Again, the solution is to show that equality does not have a large 1-monochromatic rectangle.

Claim 1.15 *If R is a 1-monochromatic rectangle, then $|R| = 1$.*

Proof Observe that if $x \neq x'$, then the points (x, x) and (x', x') cannot be in the same monochromatic rectangle. Otherwise, by Lemma 1.3, the element (x, x') would also have to be included in this rectangle. Because the rectangle is monochromatic, we would have $\text{EQ}(x, x') = \text{EQ}(x, x)$, which is a contradiction. $\square$

Because there are 2^n inputs x with $\text{EQ}(x, x) = 1$, this means 2^n rectangles are needed to cover such inputs. There is also at least one more 0-monochromatic rectangle. So, we need more than 2^n monochromatic rectangles to cover all the inputs. We conclude

Theorem 1.16 *The deterministic communication complexity of* EQ *is exactly* $n + 1$.

Inner-Product The *Hadamard* matrix is a well-known example of a matrix that has many nice combinatorial properties. See the illustration in Figure 1.11. It corresponds to the inner-product function IP : $\{0, 1\}^n \times \{0, 1\}^n \to \{0, 1\}$

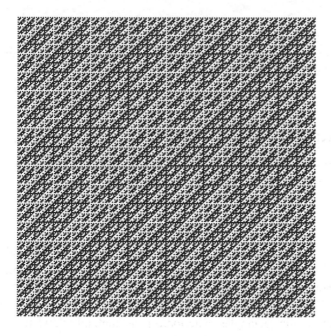

$$\mathsf{IP}(x, y) = \sum_{i=1}^{n} x_i y_i \quad \mod 2. \tag{1.3}$$

This function can be viewed as the inner-product over the finite field $\mathbb{F}_2$.

Here, we leverage linear algebra to place a bound on the size of the largest monochromatic rectangle.

We shall show in Chapter 5 that this function satisfies the strong property that the fraction of 1s is very close to the fraction of 0s in every rectangle that is not exponentially small.

Claim 1.17 *Every 0-monochromatic rectangle in the Hadamard matrix has size at most 2^n.*

Proof Suppose $R = A \times B$ is a 0-monochromatic rectangle. This means that for every $x \in A$ and $y \in B$, we have $\mathsf{IP}(x, y) = 0$. Let V be the span of the elements of A over $\mathbb{F}_2$. If the dimension of V is d_1, we have that $|A| \leq |V| = 2^{d_1}$. Moreover, we must have $B \subseteq V^\perp$, where $V^\perp$ is the dual subspace of V. If d_2 denotes the dimension of the dual, then we have $d_1 + d_2 = n$. Thus, we have $|R| = |A| \cdot |B| \leq 2^{d_1} \cdot 2^{d_2} = 2^n$. $\square$

In this proof, we use several facts from linear algebra that are discussed in the Conventions chapter of this book.

Now, let us compute the number of inputs to IP for which $\mathsf{IP}(x, y) = 0$. When $x = 0$, the inner product is always 0. This gives 2^n inputs. When $x \neq 0$, exactly half the settings of y must give 0. If $x_i = 1$ for some i, then for any input y, define y' to be the same as y except in the ith coordinate. Then we see that $\mathsf{IP}(x, y) - \mathsf{IP}(x, y') = 1 \mod 2$, so exactly one of $\mathsf{IP}(x, y), \mathsf{IP}(x, y')$ is 0. Overall, the number of inputs for which $\mathsf{IP}(x, y) = 0$ is

$$2^n + (2^n - 1)2^n/2.$$

Finally, we see that the number of 0-rectangles needed to cover the 0s is at least

$$\frac{2^n + (2^n - 1)2^n/2}{2^n} = 1 + \frac{2^n - 1}{2} > 2^{n-1}.$$

We get an almost sharp lower bound.

Theorem 1.18 *The deterministic communication complexity of* IP *is at least n.*

Fooling Sets

In some cases, the size of the largest monochromatic rectangle does not suffice to pinpoint the communication complexity. For example, the lower bound for disjointness was off by a constant factor from the upper bound. The reason, in a nutshell, was that disjointness has many large monochromatic rectangles. The *fooling set* method allows us to prove sharp lower bounds even when there are many large monochromatic rectangles.

Definition 1.19 A set $S \subset \mathcal{X} \times \mathcal{Y}$ is called a *fooling set* for a function g if every monochromatic rectangle with respect to g can share at most one element with S.

Note that any partition of the inputs into monochromatic rectangles must be at least as large as the size of a fooling set for g. Therefore, Theorem 1.6, implies the following lower bound.

Theorem 1.20 *If g has a fooling set of size s, then the communication complexity of g is at least* $\log s$.

Let us explore some concrete applications of this method:

Disjointness Fooling sets allow us to determine the communication complexity of Disj exactly.

Claim 1.21 *The set $S = \{(X, [n] - X) : X \subseteq [n]\}$ is a fooling set for* Disj.

Proof If a rectangle contains both $(X, [n] - X)$ and $(X', [n] - X')$ for $X \neq X'$, then it also contains both $(X, [n] - X')$ and $(X', [n] - X)$. However, at least one of the last pair of sets must intersect, while the first two pairs are disjoint. □

For every $(x, y) \in S$, $\mathsf{Disj}(x, y) = 1$. Because $|S| = 2^n$, and at least one more 0-monochromatic rectangle is required, this proves:

Theorem 1.22 *The deterministic communication complexity of* Disj *is* $n + 1$.

Greater-Than Our second example for using fooling sets is the greater-than function, GT $: [n] \times [n] \to \{0, 1\}$, defined as:

$$GT(x, y) = \begin{cases} 1 & \text{if } x > y, \\ 0 & \text{otherwise.} \end{cases} \tag{1.4}$$

The trivial protocol computing greater-than has length $\lceil \log n \rceil + 1$ bits. We now prove that this is tight.

Observe that GT has many large 0-monochromatic rectangles, like $R = \{(x, y) : x < n/2, y > n/2\}$, and many large 1-monochromatic rectangles, like $R = \{(x, y) : x > n/2, y < n/2\}$. See Figure 1.12. The lower bound relies on the following fooling set.

Claim 1.23 *The set of n points $S_0 = \{(x, x) : x \in [n]\}$ is a fooling set for* GT.

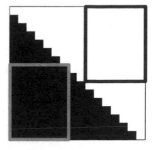

Proof If R is monochromatic and contains two distinct pairs (x, x), $(x', x') \in R$, then it also contains both (x', x) and (x, x'). However, if, say, $x' > x$, we must have $GT(x', x) \neq GT(x, x)$. □

Because S_0 is a fooling set, at least $|S_0|$ monochromatic rectangles are needed to cover the 0s. Similarly, the set

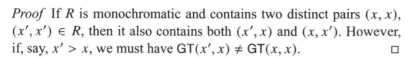

$$S_1 = \{(x + 1, x) : x \in [n - 1]\}$$

is a fooling set, and so $|S_1|$ monochromatic rectangles are needed to cover the 1s. So, $|S_0| + |S_1| = 2n - 1$ rectangles are needed in total. This proves that the communication complexity of greater-than is at least $\lceil \log(2n - 1) \rceil$. One can prove that this quantity is at least $\lceil \log n \rceil + 1$.

We leave it as an exercise to prove that $\lceil \log(2n - 1) \rceil \geq \lceil \log n \rceil + 1$.

Theorem 1.24 *The deterministic communication complexity of* GT *is* $\lceil \log(n) \rceil + 1$ *for* $n > 1$.

Asymmetric Communication

In the examples above, the scenario was symmetric – both parties had similar roles and amounts of knowledge. Now we discuss asymmetric scenarios – cases where one party has much more information than the other.

The concept of *richness* is useful for understanding asymmetric communication.[3] Intuitively, a function g is rich if there is a large set V of Bob's inputs, so that each $y \in V$ has many inputs x with $g(x, y) = 1$. See Figure 1.13 for an illustration.

[3] Miltersen et al., 1998.

Figure 1.13 A $(7, 4)$-rich function.

Definition 1.25 A function $g : \mathcal{X} \times \mathcal{Y} \to \{0, 1\}$ is said to be (u, v)-rich if there is a set $V \subseteq Y$ of size $|V| = v$ such that for all $y \in V$, we have $|\{x \in \mathcal{X} : g(x, y) = 1\}| \geq u$.

At first sight, it may seem that richness implies the existence of large 1-monochromatic rectangles. This is not true. Nevertheless, when g has an efficient asymmetric protocol, then there must be a large 1-monochromatic.

Lemma 1.26 *If $g : \mathcal{X} \times \mathcal{Y} \to \{0, 1\}$ is (u, v)-rich with $u, v > 0$, and if there is a protocol for g where Alice sends at most a bits and Bob sends at most b bits, then g admits a 1-monochromatic rectangle of dimensions $\frac{u}{2^a} \times \frac{v}{2^{a+b}}$.*

Proof The statement is proved inductively. For the base case, if the protocol does not communicate at all, then $g(x, y) = 1$ for all $x \in \mathcal{X}$, $y \in \mathcal{Y}$, and the statement holds.

If Bob sends the first bit of the protocol, then Bob partitions $\mathcal{Y}$ to $\mathcal{Y}_0 \cup \mathcal{Y}_1$. One of these two sets must have at least $v/2$ of the inputs y that show that g is (u, v)-rich. By induction, this set contains a 1-monochromatic rectangle of dimensions $\frac{u}{2^a} \times \frac{v/2}{2^{a+b-1}}$, as required.

On the other hand, if Alice sends the first bit, then this bit partitions $\mathcal{X}$ into two sets $\mathcal{X}_0, \mathcal{X}_1$. Every input $y \in \mathcal{Y}$ that has u ones must have $u/2$ ones in either $\mathcal{X}_0$ or $\mathcal{X}_1$. Thus there must be at least $v/2$ choices of inputs $y \in \mathcal{Y}$ that have $u/2$ ones for g restricted to $\mathcal{X}_0 \times \mathcal{Y}$ or for g restricted to $\mathcal{X}_1 \times \mathcal{Y}$. By induction, we get that there is a 1-monochromatic rectangle with dimensions $\frac{u/2}{2^{a-1}} \times \frac{v/2}{2^{a-1+b}}$, as required. $\square$

How can we use richness to prove lower bounds? The idea is quite simple. We need to show that g is rich and does not have 1-monochromatic rectangles that are too large. Lemma 1.26 then implies that g has no efficient asymmetric protocols. Here are a couple of examples using this approach:

Lopsided Disjointness This is an asymmetric version of disjointness, where Alice's input is promised to be a small set, while Bob's input can be an arbitrary set. Suppose Alice is given a set $X \subseteq [n]$ of size $k < n$, and Bob is given a set $Y \subseteq [n]$. Their goal is to compute the usual Disj function. See Figure 1.15. The obvious protocol is for Alice to send her input to Bob, which takes $\log \binom{n}{k}$ bits. In Chapter 2, we show that the communication complexity of this problem is at least $\log \binom{n}{k}$.

What can we say about the communication complexity of this problem if Alice is forced to send much less than $\log \binom{n}{k}$ bits?

To answer this question, we need to analyze rectangles of a certain *shape*. We restrict our attention to a special family of sets for Alice and Bob, as in Figure 1.14. We assume that the inputs are of the

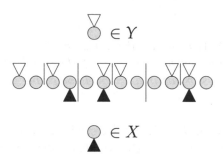

Figure 1.14 An input to the lopsided disjointness problem with $n = 12, k = 3, t = 2$.

following form. Suppose that $n = 2kt$, that X contains exactly one element from $2t(i-1)+1, \ldots, 2ti$ for each $i \in [k]$, and Y contains exactly one element of $2i - 1, 2i$ for each $i \in [kt]$.

For such inputs, we can deduce the following bound on the size of 1-monochromatic rectangles.

Claim 1.27 *If $A \times B$ is a 1-monochromatic rectangle for lopsided disjointness, then $|B| \leq 2^{kt-k|A|^{1/k}}$.*

Proof We claim that $|\bigcup_{X \in A} X| \geq k|A|^{1/k}$. Indeed, if the union $\bigcup_{X \in A} X$ has a_i elements in $\{2t(i-1)+1, \ldots, 2ti\}$, then using the arithmetic-mean geometric mean inequality:

$$\left| \bigcup_{X \in A} X \right| = \sum_{i=1}^{k} a_i \geq k \left(\prod_{i=1}^{k} a_i \right)^{1/k} \geq k|A|^{1/k}.$$

The set $\bigcup_{X \in A} X$ cannot contain both $2i, 2i + 1$ for any i because one of these two elements belongs to a set in B. Thus, the number of possible choices for sets in B is at most $2^{kt-k|A|^{1/k}}$. □

Next we argue that the lopsided disjointness function is rich:

Claim 1.28 *Lopsided disjointness is $(t^k, 2^{kt})$-rich.*

Proof Every choice for the set Y as above allows for t^k possible choices for X that are disjoint. □

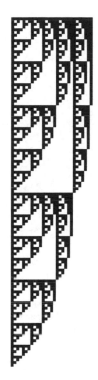

Figure 1.15 The lopsided disjointness matrix with $n = 7, k = 2$. The columns correspond to sets of size at most k from $[n]$. The rows correspond to arbitrary subsets of $[n]$.

By Lemma 1.26, any protocol where Alice sends a bits and Bob sends b bits induces a 1-monochromatic rectangle with dimensions $t^k / 2^a \times 2^{kt-a-b}$. Claim 1.27 yields

$$2^{kt-a-b} \leq 2^{kt-kt/2^{a/k}}$$

$$\Rightarrow a + b \geq \frac{n}{2^{a/k+1}}.$$

We conclude:

Theorem 1.29 *Assume that the inputs are $X, Y \subseteq [n]$ and Alice's inputs X are promised to be of size k. If Alice sends at most a bits and Bob sends at most b bits in a protocol computing* Disj*, then $a + b \geq$* $\frac{n}{2^{a/k}+1}$.

For example, when $k = 2$, if Alice sends at most $\log n$ bits to Bob, then Bob must send at least $\Omega(\sqrt{n})$ bits to Alice in order to compute lopsided disjointness.

Span Suppose Alice is given a vector $x \in \mathbb{F}_2^n$, and Bob is given an $\frac{n}{2}$-dimensional subspace $V \subseteq \mathbb{F}_2^n$, described by a basis $v_1, v_2, \ldots, v_{n/2}$ for V. Their goal is figure out whether or not $x \in V$. That is, they want to compute the Boolean function that is 1 if and only if x can be expressed as a linear combination of $v_1, \ldots, v_{n/2}$.

To prove a lower bound, we start by claiming that the inputs do not have 1-monochromatic rectangles of a certain shape:

Claim 1.30 *If $A \times B$ is a 1-monochromatic rectangle, then $|B| \leq 2^{n^2/2 - n \log |A|}$.*

Proof For every $x \in A$ and $V \in B$, we have that $x \in V$. So, for every x in the span of A, we $x \in V$ for all $V \in B$. The dimension of the span of A is at least $\log |A|$. The number of $\frac{n}{2}$-dimensional subspaces that contain this span is thus at most $\binom{2^n}{n/2 - \log |A|} \leq 2^{n^2/2 - n \log |A|}$. $\square$

> This is a loose upper bound on the number of ways we can extend the basis of the span of A to be of size $n/2$.

Next, we bound the richness:

Claim 1.31 *The span problem is $(2^{n/2}, 2^{n^2/4}/n!)$-rich.*

Proof There are at least $2^{n^2/4}$ choices for $v_1, \ldots, v_n$, and each contains $2^{n/2}$ vectors. $\square$

> For each basis vector v_i, there are at least $2^{n/2}$ available choices. So, there are at least $(2^{n/2})^{n/2} = 2^{n^2/4}$ choices for $v_1, \ldots, v_n$.

Applying Lemma 1.26, if there is a protocol where Alice sends a bits and Bob sends b bits, then

$$2^{n^2/4 - a - b} \leq 2^{n^2/2 - n \log 2^{n/2 - a}}$$

$$\Rightarrow b \geq n^2/4 - a(n + 1).$$

Theorem 1.32 *If Alice sends a bits and Bob sends b bits to solve the span problem, then $b \geq n^2/4 - a(n + 1)$.*

This shows that one of the parties must send a linear number of the bits in their input. For example, if Alice sends at most $n/8$ bits, then Bob must send at least $\Omega(n^2)$ bits in order to solve the span problem.

Lower Bounds for Relations

We have seen several methods for proving lower bounds for Boolean functions. We end this section with a method – called Krapchenko's method[4] – for proving lower bounds for relations. Here each input to Alice and Bob may have more than one valid output.

[4] Krapchenko, 1971.

Consider the following example. Let

$$\mathcal{X} = \left\{ x \in \{0,1\}^n : \sum_{i=1}^{n} x_i = 0 \mod 2 \right\},$$

and

$$\mathcal{Y} = \left\{ y \in \{0,1\}^n : \sum_{i=1}^{n} y_i = 1 \mod 2 \right\}.$$

For every $x \in \mathcal{X}, y \in \mathcal{Y}$, there is at least one index $i \in [n]$ such that $x_i \neq y_i$. The relation we are interested in is the subset of $\mathcal{X} \times \mathcal{Y} \times [n]$ consisting of all triples (x, y, i) so that $x_i \neq y_i$.

Suppose Alice is given $x \in \mathcal{X}$ and Bob is given $y \in \mathcal{Y}$, and they want to compute an index i such that $x_i \neq y_i$. How much communication is required?

In the trivial protocol, Alice sends Bob her entire string. In fact, we can use binary search to do better. Notice that

$$\sum_{i \leq n/2} x_i + \sum_{i > n/2} x_i \neq \sum_{i \leq n/2} y_i + \sum_{i > n/2} y_i \mod 2.$$

Alice and Bob can exchange two bits: $\sum_{i < n/2} x_i \mod 2$ and $\sum_{i \leq n/2} y_i \mod 2$. If these values are not the same, they can safely restrict their attention to the strings $x_{\leq n/2}, y_{\leq n/2}$ and continue. On the other hand, if the values are the same, they can continue the protocol on the strings $x_{>n/2}, y_{>n/2}$. In this way, they can eliminate half of their input strings. This yields a protocol of communication complexity $2\lceil \log n \rceil$.

It is fairly easy to see that $\log n$ bits of communication are necessary – that is the number of bits it takes to write down the answer. More formally, we need at least n monochromatic rectangles to cover the n pairs of the type $(0, e_i)$, where e_i is the ith unit vector.

Now we shall prove that $2 \log n$ bits are necessary, using a variant of fooling sets. Consider the set of inputs

$$S = \{(x, y) \in \mathcal{X} \times \mathcal{Y} : x, y \text{ differ in exactly 1 coordinate}\}.$$

The set S contains $n \cdot 2^{n-1}$ inputs because one can pick an input of S by picking $x \in \mathcal{X}$ and flipping any of the n coordinates.

We will not be able to argue that every monochromatic rectangle must contain only one or few elements of S. Instead, we prove that if a monochromatic rectangle contains many elements of S, then it must be large.

Claim 1.33 *Suppose R is a monochromatic rectangle that contains r elements of S. Then $|R| \geq r^2$.*

Proof The key observation here is that two distinct elements (x, y), (x, y') in S cannot be in the same monochromatic rectangle. For if the rectangle was labeled i, then $(x, y), (x, y')$ must disagree in the ith coordinate, but because they both belong to S we must have $y = y'$. Similarly we cannot have two distinct elements $(x, y), (x', y) \in S$ that belong to the same monochromatic rectangle.

Therefore, if $R = A \times B$ has r elements of S, we must have $|A| \geq r$ and $|B| \geq r$. So, $|R| \geq r^2$. $\square$

Now, we can prove that the binary search protocol is essentially the best one can do.

Theorem 1.34 *Any protocol computing the above relation must communicate at least $\lceil 2 \log n \rceil$ bits.*

Proof Suppose there are t monochromatic rectangles that partition the set S, and the ith rectangle covers r_i elements of S. Thus,

$$|S| = n2^{n-1} = \sum_{i=1}^{t} r_i.$$

Because the rectangles are disjoint, $|\mathcal{X} \times \mathcal{Y}| = 2^{2n-2} \geq \sum_{i=1}^{t} r_i^2$. The Cauchy-Schwartz inequality implies

$$2^{2n-2} \geq \sum_{i=1}^{t} r_i^2 \geq \left(\sum_{i=1}^{t} r_i / \sqrt{t} \right)^2 = n^2 2^{2n-2} / t.$$

So, $t \geq n^2$. $\square$

Rectangle covers have an interesting interpretation in terms of *nondeterministic* communication complexity. Here, the parties are allowed to make guesses. If a function has a 1-cover of size C, then given any input that evaluates to 1, Alice and Bob can nondeterministically guess the name of a rectangle that covers their input and then check that their inputs are consistent with the guessed rectangles. On the other hand, if their inputs correspond to a 0, no guess will convince them that their input is a 1.

Rectangle Covers

RECTANGLES ARE THE building blocks of two-party communication complexity. Every communication protocol yields a *partition* of the input space to rectangles. What happens if we count the number of monochromatic rectangles needed to *cover* all of the inputs? In other words, what if we relax the requirement that the rectangles need to be disjoint, but keep the requirement that the rectangles are monochromatic?

Definition 1.35 For $z \in \{0, 1\}$, we say that a Boolean function has a z-cover of size C if there are C monochromatic rectangles whose union contains the inputs that evaluate to z.

See Figure 1.16 for an illustration.

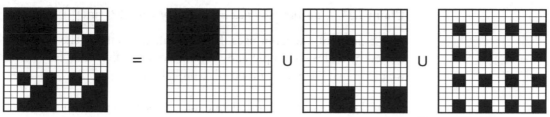

Figure 1.16 A 1-cover of size 3.

Consider the equality function. For $i \in [n], b \in \{0, 1\}$, define the rectangle

$$R_{i,b} = \{(x, y) : x_i = b, y_i \neq b\}.$$

This is a 0-cover of size $2n$. There is no 1-cover of comparable size – the fooling set method showed that at least 2^n monochromatic rectangles are needed to cover the 1s. So, equality has a 0-cover of size $2n$, but no 1-cover of size less than 2^n.

Equality was defined in (1.2).

By Theorem 1.6, every function that admits a protocol with communication c also admits a 1-cover of size at most 2^c and a 0-cover of size at most 2^c. The following extension of Theorem 1.9 shows that the converse holds as well:

Theorem 1.36 *If g has a 0-cover of size 2^{c_0} and a 1-cover of size 2^{c_1}, then there is a protocol that computes g with $O(c_0 c_1)$ bits of communication.*

One can prove Theorem 1.36 by reduction to the clique versus independent set problem – we leave the details to Exercise 1.2. Theorem 1.36 is stronger than Theorem 1.9, and it is also tight, as we show next.

For those familiar with the complexity classes P and NP, Theorem 1.36 can be interpreted as saying that in the context of two-party communication complexity $P = NP \cap coNP$.

Can the logarithm of the cover number be significantly different from the communication complexity? We have already seen that equality has a 0-cover of size $2n$, but requires communication at least $n + 1$. This gives an exponential gap between the size of the 0-cover and communication complexity. Disjointness also has small 0-cover. For $i = 1, 2, \ldots, n$, define the rectangle

An efficient partition of the 1s of the input space into rectangles also leads to an efficient protocol. See Exercise 1.1.

$$R_i = \{(X, Y) : i \in X, i \in Y\}.$$

This gives a 0-cover of size n. Yet, by Theorem 1.22 the communication complexity of disjointness is $n + 1$. So, there is an exponential gap between the logarithm of the size of a 0-cover and the communication complexity. As with equality, the fooling set method shows that every 1-cover for disjointness must have size at least 2^n.

Another interesting example is the k-disjointness function. Here Alice and Bob are given sets $X, Y \subseteq [n]$, each of size k. We shall see in Chapter 2 that the communication complexity of k-disjointness is at least $\log \binom{n}{k} \approx k \log(n/k)$. As above, there is a 0-cover of k-disjointness using n rectangles. But this time, the function has a small 1-cover as well:

In Chapter 6, we prove that actually any 1-cover of disjointness must have size at least $2^{\Omega(n)}$.

Claim 1.37 *k-disjointness has a 1-cover of size $\lceil 2^{2k} \cdot \ln(\binom{n}{k}^2) \rceil$.*

The proof of the claim uses the probabilistic method. The idea, pioneered by Erdős, is simple and elegant. To prove that an object exists, we prove that it occurs with positive probability.

Proof For every set $S \subseteq [n]$, define the monochromatic rectangle

$$R = \{(X, Y) : X \subseteq S, Y \subseteq [n] - S\}.$$

Now sample $t = \lceil 2^{2k} \cdot \ln \left(\binom{n}{k}^2 \right) \rceil$ such rectangles independently and uniformly. The probability that a particular disjoint pair (X, Y) is included in a particular sample is 2^{-2k}. So, the probability that the pair is excluded from all the rectangles is

$$(1 - 2^{-2k})^t < e^{-2^{-2k}t} \le \binom{n}{k}^{-2}.$$

Because $1 - x < e^{-x}$ for $x > 0$.

Because the number of disjoint pairs (X, Y) is at most $\binom{n}{k}^2$, the probability that there is a disjoint pair that is excluded by the t rectangles is less than 1. So there must be t rectangles that cover all the 1 inputs. $\square$

Setting $k = \log n$, we have found a 1-cover with $O(n^2 \log^2 n)$ rectangles. So, *all* the entries of the matrix can be covered with $2^{O(\log n)}$ monochromatic rectangles. However, we shall see in Chapter 2 that the communication complexity of k-disjointness is exactly $\log \binom{n}{k} = \Omega(\log^2 n)$. This proves that Theorem 1.36 is tight.

Direct-Sums in Communication Complexity

THE DIRECT-SUM QUESTION is about the complexity of solving several copies of a given problem. It can be posed in any computational model. In communication complexity, it can be phrased as follows. If a function g requires c bits of communication, how much communication is required to compute k copies of g?

More formally, given a function $g : \{0, 1\}^n \times \{0, 1\}^n \to \{0, 1\}$, define

$$g^k : (\{0, 1\}^n)^k \times (\{0, 1\}^n)^k \to \{0, 1\}^k$$

by

$$g^k((x_1, \ldots, x_k), (y_1, \ldots, y_k)) = (g(x_1, y_1), g(x_2, y_2), \ldots, g(x_k, y_k)).$$

If the communication complexity of g is c, then the communication complexity of g^k is at most kc. Can it be much lower?

No such examples are known for computing functions.

We shall describe an example where the cost of computing k copies of a relation is less than k times the cost of computing one copy.

Suppose Alice is given a set $S \subseteq [n]$ of size $n/2$, with n even. Bob has no input. The goal of the parties[5] is to output an element of S.

[5] Alon and Orlitsky, 1995.

Alice can send Bob the minimum element of her set. This can be done with communication $\lceil \log(\frac{n}{2} + 1) \rceil$ because the elements $n/2 + 2, \dots, n$ can never be the minimum of S. Moreover, $\lceil \log(\frac{n}{2} + 1) \rceil$ bits are necessary. Indeed, if fewer bits are sent, then the set of elements P that Bob could potentially output is of size at most $n/2$, and so the protocol would fail if Alice is given the complement of P as input.

On the other hand, we show that the parties can solve k copies of this problem with $k + \log(nk)$ bits of communication, while the naive protocol would take $k \log(n/2 + 1)$ bits of communication. The key claim is

Claim 1.38 *There is a set $Q \subseteq [n]^k$ of size $nk2^k$ with the property that for any $S_1, S_2, \dots, S_k$, each of size $n/2$, there is an element $q \in Q$ such that $q_i \in S_i$ for every $i = 1, 2, \dots, k$.*

This claim gives the protocol – Alice simply sends Bob the name of the element of Q with the required property. Once again, the proof of the claim relies on the probabilistic method.

Proof To find such a set Q, we pick $|Q|$ elements from $[n]^k$ by sampling each element uniformly at random. For any fixed $S_1, \dots, S_k$, the probability that Q misses this tuple is

$$(1 - (1/2)^k)^{|Q|} \leq e^{-(1/2)^k |Q|}.$$

Setting $|Q| = nk2^k$, the probability that Q does not have an element that works for some tuple is at most

$$2^{nk} e^{-(1/2)^k |Q|} \leq 2^{nk} e^{-nk} < 1.$$

Thus such a Q does exist. □

So, in some cases, some saving is possible. Nevertheless, there is a nontrivial lower bound[6] for the communication complexity of g^k in terms of the communication complexity of g.

[6] Feder et al., 1995.

Theorem 1.39 *If g requires c bits of communication, then g^k requires at least $k(\sqrt{c} - \log n - 1)$ bits of communication.*

One can show that even computing the two bits $\wedge_{i=1}^k g(x_i, y_i)$, and $\vee_{i=1}^k g(x_i, y_i)$ requires $k(\sqrt{c} - \log n - 1)$ bits of communication – see Exercise 1.14.

The proof uses the fact that we can extract a monochromatic cover for g from a monochromatic cover for g^k. This is summarized in the following lemma:

Lemma 1.40 *If the inputs to g^k can be covered with 2^ℓ monochromatic rectangles, then the inputs to g can be covered with $\lceil 2n \cdot 2^{\ell/k} \rceil$ monochromatic rectangles.*

To prove Theorem 1.39, observe that if g^k has communication ℓ, then its inputs can be covered with 2^ℓ monochromatic rectangles, by

Theorem 1.6. Theorem 1.36 and Lemma 1.40 then imply that g has a protocol with communication $(\ell/k + \log n + 1)^2$. Thus,

$$c \le (\ell/k + \log n + 1)^2$$
$$\Rightarrow \ell \ge k(\sqrt{c} - \log n - 1).$$

Proof of Lemma 1.40 We iteratively find the rectangles that cover the input space using the following claim.

Claim 1.41 *For every nonempty set $S \subseteq \{0,1\}^n \times \{0,1\}^n$, there is a rectangle that is monochromatic under g and covers at least $2^{-\ell/k}|S|$ of the inputs from S.*

Proof The set S^k can be covered by 2^ℓ monochromatic rectangles. In particular, there is a monochromatic rectangle R that covers at least $2^{-\ell}|S|^k$ of these inputs. For each $i \in [k]$, define

$$R_i = \{(x,y) \in \{0,1\}^n \times \{0,1\}^n : \exists (a,b) \in R, a_i = x, b_i = y\}.$$

The set R_i is simply the projection of the rectangle R to the ith coordinate. The set R_i is also a rectangle because R is a rectangle. Moreover, because R is monochromatic under g^k, each R_i is monochromatic under g. Finally, because

$$\prod_{i=1}^{k} |R_i \cap S| \ge |R \cap S^k| \ge 2^{-\ell}|S|^k.$$

there must be some i for which $|R_i \cap S| \ge 2^{-\ell/k}|S|$. $\qquad\square$

We repeatedly pick rectangles using Claim 1.41 until all of the inputs to g are covered. Let $S \subseteq \{0,1\}^n \times \{0,1\}^n$ denote the set of inputs to g that have not yet been covered by one of the monochromatic rectangles we have already found. Initially, S is the set of all inputs. Eventually, we reach the empty set. Indeed, after $\lceil 2n2^{\ell/k} \rceil$ steps, the number of uncovered inputs is at most

$$2^{2n} \cdot (1 - 2^{-\ell/k})^{2n2^{\ell/k}} \le 2^{2n} e^{-2^{-\ell/k} \cdot 2n2^{\ell/k}} = 2^{2n} \cdot e^{-2n} < 1.$$

Because $1 - x \le e^{-x}$ for all x.

Lemma 1.40 is proved. $\qquad\square$

Exercises

Ex 1.1 – Show that if $g : \mathcal{X} \times \mathcal{Y} \to \{0,1\}$ is such that $g^{-1}(1)$ can be partitioned into 2^c rectangles, then g has communication complexity at most $O(c^2)$.

Ex 1.2 – Prove Theorem 1.36 by reduction to the protocol for the cliques and independent sets problem. *Hint: Define a graph where the vertices correspond to rectangles in the rectangle cover.*

Ex 1.3 – Suppose Alice and Bob each get a subset of size k of $[n]$ and want to know whether these sets intersect or not. Show that at least $\log(\lfloor n/k \rfloor)$ bits are required.

Ex 1.4 – Suppose Alice gets a string $x \in \{0,1\}^n$ that has more 0s than 1s, and Bob gets a string $y \in \{0,1\}^n$ that has more 1s than 0s. They wish to communicate to find a coordinate i where $x_i \neq y_i$. Show that at least $2 \log n$ bits of communication are required.

Ex 1.5 – The chromatic number $\chi(G)$ of a graph G is the minimum number of colors needed to color the vertices of G so that no two adjacent vertices have the same color.

1. Consider the following communication problem. Alice gets a vertex x in G, Bob gets a vertex y in G, and they need to decide whether $\{x, y\}$ is an edge in G. Show that $\log \chi(G)$ is at most the deterministic communication complexity this problem. *Hint: Recall that (x, x) is never an edge of the graph.*

2. Let H denote the graph on the same vertex set as G, such that $\{x, y\}$ is an edge of H if and only if there is a path of length 2 of the form x, z, y in G. Consider the following communication problem. Alice gets x, Bob gets y, and they are promised that $\{x, y\}$ is an edge of G. Their goal is for Alice to learn y and Bob to learn x. Give a protocol with $2 \log \chi(H)$ bits for accomplishing this.

Ex 1.6 – Recall the protocol for the median of two *lists* discussed in the introduction. Consider the following variant of the median problem. Alice is given a set $X \subseteq [n]$, Bob is given a set $Y \subseteq [n]$, and their goal is to compute the median of the *set* $X \cup Y$. The difference here is that we take the union as sets, so there are no repetitions. Show that the communication complexity of this problem is at least $\Omega(n/\log n)$. *Hint: Compute the median of the union of sets, as well as the union of the lists.*

Ex 1.7 – Show that for every $0 \leq \alpha < 1/2$, any deterministic protocol for estimating the Hamming distance between two strings $x, y \in \{0,1\}^n$ up to an additive error αn must have length at least $\Omega(n)$. To do this, use an error correcting code. An error correcting code is a map $E : \{0,1\}^m \to \{0,1\}^{O(m)}$ with the property that if $x \neq y$, then $E(x)$ and $E(y)$ disagree in at least α fraction of their coordinates. Such a code exists for every $0 \leq \alpha < 1/2$. Use the code to prove the lower bound.

Ex 1.8 – Prove the following. Suppose Alice is given a string $x \in [w]^k$, and Bob is given a sequence Y of sets $Y_1, \ldots, Y_k \subseteq [w]$. If there a protocol that determines whether or not there is an i such that $x_i \in Y_i$, with Alice sending a bits and Bob sending b bits, then $a + b \geq \frac{wk}{2^{a/k}+1}$.

Ex 1.9 – In the Introduction, given a function $f : \{0,1\}^{2n} \to \{0,1\}$, and a subset $S \subseteq [2n]$, let $C(f, S)$ be the communication complexity of computing f, when Alice is given the bits of the input that correspond to S, and Bob is given the bits that correspond to the complement of S. In the Introduction, we see that the area of a chip computing f can be related to $C(f, S)$, for some set S containing roughly half of the input. Use a counting argument to show that there is a universal constant $\epsilon > 0$ such that for most functions f, it holds that $C(f, S) \geq \epsilon n$, for every set S with $2n/3 \leq |S| \leq 3n/4$.

Ex 1.10 – Give an explicit example of a function $f : \{0,1\}^{4n} \to \{0,1\}$ for which $C(f,S) \geq \Omega(n)$ for all sets S with $|S| \leq 4n/3$. Hint: Consider functions of the type $f(A,B,x) = \mathsf{IP}(x_A, x_{A^c})$, where here $A,B \subset [m]$ are disjoint subsets of size $m/10$, $x \in \{0,1\}^m$, and x_A, x_B are the projections of x onto the coordinates of A and B.

Ex 1.11 – Let $f : \{0,1\}^n \times \{0,1\}^n \to \{0,1\}$ be a function with the property that for every $x \in \{0,1\}^n$, there are exactly t choices for j with $f(x,y) = 1$, and for every $y \in \{0,1\}^n$, there are exactly t choices for x with $f(x,y) = 1$. Our goal is to show that f must admit a 0-cover of size at most $(2n)^t$.

To do this, we use *Hall's matching theorem*. Let L, R be disjoint sets of the same size. Given a bipartite graph with vertex set $L \cup R$, where every edge belongs to the set $L \times R$, Hall's theorem says that if every subset $S \subseteq L$ is connected to at least $|S|$ vertices in R, then the graph must contain a *matching*, namely $|L|$ disjoint edges.

- Use Hall's theorem to prove that there are permutations $\pi_1, \ldots, \pi_t$ such that $f(x,y) = 1$ if and only if $y = \pi_r(x)$ for some r.
- Give a 0-cover of size $(2n)^t$ for f.

Ex 1.12 – This exercise shows that an analogue of Theorem 1.36 does not hold for *partial* functions. These are functions that are defined on a subset of the domain. Consider the partial function $f : \{0,1\}^n \times \{0,1\}^n \to \{0,1\}$, where the input to each party is interpreted as two $n/2$ bit strings, defined by

$$f(x,x',y,y') = \begin{cases} 1 & \text{if } x = y \text{ and } x' \neq y', \\ 0 & \text{if } x \neq y \text{ and } x' = y'. \end{cases}$$

Show that there are $2n$ monochromatic rectangles that cover the domain of f. A rectangle is considered monochromatic if f takes on the same value on any two inputs of the rectangle where f has been defined. Show that the communication complexity of f is at least $\Omega(n)$.

Ex 1.13 – For a Boolean function g, define $g^{\wedge k}$ by

$$g(x_1, x_2, \ldots, x_k, y_1, \ldots, y_k) = \wedge_{i=1}^{k} g(x_i, y_i).$$

Show that if $g^{\wedge k}$ has a 1-cover of size 2^{ℓ}, then g has a 1-cover of size $2^{\ell/k}$.

Ex 1.14 – Show that if $g : \{0,1\}^n \times \{0,1\}^n \to \{0,1\}$ requires c bits of communication, then any protocol computing both $\wedge_{i=1}^{k} g(x_i, y_i)$ and $\vee_{i=1}^{k} g(x_i, y_i)$ requires $k(\sqrt{c/2} - \log n - 1)$ bits of communication.

2

Rank

A MATRIX IS A POWERFUL AND VERSATILE WAY to represent objects. Once an object is encoded as a matrix, the many tools of linear algebra can be put to use to reason about the object. This broad approach has a long history in mathematics, and it is useful in communication complexity as well.

The linear algebra method in combinatorics, spectral graph theory, and representation theory are just a few examples of this paradigm.

Communication problems between two parties correspond to matrices in a natural way. A function $g : \mathcal{X} \times \mathcal{Y} \to \{0, 1\}$ corresponds to an $|\mathcal{X}| \times |\mathcal{Y}|$ matrix M, where the (x, y)th entry of M is $M_{xy} = g(x, y)$. What do the linear algebraic properties of M tell us about the communication complexity of g?

Sometimes it is convenient to use $M_{xy} = (-1)^{g(x,y)}$ instead.

The *rank* of a matrix is a fundamental concept in linear algebra. It is the maximum size of a set of linearly independent rows in the matrix. We write rank(M) to denote the rank of M. One reason why rank is such a useful concept is that is has many equivalent interpretations:

If the function depends on the inputs of k parties, the natural representation is by a k-dimensional tensor rather than a matrix.

Fact 2.1 *For an $m \times n$ matrix M, the following are equivalent:*

1. rank(M) = r.

2. *r is the maximum size of a set of linearly independent columns in M.*

3. *r is the smallest number such that M can be expressed as $M = AB$, where A is an $m \times r$ matrix, and B is an $r \times n$ matrix.*

4. *r is the smallest number such that M can be expressed as the sum of r matrices of rank 1.*

Throughout this chapter, rank is over the reals, unless explicitly stated otherwise.

The rank of a matrix is invariant under several natural operations: scaling the entries of a matrix by the same nonzero number, reordering the rows, reordering the columns, or taking the transpose does not change the rank. Coincidentally, communication complexity is *also* invariant under these operations – could there be a deeper relationship between rank and communication?

Low-rank Boolean matrices have even more structure. This will be exploited several times in this chapter.

This connection is tantalizing because rank is an old concept in mathematics, one that we understand quite well. There are efficient algorithms for computing the rank, but no such algorithms for computing communication complexity. Moreover, rank satisfies many properties that do not seem to have natural analogues in communication complexity. For example, if U, V are invertible, then rank(UMV) = rank(M).

Gaussian elimination can be used to compute the rank of an $n \times n$ matrix in $O(n^3)$ steps.

Communication Complexity and Rank

When we refer to the
communication complexity of
M, we mean the
communication complexity of
the associated function.

THE MANY EQUIVALENT DEFINITIONS OF RANK discussed
above yield inequalities that relate communication complexity and rank.
We start by showing that small rank implies small communication
complexity.

Theorem 2.2 *The communication complexity of M is at most* rank
$(M) + 1$.

See Exercise 2.1.

Proof The third characterization of rank in Fact 2.1 is suggestive of
communication complexity. Alice and Bob can use a factorization $M =
AB$, where A is an $m \times r$ matrix, and B is an $r \times n$, to get a protocol for
computing g. Alice is given an input $x \in \mathcal{X}$, and Bob is given $y \in \mathcal{Y}$. If
$e_x \in \{0, 1\}^{\mathcal{X}}$ denotes the standard unit column vector that is 1 in the xth
entry, and $e_y \in \{0, 1\}^{\mathcal{Y}}$ denotes the standard unit column vector that is 1
in the yth entry, then

$$g(x, y) = e_x^{\mathsf{T}} M e_y = e_x^{\mathsf{T}} A B e_y.$$

Now, Alice can send Bob $e_x^{\mathsf{T}} A$, and then Bob can multiply this vector
with $B e_y$ and send back $M_{x,y}$. This involves transmitting a vector of at
most $r + 1$ numbers. It seems like we have shown that the communication complexity is at most $r + 1$. But there is a catch – each of the
numbers in the vector $e_x^{\mathsf{T}} A$ may require many bits to encode.

To salvage this approach, we ensure that A is also Boolean.

Claim 2.3 $M = AB$, *where A is a Boolean $m \times r$ matrix and B is an*
$r \times n$ *matrix.*

Theorem 2.2 is far from the
last word on the subject. By
the end of this chapter, we will
prove that the communication
is bounded from above by a
quantity closer to $\sqrt{r}$.

Let A be an $m \times r$ matrix consisting of r columns of M that are linearly
independent. Because r is the rank of M, every other column of M is a
linear combination of these r columns. So, there is some $r \times n$ matrix B
with $AB = M$. The parties use the same protocol as above, except that
now every entry in the vector $e_x^{T} A$ can be encoded with a bit because A
is Boolean.   □

Below we see many examples
where Theorem 2.4
immediately implies sharp
lower bounds on
communication complexity.

Conversely, the decomposition of communication protocols in terms
of combinatorial rectangles shows that large rank implies large communication complexity.

Theorem 2.4 *If M is not the all 1s matrix, then the communication
complexity of M is at least* $\log(\text{rank}(M) + 1)$.

Proof By Theorem 1.6, we know that M can be partitioned into 2^c
monochromatic rectangles. For every rectangle R of the partition, let
z denote the value of the function in the rectangle, and let M_R denote
the matrix whose (x, y)th entry is z if $(x, y) \in R$, and 0 otherwise. We
have $\text{rank}(M_R) \leq 1$. Moreover, M can be expressed as the sum of 2^c
such matrices, and at least one of these matrices is 0 because M has at
least one zero. By Fact 2.1, $\text{rank}(M) \leq 2^c - 1$.   □

How sharp are the two bounds above? Which of the two quantities rank(M) and log(rank(M)) is closer to the communication complexity of M? This is the issue we explore in the rest of this chapter.

When M is the all 1s matrix, $\log(\text{rank}(M) + 1) = 1$, but the communication complexity is 0.

Properties of Rank

IN ORDER TO BETTER UNDERSTAND the relationship between rank and communication complexity, we review some of the nice properties of rank.

A matrix R is called a *submatrix* of M if R can be obtained by repeatedly deleting rows and columns of M. In other words, it is the matrix specified by a subset of the columns of M and a subset of the rows of M. It is the matrix obtained by restricting the inputs to a rectangle.

Fact 2.5 *If R is a submatrix of M then* rank(R) $\leq$ rank(M).

Fact 2.6 rank $\left(\begin{bmatrix} A & C \\ 0 & B \end{bmatrix} \right) \geq$ rank(A) + rank(B).

Fact 2.6 follows from the definition of rank.

Fact 2.7 $|\text{rank}(A) - \text{rank}(B)| \leq \text{rank}(A + B) \leq \text{rank}(A) + \text{rank}(B)$.

A consequence of Fact 2.7 is that the constants used to represent a function $g(i, j)$ do not significantly change the rank. For example, if M is a matrix with $0/1$ entries, one can define a matrix M' of the same dimensions by

Fact 2.7 follows from the fact that the rank of M is the minimum number of rank 1 matrices that add up to M.

$$M'_{i,j} = (-1)^{M_{i,j}}.$$

This operation replaces 1s with -1s and 0s with 1s. Now observe that $M' = J - 2M$, where J is the all 1s matrix, and so

Fact 2.8 $|\text{rank}(M') - \text{rank}(M)| \leq \text{rank}(J) = 1$.

Another nice feature of rank is that monochromatic rectangles correspond to submatrices of rank at most 1. The following fact can be proved using the previous facts:

Fact 2.9 *If* rank(R) ≤ 1,

$$\text{rank} \left(\begin{bmatrix} R \\ B \end{bmatrix} \right) + \text{rank} \left(\begin{bmatrix} R & A \end{bmatrix} \right) \leq \text{rank} \left(\begin{bmatrix} R & A \\ B & C \end{bmatrix} \right) + 3.$$

See Exercise 2.2.

The *tensor product* of an $m \times n$ matrix M and an $m' \times n'$ matrix M' is the $mm' \times nn'$ matrix $T = M \otimes M'$ whose entries are indexed by tuples $(i, i'), (j, j')$ defined by

$$T_{(i,i'),(j,j')} = M_{i,j} \cdot M_{i',j'}.$$

The tensor product multiplies the rank, a fact that is very useful for proving lower bounds.

Fact 2.10 rank($M \otimes M'$) = rank(M) $\cdot$ rank(M').

Try to prove Fact 2.10.

When the matrix is both Boolean and low-rank, it often enjoys additional properties. One such property was exploited when we proved Claim 2.3. A consequence of the claim is:

Lemma 2.11 *A matrix with 0/1 entries of rank r has at most 2^r distinct rows, and at most 2^r distinct columns.*

Proof If M is a Boolean matrix, by Claim 2.3, $M = AB$ where A is a Boolean $m \times r$ matrix and B is an $r \times m$ matrix. Because A is Boolean, A can have at most 2^r distinct rows. But this means M can have at most 2^r distinct rows. A similar argument proves that M can have at most 2^r distinct columns.   □

Lower Bounds Based on Rank

THE LOGARITHM OF THE RANK always gives a lower bound on communication complexity. Here we revisit several examples from the previous chapter and see what this lower bound gives.

Note that communication complexity must be an integer. $\log 2^n = n$, and log is a strictly increasing function, so $\log(2^n + 1) > n$.

Equality We start with the equality function, defined in (1.2). The matrix of the equality function is just the identity matrix. The rank of the matrix is 2^n, proving that the communication complexity of equality is at least $\lceil \log(2^n + 1) \rceil = n + 1$.

Can you prove a sharp $1 + \lceil \log n \rceil$ lower bound using rank?

Greater-Than Consider the greater-than function, defined in (1.4). The matrix of this function is the upper-triangular matrix, which is 1 above the diagonal and 0 on all other points. Once again, the matrix has full rank. This proves that the communication complexity is at least $\log(n + 1)$.

Disjointness Consider our running example, the disjointness function, defined in (1.1). The size of rectangles did not give sharp lower bounds on the communication complexity of Disj. To prove sharp lower bounds using footings sets, we needed to carefully identify the correct fooling set. We now show that rank gives a sharp lower bound.

Let D_n be the 0/1 matrix that represents disjointness. Let us order the rows and columns of the matrix in lexicographic order so that the last rows/columns correspond to sets that contain n. We see that D_n can be expressed as:

$$D_n = \begin{bmatrix} D_{n-1} & D_{n-1} \\ D_{n-1} & 0 \end{bmatrix}.$$

In other words $D_n = D_1 \otimes D_{n-1}$ and so

$$\text{rank}(D_n) = 2 \cdot \text{rank}(D_{n-1}) = 2 \cdot 2 \cdot \text{rank}(D_{n-2}) = \cdots = 2^n,$$

by Fact 2.10. This proves that the communication complexity of disjointness is at least $\lceil \log(2^n + 1) \rceil = n + 1$.

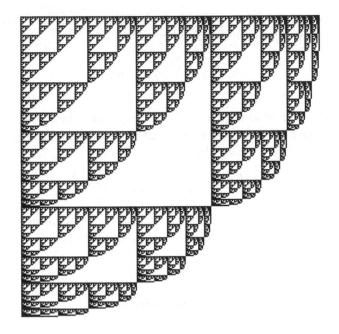

Figure 2.1 The disjointness matrix $D_{9,4}$, which represents disjointness when restricted to sets of size at most 4 on a universe of size 9. The sets are ordered lexicographically. Compare this with Figure I.2.

k-Disjointness Consider the disjointness function restricted to sets of size at most k. In this case, the matrix is a $\sum_{i=0}^{k} \binom{n}{i} \times \sum_{i=0}^{k} \binom{n}{i}$ matrix. Let us write $D_{n,k}$ to represent the matrix for this problem. See Figure 2.1.

Analyzing the rank of $D_{n,k}$ is more complicated than the three examples above. We shall use algebra to prove[1] that this matrix also has full rank. In particular, we use a powerful tool from algebra – polynomials.

[1] Gregoryev, 1982.

Polynomials are often used to prove facts in combinatorics. It may be helpful to recall the section about polynomials from the Conventions and Preliminaries chapter.

For two sets $X, Y \subseteq [n]$ of size at most k, define the monomial $m_X(z_1, \ldots, z_n) = \prod_{i \in X} z_i$, and the string $z_Y \in \{0,1\}^n$ such that $(z_Y)_i = 0$ if and only if $i \in Y$. This ensures that $\mathrm{Disj}(X, Y) = m_X(z_Y)$. The rows of the matrix are associated with the Xs. Any nonzero linear combination of the rows corresponds to a linear combination of the monomials we have defined and so gives a nonzero polynomial f. We show there must be a set Y of size at most k so that $f(z_Y) \neq 0$, so the linear combination cannot be zero. This proves that the rank of the matrix is full.

To show this, let X be a set that corresponds to a monomial of maximum degree in f. Let us restrict the values of all variables outside X to be equal to 1. This turns f into a nonzero polynomial that only depends on the variables corresponding to X. In this polynomial, let X' denote the set of variables in a minimal monomial that has a nonzero coefficient. Consider the assignment z_Y for $Y = X - X'$. Now, $f(z_Y)$ is equal to the coefficient of this minimal monomial, which is nonzero.

Can you come up with a similar proof that shows that the matrix for disjointness on sets of size *exactly* k also has full rank?

Inner-Product Our final example is the inner-product function IP : $\{0,1\}^n \times \{0,1\}^n \to \{0,1\}$ defined by

$$\mathsf{IP}(x,y) = \sum_{i=1}^{n} x_i y_i \quad \text{mod } 2. \tag{2.1}$$

Here it is helpful to use Fact 2.8. If P_n represents the IP matrix after sorting the rows and columns lexicographically, and replacing 1 with -1 and 0 with -1, we see that

$$P_n = \begin{bmatrix} P_{n-1} & P_{n-1} \\ P_{n-1} & -P_{n-1} \end{bmatrix} = \begin{bmatrix} 1 & 1 \\ 1 & -1 \end{bmatrix} \otimes P_{n-1}.$$

So, by Fact 2.10, $\text{rank}(P_n) = 2 \cdot \text{rank}(P_{n-1})$. This proves that $\text{rank}(P_n) = 2^n$, and so by Fact 2.8, the communication complexity of IP is at least n.

Try to prove a sharp $n + 1$ lower bound using rank.

Nonnegative Rank

RANK IS NOT THE ONLY WAY TO measure the complexity of matrices using linear algebra. When working with nonnegative matrices, there is another very natural measure, the *nonnegative rank*.

A matrix is called nonnegative if all of its entries are nonnegative.

The nonnegative rank of a nonnegative matrix M, denoted $\text{rank}_+(M)$, is the smallest number of nonnegative rank 1 matrices that sum to M. Equivalently, it is the smallest number r such that $M = AB$, where A is a nonnegative $m \times r$ matrix, and B is a nonnegative $r \times n$ matrix. The definitions immediately give:

Fact 2.12 *If M is an $m \times n$ nonnegative matrix then* $\text{rank}(M) \leq \text{rank}_+(M) \leq \min\{n, m\}$.

However, $\text{rank}(M)$ and $\text{rank}_+(M)$ may be quite different. For example, given a set of numbers $X = \{x_1, \ldots, x_n\}$, consider the $n \times n$ matrix defined by $M_{i,j} = (x_i - x_j)^2 = x_i^2 + x_j^2 - 2x_i x_j$. Because M is the sum of three rank 1 matrices, namely the matrices corresponding to x_i^2, x_j^2 and $-2x_i x_j$, we have $\text{rank}(M) \leq 3$. On the other hand, we can show by induction on n that $\text{rank}_+(M) \geq \log n$. Indeed, if $\text{rank}_+(M) = r$, then there must be nonnegative rank 1 matrices $R_1, \ldots, R_r$ such that $M = R_1 + \cdots + R_r$. Let the set of positive entries of R_1 correspond to the rectangle $A \times B \subset X \times X$. Then we must have that either $|A| \leq n/2$ or $|B| \leq n/2$, or else there will be an element $x \in A \cap B$, but $M_{x,x} = 0$ is not positive. Suppose without loss of generality that $|A| \leq n/2$. Let

Another example is the matrix indexed by binary strings $x, y \in \{0,1\}^n$ where $M_{x,y} = (1 - \langle x, y \rangle)^2$. Its $\text{rank}(M)$ is at most polynomial in n, but we shall see in Chapter 6 that $\text{rank}_+(M) \geq 2^{\Omega(n)}$.

M' be the submatrix that corresponds to the numbers of $X - A$. Then, by induction,

$$r - 1 \geq \text{rank}_+(M') \geq \log(n/2) = \log(n) - 1.$$

Nonnegative rank is a fundamental concept. We shall revisit it again in Chapter 12. We saw in Theorem 2.4 that the logarithm of the rank gives a lower bound on communication complexity. The same argument works for nonnegative rank:

Theorem 2.13 *If M is not the all 1s matrix, the communication complexity of M is at least* $\log(\text{rank}_+(M) + 1)$.

Because $\text{rank}(M) \leq \text{rank}_+(M)$, Theorem 2.2 implies that the communication complexity is at most $\text{rank}_+(M) + 1$. In fact,[2] there is a much more efficient communication protocol:

[2] Lovász, 1990.

Theorem 2.14 *The communication complexity of a Boolean matrix M is at most* $O(\log^2(\text{rank}_+(M)))$.

The theorem follows from a more general statement:

Recall the notion of covers from Definition 1.35.

Lemma 2.15 *If a Boolean matrix M has a 1-cover of size 2^c then the communication complexity M is at most* $O(c \cdot \log(\text{rank}(M)))$.

Let us use the lemma to prove the theorem. Suppose $\text{rank}_+(M) = r$ and write $M = R_1 + \cdots + R_r$, where $R_1, \ldots, R_r$ are nonnegative rank 1 matrices. The set of nonzero entries of each matrix R_i must form a monochromatic rectangle in M with value 1. Thus, M must have a 1-cover of size r. By the lemma, its communication complexity is at most

$$O(\log(\text{rank}_+(M)) \cdot \log(\text{rank}(M))) \leq O(\log^2(\text{rank}_+(M))).$$

Proof of Lemma 2.15 For every rectangle R in the one-cover, we can write

$$M = \begin{bmatrix} R & A \\ B & C \end{bmatrix}.$$

By Fact 2.9, either

$$\text{rank}\left(\begin{bmatrix} R & A \end{bmatrix}\right) \leq (\text{rank}(M) + 3)/2, \tag{2.2}$$

or

$$\text{rank}\left(\begin{bmatrix} R \\ B \end{bmatrix}\right) \leq (\text{rank}(M) + 3)/2. \tag{2.3}$$

So, if Alice sees a rectangle R in the cover that is consistent with her input and satisfies (2.2), she announces its name. Describing R takes at most c bits. Similarly, if Bob sees a rectangle R that is consistent with his input and satisfies (2.3), he announces its name.

If they find an R that contains their input, then they deduce that the output is 1. Otherwise, both parties then restrict their attention to the appropriate submatrix, which reduces the rank of M by a constant factor. This can continue for at most $O(\log(\text{rank}(M)))$ steps. If neither finds an appropriate R to announce, then they can safely output 0. □

Better Upper Bounds Using Rank

LOW RANK IMPLIES LOW COMMUNICATION COMPLEXITY, and vice versa. There is, however, an exponential gap between the two bounds we have seen so far. The communication complexity is at least $\log(\text{rank}(M) + 1)$ and at most $\text{rank}(M) + 1$. Given Theorem 2.14, one might be tempted to believe that the first inequality is closer to the truth. This is the log-rank conjecture due to Lovász and Saks:[3]

[3] Lovász and Saks, 1988.

Conjecture 2.16 (Log-rank conjecture) *There is a constant α such that the communication complexity of a nonconstant matrix M is at most* $\log^{\alpha}(\text{rank}(M))$.

It is known[4] that α must be at least 2 for the conjecture to hold. See Chapter 8 for more details.

[4] Göös et al., 2015; and Ambainis et al., 2016.

In fact, the log-rank conjecture can be stated in a form that has nothing to do with communication: Is it true that the logarithm of the rank of a Boolean matrix is at most polylogarithmic in the logarithm of its nonnegative rank? Is it true that a Boolean matrix of small rank has a small one-cover? Is it true that a Boolean matrix of small rank has a large submatrix of even smaller rank? All such statements are equivalent to the log-rank conjecture.

See Exercise 2.7

Here we prove[5] a weaker bound:

[5] Lovett, 2014.

Lovett actually proved that the communication is bounded from above by $O(\sqrt{r}\log r)$, but we prove the weaker bound here for ease of presentation.

Theorem 2.17 *If the rank of a matrix is $r > 1$, then its communication complexity is at most $O(\sqrt{r}\log^2 r)$.*

To prove Theorem 2.17, we need to understand something fundamental about the structure of low-rank Boolean matrices. We prove:

Lemma 2.18 *Any $m \times n$ matrix that has $0/1$ entries and rank $r \geq 0$ must contain a monochromatic submatrix of size at least $mn \cdot 2^{-O(\sqrt{r}\log r)}$.*

[6] Lovász, 1990; and Nisan and Wigderson, 1995.

Before proving the lemma, let us use[6] it to get a protocol.

Proof of Theorem 2.17 Let R be the rectangle promised by Lemma 2.18. We can write the matrix M as:

$$M = \begin{bmatrix} R & A \\ B & C \end{bmatrix}.$$

By Fact 2.9,

$$\text{rank}\left(\begin{bmatrix} R \\ B \end{bmatrix}\right) + \text{rank}\left(\begin{bmatrix} R & A \end{bmatrix}\right) \leq \text{rank}\left(\begin{bmatrix} R & A \\ B & C \end{bmatrix}\right) + 3.$$

If this does not hold, then Alice speaks.

Without loss of generality, suppose

$$\text{rank}\left(\begin{bmatrix} R \\ B \end{bmatrix}\right) \leq \text{rank}\left(\begin{bmatrix} R & A \end{bmatrix}\right).$$

In this case, Bob sends a single bit to Alice indicating whether y is consistent with R. If it is consistent, the parties set

$$M = \begin{bmatrix} R \\ B \end{bmatrix}$$

and repeat. They have essentially reduced the rank of the matrix by half. If y is not consistent with R, then the parties set

$$M = \begin{bmatrix} A \\ C \end{bmatrix}$$

Strictly speaking, the rank decreases in this step only if rank(M) > 3. However, once rank(M) ≤ 3, the parties can use the trivial protocol to finish the computation.

and repeat. In this case, the size of the matrix is less by a factor of $1 - 2^{-O(\sqrt{r}\log r)} = 1 - 2^{-k}$, for a parameter k, and the rank is still at most r.

By Lemma 2.11, we can assume that the matrix M has at most 2^r rows and columns. In each step of the protocol, one of the parties sends a bit and either reduces the rank or reduces the size of the matrix. The number of transmissions of the first type is at most $O(\log r)$ because after that many transmissions, the rank of the matrix is reduced to a constant. The number of transmissions of the second type is at most $2r \ln 2 \cdot 2^k$ because after that many steps, the number of entries in the matrix has been reduced to

$$2^{2r}(1 - 2^{-k})^{2r \cdot \ln 2 \cdot 2^k} < 2^{2r} e^{-2^{-k} \cdot 2r \cdot \ln 2 \cdot 2^k} = 1.$$

using $1 - x < e^{-x}$ for $x > 0$.

Thus, the number of leaves in this protocol is at most

$$\binom{2r \cdot \ln 2 \cdot 2^k + O(\log r)}{O(\log r)} \le 2^{O(\sqrt{r}\log^2 r)}.$$

Finally, by Theorem 1.7, we can balance the protocol tree to obtain a protocol computing M with length $O(\sqrt{r} \log^2 r)$. □

It only remains to prove Lemma 2.18. It is no loss of generality to assume that the matrix has more 0s than 1s – if this is not the case, we can always work with the matrix $J - M$. The lemma is proved with two claims. The first claim shows that M must contain a large rectangle that is *almost* monochromatic:

If we replace M with $J - M$, where J is the all 1s matrix, this can increase the rank by at most 1, but now the role of 0s and 1s has been reversed.

Claim 2.19 *If at least half of the entries in M are 0s, then there is a submatrix T of M of size at least $mn \cdot 2^{-O(\sqrt{r}\log r)}$ such that the fraction of 1s in T is at most $1/r^3$.*

The second claim[7] shows that a low-rank matrix with few ones must contain a large zero rectangle:

[7] Gavinsky and Lovett, 2014.

Claim 2.20 *If T is 0/1 matrix of rank $r \ge 2$, where at most $1/r^3$ fraction of the entries are 1s, then there is a submatrix consisting of at least half of the rows and half of the columns of T that only contains 0s.*

Proof Call a row of T *good* if the fraction of 1s in it is at most $2/r^3$. At least half the rows of T must be good, or else T would have more than $1/r^3$ fraction of 1s overall. Let T' be the submatrix obtained by restricting T to the good rows. Because $\operatorname{rank}(T') \leq r$, it has r rows $A_1, \ldots, A_r$ that span all the other rows of T'. Each row A_i has at most $2/r^3$ fraction of 1s, so at most $r \cdot 2/r^3 \leq 1/2$ fraction of the columns can contain a 1 in one of these r rows. Let T'' be the submatrix obtained by restricting T' to the columns that do not have a 1 in the rows $A_1, \ldots, A_r$. Then T'' must be 0 because every row of T' is a linear combination of $A_1, \ldots, A_r$. □

[8] Rothvoß, 2014.

[9] John, 1948.

It remains to prove Claim 2.19. The claim is proved[8] using John's theorem[9] from convex geometry. Informally, John's theorem says that if a convex set is sufficiently round, then it cannot be too long. To formally state the theorem, we need some definitions.

A set $K \subseteq \mathbb{R}^r$ is called *convex* if whenever $x, y \in K$, then all the points on the line segment between x and y are also in K. The *convex hull* of a set of points is the smallest convex body containing the points. The set is called *symmetric* if whenever x is in K, $-x$ is also in K. An ellipsoid centered at 0 is a set of the form:

$$E = \left\{ x \in \mathbb{R}^r : \sum_{i=1}^{r} \langle x, u_i \rangle^2 / \alpha_i^2 \leq 1 \right\},$$

where $u_1, \ldots, u_r$ is an orthonormal basis of $\mathbb{R}^r$, and $\alpha_1, \ldots, \alpha_r$ are nonzero numbers.

Theorem 2.21 (John) *Let $K \subseteq \mathbb{R}^r$ be a symmetric convex body such that the unit ball is the most voluminous of all ellipsoids contained in K. Then every element of K has Euclidean length at most $\sqrt{r}$.*

John's theorem can be used to show that any Boolean matrix has a useful factorization:

Lemma 2.22 *Any Boolean matrix M of rank r can be expressed as $M = AB$, where A is an $m \times r$ matrix whose rows are vectors of length at most $\sqrt{r}$, and B is an $r \times n$ matrix whose columns are vectors of length at most 1.*

The "$\sqrt{r}$" and "1" in the statement of Lemma 2.22 can be replaced by any numbers whose product is $\sqrt{r}$.

The lemma also holds for all matrices M so that $|M_{i,j}| \leq 1$ for all i, j.

Proof Because M has rank r, we know that it can be expressed as $M = A'B'$, where A' is an $m \times r$ matrix, and B' is an $r \times n$ matrix. The matrices A', B' do not necessarily satisfy the length constraints we need. To fix this, we use John's theorem.

Let $a_1, \ldots, a_m$ be the rows of A', and $b_1, \ldots, b_n$ be the columns of B. Let K' be the convex hull of $\{\pm a_1, \ldots, \pm a_m\}$. Our first goal is to modify K' to a convex body K so that the ellipsoid of maximum volume in K is the unit ball.

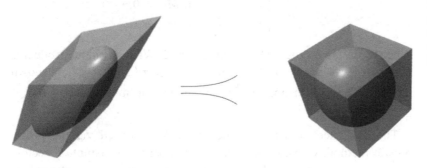

Figure 2.2 After applying a suitable linear transformation, the unit ball is the inscribed ellipsoid of maximum volume inside K.

Suppose

$$E' = \left\{ x \in \mathbb{R}^r : \sum_{i=1}^{r} \langle x, u_i \rangle^2 / \alpha_i^2 \le 1 \right\}$$

is the ellipsoid of maximum volume contained in K'. Using a linear map, we transform E' to a unit ball. We define L by its action on the basis $u_1, \ldots, u_r$ – define $L(u_i) = \alpha_i u_i$. Let K be the convex hull of the points $\{\pm L a_1, \pm L a_2, \ldots, \pm L a_m\}$. K is just the image of K' under L. After applying L, the volume of any set is multiplied by a factor of $\alpha_1 \alpha_2 \ldots \alpha_r$. This has the desired effect – the ellipsoid of maximum volume in K is now the image of E' under L, which is a unit ball:

Because A' has rank r, K' has full dimension and so contains an ellipsoid of nonzero volume.

$$E = L(E') = \left\{ x \in \mathbb{R}^r : \sum_{i-1}^{r} \langle x, u_i \rangle^2 \le 1 \right\}.$$

See Figure 2.2 for an illustration.

Let A be the matrix whose rows are $L(a_1), \ldots, L(a_m)$, and B be the matrix whose rows are $L^{-1}(b_1), \ldots, L^{-1}(b_m)$. Then, by the choice of L, we have

$$M = A'B' = AB.$$

By John's theorem, the length of all rows of A is at most $\sqrt{r}$, as desired.

It only remains to argue that columns of B are of length at most 1. This is where we use the fact that M is Boolean. Let $b \in \mathbb{R}^r$ be a row of B. Consider the unit vector in the same direction $e = b / \|b\|$. Because e is of unit length, we have $e \in K$. For every row a of A, we have $|\langle b, -a \rangle| = |\langle b, a \rangle| = |M_{i,j}| \le 1$. Because K is the convex hull of the rows and the negations of the rows of A, it follows that $\|b\| = |\langle b, e \rangle| \le 1$. $\qquad \square$

$A'B'$ is preserved because L simply scales the coefficients of each row vector of A by the factors α_i, and L^{-1} scales the corresponding coefficients of the columns of B by $1/\alpha_i$.

Now let us use Lemma 2.22 to complete the proof.

Proof of Claim 2.19 Let A, B be the two matrices guaranteed by Lemma 2.22. Let $a_1, \ldots, a_m$ be the rows of A and $b_1, \ldots, b_n$ be the columns of B. Let $\theta_{i,j} = \arccos \left(\frac{\langle a_i, b_j \rangle}{\|a_i\| \|b_j\|} \right)$ be the angle between the unit vectors in the directions of a_i and b_j. We claim that

$$\theta_{i,j} \begin{cases} = \frac{\pi}{2} & \text{if } M_{i,j} = 0, \\ \leq \frac{\pi}{2} - \frac{2\pi}{7\sqrt{r}} & \text{if } M_{i,j} = 1. \end{cases}$$

When a_i, b_j are orthogonal, the angle is $\pi/2$. When the inner product is closer to 1, we use the fact that $\arccos(\alpha) \leq \pi/2 - 2\pi\alpha/7$, as shown in Figure 2.3, which implies that the angle is at most $\arccos\left(\frac{1}{\sqrt{r}}\right) \leq \frac{\pi}{2} - \frac{2\pi}{7\sqrt{r}}$.

The existence of the rectangle we seek is proved via the probabilistic method. Consider the following experiment. Sample t vectors $z_1, \ldots, z_t \in \mathbb{R}^r$ of length 1 uniformly and independently at random. Use them to define the rectangle

$$R = \{(i, j) : \forall k \in [t] \;\; \langle a_i, z_k \rangle > 0, \langle b_j, z_k \rangle < 0\}.$$

For fixed (i, j) and k, the probability that $\langle a_i, z_k \rangle > 0$ and $\langle b_j, z_k \rangle < 0$ is exactly $\frac{1}{4} - \frac{\pi/2 - \theta_{i,j}}{2\pi}$. So for a fixed (i, j) we get

$$\Pr_{z_1, \ldots, z_t} [(i, j) \in R] \begin{cases} = \left(\frac{1}{4}\right)^t & \text{if } M_{i,j} = 0, \\ \leq \left(\frac{1}{4} - \frac{1}{7\sqrt{r}}\right)^t & \text{if } M_{i,j} = 1. \end{cases}$$

Let R_1 denote the number of 1s in R and R_0 denote the number of 0s. See Figures 2.4 and 2.5. Set $t = \lceil 7\sqrt{r} \log r \rceil$. We can conclude that

$$\mathbb{E}[R_0] \geq \frac{mn}{2 \cdot 4^t},$$

and

$$\mathbb{E}[R_1] \leq \frac{mn}{2 \cdot 4^t} \cdot \left(1 - \frac{4}{7\sqrt{r}}\right)^t \leq \frac{mn}{2 \cdot 4^t} \cdot e^{-\frac{4}{7\sqrt{r}}t} \leq \frac{mn}{2 \cdot 4^t} \cdot r^{-4 \log e},$$

because $1 - x \leq e^{-x}$ for $0 < x < 1$. Now let $Q = R_0 - r^3 R_1$. By linearity of expectation, we have

$$\mathbb{E}[Q] \geq \frac{mn}{2 \cdot 4^t} \cdot (1 - 1/r) \geq 0.$$

There must be some rectangle R for which $Q \geq 0$. For this rectangle, $R_0 \geq r^3 R_1$. The fraction of 1 entries in R is at most

$$\frac{R_1}{|R|} \leq \frac{R_0}{r^3 |R|} \leq \frac{1}{r^3}.$$

$\square$

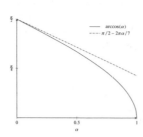

Figure 2.3 $\arccos(\alpha) \leq \pi/2 - 2\pi\alpha/7$ for $0 \leq \alpha \leq 1$.

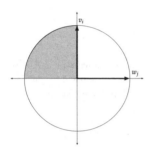

Figure 2.4 The region where all z_ks must fall to ensure that $(i, j) \in R$, when $M_{i,j} = 0$.

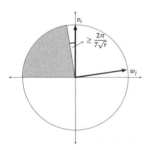

Figure 2.5 The region where all z_ks must fall to ensure that $(i, j) \in R$, when $M_{i,j} = 1$.

Exercises

Ex 2.1 – Show that there is a matrix whose rank is 1, yet its communication complexity is 2. Conclude that the +1 is necessary in Theorem 2.2.

Ex 2.2 – Prove Fact 2.9.

Ex 2.3 – The matrices we are working with have $0/1$ entries, so one can view these entries as coming from any field – for instance, we can view them as real numbers, rational numbers, or elements of the finite field $\mathbb{F}_2$. This is important because the value of the rank may depend on the field used.

1. Give an example of a 3×3 matrix whose rank over $\mathbb{F}_2$ is not the same as its rank over the reals.
2. Prove that if M has $0/1$ entries, then the rank of M over the reals is equal to its rank over the rationals, which is at least as large as its rank over $\mathbb{F}_2$.
3. For every r, show that there is matrix whose $\mathbb{F}_2$-rank and communication complexity are both r. Conclude that the log-rank conjecture is false over $\mathbb{F}_2$.

Ex 2.4 – Show that if $f(x, y)$ has fooling set S such that f evaluates to 1 on every point of S. Then, we shall show that $\text{rank}(M_f) \geq \sqrt{|S|}$.

1. Show that every row and column of M_f can contain at most one element of S. Thus, after rearranging the rows and columns, we can assume that the elements of S lie on the diagonal.
2. Consider the matrix $A = M_f \oplus M_f$. Prove that $\text{rank}(A) \geq |S|$. Conclude that $\text{rank}(M_f) \geq \sqrt{|S|}$.

Ex 2.5 – Show that there is a Boolean matrix of rank at most $2r$ with 2^r distinct rows, and 2^r distinct columns. Conclude that Lemma 2.11 is nearly sharp. *Hint: Consider the $2^r \times r$ matrix M obtained by taking all possible binary strings of length r. Construct the desired matrix using M and $M^\top$ as submatrices.*

Ex 2.6 – For any symmetric matrix $M \in \{0, 1\}^{n \times n}$ with ones in all diagonal entries, show that

$$2^c \geq \frac{n^2}{|M|},$$

where c is the deterministic communication complexity of M, and $|M|$ is the number of ones in M.

M is symmetric if $M_{i,j} = M_{j,i}$.

Ex 2.7 – Show that the protocol used to prove Theorem 2.17 works even if we weaken Lemma 2.18 to only guarantee the existence of a large submatrix with rank at most $r/8$, instead of rank at most 1. Conclude that to prove the log-rank conjecture, it is enough to show that every Boolean matrix of rank r contains a submatrix with $mn2^{-\text{polylog}(r)}$ entries and rank $r/8$.

3

Randomized Protocols

ACCESS TO RANDOMNESS is an enabling feature in many computational processes. Randomized algorithms are often easier to understand and more elegant than their deterministic counterparts. Sometimes, randomness even allows to achieve results that are impossible to achieve deterministically, like in cryptography or data structures.

In this chapter, we begin our investigation of randomized communication complexity. We show how randomness can be used to give communication protocols that are far more efficient than the best possible deterministic protocols for many problems. We start with some informal examples of randomized protocols. Later, we define randomized protocols formally and prove some basic properties.

We do not discuss any lower bounds on randomized communication complexity in this chapter. Lower bounds for randomized protocols can be found in Chapters 5 and 6.

Some Protocols

Equality Suppose Alice and Bob are given access to n bit strings x, y, and want to know if these strings are the same or not (1.2). In Chapter 1, we showed that the deterministic communication complexity of this problem is $n + 1$. There is a simple randomized protocol, where Alice and Bob use a *shared* random string. The idea is to use *hashing*. Alice and Bob use the shared randomness to sample a random function $h : \{0, 1\}^n \to \{0, 1\}^k$. Then, Alice sends $h(x)$ to Bob, and Bob responds with a bit indicating whether or not $h(y) = h(x)$. If $h(x) = h(y)$, they conclude that $x = y$. If $h(x) \neq h(y)$, they conclude that $x \neq y$.

The protocol uses $k 2^n$ shared random bits.

The number of bits communicated is $k + 1$. The probability of making an error is at most 2^{-k} – if $x = y$ then $h(x) = h(y)$, and if $x \neq y$ then the probability that $h(x) = h(y)$ is at most 2^{-k}.

The length of this protocol is short, but it requires a huge number of shared random coins. Is this necessary? It is not – we can describe similar protocols that use much less randomness. Here is one way to achieve this.

We can reduce the number of random bits used if we use an *error-correcting code*. This is a function $C : \{0, 1\}^n \to [2^k]^m$ such that if

46

$x \neq y$, then $C(x)$ and $C(y)$ differ in all but $m/2^{-\Omega(k)}$ coordinates. It can be shown that if m is set to $10n$, then for any k, most functions C will be error-correcting codes.

Given a code, Alice can pick a random coordinate of $C(x)$ and send it to Bob, who can then check whether this coordinate is consistent with $C(y)$. This takes $\log m + \log 2^k = O(\log n + k)$ bits of communication, and again the probability of making an error is at most $2^{-\Omega(k)}$. In this protocol, the parties do not require a shared random string because the choice of C is made once and for all when the protocol is constructed, and before the inputs are seen.

Greater-Than Suppose Alice and Bob are given numbers $x, y \in [n]$ and want to know which one is greater (1.4). We have seen that any deterministic protocol for this problem requires $\log n$ bits of communication. However, there is a randomized protocol that requires only $O(\log \log n)$ bits of communication. Here we describe a protocol that requires only $O(\log \log n \cdot \log \log \log n)$ communication.

The inputs x, y can be encoded by ℓ-bit binary strings, where $\ell = O(\log n)$. To determine whether $x \geq y$, it is enough to find the most significant bit where x and y differ. To find this bit, we use the randomized protocol for equality described above, along with binary search. In the first step, Alice and Bob exchange k bits according to the protocol for equality to determine whether the $\frac{n}{2}$ most significant bits of x and y are the same. If they are the same, the parties continue with the remaining $\frac{n}{2}$ bits. If not, the parties recurse on the $n/2$ most significant bits.

In this way, after $O(\log n)$ steps, they find the first bit where their inputs differ. In order to ensure that the probability of making an error in all of these $O(\log n)$ steps is small, we set $k = O(\log \log n)$. By the union bound, this guarantees that the protocol succeeds with high probability.

k-Disjointness Suppose Alice and Bob are given sets $X, Y \subseteq [n]$, each of size at most k. Their goal is to determine if these sets intersect. In Chapter 2, we used the rank method to argue that at least $\log \binom{n}{k} \approx k \log(n/k)$ bits of communication are required. Here we give a randomized protocol[1] of length $O(k)$. The randomized protocol is much more efficient than the best possible deterministic protocol when $k \ll n$.

The parties use shared randomness to sample a sequence of sets $R_1, R_2, \ldots \subseteq [n]$. Alice announces the smallest index i with $X \subseteq R_i$, and Bob announces the smallest index j with $Y \subseteq R_j$. This can be done with at most $2(\log(i) + \log(j) + 2)$ bits of communication. Now

Many beautiful explicit constructions of error-correcting codes are also known.

See Exercise 3.1.

[1] Håstad and Wigderson, 2007.

In Chapter 6, we show that $\Omega(k)$ bits are required even for randomized protocols.

Alice can send i using $2\lceil \log i \rceil$ bits by sending the binary encoding of i bit by bit. For each bit, she also sends an extra bit to indicate whether or not the transmission is over. In fact, there is a more efficient encoding using $\log(i) + O(\log \log(i))$ bits of communication.

Alice can safely replace her set with $X \cap R_j$, and Bob can replace his set with $Y \cap R_i$. If the sets were disjoint, they remain disjoint, and if they were not disjoint, they must still intersect.

They repeat the above process until they communicate $O(k)$ bits. If one of their sets eventually becomes empty, then they know that X, Y are disjoint. If both of their sets are nonempty, they conclude that X, Y must intersect. We shall prove that they arrive at the correct conclusion with probability at least $2/3$.

Let us start by analyzing the expected number of bits that are communicated in the first step.

Claim 3.1 *The expected length of the first step is at most*

$$2(|X| + |Y| + 2).$$

Proof We start by proving that $\mathbb{E}[i] = 2^{|X|}$ and $\mathbb{E}[j] = 2^{|Y|}$. The probability that the first set in the sequence contains X is exactly $2^{-|X|}$. In the event that it does not contain X, we are picking the first set that contains X from the rest of the sequence. Thus:

$$\mathbb{E}[i] = 2^{-|X|} \cdot 1 + (1 - 2^{-|X|}) \cdot (\mathbb{E}[i] + 1)$$

$$\Rightarrow \mathbb{E}[i] = 2^{|X|}.$$

The bound on the expected value of j is the same.

Convexity now implies that the expected length of the first step is at most

$$\mathbb{E}[2(\log(i) + \log(j) + 2)] \leq 2(\log(\mathbb{E}[i]) + \log(\mathbb{E}[j])) + 4$$

$$= 2(|X| + |Y| + 2).$$

$\square$

The intuition is that although $2(k + 2)$ bits are sent in the first round, when X, Y are disjoint, the sets in the second round are half as large. So, roughly $2(k/2 + 2)$ bits are sent in the second round, and again the sets are halved. See Figure 3.1. The expected length of the protocol should look like a geometric sum of the form $2k \cdot \sum_{i=0}^{\infty} 2^{-i}$, which is at most $4k$. Let us make this more formal.

$X_{i,s} = 1$ if $i \in X$ before step s, and $X_{i,s} = 0$ otherwise.

For each $i \in [n]$, let $X_{i,s}$ be the indicator random variable for the event that $i \in X$ before step s of the above process. Define $Y_{i,s}$ similarly.

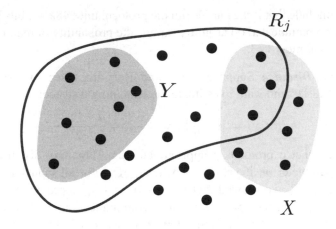

If $X \cup Y$ is not empty before step s, Claim 3.1 shows that the expected number of bits communicated in step s is at most

$$2 \cdot \left(2 + \sum_{i \in [n]} X_{i,s} + Y_{i,s} \right) \leq 4 \cdot \left(\sum_{i \in [n]} X_{i,s} + Y_{i,s} \right).$$

Moreover, the expected value of this sum is small when X, Y are disjoint:

Claim 3.2 *If X, Y are disjoint, then*

$$\mathbb{E}\left[\sum_{i \in [n]} \sum_{s=1}^{\infty} X_{i,s} + Y_{i,s} \right] \leq 4k.$$

Proof By linearity of expectation,

$$\mathbb{E}\left[\sum_{i \in [n]} \sum_{s=1}^{\infty} X_{i,s} + Y_{i,s} \right] = \sum_{i \in [n]} \sum_{s=1}^{\infty} \mathbb{E}\left[X_{i,s} \right] + \mathbb{E}\left[Y_{i,s} \right].$$

If $X_{i,1} = 0$, then $X_{i,s} = 0$ for all s. If $X_{i,1} = 1$, then the probability that $X_{i,s} = 1$ is exactly 2^{-s+1}, so

$$\sum_{i \in X} \sum_{s=1}^{\infty} \mathbb{E}\left[X_{i,s} \right] = \sum_{i \in X} \sum_{s=1}^{\infty} 2^{-s+1} = 2|X| \leq 2k.$$

Indeed, because X, Y are disjoint, in each step the probability that an element of X survives is exactly $1/2$.

The same bound holds for $\mathbb{E}\left[\sum_{i \in [n]} \sum_{s=1}^{\infty} Y_{i,s} \right]$. □

When X, Y are disjoint, Claim 3.2 implies that the expected number of bits communicated during all the steps where the parties still have elements is at most $16k$. By Markov's inequality, the probability that the protocol communicates more than $3 \cdot 16k = 48k$ bits in such steps is at most $1/3$.

We conclude that if the parties run the protocol until $48k + 2$ bits have been communicated on arbitrary inputs, the probability of making an error is at most $1/3$.

Hamming Distance Suppose Alice and Bob are given two strings $x, y \in \{\pm 1\}^n$ and want to estimate the Hamming distance:

$$\Delta(x, y) = |\{i \in [n] : x_i \neq y_i\}| = \frac{n - \langle x, y \rangle}{2}.$$

We say that a protocol π approximates the Hamming distance up to a parameter m, if $|\pi(x, y) - \Delta(x, y)| \leq m$ for all inputs x, y. In Exercise 1.7, we showed that for any $\alpha < 1/2$, approximating the Hamming distance up to αn requires communication $\Omega(n)$. There is a significantly better randomized protocol, as we will see below.

Alice and Bob use shared randomness to sample $i_1, \dots, i_k \in [n]$ independently and uniformly at random. They communicate $2k$ bits to compute the *empirical distance*

$$\gamma = (1/k) \cdot |\{j \in [k] : x_{i_j} \neq y_{i_j}\}|,$$

and output γn.

We now analyze the approximation factor of this algorithm. Assume $\Delta(x, y) \leq n/2$. Define $Z_1, \dots, Z_k$ by

If $\Delta(x, y) > n/2$, replace in the analysis the vector x by its complement vector.

$$Z_j = \begin{cases} 1 & \text{if } x_{i_j} \neq y_{i_j}, \\ 0 & \text{otherwise.} \end{cases}$$

The expected value of each Z_j is $\Delta(x, y)/n$. So if $m \leq \Delta(x, y)$, we can apply the Chernoff-Hoeffding bound to conclude:

$$\Pr[|\gamma k - \Delta(x, y)k/n| > mk/n] \leq e^{-\left(\frac{m}{\Delta(x,y)}\right)^2 \cdot \frac{\Delta(x,y)k}{n} \cdot \frac{1}{3}}$$

$$\leq e^{-\frac{m^2 k}{3\Delta(x,y)n}}.$$

If $m > \Delta(x, y)$, we have

$$\Pr[\gamma k > \Delta(x, y)k/n + mk/n] \leq e^{-\frac{m}{\Delta(x,y)} \cdot \frac{\Delta(x,y)k}{n} \cdot \frac{1}{3}}$$

$$\leq e^{-\frac{mk}{3n}}.$$

Because $m \leq n$ and $\Delta(x, y) \leq n$, in either case this probability is at most $e^{-\frac{m^2 k}{3n^2}}$. Thus, if we set $k = 3n^2/m^2$, we obtain a protocol whose probability of making an error is at most $1/e$.

For $m = n^{0.6}$ we get a protocol of length $O(n^{0.8})$, and for $m = \sqrt{n}/\epsilon$ the length is $O(\epsilon^2 n)$.

Randomized Communication Complexity

RANDOMNESS CAN APPEAR in several ways in communication protocols. The parties could use shared randomness, each party could toss some private coins, and the inputs could be random as well. We now discuss definitions that capture these different uses of randomness.

We say that a protocol uses *public coins* if all parties have access to a common shared random string. We usually denote the public randomness of the protocol by R. We say that the protocol uses *private coins* if each party privately samples an independent random string. We denote the private coins of Alice and Bob by R_a and R_b.

So there are four potential sources of randomness – R, R_a, R_b and the input (X, Y). These four random variables are always assumed to be independent. A randomized protocol is simply a distribution over deterministic protocols. Once R, R_a, R_b are fixed, we are left with a deterministic protocol, which we already defined. That is, for all R, R_a, R_b, there is a deterministic protocol π_{R,R_a,R_b} that operates on the input (X, Y). The distribution of R, R_a, R_b can always be assumed to be uniform over some domain.

Every private coin protocol can be easily simulated by a public coin protocol. We shall soon see a partial converse – every public coin protocol can be simulated with private coins, albeit with a small increase in the length of the protocol.

There are two standard ways to measure the probability that a randomized protocol makes an error:

> If a randomized protocol never makes an error, we can fix the randomness to obtain a deterministic protocol that is always correct.

Worst-Case We say that a randomized protocol has error ϵ in the *worst-case* if for *every* input, the probability that the protocol makes an error is at most ϵ. That is, for all x, y,

$$\Pr_{R,R_a,R_b} \left[\pi_{R,R_a,R_b}(x, y) \text{ is wrong} \right] \le \epsilon.$$

Average-Case Given a distribution on inputs μ, we say that a protocol has error ϵ with respect to μ if the probability that the protocol makes an error is at most ϵ when the inputs are sampled from μ. That is,

$$\Pr_{R,R_a,R_b,(X,Y)} \left[\pi_{R,R_a,R_b}(X, Y) \text{ is wrong} \right] \le \epsilon.$$

In both cases, the length of the protocol is defined to be the maximum depth of all of the deterministic protocol trees that the protocol may generate.

> In some contexts, it makes sense to measure the expected length.

Error Reduction

The error in worst-case protocols can be reduced by repetition. When a protocol has error $\epsilon < 1/2$ in the worst-case, we can run it several times and output the most common outcome that we see. This reduces the probability of making an error. If we run the protocol k times, and output the most frequent output in all of the runs, there will be an error in the output only if at least $k/2$ of the runs computed the wrong answer. By the Chernoff bound, the probability of error is thus reduced to at most $2^{-\Omega(k(1/2-\epsilon)^2)}$. For this reason, we often restrict our attention to protocols with error $1/3$. The error can be made an arbitrarily small constant with a constant number of rounds of repetition.

> Is it possible to reduce the error in an average-case protocol over some fixed distribution μ?

> For example, if the error is $1/3$, then repeating the protocol $O(\log(1/\delta))$ reduces the error to at most δ.

Minimax

The minimax principle can be applied to almost any randomized computational process. It does not rely on any features of the communication model.

Amazingly, the worst-case and average-case complexity of a problem are related. This principle is called Yao's minimax principle.

Theorem 3.3 *The worst-case randomized communication complexity of a function g with error at most ϵ is equal to the maximum, over all distributions μ on inputs, of the average-case communication complexity of g with error at most ϵ with respect to μ.*

[2] von Neumann, 1928.

To prove Theorem 3.3, we appeal to a famous minimax principle due to von Neumann:[2]

von Neumann's minimax principle can be seen as a consequence of duality in linear programming.

Theorem 3.4 *Let M be an $m \times n$ matrix with entries that are real numbers. Let A denote the set of $1 \times m$ row vectors with nonnegative entries such that $\sum_i x_i = 1$. Let B denote the set of $n \times 1$ column vectors with nonnegative entries such that $\sum_j y_j = 1$. Then*

$$\min_{x \in A} \max_{y \in B} xMy = \max_{y \in B} \min_{x \in A} xMy.$$

It may seem overly simplistic to model two-player games using a matrix. How can we possibly model an interactive game like chess using a matrix? The idea is that each row of the matrix represents the *entire strategy* of the player, encoding how he might respond at every point during the play. Each pair of strategies then leads to a winner (or a draw), and the entries of the matrix can be set appropriately. As von Neumann said, "In other words, the player knows before hand how he is going to act in a precisely defined situation: he enters the game with a theory worked out in detail."

Theorem 3.4 has an intuitive but surprising interpretation in terms of *zero-sum games*. A zero-sum game is specified by a matrix M and is played between two players: a row player and a column player. The row player privately chooses a row i of the matrix. The column player privately chooses a column j. The parties then announce i and j. The outcome of the game is determined by i and j. The column player gets a payoff of $M_{i,j}$, and the row player gets a payoff of $-M_{i,j}$. This is why it is a zero-sum game – the sum of payoffs is zero. The column player chooses i in order to maximize $M_{i,j}$, and the row player chooses j in order to minimize $M_{i,j}$.

We see that the matrix M encodes the payoffs of the game, and the vectors x and y represent *randomized strategies* for playing the game. The vector x in the theorem corresponds to a distribution on the rows that the row player may use to choose his row, and the vector y corresponds to a distribution that the column player may use.

The quantity $\min_{x \in A} \max_{y \in B} xMy$ gives the expected value of the payoff when the row player announces his choice for x first, and commits to it before the column player picks y. In this case, the row player picks x to minimize $\max_{y \in B} xMy$, and the column player then picks y to maximize xMy. Similarly, the quantity $\max_y \min_x xMy$ measures the expected payoff if the column player commits to a strategy y first, and the row player gets to pick the best strategy x after seeing y.

The classic Rock-Paper-Scissors game is a zero-sum game with the following payoff matrix:

$$\begin{array}{c} \\ R \\ P \\ S \end{array} \begin{array}{c} \begin{array}{ccc} R & P & S \end{array} \\ \left[\begin{array}{ccc} 0 & -1 & 1 \\ 1 & 0 & -1 \\ -1 & 1 & 0 \end{array} \right] \end{array}$$

The first quantity $\min_x \max_y xMy$ can only be larger than the second $\max_y \min_x xMy$. The column player wishes to maximize xMy. In the first case, the column player has more information than in the second case, so she can choose a more profitable strategy.

The minimax theorem states that the two quantities are always equal. There is a strategy y^* for the column player that guarantees a payoff that is equal to the amount she would get if she knew the strategy of the row player. Similarly there is a strategy x^* for the row player.

Now we leverage this powerful theorem to prove Yao's min-max principle:

Proof of Theorem 3.3 The average-case complexity is at most the worst-case complexity. If there is a protocol that computes g with error ϵ in the worst case, then the same protocol must compute g with error ϵ in the average case, no matter what the input distribution is.

Conversely, suppose that for every distribution on inputs, the average-case complexity of the problem with error ϵ is at most c. Consider the matrix M, where every row corresponds to an input to the protocol, and every column corresponds to a deterministic communication protocol of length at most c, defined by

$$M_{i,j} = \begin{cases} 1 & \text{if protocol } j \text{ computes } g \text{ correctly on input } i, \\ 0 & \text{otherwise.} \end{cases}$$

A distribution on the inputs corresponds to a choice of x. Because a randomized protocol is a distribution on deterministic protocols, a randomized protocol corresponds to a choice of y. The success probability of a fixed randomized protocol y on inputs distributed according to x is exactly xMy. So, by assumption, we know that $\min_x \max_y xMy \geq 1 - \epsilon$. Theorem 3.4 implies that $\max_y \min_x xMy \geq 1 - \epsilon$ as well. There is a fixed randomized protocol y^* that has error at most ϵ under every distribution on inputs. □

The pair of strategies (x^*, y^*) is called an *equilibrium*. Neither player has an incentive to unilaterally deviate from this pair of strategies. What are the equilibrium strategies for Rock-Paper-Scissors?

Public Coins versus Private Coins

EVERY PRIVATE COIN PROTOCOL can certainly be simulated by a public coin protocol, by making the private randomness visible to both parties. It turns out that every public coin protocol can also be simulated by a private coin protocol with only a small increase in communication.[3]

[3] Newman, 1991.

Theorem 3.5 *If $g : \{0, 1\}^n \times \{0, 1\}^n \rightarrow \{0, 1\}$ can be computed with c bits of communication, and error ϵ in the worst-case, then it can be computed by a private coin protocol with $c + \log(n/\epsilon^2) + O(1)$ bits of communication, and error 2ϵ in the worst-case.*

Proof We use the probabilistic method to find the required private coin protocol. Suppose the public coin protocol uses a random string R as the source of all randomness. To design the private coin protocol, we start by picking t independent random strings $R_1, \ldots, R_t$ each distributed like R.

It is known that computing whether or not two n-bit strings are equal requires $\Omega(\log n)$ bits of communication if only private coins are used. This shows that Theorem 3.5 is tight.

For any fixed input (x, y), some of these t random strings lead to the public coin protocol computing the right answer, and some lead to the protocol computing the wrong answer. However, the probability that R_i gives the right answer is at least $1 - \epsilon$. Thus, by the Chernoff bound, the probability that $1 - 2\epsilon$ fraction of the t strings lead to the wrong answer is at most $2^{-\Omega(\epsilon^2 t)}$. We set $t = O(n/\epsilon^2)$ to be large enough so that this probability is less than 2^{-2n}. By the union bound, we get that the probability that more than $2\epsilon t$ of these strings give the wrong answer for *some* input is less than 1. Thus, there must be some fixed strings with this property.

The private coin protocol is now simple. We fix $R_1, \ldots, R_t$ with the property that for any input (x, y), the fraction of strings giving the wrong answer is at most 2ϵ. Alice samples a uniformly random element $i \in \{1, 2, \ldots, t\}$ and sends i to Bob. This takes at most $\log(n/\epsilon^2) + O(1)$ bits of communication. Alice and Bob then run the original protocol using the randomness R_i.   □

Only one party uses randomness!

Nearly Monochromatic Rectangles

MONOCHROMATIC RECTANGLES PROVED to be a very useful concept for understanding deterministic protocols. A similar role is played by *nearly monochromatic* rectangles when trying to understand randomized protocols. Here we provide one example of this connection. This is studied in greater detail in future chapters, where lower bounds on randomized communication complexity are proved.

Given a randomized protocol, and a distribution μ on inputs, one can always fix the randomness of the protocol in the way that minimizes the probability of error under μ. The result is a deterministic protocol whose error under μ is at most the error of the randomized protocol.

The following theorem shows that average-case protocols yields nearly monochromatic rectangles.

Theorem 3.6 *If there is a deterministic c-bit protocol π with error at most ϵ under a distribution μ, and a set S such that*

$$\Pr[\pi(X, Y) \in S] > 2\sqrt{\epsilon},$$

then there exists a rectangle R such that

- *π has the same outcome for all inputs in R, and this outcome is in S.*
- *$\Pr[(X, Y) \in R] \geq \sqrt{\epsilon} \cdot 2^{-c}$.*
- *$\Pr[\pi \text{ makes an error} | (X, Y) \in R] \leq \sqrt{\epsilon}$.*

Proof By Theorem 1.6, we know that the protocol induces a partition of the space into $t \leq 2^c$ rectangles $R_1, R_2, \ldots, R_t$. In each of these rectangles, the outcome of the protocol is determined.

For each rectangle R_i in the collection, define the number

$$\epsilon(R_i) = \Pr[\text{the protocol makes an error} | (X, Y) \in R_i].$$

Let $\rho(R_i)$ denote the number $\Pr[(X, Y) \in R_i]$. If R denotes the rectangle that the inputs X, Y belong to, we have that $\mathbb{E}[\epsilon(R)] \leq \epsilon$. Markov's inequality gives $\Pr[\epsilon(R) > \sqrt{\epsilon}] < \sqrt{\epsilon}$. In addition,

$$\mathbb{E}\left[1/\rho(R)\right] = \sum_{i=1}^{t} \Pr[R = R_i] \cdot \frac{1}{\Pr[(X,Y) \in R_i]} = t.$$

By Markov's inequality, we get $\Pr[1/\rho(R) > t/\sqrt{\epsilon}] \le \sqrt{\epsilon}$. Therefore,

$$\Pr[\pi(X,Y) \in S] > 2\sqrt{\epsilon} > \Pr[\epsilon(R) > \sqrt{\epsilon}] + \Pr[1/\rho(R) > t/\sqrt{\epsilon}].$$

By the union bound, there must be a rectangle R^* in the collection corresponding to an outcome in S, with $\epsilon(R^*) \le \sqrt{\epsilon}$ and $\rho(R^*) \ge \sqrt{\epsilon}/t \ge \sqrt{\epsilon} \cdot 2^{-c}$. □

Exercises

Ex 3.1 – In this exercise, we design a randomized protocol[4] for finding the first difference between two n-bit strings. Alice and Bob are given n bit strings $x \ne y$ and want to find the smallest i such that $x_i \ne y_i$. We already saw how to accomplish this using $O(\log n \log \log n)$ bits of communication. Here we do it with $O(\log n)$ bits of communication. For simplicity, assume that n is a power of two.

[4] Feige et al., 1994; and Viola, 2015.

$\Omega(\log n)$ bits are required just to output the index.

Define a rooted binary tree as follows. Every vertex v in the tree corresponds to an interval I_v of coordinates from $[n]$. The root corresponds to the interval $I_{root} = [n]$. Every leaf in the tree corresponds to an interval of size 1. Every internal vertex v has two children. The left child corresponds to the left half of I_v, and the right child corresponds to the right half of I_v.

Extend the tree as follows. At each leaf of the binary tree, attach a path of length $3 \log n$. Every vertex of this path represents the same interval of size 1. The depth of the overall tree is now $4 \log n$.

Fill in the details of the following protocol. The parties use their inputs and hashing to start at the root of the tree and try to navigate to the smallest interval that contains the index i that they seek. In each step, the parties either move to a parent or move to a child of the node that they are currently at. When the parties are at a vertex v that corresponds to the interval I_v, they exchange $O(1)$ hash bits to confirm that the first difference lies in I_v. If this hash shows that the first difference does not lie in I_v, they move to the parent of the current node. Otherwise, they exchange $O(1)$ hash bits to decide to which child of v to move to.

Prove an upper bound on the expected number of bits communicated and a lower bound on the success probability:

1. Argue that as long as the number of nodes where the protocol made the *correct* choice exceeds the number of nodes where the parties made the *wrong* choice by $\log n$, the protocol you defined succeeds in computing i.
2. Use the Chernoff-Hoeffding bound to argue that the number of hashes that give the correct answer is high enough to ensure that the protocol succeeds with high probability on any input.

Ex 3.2 – Show that there is a protocol for computing greater-than with communication complexity $\lceil \log(1/\epsilon) \rceil$ such that if the inputs are sampled uniformly and independently, then the average case error of the protocol is at most ϵ.

Can you guess a distribution on inputs for which the average case communication complexity of greater-than with error $1/3$ is $\Omega(\log n)$?

Ex 3.3 – In this exercise, we explore the concept of *locality sensitive hashing*. Suppose Alice and Bob are given inputs $x, y \in \{0, 1\}^n$ and they want to know whether the two strings are close in Hamming distance, or far apart. Show that for every $t < n/2$, there is a public-coin protocol of length $O(1)$ with the property that if the Hamming distance between x, y is at most t, the protocol outputs 1 with probability $2/3$, and if the Hamming distance is at least $2t$, the protocol outputs 0 with probability at least $2/3$. *Hint: Consider taking the inner product of x, y with random strings z generated using a biased coin, and compute* $\mathbb{E}\left[(-1)^{\langle x-y, z \rangle}\right]$.

Ex 3.4 – In this exercise, we design a randomized protocol for the lopsided disjointness problem. Suppose Alice and Bob are given sets $X, Y \subseteq [n]$ with the promise that $|X| \leq k$, and Y is allowed to have arbitrary size. They wish to determine whether the sets are disjoint. Give a randomized protocol for the worst-case, with error $1/3$ such that in every execution of the protocol, Alice sends at most $O(k)$ bits, and Bob sends at most $O(n)$ bits.

Ex 3.5 – For a real matrix M and $\epsilon > 0$ define the ϵ-approximate rank of M to be $\text{rank}_\epsilon(M) = \min\{\text{rank}(A) : |A_{i,j} - M_{i,j}| \leq \epsilon \text{ for all } i, j\}$.

1. Find a Boolean matrix with rank r and $1/3$-approximate rank at most $O(\log r)$. *Hint: The equality function.*
2. More generally, suppose there is a private coin protocol computing a Boolean function with communication complexity c and error ϵ. Then show that $\text{rank}_\epsilon(M) \leq 2^c$.
3. Prove the following strengthening of Theorem 2.17. The communication complexity of a matrix M is at most

$$O(\sqrt{\text{rank}_{1/3}(M)} \log^2 \text{rank}(M)).$$

4

Numbers on Foreheads

WHEN MORE THAN TWO PARTIES COMMUNICATE, there are several ways to model the communication. The number-on-forehead model[1] is one way to generalize the case of two-party communication to the multiparty setting. In this model, there are k parties communicating, and the ith party has her input *written on her forehead*. Namely, the input to all the parties is of the form $(X_1, X_2, \ldots, X_k)$, and each party can see $k - 1$ of the k inputs – all of the k inputs except the one written on her forehead.

Because each party can see most of the inputs, the parties often do not need to communicate much. This makes proving lower bounds for this model more difficult than for the two-party case. In stark contrast to the models we have discussed before, we do not yet know of any explicit functions that require the maximum communication complexity in this model. The challenge of proving strong lower bounds in this model is related to other deep and difficult questions in computational complexity theory and combinatorics. For example, optimal lower bounds in this model imply interesting consequences in the study of circuit complexity.

[1] Chandra et al., 1983.

There is also the *number-in-hand* model, where each party has a private input known only to them. This model is meaningful as well, but it is sufficiently similar to the two-party case that we discuss it only in the exercises.

When there are only $k = 2$ parties, this model is identical to the model of two-party communication we have already discussed.

Some Protocols

We start with some examples of clever number-on-forehead protocols.

Equality We have seen that every deterministic protocol for computing equality in the two-party setting must have complexity $n + 1$. The complexity of equality is quite different in the number-on-forehead model. Suppose there are three parties. Each party has an n-bit string written on her forehead. How many bits do they need to exchange in order to figure out if all three strings are the same?

Just two bits! Alice announces whether or not Bob's and Charlie's strings are the same, and Bob announces whether or not Alice's and Charlie's strings are the same.

Intersection Size Suppose there are k parties. The ith party has a set $X_i \subseteq [n]$ on her forehead. The parties want to compute the size of the

A protocol solving this problem would compute both the disjointness function and the inner product function.

[2] Grolmusz, 1998; and Babai et al., 2003.

In Chapter 5, we prove that at least $\Omega(n/4^k)$ bits of communication are required.

intersection $\bigcap_{i=1}^{k} X_i$. There is a protocol[2] that requires only $O(k^4(1 + n/2^k))$ bits of communication.

We start by describing a protocol that requires only $O(k^2 \log n)$ bits of communication, as long as $n < \binom{k}{\lceil k/2 \rceil}$. It is helpful to think of the input as a $k \times n$ Boolean matrix, where each row is the indicator vector of one of the sets. Each of the parties knows all but one row of this matrix. They wish to compute the number of all 1s columns. Let $C_{i,j}$ denote the number of columns containing exactly j ones that are visible to the ith party. The parties compute and announce the values of $C_{i,j}$, for each i, j. Because this involves each party announcing $k + 1$ numbers between 0 and n, the communication complexity of the protocol is at most $O(k^2 \log n)$.

It remains to prove that given $C_{i,j}$ for all i, j, there is a unique possible count for the number of all 1s columns. Let Z_r denote the number of columns with r ones. We show that there is actually a unique tuple $Z = (Z_0, \ldots, Z_k)$ consistent with the $C_{i,j}$s. We first prove:

Claim 4.1 *Suppose $Z = A$ and $Z = B$ are two solutions that are both consistent with the $C_{i,j}$s. Then*

$$|A_r - B_r| = \binom{k}{r} \cdot |A_0 - B_0|,$$

for each $r \in \{0, 1, \ldots, k\}$.

Proof Because a column of weight r is observed as having weight $r - 1$ by r parties and having weight r by $k - r$ parties, we have

$$(k - r + 1)A_{r-1} + rA_r = \sum_{i=1}^{k} C_{i,r-1} = (k - r + 1)B_{r-1} + rB_r.$$

Rearranging,

$$|A_r - B_r| = \left(\frac{k - r + 1}{r} \right) |A_{r-1} - B_{r-1}|$$

repeating the same argument for $r - 2$.

$$= \left(\frac{(k - r + 1)(k - r + 2)}{(r)(r - 1)} \right) |A_{r-2} - B_{r-2}|$$

$$= \cdots$$

$$= \binom{k}{r} \cdot |A_0 - B_0|. \qquad \square$$

Claim 4.1 implies that there can only be one possible value for $Z_0, Z_1, \ldots, Z_k$ – if there were two solutions $A \neq B$, then because $A_r \neq B_r$ for some r, we must have $|A_0 - B_0| > 0$, which implies that $|A_0 - B_0| \geq 1$, because these are integers. But then we get

$n \geq |B_{k/2} - A_{k/2}| \geq \binom{k}{\lceil k/2 \rceil}$, which is not possible because $n < \binom{k}{\lceil k/2 \rceil}$ by assumption.

To obtain a protocol for general n, the parties divide the columns of the matrix into blocks of size $\binom{k}{\lceil k/2 \rceil} - 1$. They count the number of all 1s columns in each block using the above idea separately. The total communication is at most

$$\left(\frac{n}{\binom{k}{\lceil k/2 \rceil}} + 1 \right) \cdot k^2 \log \binom{k}{\lceil k/2 \rceil} \leq O(k^4(1 + n/2^k)).$$

because $\binom{k}{k/2} \approx 2^k / \sqrt{k}$.

Exactly n Suppose there are three parties. Each party has a number from $[n]$ written on the forehead. They want to know whether these numbers sum to n or not.

A trivial protocol is for one of the parties to announce one of the numbers she sees, and then the relevant party announces the answer. This takes $O(\log n)$ bits of communication.

There is a more efficient protocol that uses just $O(\sqrt{\log n})$ bits of communication. The protocol is based on a construction of Behrend.[3] Behrend constructed a large set of integers that avoids three-term arithmetic progressions. His ideas can be used to show:

Theorem 4.2 *One can color the set $[m]$ with $2^{O(\sqrt{\log m})}$ colors with no monochromatic three-term arithmetic progression. Namely, for each $a, b \in [m]$, if all three numbers $a, a + b$, and $a + 2b$ are in $[m]$, then they do not have the same color.*

First we explain how Berhend's coloring yields a protocol. Suppose the three inputs are x, y, and z. Consider the numbers

$$x' = n - y - z, \qquad y' = n - x - z.$$

Alice can compute x', and Bob can compute y'. Observe that

$$x - x' = y - y' = x + y + z - n.$$

This means that the numbers $x + 2y', x' + 2y$, and $x + 2y$ form an arithmetic progression, and this progression is nontrivial if and only if $x + y + z \neq n$. In the protocol, the parties set $m = 3n$ and check that the three numbers above have the same color in the coloring promised by Theorem 4.2. If all three colors are the same, the parties conclude that the sum of their numbers is n. If the colors are not the same, they conclude that the sum is not n. The length of the protocol is at most $O(\sqrt{\log n})$.

Now we turn to proving Theorem 4.2. We start with some intuition from Euclidean geometry. A triple of points $a, a + b$, and $a + 2b$ can

The randomized communication of exactly n is only a constant because Alice can use the randomized protocol for equality to check whether the number on her forehead is equal to what it needs to be for all numbers to sum to n.

[3] Behrend, 1946.

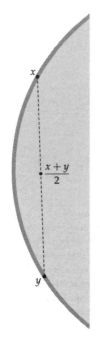

be also thought of as a triple of the form $x, (x + y)/2, y$. In other words, we want to find a coloring of $[m]$ so that if x, y have the same color, then $(x + y)/2$ has a different color.

The basic observation is that the points on a sphere satisfy a similar property. If x, y are two distinct vectors of the same length, then $(x + y)/2$ is shorter, as in Figure 4.1. If we color each vector by its Euclidean length, then we get the desired property. The idea is to think of integers as high-dimensional vectors and then color an integer by the length of the corresponding vector.

Proof of Theorem 4.2 We shall choose parameters d, r with $d^r > m$ and d is divisible by 4. To carry out the above intuition, we need to convert each number $x \in [m]$ into a vector. To do this, we write each number $x \in [m]$ in base d, using at most r digits. Express x as $x = \sum_{i=0}^{r-1} x_i d^i$, where $x_i \in \{0, 1, \ldots, d - 1\}$. Interpret $x \in [m]$ as a vector $v(x) \in \mathbb{R}^r$ whose ith coordinate x_i.

We would like to color x by the norm of $v(x)$. This could potentially give a very efficient coloring – when d is a constant, the square of the norm of $v(x)$ can be at most $\lceil \log_d m \rceil d^2 = O(\log m)$, so we need only $O(\log m)$ colors to encode the norm of $v(x)$. Unfortunately, this fails. The reason is that algebra over the integers does not quite correspond to algebra over the vectors – $v(x + y) \neq v(x) + v(y)$ in general. However, we do have that $v(x + y) = v(x) + v(y)$ when x, y only involve small digits.

We add the following data to ensure that the digits used in the analysis are small. Let $w(x)$ be the vector whose ith coordinate is the largest number of the form $jd/4$ such that $jd/4 \leq x_i$ and j is an integer. $w(x)$ simply rounds each coordinate of $v(x)$ to the closest multiple of $d/4$.

Color each number $x \in [n]$ by the integer $\|v(x)\|^2 = \sum_{i=0}^{r-1} x_i^2$ and by the whole vector $w(x)$. The number of possible values for $\|v(x)\|^2$ is at most $O(rd^2)$. The number of choices for $w(x)$ is at most $2^{O(r)}$. The total number of possible colors is at most $2^{O(r + \log d)}$. Setting $r = \sqrt{\log m}$ and $d = 2^{O(\sqrt{\log m})}$ gives the required bound.

It only remains to check that the coloring avoids arithmetic progressions. For the sake of finding a contradiction, suppose $a, b \in [m]$ are such that $a, a + b$, and $a + 2b$ all get the same color. Then we must have $\|v(a)\| = \|v(a + b)\| = \|v(a + 2b)\|$. So, $v(a), v(a + b)$, and $v(a + 2b)$ all lie on a sphere. We get a contradiction by proving that

$$v(a + 2b) + v(a) = 2v(a + b).$$

To prove this, we need to use the fact that the points also satisfy $w(a) = w(a + b) = w(a + 2b)$. Given that these are the same, it is enough to prove

Figure 4.1 The average of two distinct points on a sphere must lie in the interior.

$$(v(a+2b) - w(a+2b)) + (v(a) - w(a)) = 2(v(a+b) - w(a+b)).$$

Let W denote the integer whose d-ary digit representation corresponds to $w(a)$. Then the left-hand side above is the d-ary representation of the integer $(a + 2b - W) + (a - W)$, and the right-hand side is the d-ary representation of $2(a + b - W)$. These are the same integer, so the two sides are equal. □

All three d-ary representations here involve digits of magnitude at most $d/4$.

Defining Protocols in the Number-on-Forehead Model

COMMUNICATION PROTOCOLS IN THE NUMBER-ON-FORE-HEAD MODEL are also represented by trees. The formal definitions are similar to the two-party case, so we provide just a brief overview.

A protocol tree is a rooted directed binary tree. Every inner vertex in the protocol tree is associated with one of the k parties and with a function that maps this party's input to $\{0, 1\}$. Each leaf in the tree is labeled by some output of the protocol.

Every input $x = (x_1, x_2, \ldots, x_k)$ defines a path from the root to the leaf $\pi(x)$ of the protocol tree. This path corresponds to the bits communicated during the execution of the protocol on this input. The label of the leaf $\pi(x)$ is the output of the protocol on this input.

A protocol π computes a function $g : \mathcal{X}_1 \times \cdots \times \mathcal{X}_k \to \{0, 1\}$ if the label of $\pi(x)$ is $g(x)$ for all inputs x. The length of a protocol is the depth of the protocol tree. The communication complexity of a function g is the minimum length of a protocol that computes g.

Cylinder Intersections

COMBINATORIAL RECTANGLES are the basic building blocks of two-party communication protocols. The corresponding building blocks in the number-on-forehead model are *cylinder intersections*. Any set $S \subseteq \mathcal{X}_1 \times \cdots \times \mathcal{X}_k$ can be described using its characteristic function:

$$\chi_S(x_1, \ldots, x_k) = \begin{cases} 1 & \text{if } (x_1, \ldots, x_k) \in S, \\ 0 & \text{otherwise.} \end{cases}$$

Cylinders are set that are constant in one dimension:

Definition 4.3 A set $S \subseteq \mathcal{X}_1 \times \cdots \times \mathcal{X}_k$ is called a *cylinder* if χ_S does not depend on one of its inputs.

Cylinder intersections are defined as the intersection of cylinders:

Definition 4.4 A set S is called a *cylinder intersection* if it can be expressed as an intersection of cylinders. Namely,

$$\chi_S(x_1, \ldots, x_k) = \prod_{i=1}^{k} \chi_i(x_1, \ldots, x_k),$$

where χ_i is a Boolean function that does not depend on x_i.

Figure 4.2 A cylinder
intersection.

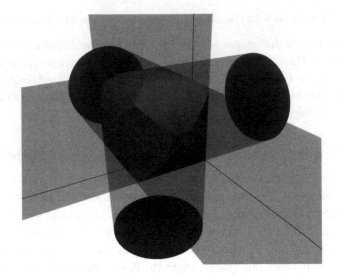

Figure 4.3 Figure 4.2 viewed
from above.

Figures 4.2–4.6 show some examples of cylinder intersections. Just
as for rectangles, we say that a cylinder intersection is *monochromatic*
with respect to a function g, if $g(x) = g(y)$ for every two inputs x, y in
the cylinder intersection.

When $k = 2$, cylinder intersections are the same as rectangles. However, when $k > 2$, they are much more complicated to understand than
rectangles. Nevertheless, in analogy with the two-party case, we have
the following theorem:

Theorem 4.5 *If the deterministic communication complexity of $g : \mathcal{X}_1 \times$
$\cdots \times \mathcal{X}_k \to \{0, 1\}$ in the number-on-forehead model is c, then $\mathcal{X}_1 \times$
$\cdots \times \mathcal{X}_k$ can be partitioned into at most 2^c monochromatic cylinder
intersections with respect to g.*

Proof Sketch It follows by induction that the set of inputs that are
consistent with every vertex in the protocol tree form a cylinder
intersection.   □

Lower Bounds from Ramsey Theory

CYLINDER INTERSECTIONS ARE MORE COMPLICATED than
rectangles. This makes proving lower bounds in the number-on-forehead
model challenging. Here we use *Ramsey theory* to prove a lower bound
in this model. The main message of Ramsey theory is that every large
enough system must contain small pieces that are structured. Let us
see how to use this idea to prove lower bounds in communication
complexity.

In Chapter 5 we discuss the
discrepancy method, which
leads to the strongest known
lower bounds in the
number-on-forehead model.

Consider the *Exactly n* problem. Alice, Bob, and Charlie are each
given a number from $[n]$, written on their foreheads. They want to know
if their numbers sum to n. We have shown that there is a protocol that

Figure 4.4 A cylinder intersection.

computes this function using $O(\sqrt{\log n})$ bits of communication. Here we show that $\Omega(\log \log \log n)$ bits of communication are required.[4]

[4] Chandra et al., 1983.

Denote by c_n the deterministic communication complexity of the exactly n problem. We need to identify an obstacle that makes c_n large. The key idea is to focus on a structured subset called a *corner*.

Three points in $[n] \times [n]$ form a corner if they are of the form $(x, y), (x + d, y), (x, y + d)$ for some integer d. See Figure 4.7. A *coloring* of $[n] \times [n]$ with C colors is a map from $[n] \times [n]$ to $[C]$. A corner is monochromatic with respect to the coloring if its three points get the same color. Let C_n be the minimum number of colors required to avoid having any monochromatic corners in $[n] \times [n]$.

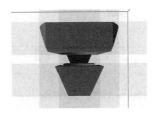

Figure 4.5 Figure 4.4 viewed from above.

First we show that C_n captures the value of c_n:

Lemma 4.6 $\log C_{n/3} \le c_n \le 2 + \log C_n$.

Proof of Lemma 4.6 To prove $2 + \log C_n \ge c_n$, suppose there is a coloring with C_n colors that avoids monochromatic corners. Alice announces the color of $(n - y - z, y)$. Bob and Charlie then send a bit indicating if this color is the same as the color of $(x, n - x - z)$ and (x, y). The three points $(x, y), (x, n - x - z), (n - y - z, y)$ form a corner with $d = n - x - y - z$. So all three points have the same color if and only if all three points are the same, which can only happen when $x + y + z = n$.

Figure 4.6 Figure 4.4 viewed from the right.

The second inequality in the lemma is not needed for the lower bound. We state and prove it here because it shows that the communication problem is equivalent to a this purely combinatorial problem.

To prove that $\log C_{n/3} \le c_n$, suppose there is a protocol solving the Exactly n problem with c bits of communication. By Theorem 4.5, every input to the protocol can be colored by one of 2^c colors that is the name of the corresponding cylinder intersection. This induces a coloring of $[n/3] \times [n/3]$: color (x, y) by the name of the cylinder intersection containing the point $(x, y, n - x - y)$. We claim that this coloring avoids monochromatic corners. Indeed, assume that

$$(x, y), (x + d, y), (x, y + d)$$

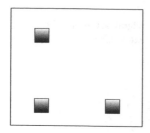

Figure 4.7 A monochromatic corner.

[5] Graham, 1980; and Graham et al., 1980.

In fact, one can prove that every large enough subset of $[n] \times [n]$ contains a corner.

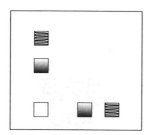

Figure 4.8 A rainbow-corner.

is a monochromatic corner with $d \neq 0$. That is,

$$(x, y, n - x - y), (x + d, y, n - (x + d) - y), (x, y + d, n - x - (y + d))$$

belong to the same cylinder intersection. The point $(x, y, n - x - y - d)$ must *also* be in the same cylinder intersection because it agrees with each of the three points in two coordinates. This contradicts the correctness of the protocol: $x + y + n - x - y = n$ but $x + y + n - x - y - d \neq n$.   □

The second step in the proof uses ideas from Ramsey theory.[5] We show that the number of colors that are needed to avoid monochromatic corners is large:

Theorem 4.7 $C_n \geq \Omega\left(\frac{\log\log n}{\log\log\log n}\right)$.

Proof We prove the theorem by induction. We need to strengthen the statement in order for the induction to go through. We prove that the matrix must either contain a monochromatic corner, or a structure called a rainbow-corner. A *rainbow-corner* with r colors and center (x, y) is specified by a set of r distinct colors, and numbers $d_1, \ldots, d_{r-1}$, such that $(x + d_i, y)$ and $(x, y + d_i)$ are both colored using the ith color, and (x, y) is colored by the rth color. See Figure 4.8 for an illustration.

We prove that if $C > 3$ and $n \geq 2^{C^{2r}}$, then any coloring of $[n] \times [n]$ with C colors must contain either a monochromatic corner, or a rainbow-corner with r colors. When $r = C + 1$, this means that if $n \geq 2^{C^{2(C+1)}}$, then $[n] \times [n]$ must contain a monochromatic corner. Thus, $C_n \geq \Omega\left(\frac{\log\log n}{\log\log\log n}\right)$.

The base case is when $r = 2$. There are n points of the form $(x, n - x)$. Because $n \geq 2^{C^{2r}} > C$, two points of the form $(x, n - x)$ and $(x', n - x')$ with $x > x'$ have the same color. It follows that $(x', n - x), (x, n - x)$, and $(x', n - x')$ are either a monochromatic corner, or a rainbow-corner with two colors.

For the inductive step, assume $n = 2^{C^{2r}}$. The set $[n]$ contains $m = 2^{C^{2r} - C^{2(r-1)}}$ disjoint intervals $I_1, I_2, \ldots, I_m$, each of size exactly $2^{C^{2(r-1)}}$. By induction, each of the sets $I_j \times I_j$ must have either a monochromatic corner or a rainbow-corner with $r - 1$ colors. If one of them has a monochromatic corner, then we are done. So, suppose they all have rainbow-corners with $r - 1$ colors. A rainbow-corner is specified by choosing the center, choosing the colors, and choosing the offsets for each color. Thus, there are at most

$$(2^{C^{2(r-1)}})^2 \cdot C^r \cdot (2^{C^{2(r-1)}})^C = 2^{2C^{2(r-1)} + r\log C + C^{2r-1}} < m$$

potential rainbow-corners in each of these sets. Because the number of possible rainbow corners is less than m, there must be some $j < j'$ that have exactly the *same* rainbow-corner with the same coloring. These two rainbow-corners induce a monochromatic corner centered in the box $I_j \times I_{j'}$, or a rainbow-corner with r colors. See Figure 4.9.   □

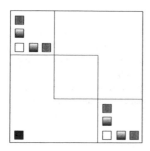

Figure 4.9 A rainbow-corner induced by two smaller rainbow-corners.

Exercises

Ex 4.1 – Suppose there are k parties in the number-on-forehead model. The ith party has the bit $X_i \in \{0, 1\}$ written on their forehead, and $X_1, \ldots, X_k$ are sampled independently and uniformly at random. Show that there is a protocol for each party to privately write down a guess for the bit on their own forehead, without *any* communication, in such a way that the probability that all parties guess correctly is $1/2$.

Ex 4.2 – Define the generalized inner product function GIP as follows. For k inputs $x_1, \ldots, x_k \in \{0, 1\}^n$,

$$\mathsf{GIP}(x) = \sum_{j=1}^{n} \prod_{i=1}^{k} x_{i,j} \bmod 2.$$

This exercise outlines a number-on-forehead GIP protocol using $O(n/2^k + k)$ bits. It is convenient to think about the input X as a $k \times n$ matrix with rows corresponding to $x_1, \ldots, x_k$.

- For $\ell \in \{0, 1, \ldots, k - 1\}$ define c_ℓ as the number of columns in X that start with ℓ zeroes, followed by either a one or zero, followed by $k - \ell - 1$ ones. Prove that $\sum_{\ell=0}^{t-1} c_\ell = \mathsf{GIP}(x) \bmod 2$.
- Suppose the parties know a string $z \in \{0, 1\}^k$ with the property that no column of X is equal to z. Find a protocol to compute $\mathsf{GIP}(x)$ using $O(k)$ bits *assuming the parties know z.*
- Exhibit an overall protocol for GIP by showing that the parties can agree upon a vector z and communicate to determine $c_\ell \pmod 2$ using $O(n/2^k + k)$ bits.

Ex 4.3 – This exercise explores the direct sum question in the number-on-forehead model. Given a function g, recall that g^n is the function that computes n copies of g. What can we say about the communication complexity of g^n knowing the communication complexity of g?

The approach taken in the proof of Theorem 1.39 does not work because cylinder intersections do not "tensorize" nicely like rectangles do. However, ideas from Ramsey theory can be used to show that the communication complexity of g^r must increase as r increases.

The key ingredient is the *Hales-Jewett* theorem.[6] The theorem gives insight into the structure of the Cartesian product $S^n = S \times S \times \cdots S$ as n grows, for an *arbitrary* finite set S. For the precise statement we need the notion of a combinatorial line. The *combinatorial line* specified by a nonempty set of indices $I \subseteq [n]$ and a vector $v \in S^n$ is the set of all $x \in S^n$ so that $x_i = v_i$ for every $i \notin I$ and $x_i = x_j$ for every $i, j \in I$.

Given a set S and a number t, the Hales-Jewett theorem says that as long as n is large enough, any coloring of S^n with t colors must contain a monochromatic combinatorial line.

Assume that the communication complexity of g is strictly greater than the number of parties. Define c_n to be communication required to compute the AND of n copies of g. Prove that

$$\lim_{n \to \infty} c_n = \infty.$$

[6] Hales and Jewett, 1963.

For example, when $S = [3]$ and $n = 4$ then the set $\{1132, 2232, 3332\}$ is a combinatorial line with $I = \{1, 2\}$ and $v_3 = 3, v_4 = 2$.

Ex 4.4 – A three-party number-on-forehead puzzle demonstrates that unexpected efficiency is sometimes possible.

Alice has a number $i \in [n]$ on her forehead, Bob has a number $j \in [n]$ on his forehead, and Charlie has a string $x \in \{0, 1\}^n$ on his forehead. On input (i, j, x) the goal is for Charlie to output the bit x_k where $k = i + j \mod n$.

Find a deterministic protocol in which Bob sends one bit to Charlie, and Alice sends $\lceil \frac{n}{2} \rceil$ bits to Charlie. Alice and Bob must send Charlie their message *simultaneously*. Charlie is then able to output the correct answer.

Ex 4.5 – In this exercise, we find an even more surprising protocol than in the last exercise. Suppose Alice has a number $i \in [n]$ on her forehead, Bob has a permutation $\pi : [n] \to [n]$ on his forehead, and Charlie has a string $x \in \{0, 1\}^n$ on his forehead. Their goal is to compute $x_{\pi(i)}$. We show that there is a protocol where Alice sends Charlie at most $O(n/\log n)$ bits, and Bob sends Charlie at most $n/2$ bits.

To do this, we appeal to a bound on the chromatic number of random graphs. Recall that the chromatic number is $\chi(G)$ if the vertices can be colored with $\chi(G)$ colors so that adjacent vertices get different colors. It is a theorem that if a graph on n vertices is sampled by including each edge independently with probability $1/50$, then the chromatic number of the graph is $O(n/\log n)$, except with probability $2^{-\Omega(n^{1.1})}$.

1. Use the bound on the chromatic number of random graphs discussed above to show that there exist sets $S_1, \ldots, S_n \subseteq [n]$ with the property that $|S_i| \leq n/2$ for all i, and yet, for any $\pi : [n] \to [n]$, one can color $[n]$ with $O(n/\log n)$ colors so that if i, j get the same color, then $\pi(j) \in S_i$. *Hint: Use the probabilistic method.*
2. Use the above property to give the desired protocol.

Ex 4.6 – Let f be a polynomial of total degree d in n variables $x_1, \ldots, x_n$ over the field $\mathbb{F}_2$. There are $d + 1$ parties in the number-on-forehead model. The set of coordinates $[n]$ is partition to $d + 1$ parts $I_1, \ldots, I_{d+1}$. Party j has x_{I_j} written on the forehead. Show that the parties can compute $f(x_1, \ldots, x_n)$ with $O(d)$ bits of communication.

5

Discrepancy

IF THE ELEMENTS OF A LARGE SET are randomly colored either red or blue, we would expect the coloring to be roughly balanced. Namely, approximately half of the elements would be red and half would be blue. Discrepancy is a way to measure the degree to which the coloring is balanced. It quantifies how "random" the coloring is. Discrepancy is used in several different areas, such as in geometry and learning theory. Here we use it to prove lower bounds on communication complexity.

The techniques we have developed for proving lower bounds in prior chapters all rely on the fact that efficient communication protocols lead to partitions of the space into a small number of monochromatic sets. A monochromatic set has large discrepancy; it does not look like it was randomly colored at all. For a given Boolean function, lower bounds on communication complexity can be proved by arguing that the discrepancy of large rectangles or cylinder intersections must be small.

The ideas we develop in this chapter lead to lower bounds for randomized protocols and the best-known lower bounds in the number-on-forehead model.

Definitions

SUPPOSE $g : D \to \{0, 1\}$ is a Boolean function, and μ is a distribution on the inputs D. Suppose $S \subseteq D$ is a subset of the domain, and let χ_S be the characteristic function of the set S. We define the *discrepancy* of g with respect to S and μ as

$$\left| \mathop{\mathbb{E}}_{\mu} \left[\chi_S(x) \cdot (-1)^{g(x)} \right] \right|.$$

$$\chi_S(x) = \begin{cases} 1 & \text{if } x \in S, \\ 0 & \text{otherwise.} \end{cases}$$

When the distribution μ is understood from the context, we refer to this quantity as the discrepancy of g with respect to S.

There are two obvious reasons why the discrepancy could be small – either the set S is small, or g corresponds to a balanced coloring of S. Moreover, if the discrepancy is very small, then it must be the case that either S has small measure under μ, or g corresponds to a very balanced coloring of S.

If μ is relatively well behaved, a random function g will have low discrepancy with high probability. However, the choice of the low discrepancy function g certainly depends on S. Indeed, every $g : D \to$

See Exercise 5.1.

$\{0, 1\}$ is monochromatic on a set of μ-measure at least $1/2$, so given g, the discrepancy is certainly large with respect to many sets. Nevertheless, we can hope to establish that a fixed function g has small discrepancy with respect to sets of a specific structure, like rectangles or cylinder intersections. For example, we shall consider the domain $D = \mathcal{X} \times \mathcal{Y}$ and the maximum of the discrepancy with respect to all the rectangles in D.

A large set with large bias must lead to high discrepancy. The bias of a function g with respect to a set S is defined to be

$$\mathsf{bias}_g(S) = \max_b \Pr[g(x) = b | x \in S].$$

Claim 5.1 *If S is so that $\Pr_\mu[x \in S] \geq \delta$ and $\mathsf{bias}_g(S) \geq 1 - \epsilon$, then the discrepancy of g with respect to S is at least $(1 - 2\epsilon)\delta$.*

Proof Only points inside S contribute to its discrepancy. Because a $1 - \epsilon$ fraction of these points have the same value under g, the discrepancy is at least $\delta(1 - \epsilon - \epsilon) = \delta(1 - 2\epsilon)$. □

Discrepancy and Communication

DISCREPANCY CAN BE USED to prove lower bounds on randomized communication complexity. The idea is that any function that has small discrepancy with respect to all rectangles must have large communication complexity:

The same result applies in the number-on-forehead model when we have a bound on the discrepancy with respect to cylinder intersections.

Theorem 5.2 *For a fixed distribution μ, if the discrepancy of g with respect to every rectangle is at most γ, then any protocol computing g with error ϵ when the inputs are drawn from μ must have communication complexity at least $\log\left(\frac{1-2\epsilon}{\gamma}\right)$.*

Proof Suppose π is a protocol of length c with error ϵ with respect to μ. We can assume without loss of generality that π is deterministic. Let $\pi(x, y)$ denote the output of the protocol.

By Lemma 1.4, the leaves of the protocol π correspond to rectangles $R_1, \ldots, R_t$ that partition the input space. Moreover, we have $t \leq 2^c$ because the length of the protocol is c. Thus,

$$1 - 2\epsilon \leq \Pr_\mu[\pi(x, y) = g(x, y)] - \Pr_\mu[\pi(x, y) \neq g(x, y)]$$
$$= \mathbb{E}_\mu\left[(-1)^{\pi(x,y)} \cdot (-1)^{g(x,y)}\right]$$
$$= \mathbb{E}_\mu\left[\left(\sum_{i=1}^t \chi_{R_i}(x, y) \cdot \varphi(R_i)\right) \cdot (-1)^{g(x,y)}\right],$$

where $\varphi(R_i) = -1$ if the protocol outputs 1 on inputs from R_i, and $\varphi(R_i) = 1$ if the protocol outputs 0. By the triangle inequality,

$$1 - 2\epsilon \leq \sum_{i=1}^{t} \left| \mathbb{E}_{\mu} \left[\chi_{R_i}(x, y) \cdot (-1)^{g(x,y)} \right] \right|$$

$$\leq 2^c \cdot \max_R \left| \mathbb{E}_{\mu} \left[\chi_R(x, y) \cdot (-1)^{g(x,y)} \right] \right| \leq 2^c \gamma,$$

where the maximum is taken over all choices of rectangles. Rearranging, we get $2^c \geq \frac{1-2\epsilon}{\gamma}$, proving the theorem.   □

To prove lower bounds on randomized communication complexity, it suffices to give upper bounds on the discrepancy with respect to rectangles and cylinder intersections. Simple counting arguments show that most functions have small discrepancy with respect to rectangles and cylinder intersections. Our goal in this chapter is to prove that there are explicit functions g that have small discrepancy.   See Exercise 5.2.

We explore two general techniques that can be used to bound the discrepancy. First, we show how to use *convexity* to bound discrepancy. Later, we show how one can use concentration bounds from probability theory to control it. As a warm-up, let us explore some examples where convexity is useful in combinatorics.

Convexity in Combinatorics

CONVEXITY PLAYS a key role in solving many combinatorial problems. At a high level, the approach is to represent a given quantity of interest in an analytic form, as a sum of real numbers. Convexity is then used to move from the *specific* object we started with to an *average case* object where the quantity is much easier to bound.

Let us illustrate this general principle by applying it to the following question: how many edges must a graph have before it is forced to contain a small cycle? A graph on n vertices can have up to $\binom{n}{2}$ edges. We say that the graph has edge density ϵ if it has $\epsilon \cdot \binom{n}{2}$ edges. There are graphs with constant edge density that have no three-cycles, like the complete bipartite graph, see Figure 5.1. However, as we show below, there are no graphs with constant density without four-cycles.

Lemma 5.3 *Every graph with n vertices and edge density at least $\frac{3}{\sqrt{n}}$ contains a 4-cycle.*

Proof Let $E(x, y)$ be the indicator function for the edges of the graph – for two vertices x, y, we have $E(x, y) = 1$ when there is an edge between the vertices x and y, and $E(x, y) = 0$ otherwise.

Let x, x', y be three vertices chosen independently and uniformly at random from the graph. By convexity,

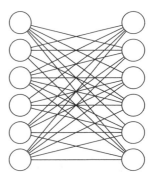

Figure 5.1 A dense graph with no three-cycles.

$$\underset{x,x'}{\mathbb{E}}\left[\underset{y}{\mathbb{E}}\left[E(x,y)\cdot E(x',y)\right]\right] = \underset{y}{\mathbb{E}}\left[\underset{x}{\mathbb{E}}\left[E(x,y))\right]^2\right] \geq \underset{x,y}{\mathbb{E}}\left[E(x,y)\right]^2.$$

The point-line incidence graph of a projective plane has n vertices, approximately $n^{3/2}$ edges, and no four-cycles. This shows that the lemma is sharp up to constants.

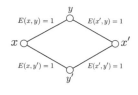

$E(x,y)\cdot E(x',y)$ is the indicator for a path of length 2.

$E(x,y)$ is 0 only when $x = y$ or $\{x, y\}$ is not an edge. Because $x = y$ with probability $1/n$ and the edge density is at least $3/\sqrt{n}$, this last quantity is at least

$$\left(\frac{3}{\sqrt{n}} - \frac{1}{n}\right)^2 \geq \left(\frac{2}{\sqrt{n}}\right)^2 \geq \frac{4}{n}.$$

For the sake of reaching a contradiction, suppose that the graph has no 4-cycles. Then, for each $x \neq x'$, there can be at most one y with $E(x,y)\cdot E(x',y) = 1$. Otherwise, if $E(x,y)\cdot E(x,y) = E(x,y')\cdot E(x,y') = 1$, then the vertices x, y, x', y' must form a four-cycle. So, whenever $x \neq x'$, $\mathbb{E}_y\left[E(x,y)\cdot E(x',y)\right] \leq \frac{1}{n}$. The probability that $x = x'$ is exactly $1/n$. So, we get

$$\underset{x,x'}{\mathbb{E}}\left[\underset{y}{\mathbb{E}}\left[E(x,y)\cdot E(x',y)\right]\right] \leq \frac{1}{n} + \frac{1}{n} \leq \frac{2}{n},$$

contradicting the bound we proved above.   □

We have just seen that dense graphs contain four-cycles. What can we say about structures that are more complicated than cycles? We now show that dense bipartite graphs contain large bipartite cliques. For example, every bipartite graph with constant edge density contains a complete bipartite graph of logarithmic size.

Lemma 5.4 *Suppose G is a bipartite graph with edge density $\epsilon > 0$, and bipartition A, B with $|A| = m$ and $|B| = n$. Let $k \leq \frac{\log n}{2\log(2e/\epsilon)}$. If $\epsilon \geq 2k/m$, then there are subsets $A' \subseteq A$ and $B' \subseteq B$ of sizes*

$$|A'| \geq k \quad and \quad |B'| \geq \sqrt{n}$$

such that every pair of vertices $a \in A', b \in B'$ is connected by an edge.

Proof Pick a uniformly random subset $Q \subseteq A$ of size k. Let R be all the common neighbors of Q. The induced graph on $Q \times R$ is a complete bipartite clique, which is the structure we are looking for. We just need to prove that R is large with nonzero probability.

Given any vertex $b \in B$ with degree $d_b \geq k$, the probability that b is included in R is exactly

because $(\frac{n}{k})^k \leq \binom{n}{k}$
$\leq (\frac{en}{k})^k$ for $0 < k \leq n$.

$$\frac{\binom{d_b}{k}}{\binom{m}{k}} \geq \frac{(d_b/k)^k}{(em/k)^k} = \left(\frac{d_b}{em}\right)^k.$$

The expected size of the set R is at least

$$\mathbb{E}\left[|R|\right] \geq \sum_{b \in B:d_b \geq k} \left(\frac{d_b}{em}\right)^k \geq n \cdot \left(\frac{1}{n} \cdot \sum_{b \in B:d_b \geq k} \frac{d_b}{em}\right)^k \qquad \text{because the function } x \mapsto x^k \text{ is convex.}$$

$$= n \cdot \left(\frac{1}{emn} \cdot \sum_{b \in B:d_b \geq k} d_b\right)^k.$$

Observe that $\sum_{b \in B:d_b \geq k} d_b$ is the number of the edges of the graph, except those that touch vertices in B of degree less than k. This quantity is at least $\epsilon mn - kn \geq \frac{\epsilon mn}{2}$ because $\epsilon \geq \frac{2k}{m}$. Thus,

$$\mathbb{E}\left[|R|\right] \geq n \cdot \left(\frac{1}{emn} \cdot \frac{\epsilon mn}{2}\right)^k = n \cdot \left(\frac{\epsilon}{2e}\right)^k \geq \sqrt{n}.$$

So, there must be some choice of Q, R that proves the lemma. $\square$

Lower Bounds for Inner-Product

MOVING BACK TO COMMUNICATION COMPLEXITY, imagine Alice and Bob are given $x, y \in \{0, 1\}^n$ and want to compute the inner-product

$$\mathsf{IP}(x, y) = \langle x, y \rangle \quad \mod 2.$$

We have seen that this requires $n + 1$ bits of communication using a deterministic protocol. Here we show that it requires at least $\approx n/2$ bits of communication even using a randomized protocol. To prove this, we use convexity to show that the discrepancy of IP is small.

Lemma 5.5 *For any rectangle R, the discrepancy of IP with respect to R over the uniform distribution is at most $2^{-n/2}$.*

Proof Because R is a rectangle, we can write its characteristic function as the product of two functions $A : \{0, 1\}^n \to \{0, 1\}$ and $B : \{0, 1\}^n \to \{0, 1\}$. The square of the discrepancy with respect to R can be written as

$$\left(\mathbb{E}_{x,y}\left[\chi_R(x, y) \cdot (-1)^{\langle x,y \rangle}\right]\right)^2 = \left(\mathbb{E}_{x,y}\left[A(x) \cdot B(y) \cdot (-1)^{\langle x,y \rangle}\right]\right)^2$$

$$= \left(\mathbb{E}_x\left[A(x) \mathbb{E}_y\left[B(y) \cdot (-1)^{\langle x,y \rangle}\right]\right]\right)^2$$

$$\leq \mathbb{E}_x\left[A(x)^2 \left(\mathbb{E}_y\left[B(y) \cdot (-1)^{\langle x,y \rangle}\right]\right)^2\right]. \qquad \text{by convexity of } z \mapsto z^2.$$

Because $0 \le A(x) \le 1$, we can drop $A(x)$ from this expression to get:

$$\left(\mathop{\mathbb{E}}_{x,y} \left[\chi_R(x,y) \cdot (-1)^{\langle x,y \rangle} \right] \right)^2 \le \mathop{\mathbb{E}}_{x} \left[\left(\mathop{\mathbb{E}}_{y} \left[B(y) \cdot (-1)^{\langle x,y \rangle} \right] \right)^2 \right]$$

$$= \mathop{\mathbb{E}}_{x,y,y'} \left[B(y)B(y') \cdot (-1)^{\langle x,y \rangle + \langle x,y' \rangle} \right]$$

$$= \mathop{\mathbb{E}}_{x,y,y'} \left[B(y)B(y') \cdot (-1)^{\langle x,y+y' \rangle} \right].$$

In this way, we have completely eliminated the dependence on the set A from the calculation! We can also eliminate the set B using the triangle inequality to bound:

$$\left(\mathop{\mathbb{E}}_{x,y} \left[\chi_R(x,y) \cdot (-1)^{\langle x,y \rangle} \right] \right)^2 \le \mathop{\mathbb{E}}_{x,y,y'} \left[B(y)B(y') \cdot (-1)^{\langle x,y+y' \rangle} \right]$$

$$\le \mathop{\mathbb{E}}_{y,y'} \left[\left| \mathop{\mathbb{E}}_{x} \left[(-1)^{\langle x,y+y' \rangle} \right] \right| \right]$$

$$= \mathop{\mathbb{E}}_{y,y'} \left[\prod_{i=1}^{n} \left(\frac{1+(-1)^{y_i+y'_i}}{2} \right) \right].$$

Now, whenever $y + y'$ is not zero modulo 2, the inner expression is 0. The probability that $y + y'$ is zero modulo 2 is exactly 2^{-n}. So

$$\left(\mathop{\mathbb{E}}_{x,y} \left[\chi_R(x,y) \cdot (-1)^{\langle x,y \rangle} \right] \right)^2 \le 2^{-n}.$$

□

Lemma 5.5 and Theorem 5.2 together imply the desired lower bound on the randomized communication complexity of the inner-product function:

Theorem 5.6 *Any two-party protocol that computes the inner-product function with error at most ϵ over the uniform distribution must have length at least $n/2 - \log(1/(1 - 2\epsilon))$.*

So, we have reasonably tight bounds on the communication complexity of IP in the two-party setting. What happens when more parties are involved?

It turns out that similar ideas can be used to analyze the *generalized inner-product* in the number-on-forehead model,[1] Here each of the k parties is given a binary string $x_i \in \{0,1\}^n$. They want to compute

[1] Babai et al., 1989.

Each vector x_i can be interpreted as a subset of $[n]$. The protocol for computing the set intersection size gives a protocol for computing generalized inner-product with communication $O(k^4(1 + n/2^k))$.

$$\mathsf{GIP}(x) = \sum_{j=1}^{n} \prod_{i=1}^{k} x_{i,j} \quad \bmod 2.$$

Once again, we can use discrepancy to prove a strong lower bound on the communication complexity of generalized inner-product. This time, we need to analyze the discrepancy with respect to cylinder intersections.

Lemma 5.7 *The discrepancy of* GIP *with respect any cylinder intersection over the uniform distribution is at most* $e^{-n/4^{k-1}}$.

Proof Let S be a cylinder intersection. Its characteristic function can be expressed as the product of k Boolean functions $\chi_S = \prod_{i=1}^{k} \chi_i$, where χ_i does not depend on x_i. Express the square of the discrepancy as

$$\left(\mathop{\mathbb{E}}_{x} \left[\chi_S(x) \cdot (-1)^{\mathrm{GIP}(x)} \right] \right)^2$$

$$= \left(\mathop{\mathbb{E}}_{x_1,\ldots,x_{k-1}} \left[\chi_k(x) \mathop{\mathbb{E}}_{x_k} \left[\prod_{i=1}^{k-1} \chi_i(x) \cdot (-1)^{\mathrm{GIP}(x)} \right] \right] \right)^2$$

$$\leq \mathop{\mathbb{E}}_{x_1,\ldots,x_{k-1}} \left[\chi_k(x)^2 \left(\mathop{\mathbb{E}}_{x_k} \left[\prod_{i=1}^{k-1} \chi_i(x) \cdot (-1)^{\mathrm{GIP}(x)} \right] \right)^2 \right]. \qquad \text{by convexity of } z \mapsto z^2.$$

Now, we can drop $\chi_k(x)$ from this expression to get:

$$\left(\mathop{\mathbb{E}}_{x} \left[\chi_S(x) \cdot (-1)^{\mathrm{GIP}(x)} \right] \right)^2$$

$$\leq \mathop{\mathbb{E}}_{x_1,\ldots,x_{k-1}} \left[\left(\mathop{\mathbb{E}}_{x_k} \left[\prod_{i=1}^{k-1} \chi_i(x) \cdot (-1)^{\mathrm{GIP}(x)} \right] \right)^2 \right]$$

$$= \mathop{\mathbb{E}}_{x_1,\ldots,x_k,x_k'} \left[\prod_{i=1}^{k-1} \chi_i(x)\chi_i(x') \cdot (-1)^{\sum_{j=1}^{n}(x_k+x_k')\prod_{i=1}^{k-1} x_{i,j}} \right],$$

where x_k' is uniformly distributed and independent of $x_1,\ldots,x_k$, and $x' = (x_1,\ldots,x_{k-1},x_k')$. In this way, we have completely eliminated the function χ_k from the calculation! Repeating this $k-1$ times gives the bound

$$\left(\mathop{\mathbb{E}}_{x} \left[\chi_S(x) \cdot (-1)^{\mathrm{GIP}(x)} \right] \right)^{2^{k-1}}$$

$$\leq \mathop{\mathbb{E}}_{x_2,x_2',\ldots,x_k,x_k'} \left[\left| \mathop{\mathbb{E}}_{x_1} \left[(-1)^{\sum_{j=1}^{n} x_1 \prod_{i=2}^{k}(x_i+x_i')} \right] \right| \right].$$

Whenever there is a coordinate j for which

$$\prod_{i=2}^{k-1} (x_{i,j} + x_{i',j}) \neq 0 \mod 2,$$

the inner expectation is 0. The probability that there is no such j is exactly $(1 - 2^{-k+1})^n$. So we get

$$\left(\mathop{\mathbb{E}}_{x} \left[\chi_S(x) \cdot (-1)^{\mathrm{GIP}(x)} \right] \right)^{2^{k-1}} \leq (1 - 2^{-k+1})^n \leq e^{-n/2^{k-1}}. \qquad \text{because } 1 - z \leq e^{-z} \text{ for all } z.$$

$\square$

By Lemma 5.7 and the analog of Theorem 5.2 in the number-on-forehead model:

Theorem 5.8 *Any randomized protocol for computing the generalized inner-product in the number-on-forehead model with error ϵ over the uniform distribution requires at least $n/4^{k-1} - \log(1/(1 - 2\epsilon))$ bits of communication.*

Disjointness and Discrepancy

IT IS TIME TO CONSIDER THE DISCREPANCY OF our favorite function, the disjointness function. Can we use discrepancy to prove lower bounds on its communication complexity? We certainly cannot do this using the discrepancy of disjointness with respect to the uniform distribution because disjointness has quite large monochromatic rectangles, like $R = \{(X, Y) : 1 \in X, 1 \in Y\}$. The discrepancy of disjointness with respect to R over the uniform distribution is $\frac{1}{4}$. This only gives us a constant lower bound.

What if we carefully choose some other distribution on inputs? Can we hope to get a better bound on the discrepancy of rectangles? If we use a distribution on inputs that gives intersecting sets with probability at most ϵ, then the parties could just *guess* that the sets intersect without communicating. On the other hand, if the probability of intersections is at least ϵ, then by averaging there must be some fixed coordinate i such that the sets both contain i with probability at least ϵ/n. Setting $R = \{(X, Y) : i \in X, i \in Y\}$, we get

If the probability of intersections is at most ϵ, then the trivial rectangle $R = \mathcal{X} \times \mathcal{Y}$ has high discrepancy:

$$\left| \mathbb{E}\left[\chi_R(X, Y) \cdot (-1)^{\text{Disj}(X,Y)} \right] \right|$$
$$= |\Pr[X \cap Y = \emptyset]$$
$$- \Pr[X \cap Y \neq \emptyset]|$$
$$\geq 1 - 2\epsilon.$$

$$\left| \mathbb{E}\left[\chi_R(X, Y) \cdot (-1)^{\text{Disj}(X,Y)} \right] \right| = \mathbb{E}\left[\chi_R(X, Y) \right] \geq \epsilon/n.$$

This suggests that the discrepancy method can only give a lower bound of $\Omega(\log n)$ if we follow the same approach that was used for the inner-product function.

[2] Sherstov, 2012; and Rao and Yehudayoff, 2015.

Nevertheless, one *can* use discrepancy to give a lower bound on the communication complexity of disjointness,[2] even when the protocol is allowed to be randomized. The idea is to study the discrepancy of a function that is related to disjointness under a suitably chosen distribution.

Above we showed that the discrepancy with respect to rectangles must be $\Omega(1/n)$. Let us start by proving an upper bound of $1/\sqrt{n}$ on the discrepancy. Consider the following distribution on sets. Suppose Alice gets a uniformly random set $X \subseteq [n]$, and Bob gets an independent, uniformly random set $Y \subseteq [n]$ *of size* 1.

Lemma 5.9 *For any rectangle R,*

$$\left| \mathbb{E}\left[\chi_R(X, Y) \cdot (-1)^{\text{Disj}(X,Y)} \right] \right| \leq \frac{1}{\sqrt{n}}.$$

Proof As usual, we express $\chi_R(X,Y) = A(X) \cdot B(Y)$ and carry out a convexity argument. Express the square of the discrepancy as

$$\left(\mathbb{E}\left[\chi_R(X,Y) \cdot (-1)^{\mathsf{Disj}(X,Y)}\right]\right)^2$$

$$= \left(\mathbb{E}\left[A(X) \cdot B(Y) \cdot (-1)^{\mathsf{Disj}(X,Y)}\right]\right)^2$$

$$\leq \mathbb{E}\left[A(X)^2 \left(\mathbb{E}\left[B(Y) \cdot (-1)^{\mathsf{Disj}(X,Y)}\right]\right)^2\right]$$

$$\leq \mathop{\mathbb{E}}_{X,Y,Y'}\left[B(Y)B(Y') \cdot (-1)^{\mathsf{Disj}(X,Y)+\mathsf{Disj}(X,Y')}\right]$$

$$\leq \mathop{\mathbb{E}}_{Y,Y'}\left[\left|\mathop{\mathbb{E}}_{X}\left[(-1)^{\mathsf{Disj}(X,Y)+\mathsf{Disj}(X,Y')}\right]\right|\right],$$

where Y' is an independent copy of Y. Now observe that for any fixing of Y, Y', the inner expectation is 0 as long as $Y \neq Y'$ because $|Y_j| = |Y'_j| = 1$ for each j. The probability that $Y = Y'$ is exactly $1/n$. So, the square of the discrepancy is at most $1/n$. $\square$

Although this bound looks quite weak, we actually can use it to prove a linear lower bound on the communication complexity of disjointness. The key observation is that discrepancy *tensorizes* – the techniques we have used to bound the discrepancy behave very nicely when we attempt to compute our function on independent copies drawn from the same distribution. Specifically, suppose $n_1, \ldots, n_m$ are nonnegative integers, and

$$(X_1, Y_1) \subseteq [n_1] \times [n_1], \ldots, (X_m, Y_m) \subseteq [n_m] \times [n_m]$$

are pairs of sets, each drawn independently from the same distribution as above, although on universes of different sizes. Let $X = X_1, \ldots, X_m$, and $Y = Y_1, \ldots, Y_m$. The variables X and Y are lists of sets, but we can also think of X, Y as subsets of $[n_1 + n_2 + \cdots + n_m]$, by partitioning the space into m intervals of sizes $n_1, n_2, \ldots, n_m$, and letting X_j be the intersection of X with the jth interval. Then the equations we used above can be easily modified to show that the discrepancy of the function $\sum_{j=1}^m \mathsf{Disj}(X_j, Y_j)$ is at most $\prod_{i=1}^m (1/\sqrt{n_i})$:

Lemma 5.10 *For any rectangle R,*

$$\left|\mathbb{E}\left[\chi_R(X,Y) \cdot (-1)^{\sum_{j=1}^m \mathsf{Disj}(X_j,Y_j)}\right]\right| \leq \prod_{i=1}^m \frac{1}{\sqrt{n_i}}.$$

Proof Express the square of the discrepancy as

$$\left(\mathbb{E}\left[\chi_R(X,Y) \cdot (-1)^{\sum_{j=1}^m \mathsf{Disj}(X_j,Y_j)}\right]\right)^2$$

$$= \left(\mathbb{E}\left[A(X) \cdot B(Y) \cdot (-1)^{\sum_{j=1}^m \mathsf{Disj}(X_j,Y_j)}\right]\right)^2$$

$$\leq \mathbb{E}\left[A(X)^2 \left(\mathbb{E}\left[B(Y) \cdot (-1)^{\sum_{j=1}^m \mathsf{Disj}(X_j,Y_j)}\right]\right)^2\right]$$

This bound is tight. Set $R = \{(x,y) : |x| \geq n/2\}$.

Then R has density $1/2$, and for X, Y chosen randomly from R, the probability that $Y \subseteq X$ is at least $1/2 + \Omega(1/\sqrt{n})$. This gives discrepancy $\Omega(1/\sqrt{n})$.

by convexity of $z \mapsto z^2$.

by convexity of $z \mapsto z^2$.

$$\leq \mathop{\mathbb{E}}_{X,Y,Y'} \left[B(Y)B(Y') \cdot (-1)^{\sum_{j=1}^{m} \mathrm{Disj}(X_j,Y_j) + \mathrm{Disj}(X_j,Y'_j)} \right]$$

$$\leq \mathop{\mathbb{E}}_{Y,Y'} \left[\left| \mathop{\mathbb{E}}_{X} \left[(-1)^{\sum_{j=1}^{m} \mathrm{Disj}(X_j,Y_j) + \mathrm{Disj}(X_j,Y'_j)} \right] \right| \right],$$

where Y' is an independent copy of Y. For any fixing of Y, Y', the inner expectation is 0 as long as $Y \neq Y'$ because $|Y_j| = |Y'_j| = 1$ for each j. The probability that $Y = Y'$ is exactly $\prod_{i=1}^{m}(1/n_i)$, so the square of the discrepancy is at most $\prod_{i=1}^{m}(1/n_i)$. □

Lemma 5.10 may not seem useful at first because under the given distribution, the probability that X, Y are disjoint is 2^{-m}. However, we can actually use it to give a linear lower bound on the communication of two-party deterministic protocols.

Set $n = m\ell$, and partition the universe $[n]$ into m disjoint sets of size ℓ. Consider the distribution on sets $X, Y \subseteq [n]$ where (X_j, Y_j) are subsets of the ℓ elements in the jth part of the universe sampled as above, and $X = X_1 \cup \cdots \cup X_m, Y = Y_1 \cup \cdots \cup X_m$.

We know that if there is a deterministic protocol for disjointness over a universe of size $n = m\ell$ of length c, then there are $T \leq 2^c$ monochromatic 1-rectangles $R_1, \ldots, R_T$ that cover all the 1s of Disj. Now, whenever X, Y are disjoint, we must have $\sum_{j=1}^{m} \mathrm{Disj}(X_j, Y_j) = m$ and $\sum_{t=1}^{T} \chi_{R_t}(X, Y) \geq 1$. The probability that X, Y are disjoint is exactly 2^{-m}. Whenever X, Y are not disjoint, we have that $\sum_{t=1}^{T} \chi_{R_t}(X, Y) = 0$. So,

$$2^{-m} \leq \left| \mathbb{E} \left[\sum_{t=1}^{T} \chi_{R_t}(X, Y) \cdot (-1)^{\sum_{j=1}^{m} \mathrm{Disj}(X_j,Y_j)} \right] \right|$$

$$\leq \sum_{t=1}^{T} \left| \mathbb{E} \left[\chi_{R_t}(X, Y) \cdot (-1)^{\sum_{j=1}^{m} \mathrm{Disj}(X_j,Y_j)} \right] \right|$$

$$\leq 2^c \cdot \frac{1}{\sqrt{\ell^m}}.$$

If $\ell = 16$, we get the lower bound $c \geq m = n/16$.

We have already seen several approaches for proving lower bounds on the two-party communication complexity of disjointness. The discrepancy approach, however, has a unique advantage over all the methods we have discussed before – it works even in the number-on-forehead model.

Suppose that there are k parties in the number-on-forehead model. We shall define a distribution on k sets $X_1, \ldots, X_k \subseteq [n]$. Let $n = n_1 + n_2 + \cdots + n_m$, and partition the universe into disjoint sets of size $n_1, n_2, \ldots, n_m$. Consider the distribution where for each $j = 1, \ldots, m$, the set of the first party $X_{1,j}$ is picked uniformly at random from the jth part of the universe. The sets of the other parties $X_{2,j}, \ldots, X_{k,j}$ are picked uniformly and independently at random from the jth part of the

Previously, we used discrepancy to prove lower bounds on randomized communication complexity. Here we use it to prove a lower bound where the proof only gives lower bounds on deterministic communication complexity.

The argument we present here even gives a lower bound on the size of a one-cover for disjointness.

by the triangle inequality.

universe, subject to the constraint that their intersection contains exactly one element. The set X_i is the union $X_{i,1} \cup \cdots \cup X_{i,m}$.

We can generalize Lemma 5.10 to show:

Lemma 5.11 *For any cylinder intersection S,*

$$\left| \mathbb{E}\left[\chi_S(X) \cdot (-1)^{\sum_{j=1}^{m} \mathsf{Disj}(X_{1,j},\ldots,X_{k,j})} \right] \right| \le \prod_{j=1}^{m} \frac{8^k}{\sqrt{n_j}}.$$

Proof We prove the lemma by induction on k. When $k = 2$, the statement was already proved in Lemma 5.10. So, let us assume that $k > 2$ and perform the induction step. To do so, let X'_k be an independent copy of X_k conditioned on $X_1, \ldots, X_{k-1}$. It is helpful to introduce the following notation. Let $T_j = X_{1,j}, \ldots, X_{k,j}$ denote all the sets in the jth part of the universe. Let $X' = X_1, \ldots, X_{k-1}, X'_k$, and let $T'_j = X_{1,j}, \ldots, X_{k-1,j}, X'_{k,j}$.

As usual, we use convexity to bound the discrepancy. Write the characteristic function of the cylinder intersection as $\chi_S = \prod_{i=1}^{k} \chi_i$, where χ_i does not depend on X_i. The square of the discrepancy is

$$\left(\mathbb{E}\left[\chi_S(X) \cdot (-1)^{\sum_{j=1}^{m} \mathsf{Disj}(X_{1,j},\ldots,X_{k,j})} \right] \right)^2$$

$$\le \mathop{\mathbb{E}}_{X_1,\ldots,X_{k-1}} \left[\chi_k(X)^2 \cdot \left(\mathop{\mathbb{E}}_{X_k}\left[\prod_{i=1}^{k-1} \chi_i(X) \cdot (-1)^{\sum_{j=1}^{m} \mathsf{Disj}(T_j)} \right] \right)^2 \right]$$

$$\le \mathop{\mathbb{E}}_{X_1,\ldots,X_{k-1}} \left[\left(\mathop{\mathbb{E}}_{X_k}\left[\prod_{i=1}^{k-1} \chi_i(X) \cdot (-1)^{\sum_{j=1}^{m} \mathsf{Disj}(T_j)} \right] \right)^2 \right]$$

$$= \mathop{\mathbb{E}}_{X_1,\ldots,X_{k-1},X_k,X'_k} \left[\prod_{i=1}^{k-1} \chi_i(X)\chi_i(X') \cdot (-1)^{\sum_{j=1}^{m} \mathsf{Disj}(T_j)+\mathsf{Disj}(T'_j)} \right]. \quad (5.1)$$

Focus on the expression $\mathsf{Disj}(T_j) + \mathsf{Disj}(T'_j)$ for some fixed j. Let v_j denote the common intersection point of $X_{2,j}, \ldots, X_{k,j}$. Let v'_j denote the common intersection point of $X_{2,j}, \ldots, X_{k-1,j}, X'_{k,j}$. When $v_j = v'_j$, we have $\mathsf{Disj}(T_j) = \mathsf{Disj}(T'_j)$, and so this expression is 0 modulo 2. When $v_j \ne v'_j$, any intersection in T_j must take place in the set $X_{k,j} - X'_{k,j}$, and any intersection in T'_j must take place in $X'_{k,j} - X_{j,k}$. See Figure 5.2 for an illustration. So, we can ignore the part of the sets $X_1, \ldots, X_{k-1}$ that is not in the symmetric difference of $X_{k,j}$ and $X'_{k,j}$. Effectively, after fixing $X_{k,j}$ and $X'_{k,j}$, the intersection of all sets with the points outside the symmetric difference of $X_{k,j}$ and $X'_{k,j}$, and whether or not $v_j = v'_j$, we are left with bounding the discrepancy of a $(k-1)$-dimensional cylinder intersection on sets that are sampled from the universe consisting of all elements that are in $(X_{k,j} - X'_{k,j}) \cup (X'_{k,j} - X_{k,j})$ for some j with $v_j \ne v'_j$. We can use induction to bound the discrepancy.

Let E_j be the indicator random variable for the event that one of the following holds

> A more careful analysis gives the bound $\prod_{j=1}^{m} \frac{(2^{k-1}-1)}{\sqrt{n_j}}$.

Figure 5.2 $X_{k,j}$ and $X'_{k,j}$
intersect the rest of the sets in
unique points with high
probability.

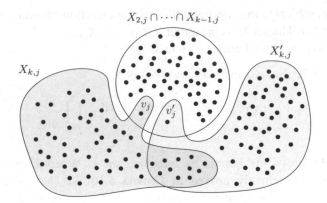

- $v_j = v'_j$, or
- $|X_{k,j} - X'_{k,j}| < n_j/32$, or
- $|X'_{k,j} - X_{k,j}| < n_j/32$.

We shall prove below that

$$\mathbb{E}\,[E_j] = \Pr[E_j = 1] \le \frac{1}{2} \cdot \frac{8^{2k}}{n_j}. \qquad (5.2)$$

When $E_j = 0$, we can use induction to bound the contribution of the jth part of the universe to the discrepancy by $\frac{8^{k-1}}{\sqrt{n_j/32}} \cdot \frac{8^{k-1}}{\sqrt{n_j/32}}$. This is because in the jth part of the universe, the only elements that could still contain an intersection are the elements belonging to two disjoint sets: $X_{k,j} - X'_{k,j}$ and $X'_{k,j} - X_{k,j}$. Each of these sets is of size at least $n_j/32$, and the distribution is independent on these sets. Let Z_j be the random variable defined as

$$Z_j = E_j + \frac{8^{k-1}}{\sqrt{n_j/32}} \cdot \frac{8^{k-1}}{\sqrt{n_j/32}}$$

$$= E_j + \frac{1}{2} \cdot \frac{8^{2k}}{n_j}.$$

Then, (5.2) and the inductive hypothesis give

because the Z_js are
independent of each other.

$$(5.1) \le \mathbb{E}\left[\prod_{j=1}^{m} Z_j\right] \le \prod_{j=1}^{m} \mathbb{E}\,[Z_j] \le \prod_{j=1}^{m} \left(\frac{1}{2} + \frac{1}{2}\right) \cdot \frac{8^{2k}}{n_j} \le \prod_{j=1}^{m} \frac{8^{2k}}{n_j}.$$

It only remains to prove (5.2). Without loss of generality, we can assume that $n_j \ge 8^{2k}/2$, or the bound is trivial. Because v_j and v'_j are uniformly random elements of $X_{2,j} \cap \cdots \cap X_{k-1,j}$, the probability that they are equal is $\frac{1}{|X_{2,j} \cap \cdots \cap X_{k-1,j}|}$. We shall argue that $|X_{2,j} \cap \cdots \cap X_{k-1,j}|$ is typically of size at least $n_j/2^{k+1}$. Indeed, once we fix v_j, every other element of the universe is included in $X_{2,j} \cap \cdots \cap X_{k-1,j}$ with probability at least $\frac{1}{2^{k-1}-1}$. Thus, the expected size of the intersection (not counting v_j) is at least

$$\frac{n_j - 1}{2^{k-1} - 1} \geq \frac{n_j}{2^k}$$

because $n_j \geq 2^k$. By the Chernoff-Hoeffding bound, the probability that the size of the intersection is less than $n_j / (2 \cdot 2^k)$ is at most

$$\exp\left(-\frac{n_j}{4 \cdot 3 \cdot 2^k}\right) = \exp\left(-\frac{n_j}{3 \cdot 2^{k+2}}\right).$$

So, we get that the probability that $v_j \neq v'_j$ is at most

$$\exp\left(-\frac{n_j}{3 \cdot 2^{k+2}}\right) + \frac{2^{k+1}}{n_j} \leq \frac{3 \cdot 2^{k+2}}{n_j} + \frac{2^{k+2}}{n_j} = \frac{2^{k+4}}{n_j}.$$

Next, let us bound the probability that $|X_{k,j} - X'_{k,j}| < n_j / 32$. Observe that once v_j is fixed, every other element in the universe is included in $X_{k,j}$ with probability exactly $\frac{2^{k-2}-1}{2^{k-1}-1}$. Once the element is included in $X_{k,j}$, it must be missing from $X_{2,j} \cap \cdots \cap X_{k-1,j}$, and so it is included in $X'_{k,j}$ with probability exactly $1/2$. Thus, the probability that the element contributes to $X_{k,j} - X'_{k,j}$ is exactly $\frac{1}{2} \cdot \frac{2^{k-2}-1}{2^{k-1}-1}$, and the expected number of elements in $X_{k,j} - X'_{k,j}$, not counting v_j, is at least

$$(n_j - 1) \cdot \frac{2^{k-2} - 1}{2(2^{k-1} - 1)} \geq \frac{n_j}{16}.$$

By the Chernoff-Hoeffding bound, the probability that $|X_{k,j} - X'_{k,j}|$ is of size less than $n_j / 32$ is at most $\exp(-n_j / 384)$. By symmetry, the same bound applies to the probability that $|X'_{k,j} - X_{k,j}| < n / 32$.

Putting it all together, we have shown:

$$\Pr[E_j = 1] \leq 2 \exp\left(-\frac{n_j}{384}\right) + \frac{2^{k+4}}{n_j}$$

$$\leq \frac{768}{n_j} + \frac{2^{k+4}}{n_j}$$

$$\leq \left(\frac{768}{8^6} + \frac{1}{2^{5k-4}}\right) \cdot \frac{8^{2k}}{n_j} \leq \frac{1}{2} \cdot \frac{8^{2k}}{n_j}.$$

□

The discrepancy estimate implies a lower bound on the deterministic communication complexity of disjointness in the number-on-forehead model.

There are exactly 2^{k-1} possible ways in which an element that is not v_j can belong to $X_{2,j}, \ldots, X_{k-1,j}$, and one of these ways – where the element belongs to all the sets – is forbidden.

using $\exp(-x) \leq 1/(1 + x) \leq 1/x$ for $x > 0$.

There are $2^{k-1} - 1$ possibly configurations for each element, and $2^{k-2} - 1$ of them involve the element belonging to $X_{k,j}$.

again using $\exp(-x) \leq 1/x$ for $x > 0$.

because $k \geq 3$.

In fact, it proves a lower bound on the number of monochromatic cylinder intersections needed to cover the 1s of disjointness.

Theorem 5.12 *Any deterministic protocol for computing disjointness in the number-on-forehead model with k parties over a universe of size n requires $\frac{n}{16 \cdot 8^{2k}}$ bits of communication.*

Proof Suppose a deterministic protocol for disjointness has length c. There are at most 2^c monochromatic cylinder intersections $S_1, \ldots, S_T$ that cover all the 1s. Whenever $X_1, \ldots, X_k$ are disjoint, we have that $\sum_{j=1}^{m} \text{Disj}(X_{1,j}, X_{2,j}, \ldots, X_{k,j}) = m$. On the other hand, the probability that $X_1, \ldots, X_k$ are disjoint is exactly 2^{-m}. Thus, we get

$$2^{-m} \leq \mathbb{E} \left[\sum_{t=1}^{T} \chi_{S_t}(X) \cdot (-1)^{\sum_{j=1}^{m} \text{Disj}(X_{1,i}, \ldots, X_{k,j})} \right]$$

$$\leq \sum_{t=1}^{T} \left| \mathbb{E} \left[\chi_{S_t}(X) \cdot (-1)^{\sum_{j=1}^{m} \text{Disj}(X_{1,i}, \ldots, X_{k,j})} \right] \right|$$

$$\leq 2^c \cdot \left(\prod_{j=1}^{m} \frac{8^k}{\sqrt{n_j}} \right).$$

Setting $n_j = 16 \cdot 8^{2k}$ for all j, we get that

$$c \geq m = \frac{n}{16 \cdot 8^{2k}}.$$

$\square$

The best-known lower bound on the randomized communication complexity is not linear:[3]

[3] Sherstov, 2014; and Rao and Yehudayoff, 2015.

Proving sharp bounds on the randomized communication complexity of disjointness in the number-on-forehead model is an important open problem.

Theorem 5.13 *Any randomized protocol for computing disjointness in the worst case with error $1/3$ in the number-on-forehead model with k parties over a universe of size n requires $\Omega\left(\frac{\sqrt{n}}{k2^k}\right)$ bits of communication.*

Theorem 5.13 is proved using discrepancy estimates as above, combined with ideas from approximation theory. We do not include the proof here.

Concentration of Measure

THERE ARE SEVERAL TECHNIQUES for controlling discrepancy. Here we explore two techniques from probability theory: the Chernoff-Hoeffding bound and Talagrand's inequality.

Disjointness

We start by proving a lower bound on the randomized communication complexity of two-party protocols computing the disjointness function. We have already discussed a major obstacle for this approach – disjoint-

ness has large discrepancy. Nevertheless, discrepancy can still be used
to prove the following lower bound:[4]

[4] Babai et al., 1986.

Theorem 5.14 *Any randomized two-party protocol computing disjointness with error* $1/3$ *must have communication* $\Omega(\sqrt{n})$.

To prove this theorem, we define a *hard* distribution on inputs. For a
parameter γ, we independently sample sets $X, Y \subseteq [n]$ by including each
element in each set independently with probability γ. We set $\gamma \approx 1/\sqrt{n}$
so that the probability that the sets are disjoint is exactly

$$(1 - \gamma^2)^n = \frac{1}{2}.$$

The heart of the proof is the following upper bound on discrepancy over
rectangles with many disjoint pairs of inputs.

Lemma 5.15 *There are constants* $\alpha, \beta > 0$ *such that for any rectangle
R with*

$$\Pr[(X, Y) \in R] \geq e^{-\alpha \sqrt{n}},$$

we have

$$\Pr[X, Y \text{ are disjoint} | (X, Y) \in R] < 1 - \beta.$$

The lemma implies the theorem:

Proof of Theorem 5.14 We actually prove a stronger, average case
lower bound for the distribution on inputs described above. Let α, β
be as in Lemma 5.15. Without loss of generality, we can assume that
$\beta < 1/8$ because if the Lemma is true with a large value of β then it
is true with a smaller value as well. Suppose that there is a protocol of
length c for disjointness with error at most $\beta^2/4$ over the distribution
defined above.

Because the probability that X, Y are disjoint is $\frac{1}{2}$, the protocol must
output that the sets are disjoint with probability at least $\frac{1}{2} - \beta^2/4 > \beta$
because $\beta < 1/8$. Theorem 3.6 implies that there is a rectangle of
density $(\beta/2) \cdot 2^{-c}$ that consists almost entirely of disjoint inputs – the
probability that the inputs intersect is at most $\beta/2$. By Lemma 5.15, any
such rectangle must have density at most $e^{-\alpha \sqrt{n}}$. So, $c \geq \Omega(n)$. $\qquad \square$

To prove Lemma 5.15, we use the Chernoff-Hoeffding bound to find a
useful subset of the rectangle. The Chernoff-Hoeffding bound controls
the deviation of a sum of independent identically distributed Boolean
random variables from its expectation. In the proof, the bound is used
in two different ways. Suppose $R = A \times B$. In the first step, the bound
shows that most choices $x_1, \ldots, x_k \in A$ are *far away from each other*.

Later on we shall prove a
sharp $\Omega(n)$ lower bound on
the randomized
communication complexity of
disjointness. We present this
proof here for two reasons.
First, it applies to a product
distribution on the inputs and
is tight for this case. Second, it
sets the stage for the lower
bound on the Gap-Hamming
problem that is explained in
the next section.

For $\gamma \leq 1/2$,

$$2^{-2\gamma^2 n} \leq (1 - \gamma^2)^n \leq e^{-\gamma^2 n}.$$

So, we have the estimates:

$$\frac{1}{\sqrt{2n}} \leq \gamma \leq \frac{\ln 2}{\sqrt{n}}.$$

Can you think of a rectangle
that shows that the lemma is
tight?

In the second step, the bound shows that it is unlikely for $y \in B$ to be disjoint from all of the sets $x_1, \ldots, x_k$.

Proof of Lemma 5.15 We shall set α, β to be small enough constants during the proof. Let $R = A \times B$ be any rectangle of density at least $e^{-\alpha \sqrt{n}}$ violating the statement of the lemma. So, we must have $\beta \geq \Pr[X, Y \text{ are intersecting} | (X, Y) \in R]$. Define

$$A' = \{x \in A : \Pr_Y[x, Y \text{ are intersecting} | Y \in B] \leq 2\beta\}.$$

See Figure 5.3 for an illustration. By Markov's inequality,

$$\Pr[X \in A'] \geq \Pr[X \in A' | (X, Y) \in R] \cdot \Pr[(X, Y) \in R]$$

$$\geq \frac{1}{2} \cdot \Pr[(X, Y) \in R] \geq \frac{e^{-\alpha \sqrt{n}}}{2}.$$

Claim 5.16 *Let $k = \lceil \frac{1}{9\gamma} \rceil$. If α is small enough, there are sets*

$$X_1, X_2, \ldots, X_k \in A'$$

such that for all $i = 1, 2, \ldots, k$,

$$\frac{1}{2} \cdot \gamma n \leq |X_i| \leq \frac{3}{2} \cdot \gamma n,$$

and

$$\left| X_i - \bigcup_{j=1}^{i-1} X_j \right| \geq \frac{\gamma n}{4}.$$

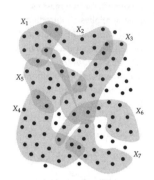

Figure 5.3 The set A' contains many sets that do not intersect each other too much.

Proof We find the sequence of sets $X_1, \ldots, X_k$ inductively. Assume we have already picked $X_1, \ldots, X_{i-1}$. Pick the next set X_i according to the distribution where each element is included in X_i independently with probability γ. Note that this distribution docs not depend on A'. The expected size of X_i is γn. By the Chernoff-Hoeffding bound,

$$\Pr[||X_i| - \gamma n| > \gamma n/2] \leq 2e^{-(1/2)^2 \gamma n/3}.$$

The size of the union $\bigcup_{j=1}^{i-1} X_j$ is at most $\frac{1}{9\gamma} \cdot \frac{3\gamma n}{2} = \frac{n}{6}$. So the expected number of elements in X_i that are not in $\bigcup_{j=1}^{i-1} X_j$ is at least $5\gamma n/6$. So,

$$\Pr\left[\left| X_i - \bigcup_{j=1}^{i-1} X_j \right| < \gamma n/4\right] \leq e^{-(\frac{5/6 - 1/4}{5/6})^2 5\gamma n/18}.$$

Set $\alpha > 0$ to be small enough so that

$$\Pr[X \in A'] \geq \frac{e^{-\alpha \sqrt{n}}}{2} > 2e^{-(1/2)^2 \gamma n/3} + e^{-(\frac{5/6 - 1/4}{5/6})^2 5\gamma n/18}.$$

This ensures that there is some $X_i \in A$ with the claimed properties.   □

Let $X_1, \ldots, X_k$ be as promised by Claim 5.16. For each i, define

$$Z_i = X_i - \bigcup_{j=1}^{i-1} X_j.$$

The sets $Z_1, \ldots, Z_k$ are disjoint, and each is of size at least $\gamma n/4$.

Now, assume toward a contradiction that $\beta < (1 - e^{-1/8})/8$. Define

$$B' = \{y \in B : y \text{ intersects at most } 4\beta k \text{ of the sets } Z_1, \ldots, Z_k\}$$

$$\supseteq \{y \in B : y \text{ intersects at most } 4\beta k \text{ of the sets } X_1, \ldots, X_k\}.$$

We claim that

$$\Pr[Y \in B'] \leq e^{-(1/2)^2 k(1-e^{-1/8})/3} < e^{-\alpha\sqrt{n}}/2,$$

if we choose α to be a small enough constant. See Figure 5.4 for an illustration.

Indeed, if we pick Y at random by including each element in Y with probability γ, then the probability that Y is disjoint from a specific Z_i is at most

$$(1 - \gamma)^{\gamma n/4} \leq e^{-\gamma^2 n/4} \leq e^{-1/8}.$$

So, the expected number of the sets $Z_1, \ldots, Z_k$ that Y intersects is at least $k(1 - e^{-1/8})$. Applying the Chernoff-Hoeffding bound gives

$$\Pr[Y \in B'] \leq e^{-(1/2)^2 k(1-e^{-1/8})/3} < e^{-\alpha\sqrt{n}}/2,$$

if we choose α to be a small enough constant.

On the other hand, by the definition of A', a random element $Y \subset B$ intersects less than $2\beta k$ of the sets $X_1, \ldots, X_k$ in expectation, and so less than $2\beta k$ of the sets $Z_1, \ldots, Z_k$. By Markov's inequality, the probability that Y intersects more than $4\beta k$ of the sets is at most $1/2$. We finally get a contradiction:

$$\Pr[Y \in B'] = \Pr[Y \in B' | Y \in B] \cdot \Pr[Y \in B]$$

$$\geq \frac{1}{2} \cdot \Pr[(X, Y) \in R] \geq e^{-\alpha\sqrt{n}}/2.$$

$\square$

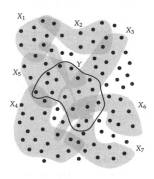

Figure 5.4 There will be a set in B that intersects many of the sets $X_1, \ldots, X_k$.

The Gap-Hamming Problem

The lower bound on the randomized communication complexity of disjointness we just proved is not tight. Nevertheless, a similar approach gives sharp bounds for the Gap-Hamming problem.

The Hamming distance between x and y is $\Delta(x, y) = |\{i \in [n] : x_i \neq y_i\}|$.

This is a *promise* problem. The parties are promised that their inputs satisfy some property. No correctness guarantees are required when the inputs do not satisfy the promise. In other words, the parties are trying to compute a function that is only partially defined on its inputs. It does not matter what they compute on inputs where the function is not defined.

The fooling set method can be used to show that the deterministic communication complexity of approximating the Hamming distance is $\Omega(n)$. See Exercise 1.7.

[5] Chakrabarti and Regev, 2012; Sherstov, 2012; Vidick, 2012; and Rao and Yehudayoff, 2019.

One can show that in this rectangle, the coordinates that are not fixed are very likely to have Hamming distance h with $|h - n/2| \leq 4\sqrt{n}$, so the overall Hamming distance is very likely to be at least $n/2 + \sqrt{n}$.

[6] Sherstov, 2012.

In the Gap-Hamming problem, Alice and Bob get inputs $x, y \in \{\pm 1\}^n$. They are promised that the Hamming distance between x and y satisfies either

- $\Delta(x, y) \geq \frac{n}{2} + \sqrt{n}$, or
- $\Delta(x, y) \leq \frac{n}{2} - \sqrt{n}$.

Their goal is to determine which case holds for x, y.

In Chapter 3, we showed that there is a randomized protocol that can estimate the Hamming distance up to an additive factor of $\sqrt{n}/\epsilon$, with communication $O(\epsilon^2 n)$. Here we prove[5] that this protocol is essentially the best we can hope for, even when the inputs are promised to exhibit this gap.

Theorem 5.17 *Any randomized protocol that solves the Gap-Hamming problem must have communication complexity* $\Omega(n)$.

The Gap-Hamming problem does have large nearly monochromatic rectangles under the uniform distribution. For example, one can show that the rectangle

$$\{x : x_1 = x_2 = \cdots = x_{5\sqrt{n}} = 1\} \times \{y : y_1 = y_2 = \cdots = y_{5\sqrt{n}} = -1\}$$

is nearly monochromatic and has density $2^{-O(\sqrt{n})}$. Therefore, discrepancy cannot be directly used to prove a linear lower bound on the communication complexity of Gap-Hamming under the uniform distribution.

The first step in the proof of the lower bound is to replace the Gap-Hamming problem with the Gap-Orthogonality problem.[6] In the Gap-Orthogonality problem, the parties are promised that $|\langle x, y \rangle|$ is either less than $\sqrt{n}$ or at least $2\sqrt{n}$. Their goal is to determine which of these is the case.

The two problems are closely related because we have

$$\Delta(x, y) = (n - \langle x, y \rangle)/2,$$

and so

$$|\Delta(x, y) - n/2| = |\langle x, y \rangle|.$$

This relationship allows us to use any protocol solving the Gap-Hamming problem to solve Gap-Orthogonality as well. Run the protocol for Gap-Hamming twice on the inputs $(x^a(1)^b, y^a(1)^b)$ and $(x^a(1)^b, y^a(-1)^b)$ for suitably chosen constants a, b. Here $x^a(1)^b$ is a vector of length $na + b$ obtained by concatenating x with itself a times followed by the all 1s string of length b. If a, b are chosen carefully, the outcomes on these two inputs determine the outcome for Gap-Orthogonality. For the rest of this section we study the Gap-Orthogonality problem.

Let $X, Y \in \{\pm 1\}^n$ be independent and uniformly random. As in the lower bound for disjointness, the key step in the argument is to prove that there are no large rectangles where the magnitude of the inner-product is small.

Lemma 5.18 *There are constants $\alpha, \beta > 0$ and an integer t such that if R is a rectangle with*

$$\Pr[(X, Y) \in R] > 2^{-\alpha n},$$

then

$$\Pr\left[|\langle X, Y \rangle| \le \sqrt{n}/t \,|\, (X, Y) \in R\right] \le 1 - \beta.$$

The proof strategy of Lemma 5.18 is similar to that of Lemma 5.15 from the lower bound for disjointness. Instead of the Chernoff-Hoeffding bound, the main tool used in this proof is a beautiful result from convex geometry called *Talagrand's inequality*. The proof also relies on the *singular value decomposition* of matrices. Before proving the lemma, let us see how to use it to prove the lower bound.

Proof of Theorem 5.17 We prove a stronger, average case lower bound. Let α, β, t be as given in Lemma 5.18. Choose $X, Y \in \{\pm 1\}^n$ independently and uniformly at random. Let $X' = X^{2t}$ and $Y' = Y^{2t}$ – namely, X', Y' are obtained from X, Y by repeating each coordinate $2t$ times. Let $\epsilon > 0$ be a small enough constant to be determined. Assume that there is a protocol of length c that solves Gap-Orthogonality for inputs in $\{\pm 1\}^{2tn}$ with error ϵ over (X', Y'). We may assume that the protocol is deterministic.

There is a significant probability that $|\langle X, Y \rangle| \le \sqrt{n}/2t$. To see this, let $Z_1, \dots, Z_n$ be bits defined by

$$Z_i = \begin{cases} 1 & \text{if } X_i \ne Y_i, \\ 0 & \text{otherwise.} \end{cases}$$

Then $Z = \sum_{i=1}^n Z_i = \frac{n - \langle X, Y \rangle}{2}$. The expected value of Z is $n/2$. So, by the Chernoff-Hoeffding bound,

$$\Pr[|\langle X, Y \rangle| > \sqrt{n}/2t] = \Pr\left[\left|Z - \frac{n}{2}\right| > \sqrt{n}/4t\right] \le 1 - p,$$

for some p that depends only on t. Because $\langle X', Y' \rangle = 2t \cdot \langle X, Y \rangle$,

$$\Pr[|\langle X', Y' \rangle| \le \sqrt{n}] \ge p.$$

This means that the protocol must conclude that $|\langle X', Y' \rangle| \le \sqrt{n}$ with probability at least $p - \epsilon$. Choose ϵ so that $p - \epsilon > 2\sqrt{\epsilon}$. By Theorem 3.6, there is a rectangle R so that

$$\Pr[(X, Y) \in R] \ge \sqrt{\epsilon} \cdot 2^{-c}$$

Because $|\langle x, y \rangle| \ge 2\sqrt{n} \Rightarrow |\Delta(x^a, y^a) - na/2| \ge 2a\sqrt{n}$, and $|\langle x, y \rangle| \le \sqrt{n} \Rightarrow |\Delta(x^a, y^a) - na/2| \le a\sqrt{n}$, the idea is to choose a, b so that the outcome of Gap-Hamming is the same on both pairs of inputs in the first case and different on both pairs of inputs in the second case. Set $b = 3a\sqrt{n}$, and set a to be a large enough constant so that

$$\sqrt{na + b} = \sqrt{na + 3a\sqrt{n}}$$
$$\le a\sqrt{n}/2.$$

When $|\Delta(x^a, y^a) - na/2| \ge 2a\sqrt{n}$, the outcome of Gap-Hamming must be the same on both pairs of inputs because $2a\sqrt{n} - b/2 = a\sqrt{n}/2$. When $|\Delta(x^a, y^a) - na/2| \le a\sqrt{n}$, the outcome of Gap-Hamming will be different on both pairs of inputs because $b/2 - a\sqrt{n} \ge a\sqrt{n}/2$.

The lemma shows that inner-product is *anti-concentrated* when the inputs come from a large enough rectangle. Namely, the value of the inner-product is not concentrated in any interval of length $\approx \sqrt{n}$.

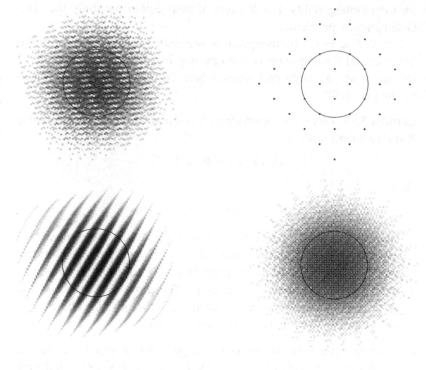

and

$$\Pr[|\langle X, Y \rangle| > \sqrt{n}/t|(X,Y) \in R] \le \sqrt{\epsilon}.$$

For $\epsilon < \beta^2$, Lemma 5.18 implies that $c \ge \alpha n$. $\qquad\qquad\square$

It only remains to prove Lemma 5.18. We start with a preliminary description of two ingredients in the proof: Talagrand's inequality and the singular value decomposition (SVD) of matrices.

Talagrand's Inequality Talagrand's inequality allows us to control the length of the projection of a uniformly random vector $X \in \{\pm 1\}^n$ to a given vector space V. Let $\text{proj}_V(x)$ denote the projection of a vector $x \in \mathbb{R}^n$ to a d-dimensional vector space $V \subseteq \mathbb{R}^n$. It is the vector in V that is closest to x. It is also the unique vector in V such that that two vectors $\text{proj}_V(x)$ and $x - \text{proj}_V(x)$ are orthogonal. Figure 5.5, shows various ways of projecting the cube $\{\pm 1\}^{15}$ to different two-dimensional subspaces.

The expected value of $\|\text{proj}_V(X)\|^2$ is d: if $e_1, e_2, \ldots, e_d$ is an orthonormal basis for V, then

$$\mathbb{E}\left[\|\text{proj}_V(x)\|^2\right] = \mathbb{E}\left[\sum_{i=1}^{d} \langle x, e_i \rangle^2\right] = \sum_{i=1}^{d} \mathbb{E}\left[\langle x, e_i \rangle^2\right],$$

and for each e_i,

$$
\begin{aligned}
\mathbb{E}\left[\langle x, e_i \rangle^2\right] &= \mathbb{E}\left[\left(\sum_{j=1}^{n} e_{i,j} x_j\right)^2\right] \\
&= \sum_j \mathbb{E}\left[(e_{i,j} x_j)^2\right] + \sum_{j \neq j'} \mathbb{E}\left[(e_{i,j} x_j)(e_{i,j'} x_{j'})\right] \\
&= \sum_{j=1}^{n} \mathbb{E}\left[e_{i,j}^2\right] = \|e_i\|^2 = 1.
\end{aligned}
$$

the expected value of $X_j X_{j'}$ is 0 for $j \neq j'$.

This might lead us to guess that length of the projection should typically be about $\sqrt{d}$. Talagrand's inequality shows that this intuition is correct.

Theorem 5.19 *There is a constant $\gamma > 0$ such that for any d-dimensional vector space $V \subseteq \mathbb{R}^n$,*

$$
\Pr\left[\left|\|\mathrm{proj}_V(X)\| - \sqrt{d}\right| \geq s\right] < 4e^{-\gamma s^2},
$$

where X is uniformly distributed in $\{\pm 1\}^n$.

To prove Lemma 5.18, we apply Talagrand's inequality in two different ways. This is analogous to how the Chernoff-Hoeffding bound was used in the proof of Lemma 5.15. Suppose $R = A \times B$. In the first step, we use Talagrand's inequality to find vectors $k = \Omega(n)$ vectors $x_1, \ldots, x_k \in A$ that are essentially orthogonal to each other. We choose $x_1, \ldots, x_k$ iteratively. A uniformly random vector $x_i \in \{\pm 1\}^n$ has a small projection onto the span of the previous vectors $x_1, \ldots, x_{i-1}$, except with exponentially small probability. Because A is not so small, we will always be able to find an x_i that works.

In the second step, we use the inequality with B. Let us assume for now that $x_1, \ldots, x_k$ are perfectly orthogonal. Consider the experiment of picking a uniformly random $Y \in \{\pm 1\}^n$. The inequality promises that the projection of Y to the space spanned by $x_1, \ldots, x_k$ must be of length at least $\Omega(\sqrt{k}) = \Omega(\sqrt{n})$ with significant probability. So $|\langle Y, x_i \rangle| > \Omega(\sqrt{n})$ for most is, except with exponentially small probability. Because B is not so small, the probability that Y is in B and still has the above properties is significant.

Of course, $x_1, \ldots, x_k$ need not be perfectly orthogonal, so to turn these intuitions into a proof, we need one more idea.

Singular Value Decomposition (SVD) Let M be an arbitrary $m \times n$ matrix with real valued entries and $m \leq n$. One can always express M as

If $m > n$, one can apply the decomposition to the transpose of M to get a similar statement.

$$
M = \sum_{i=1}^{m} \sigma_i \cdot u_i v_i^{\mathsf{T}},
$$

where $u_1, \ldots, u_m$ are orthogonal $m \times 1$ column vectors with $\|u_i\| = 1$, $v_1, \ldots, v_m$ are orthogonal $n \times 1$ column vectors with $\|v_i\| = 1$, and $\sigma_1 \geq \sigma_2 \geq \cdots \geq \sigma_m \geq 0$ are real numbers called the *singular values* of M. This decomposition gives a nice way to interpret the action of M on an $n \times 1$ column vector y:

The vectors $u_1, \ldots, u_m$ are the eigenvalues of the symmetric matrix MM^T, the vectors $v_1, \ldots, v_m$ are the eigenvectors of $M^T M$, and the singular values are square roots of the eigenvalues of both MM^T and $M^T M$.

$$My = \sum_{i=1}^{m} \sigma_i u_i v_i^T y = \sum_{i=1}^{m} \sigma_i \langle v_i, y \rangle \cdot u_i.$$

The singular values thus characterize how much the matrix M can stretch an $n \times 1$ column vector y:

$$\|My\|^2 = y^T M^T M y$$

$$= y^T \left(\sum_{i=1}^{m} \sigma_i \cdot v_i u_i^T \right) \left(\sum_{j=1}^{m} \sigma_j \cdot u_j v_j^T \right) y$$

$$= y^T \left(\sum_{i=1}^{m} \sigma_i^2 \cdot v_i v_i^T \right) y = \sum_{i=1}^{m} \sigma_i^2 \cdot (y^T v_i)^2. \tag{5.3}$$

To find the singular value decomposition, one can compute v_1 by identifying the unit vector that maximizes $\|Mv_1\|$ and repeat this process.

Moreover, this implies that $\|My\| \leq \sigma_1 \cdot \|y\|$. Thus, for a given value of $\|y\|$, the length $\|My\|$ is maximized when y is proportional to v_1.

Proof of Lemma 5.18 Let $R = A \times B$ be the given rectangle. We shall set α, β, t as needed in the proof. We assume toward a contradiction that R has density at least $2^{-\alpha n}$, and yet a uniformly random (X, Y) in R satisfy $|\langle X, Y \rangle| \leq \sqrt{n}/t$ with probability at least $1 - \beta$. In the first step of the proof, we isolate the part of A where anti-concentration fails to hold. Define:

$$A' = \left\{ x \in A : \Pr_{Y \in B}[|\langle x, Y \rangle| > \sqrt{n}/t] \leq 2\beta \right\}.$$

For simplicity of notation, and without loss of generality, we assume that several expressions of the form δn for some δ are integers.

By Markov's inequality, we must have that

$$\Pr[X \in A'] \geq \frac{1}{2} \cdot \Pr[(X, Y) \in R] \geq 2^{-\alpha n - 1}.$$

We use Talagrand's inequality to find a set of nearly orthogonal vectors in A':

In the proof, (X, Y) are sometimes uniform in $\{\pm 1\}^n$ and sometimes uniform in R. The meaning will be clear from context.

Claim 5.20 *If $k = \frac{n}{16}$, there are strings $x_1, x_2, \ldots, x_k \in A'$ such that for all i, if V_i denotes the span of $x_1, \ldots, x_i$, then*

$$\|\mathrm{proj}_{V_i}(x_{i+1})\| \leq \frac{\sqrt{n}}{2}.$$

Proof We find the sequence $x_1, \ldots, x_k \in \{\pm 1\}^n$ inductively. In the ith step, consider the experiment of picking x_i according to the uniform distribution. The dimension of V_{i-1} is at most k, so by Theorem 5.19, the probability that the length of the projection exceeds $\sqrt{n}/2$ is at most $4e^{-\gamma(\sqrt{n}/4)^2}$. We set α to be a small enough constant such that $\Pr[X \in A'] \geq 2^{-\alpha n - 1} > 4e^{-\gamma(\sqrt{n}/4)^2}$ to guarantee that there must be some $x_i \in A'$ satisfying the requirement. $\square$

Let $x_1, \ldots, x_k$ be as in the claim above. The second part of the proof focuses on B. The idea is to use Talagrand's inequality again to show that the inner-product with the x_is is typically large.

For each subset $S \subseteq [k]$ of size $|S| = m$ with $m = k - 4\beta k$, we define the set

$$B_S = \left\{ y \in B : |\langle x_i, y \rangle| \leq \sqrt{n}/t \text{ for all } i \in S \right\}.$$

By definition of A' and Markov's inequality, at least half the ys in B must satisfy the property that the number of $i \in [k]$ for which $|\langle x_i, y \rangle| > \sqrt{n}/t$ is at most $4\beta k$. So, by averaging, there must be a set S for which

$$\Pr[Y \in B_S] \geq \frac{2^{-\alpha n - 1}}{\binom{k}{m}} = \frac{2^{-\alpha n - 1}}{\binom{k}{\beta k}}. \tag{5.4}$$

Without loss of generality, we may assume that $\{1, 2, \ldots, m\}$ is such a set.

Now, we use the singular value decomposition. Define the $m \times n$ matrix M whose rows are $x_1, \ldots, x_m$. Express it as

$$M = \sum_{i=1}^{m} \sigma_i \cdot u_i^{\mathsf{T}} v_i.$$

We claim that the largest singular values of M cannot be too different from each other, by establishing two bounds:

$$\sum_{i=1}^{m} \sigma_i \geq m\sqrt{n}/2, \tag{5.5}$$

and

$$\sum_{i=1}^{m} \sigma_i^2 = mn. \tag{5.6}$$

Let us first see how to use these bounds to complete the proof of the lemma. We claim that there must be at least $m/16$ singular values of magnitude at least $\sqrt{n}/4$. Indeed,

$$\sum_{i > m/16} \sigma_i = \sum_{i=1}^{m} \sigma_i - \sum_{i=1}^{m/16} \sigma_i$$

$$\geq \frac{m\sqrt{n}}{2} - \sqrt{\sum_{i=1}^{m/16} \sigma_i^2} \cdot \sqrt{m/16} \qquad \text{by Cauchy-Schwartz and (5.5).}$$

$$\geq \frac{m\sqrt{n}}{2} - \sqrt{mn} \cdot \sqrt{m}/4 = m\sqrt{n}/4. \qquad \text{by (5.6).}$$

So, $\sigma_{m/16} > \sqrt{n}/4$.

Now, let V denote the span of $v_1, \ldots, v_{m/16}$. Theorem 5.19 implies that if $Y \in \{\pm 1\}^n$ is uniformly random, then

if α, β are small enough.

$$\Pr\left[\left| \|\text{proj}_V(y)\| - \sqrt{m}/4 \right| \geq \sqrt{m}/8 \right] < 4e^{-\gamma m/64} < \frac{2^{-\alpha n - 1}}{\binom{k}{\beta k}}.$$

Thus, by (5.4) there must be $y \in B_S$ with $\|\text{proj}_V(y)\| \geq \sqrt{m}/8$. But, on the other hand, by (5.3) and the definition of B_S,

$$\frac{mn}{t^2} \geq \sum_{i=1}^{m} \langle x_i, y \rangle^2 = \|My\|^2 \geq \sum_{i=1}^{m/16} \sigma_i^2 \cdot (y^{\mathsf{T}} v_i)^2$$

$$\geq \frac{n}{16} \cdot \sum_{i=1}^{m/16} (y^{\mathsf{T}} v_i)^2$$

$$= \frac{n}{16} \cdot \|\text{proj}_V(y)\|^2,$$

These are the vectors obtained in the Gram-Schmidt process.

which is a contradiction if $t \geq 32$.

It only remains to prove (5.5) and (5.6). To prove (5.5), let $z_1, \ldots, z_m$ be the orthogonal vectors obtained by setting $z_1 = x_1$, and for $i > 1$,

The trace of a square matrix is the sum of the entries on its diagonal. It has many useful properties.

$$z_i = x_i - \text{proj}_{V_{i-1}}(x_i).$$

Now, let Z be the matrix with rows $z_1, \ldots, z_m$. On the one hand,

$$\text{trace}(MZ^{\mathsf{T}}) = \sum_{i=1}^{m} \langle x_i, z_i \rangle$$

$$= \sum_{i=1}^{m} \langle x_i, x_i \rangle - \sum_{i=1}^{m} \left\langle x_i, \text{proj}_{V_{i-1}}(x_i) \right\rangle$$

by Cauchy-Schwartz.

$$\geq mn - \sum_{i=1}^{m} \|x_i\| \cdot \|\text{proj}_{V_{i-1}}(x_i)\|$$

$$\geq mn - m \cdot \sqrt{n} \cdot \frac{\sqrt{n}}{2} = mn/2.$$

On the other hand,

$$\text{trace}(MZ^{\mathsf{T}}) = \text{trace}\left(\left(\sum_{i=1}^{m} \sigma_i \cdot u_i v_i^{\mathsf{T}}\right) Z^{\mathsf{T}}\right)$$

$$= \sum_{i=1}^{m} \sigma_i \cdot \text{tr}(u_i v_i^{\mathsf{T}} Z^{\mathsf{T}})$$

by Cauchy-Schwartz.

$$= \sum_{i=1}^{m} \sigma_i \cdot \langle u_i, Zv_i \rangle \leq \sum_{i=1}^{m} \sigma_i \cdot \|Zv_i\|.$$

The rows of Z are orthogonal and of length at most $\sqrt{n}$, so we get:

$$\|Zv_i\|^2 = v_i ZZ^{\mathsf{T}} v_i^{\mathsf{T}} = \sum_{j=1}^{n} v_{i,j}^2 \|z_i\|^2 \leq \sum_{j=1}^{n} v_{i,j}^2 n \leq n.$$

Thus, we have

$$\text{trace}(MZ^\mathsf{T}) \le \sqrt{n} \cdot \sum_{i=1}^{m} \sigma_i,$$

which proves (5.5).

To prove (5.6), on the one hand,

$$\text{trace}(MM^\mathsf{T}) = \sum_{i=1}^{m} x_i^\mathsf{T} x_i = mn.$$

On the other hand, it is the same as the trace

$$\text{trace}\left(\sum_{i=1}^{m} \sigma_i^2 u_i u_i^\mathsf{T}\right) = \sum_{i=1}^{m} \sigma_i^2 \cdot \text{trace}\left(u_i u_i^\mathsf{T}\right) = \sum_{i=1}^{m} \sigma_i^2.$$

$\square$

Exercises

Ex 5.1 – Let D be an arbitrary domain, and μ be a distribution on the points of D such that for every $x \in D$, the probability that x is sampled under μ is at most ϵ. Let $S \subseteq D$ be an arbitrary set. Prove that if $g : D \to \{0, 1\}$ is sampled uniformly at random, the probability that the discrepancy of g with respect to μ and S exceeds $\epsilon \ell \sqrt{|D|}$ is at most $\exp(-\Omega(\ell^2))$.

Ex 5.2 – Let M be a uniformly random $\{0, 1\}^n \times \{0, 1\}^n$ matrix with entries in $\{0, 1\}$, and let R be a rectangle in the entries of M. Prove that for any constant $\delta > 0$, the probability that the discrepancy of M exceeds $2^{-(1/2-\delta)n}$ with respect to the uniform distribution and R is at most $\exp(-\Omega(\delta n))$. Compare this to the discrepancy of the inner-product function.

Ex 5.3 – Here we show how to construct a function $f : \{0, 1\}^{2n} \to \{0, 1\}$ such that Alice and Bob must communicate $\Omega(n)$ bits to compute $f(x)$, *no matter how the bits of x are partitioned between them.*

For a constant d, let $G = (V, E)$ be a graph on $2n$ vertices that is d-*regular* and an *expander* graph. d-regular means that every vertex in the graph has exactly d neighbors. The fact that the graph is an expander means that for every $A \subseteq V$ of size $|A| \le n$, the number of edges of the form $\{\{a, b\} : a \in A, b \notin A\}$ is at least $|A| / 10$. There are explicit constructions of such graphs, even with $d = 3$. Define a version of the inner-product function over G as follows. For an assignment to the vertices $x : V \to \{0, 1\}$ set

$$f(x) = \sum_{\{v,u\} \in E} x_u x_v \mod 2.$$

Prove that if the vertices of the graph are partitioned into sets A, B, each of size n, and Alice knows the values of x in A, and Bob knows the values of x in B, the discrepancy of f with respect to any rectangle R and the uniform distribution is at most $2^{-\Omega(n)}$. *Hint: Use the expansion of the graph and the fact that it is d-regular to show that there is an induced matching in the graph of size $\Omega(n)$ –*

there are subsets $A' \subset A, B' \subset B$ such that every vertex of A' has a unique neighbor in B'. Bound the discrepancy for every fixing of the assignment to x outside A', B'.

Ex 5.4 – Let $S_1, S_2, \ldots, S_n \subseteq [n]$. Show that there is an element $x \in \{\pm 1\}^n$ such that the maximum discrepancy

$$\max_{i \in [n]} \left| \sum_{j \in S_i} x_j \right| \leq O(\sqrt{n} \log n).$$

In the margin:

In fact, there is an x whose discrepancy is at most $6\sqrt{n}$. This is Spencer's result that *six standard deviations suffice.*

Let $n = 2^m$, and let $2n$ sets be defined by the identity $j \in S_{i,a}$ if and only if $\langle i, j \rangle = a \mod 2$, for $i, j \in \{0, 1\}^m$ and $a \in \{0, 1\}$. Then show that for every $x \in \{\pm 1\}^n$,

$$\max_{i \in \{0,1\}^m, a \in \{0,1\}} \left| \sum_{j \in S_{i,a}} x_j \right| \geq \sqrt{n}.$$

Hint: Consider the Hadamard matrix H defined by $H_{i,j} = (-1)^{\langle i,j \rangle}$, and show that $H^\intercal H = n \cdot I$. Use this to compute $x^\intercal H^\intercal H x$ for every x. Conclude that some set must have large discrepancy.

Ex 5.5 – Given a prime number p and an integer a with $0 \leq a \leq p - 1$, the Legendre symbol $\left(\frac{a}{p}\right)$ is defined to be the value $a^{\frac{p-1}{2}} \mod p$. It has the following properties:

- $\left(\frac{a}{p}\right) \in \{-1, 0, 1\}$.
- $\left(\frac{ab}{p}\right) = \left(\frac{a}{p}\right)\left(\frac{b}{p}\right)$.
- $\left(\frac{a}{p}\right)$ is 0 only if $a = 0$. When $a \neq 0 \mod p$, $\left(\frac{a}{p}\right) = 1$ only if there is some z such that $a = z^2 \mod p$.

We also have the Weil bound: If $f(x)$ is any degree d polynomial with coefficients from $\mathbb{F}_p$, such that f is not of the form $c \cdot g(x)^2$ for some polynomial g, then

$$\sum_{x \in \mathbb{F}_p} \left(\frac{f(x)}{p}\right) \leq \sqrt{d-1}/p.$$

[7] Babai et al., 1989.

Use these properties to show[7] that if k parties are given numbers $x_1, \ldots, x_k \in \{0, 1, 2, \ldots, p - 1\}$ in the number-on-forehead model, and wish to compute the Legendre symbol $\left(\frac{\sum_{i=1}^k x_i}{p}\right)$, then they must communicate at least $\Omega(((\log p) - k)/2^k)$ bits.

6

Information

SOME CONVERSATIONS ARE MORE INFORMATIVE than others. A short conversation can be very enlightening, and a long conversation can be completely predictable. What is the best way to quantify how much information is conveyed?

In Shannon's seminal work,[1] he defined the notion of *entropy* as a measure of information content. The definition quantifies the amount of information contained in a single message. This concept leads to a theory that is both elegant and widely useful. It has many applications in communication complexity.

We begin this chapter with some simple examples that help to demonstrate the utility of this theory. Later, we show how these concepts can be used to understand communication complexity.

Entropy

THE AMOUNT OF INFORMATION contained in a message is not always the same as the length of the message. For example:

- Suppose Alice sends Bob an n-bit string that is *always* 0^n, no matter what her input is. This message is long but not informative. Alice and Bob might as well imagine that this first message has already been sent and reduce the length of the communication to 0.

- Suppose Alice sends Bob a uniformly random n-bit string sampled from a set $S \subseteq \{0,1\}^n$ known to Bob. The parties could instead use $\lceil \log |S| \rceil$ bits to index the elements of the set. This potentially reduces the communication from n to $\lceil \log |S| \rceil$.

- Suppose Alice sends Bob the string 0^n with probability $1 - \epsilon$ and a uniformly random n bit string with the probability ϵ. One cannot encode every potential message using fewer than n bits. However, Alice can send the bit 0 to encode the string 0^n and the string $1x$ to encode the n bit string x. The message is still long in the worst case, but its expected length is $1 - \epsilon + \epsilon(n + 1) = 1 + \epsilon n \ll n$.

The Shannon entropy provides a good estimate for the optimal encoding length required for any message. Given a random variable X with probability distribution $p(x)$, the *entropy* of X is defined to be

The term *entropy* was first coined by the physicist Rudolph Clausius in the context of thermodynamics, to measure the amount of disorder in a physical system. In his words, "... I propose to call the magnitude S the entropy of the body, from the Greek word $\tau\rho o\pi\acute{\eta}$, *transformation*. I have intentionally formed the word entropy so as to be as similar as possible to the word energy; for the two magnitudes to be denoted by these words are so nearly allied in their physical meanings, that a certain similarity in design appears to be desirable." The physicists Boltzmann and Gibbs gave formulas involving entropy that look nearly identical to the formula given by Shannon.

[1] Shannon, 1948.

The *entropy* of the message is 0.

The *entropy* of the message is $\log |S|$.

The *entropy* of the message is $\approx \epsilon n$.

93

Figure 6.1 The entropy of a
bit B with distribution p.

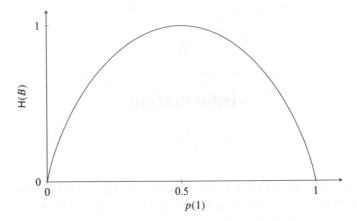

Figure 6.1 The entropy of a bit B with distribution p.

$$H(X) = \sum_x p(x) \cdot \log \frac{1}{p(x)} = \mathop{\mathbb{E}}_{p(x)}\left[\log \frac{1}{p(x)}\right], \qquad (6.1)$$

where by convention $0\log(1/0) = 0$. This definition may seem technical at first sight, but as we shall see, it enjoys some intuitive and useful
properties.

The entropy is always nonnegative because every term in the sum is
nonnegative. The entropy of a single bit is illustrated in Figure 6.1. If X
is uniformly distributed in $[n]$, then its entropy is

$$H(X) = \sum_{x \in [n]} \frac{1}{n} \log n = \log n.$$

The uniform distribution has the largest possible entropy – if $X \in [n]$
then

$$H(X) = \mathop{\mathbb{E}}_{p(x)}\left[\log \frac{1}{p(x)}\right] \le \log \mathop{\mathbb{E}}_{p(x)}\left[\frac{1}{p(x)}\right] = \log n, \qquad (6.2)$$

where the inequality follows by concavity of $\log(\cdot)$. This property of
entropy makes it particularly useful as a tool for counting. It relates
entropy to the size of sets.

Most of the properties of
entropy follow from
convexity.

An Axiomatic Definition

[2] Shannon, 1948.

Shannon's notion of entropy can be axiomatically defined[2] – it is
essentially the only quantity satisfying some natural axioms that one
might expect from a measure of information. Suppose we want to find
a notion of entropy that assigns a real number to each distribution, and
satisfies:

Symmetry $H(\pi(X)) = H(X)$ for all permutations π of the domain of X.
Intuitively, an invertible transformation should not change the amount
of information in X.

Continuity H() should be continuous in the distribution of X. Intuitively, an infinitesimally small change to the distribution of X should result in an infinitesimally small change in the information contained in X.

Monotonicity If X is uniform over a set of size n, then H(X) increases as n increases. This axiom ensures that larger strings have higher entropy.

Chain Rule If $X = (Y, Z)$ then

$$H(X) = H(Y) + \sum_y p(Y = y) \cdot H(Z|Y = y).$$

This axiom asserts that the entropy of a random variable X that consists of Y and Z equals the entropy of Y plus the expected entropy of Z given that we know Y. Intuitively X can be described by describing Y and then describing Z after Y has been determined.

Shannon proved that any notion satisfying these axioms must be proportional to the entropy function defined in (6.1) above. So, up to normalization, there is a unique notion of entropy that satisfies these axioms. Several other axiomatic definitions of the entropy are known. For example, Gromov[3] gives an axiomatic definition that extends to a quantum notion of entropy.

[3] Gromov, 2012.

Coding

Shannon[4] showed that the entropy of X characterizes the expected number of bits needed to encode X. Intuitively, we should encode the value x using roughly $\log(1/p(x))$ bits. Then the expected length of the encoding will be the entropy of X. Shannon showed that such an encoding is possible, and any shorter encoding is impossible.

We want to associate shorter strings with the most likely elements in the support of X. One idea is to associate the elements with the integers $[n]$, so that $p(1) \geq p(2) \geq \cdots \geq p(n)$. Then $1 \geq p(1) + p(2) + \cdots + p(i) \geq ip(i)$, so $1/p(i) \geq i$. If the integer i can be encoded with roughly $\log i$ bits, then the length for encoding i is $\log i \leq \log(1/p(i))$.

Theorem 6.1 *Every random variable X can be encoded using a message whose expected length is at most* H(X) + 1. *Conversely, every encoding of X has an expected length of at least* H(X).

Proof Let X be a random variable taking values in $[n]$. Without loss of generality, assume $p(x) \geq p(x + 1)$ for all $x \in [n]$. For x with $p(x) > 0$, let $\ell_x = \lceil \log(1/p(x)) \rceil$. To prove that X can be encoded using messages of length H(X) + 1, we shall describe a protocol tree. The message length for input x is going to be ℓ_x. The expected length of the message is therefore

[4] Shannon, 1948.

It is possible to encode the integers so that that i has length $\log i + O(\log \log i)$.

Here encoding X means that Alice gets X as input and needs to deterministically send X to Bob using a one-round protocol. Such an encoding is sometimes called a *prefix-free* encoding.

Can you think of an example where the expected length of the encoding needs to be at least H(X) + 0.9?

$$\sum_x p(x) \cdot \ell_x \le \sum_i p(x)(1 + \log(1/p(x))) = \mathsf{H}(X) + 1.$$

The encoding is done greedily. Start with the complete binary tree of depth n. In the first step, pick a vertex v_1 at depth ℓ_1. The vertex v_1 represents the encoding of 1. Delete all of v_1's descendants in the tree, so that v_1 becomes a leaf. Next, find an arbitrary vertex v_2 at depth ℓ_2 that has not been deleted, and use it to encode 2. Delete all of v_2's descendants as well. Continue in this way, until every element of $[n]$ has been encoded. Because $\ell_i \le \ell_j$ for $i \le j$, the above process always gives a valid encoding – the vertex encoding j cannot be a parent of the vertex encoding i.

This process can fail only if for some j there are no available vertices at depth ℓ_j. We show that this never happens. For $i < j$, we have $\ell_i \le \ell_j$, and so the number of vertices at depth ℓ_j that are deleted in the ith step is exactly $2^{\ell_j - \ell_i}$. So, the number of vertices at depth j that are deleted before the jth step is

$$\sum_{i=1}^{j-1} 2^{\ell_j - \ell_i} = 2^{\ell_j}\left(\sum_{i=1}^{j-1} 2^{-\ell_i}\right) \le 2^{\ell_j}\sum_{i=1}^{j-1} p(i) < 2^{\ell_j}.$$

This proves that some vertex is always available at the jth step.

It remains to show that no encoding can have an expected length less than $\mathsf{H}(X)$. Suppose X can be encoded in such a way that x is encoded using ℓ_x bits. The expected length of the encoding is

$$\mathop{\mathbb{E}}_{p(x)}[\ell_x] = \mathop{\mathbb{E}}_{p(x)}[\log(1/p(x))] - \mathop{\mathbb{E}}_{p(x)}\left[\log(2^{-\ell_x}/p(x))\right]$$

$$\ge \mathsf{H}(X) - \log\left(\mathop{\mathbb{E}}_{p(x)}\left[2^{-\ell_x}/p(x)\right]\right)$$

by concavity of the log function.

$$= \mathsf{H}(X) - \log\left(\sum_x 2^{-\ell_x}\right).$$

We claim that $\sum_x 2^{-\ell_x} \le 1$. Imagine sampling a random path by starting from the root of the protocol tree and picking one of the two children uniformly at random until we reach a leaf. This random path hits the leaf encoding x with probability $2^{-\ell_x}$. Thus, the sum $\sum_x 2^{-\ell_x}$ is the probability of hitting a leaf encoding some x. □

Chain Rule and Conditional Entropy

The entropy function has several properties that make it particularly useful. To illustrate some of the properties, we use an example from geometry. Let S be a set of n^3 points in $\mathbb{R}^3$, and let S_x, S_y, and S_z denote the projections of S onto the x, y, and z axes.

Claim 6.2 *One of $S_x, S_y,$ and S_z must have size at least n.*

This claim has an easy proof:

$$n^3 = |S| \leq |S_x| \cdot |S_y| \cdot |S_z|,$$

and so one of the three projections must be of size n. However, to introduce some properties of entropy, we present a second proof.

The property of the entropy function we need is called *subadditivity*. For any random variables A, B, we have:

$$H(AB) \leq H(A) + H(B).$$

This follows from the concavity of the log function:

$$H(A) + H(B) - H(AB)$$

$$= \underset{p(ab)}{\mathbb{E}} \left[\log \frac{1}{p(a)} \right] + \underset{p(ab)}{\mathbb{E}} \left[\log \frac{1}{p(b)} \right] - \underset{p(ab)}{\mathbb{E}} \left[\log \frac{1}{p(ab)} \right]$$

$$= - \underset{p(ab)}{\mathbb{E}} \left[\log \frac{p(a) \cdot p(b)}{p(ab)} \right]$$

$$\geq - \log \underset{p(ab)}{\mathbb{E}} \left[\frac{p(a) \cdot p(b)}{p(ab)} \right] = - \log \sum_{a,b} p(a) \cdot p(b) = - \log 1 = 0.$$

In the margin: In information theory, it is common to write AB to denote the tuple (A, B). This makes many complicated expressions easier to read. So, for example, on the left AB is the concatenation of the random variables A, B rather than their product.

Induction implies that subadditivity holds even when many variables are involved:

$$H(A_1 A_2 \ldots A_k) \leq H(A_1) + H(A_2 \ldots A_k)$$

$$\leq H(A_1) + H(A_2) + H(A_3 \ldots A_k)$$

$$\leq \cdots \leq \sum_{i=1}^{k} H(A_i).$$

Proof of Claim 6.2 Let (X, Y, Z) be a uniformly random element of S. Then

$$3 \log n = \log |S| = H(XYZ) \leq H(X) + H(Y) + H(Z).$$

In the margin: by subadditivity.

So, one of the three terms $H(X), H(Y), H(Z)$ must be at least $\log n$. By (6.2), the projection onto the corresponding coordinate must be supported on at least n points. □

Things become more interesting when we study more complicated projections. Let S_{xy}, S_{yz}, S_{zx} denote the projections of S to the xy, yz, and zx planes. See Figure 6.2 for an illustration. Now, the claim is

Claim 6.3 *One of S_{xy}, S_{yz}, S_{zx} must have size at least n^2.*

To proceed, we use the notion of *conditional entropy*. For two random variables A and B, the entropy of B conditioned on A is the number

In the margin: This claim is a special case of the Loomis-Whitney inequality.

Figure 6.2 A finite set in $\mathbb{R}^3$ projected onto the three planes.

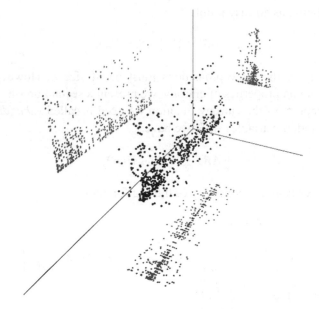

If A is a random variable and E is an event, then the notation $\mathsf{H}(B|A, E)$ denotes the entropy of B conditioned on A, where the distributions of both B and A are conditioned on the event E.

$$\mathsf{H}(B|A) = \mathop{\mathbb{E}}_{p(ab)}\left[\log\frac{1}{p(b|a)}\right] = \mathop{\mathbb{E}}_{p(a)}\left[\mathsf{H}(B|A = a)\right].$$

This is the expected entropy of B, conditioned on the event $A = a$, where the expectation is over a. The chain rule for entropy states that:

$$\mathsf{H}(AB) = \mathsf{H}(A) + \mathsf{H}(B|A).$$

In words, the entropy of (A, B) is the entropy of A plus the entropy of B given that we know A. Its proof follows from Bayes's rule and linearity of expectation:

$$\begin{aligned}
\mathsf{H}(AB) &= \mathop{\mathbb{E}}_{p(ab)}\left[\log\frac{1}{p(ab)}\right] \\
&= \mathop{\mathbb{E}}_{p(ab)}\left[\log\frac{1}{p(a)\cdot p(b|a)}\right] \\
&= \mathop{\mathbb{E}}_{p(ab)}\left[\log\frac{1}{p(a)} + \log\frac{1}{p(b|a)}\right] = \mathsf{H}(A) + \mathsf{H}(B|A).
\end{aligned}$$

The chain rule is an extremely useful property of entropy. It allows us to express the entropy of a collection of random variables in terms of the entropy of individual variables.

Suppose A, B, C are three uniformly random bits conditioned on $A + B + C$ being even. Then $\mathsf{H}(ABC) = 2$, $\mathsf{H}(A) = \mathsf{H}(B) = \mathsf{H}(C) = 1$ and $\mathsf{H}(ABC) = \mathsf{H}(A) + \mathsf{H}(B|A) + \mathsf{H}(C|AB) = 1 + 1 + 0$.

To better understand this notion, consider the following example. Suppose A, B are two uniformly random bits conditioned on being equal. Then $\mathsf{H}(AB) = \mathsf{H}(A) = \mathsf{H}(B) = 1$ and $\mathsf{H}(B|A) = 0$. So,

$$\mathsf{H}(AB) = \mathsf{H}(A) + \mathsf{H}(B|A) < \mathsf{H}(A) + \mathsf{H}(B).$$

Conditional entropy satisfies another intuitive property – conditioning can only decrease entropy:

$$H(B|A) \leq H(B). \tag{6.3}$$

The entropy of B when we know A cannot be any larger than the entropy of B when we do not know A. This follows from the chain rule and subadditivity:

$$H(A) + H(B|A) = H(AB) \leq H(A) + H(B).$$

We now have enough tools to prove the geometric claim.

Proof of Claim 6.3 As before, let (X, Y, Z) be a uniformly random element of S. Then $H(XYZ) = \log |S| = 3 \log n$. Repeatedly using the fact that conditioning cannot increase entropy (6.3):

$$
\begin{aligned}
H(X) + H(Y|X) &\leq H(X) &+ H(Y|X) \\
H(X) &+ H(Z|XY) \leq H(X) &+ H(Z|X) \\
H(Y|X) &+ H(Z|XY) \leq &H(Y) + H(Z|Y)
\end{aligned}
$$

Adding these inequalities together and applying the chain rule gives

$$6 \log n = 2 \cdot H(XYZ) \leq H(XY) + H(XZ) + H(YZ).$$

Thus, one of three terms on the right-hand side must be at least $2 \log n$. The projection onto the corresponding plane must be of size at least n^2.

□

Combinatorial Applications

THE ENTROPY FUNCTION has found many applications in combinatorics. Here are a few examples that illustrate its power and versatility.

Paths and Cycles in Graphs How many paths or cycles can a graph with n vertices and m edges have? Here we use entropy to prove lower bounds on these numbers.[5]

Because the sum of the degrees of the vertices is $2m$, the average degree in the graph is $d = 2m/n$. Now if the graph is d-regular, meaning that every vertex has exactly d neighbors, then the number of paths of length two in the graph is exactly $m(d-1)$. This is because each edge can be extended to a path of length two in $2(d-1)$ ways, and this counts every path twice.

We use entropy to prove a lower bound that applies to general graphs:

Claim 6.4 *The number of paths of length* 2 *in the graph is at least* $m\left(\frac{d}{2} - 1\right)$.

Proof Sample a random path X, Y, Z of length 2 as follows. The pair X, Y is a uniformly random edge, and Z is a uniform random neighbor

[5] Szegedy, 2014.

In Lemma 5.3, we proved a lower bound on the number of 4-cycles in the graph.

Claim 6.4 can be strengthened to match the count for d-regular graphs. See Exercise 6.1.

of Y. Conditioned on the value of Y, the vertex Z is independent of the choice of X. Thus, we can use the chain rule to write:

If A, B are independent then
$H(A|B) = H(A)$.

$$H(XYZ) = H(XY) + H(Z|XY) = \log m + H(Z|Y).$$

To bound $H(Z|Y)$, we use convexity. If d_v denotes the degree the vertex v, we have:

$$H(Z|Y) = \sum_v \frac{d_v}{2m} \cdot \log d_v$$

$$= \frac{n}{2m} \cdot \sum_v \frac{1}{n} \cdot d_v \log d_v$$

the function $x \log x$ is convex.

$$\geq \frac{n}{2m} \cdot d \cdot \log d = \log \frac{2m}{n}.$$

Thus,

$$H(XYZ) \geq \log \frac{2m^2}{n},$$

proving that the support of XYZ must contain at least $\frac{2m^2}{n}$ elements.

Some of the elements in the support of XYZ do not correspond to paths of length 2 because we could have $x = z$. However, there are at most $2m$ sequences x, y, z that correspond to such a redundant choice. After correcting for this, we are left with at least

$$\left(\frac{2m^2}{n} - 2m \right) / 2 = m \left(\frac{m}{n} - 1 \right) = m \left(\frac{d}{2} - 1 \right)$$

paths of length 2.   □

Next, we turn to proving a lower bound on the number of cycles of length four.

Claim 6.5 *The number of four-cycles in the graph is at least* $\frac{d^4}{16} - \frac{n^3}{2}$.

Proof Sample X, Y, Z as before, and then independently sample W using the distribution of Y conditioned on the values of X, Z. Then,

because W, Y are independent given XZ.

$$H(XYZW) = H(XYZ) + H(W|XZ)$$

$$= H(XYZ) + H(XWZ) - H(XZ)$$

because XYZ and XWZ are identically distributed and $H(XZ) \leq 2 \log n$.

$$\geq 2 \cdot H(XYZ) - 2 \log n.$$

Combining this with our bound for $H(XYZ)$ from Claim 6.4, we get

$$H(XYZW) \geq \log \frac{4m^4}{n^4}.$$

This does not quite count the number of four-cycles because there could be some settings of $XYZW$ where two of the vertices are the same. We could have $X = Z$ or $Y = W$. However, there are at most $2n^3$ possible elements in the support of $XYZW$ where that can happen. Each cycle can be expressed in at most four different ways as $XYZW$. After accounting for these facts, we are left with at least

There are at most n^3 choices for $XYZW$ with $X = Z$, and at most n^3 with $Y = W$.

$$\left(\frac{4m^4}{n^4} - 2n^3\right) / 4 = \frac{m^4}{n^4} - \frac{n^3}{2}$$

distinct cycles. □

Bounding the Girth The girth of a graph is the length of its smallest cycle. Graphs with large girth are locally like trees – you have to look at a large ball around a vertex to observe a cycle. This property makes these graphs useful in applications. How large can the girth of a graph with a given number of edges be?

We prove that the girth g cannot be too large. This is fairly easy to do when the graph is d-regular. Suppose we have a graph with n vertices and m edges. If every vertex in the graph has the same degree d, then the vertices at distance $\frac{g-1}{2}$ from some fixed vertex must form a rooted tree, or else the graph would have a cycle of length less than g. See Figure 6.3 for an illustration. The number of vertices in this tree is at least $(d-1)^{\frac{g-1}{2}}$ but at most n. So,

Figure 6.3 If the vertices near a fixed vertex do not form a tree, then the graph contains a short cycle.

$$g \le \frac{2 \log n}{\log(d-1)} + 1.$$

Now let us see how to use information theory to prove a similar bound when the graph is not necessarily regular.[6]

[6] Alon et al., 2002; and Babu and Radhakrishnan, 2010.

Claim 6.6 *Let $d = 2m/n$ denote the average degree in a graph with n vertices. Then the girth g of the graph satisfies $g \le \frac{2 \log n}{\log(d-1)} + 1$.*

Can you think of a graph with $d = 2$ that has large girth?

Proof Start by observing that we may assume that $d_v \ge 2$ for each vertex v. Indeed, if the degree of some vertex v is less than 2, then by deleting v and its neighbor from the graph, we obtain a graph with fewer vertices, larger average degree, and yet the same girth.

To give a lower bound on the number of paths, we used a random walk in the graph. To get tight bounds here, we need to use a *non-backtracking random walk*. The walk never returns along an edge that it took in the last step. Let

$$X = (X_0, X_1, \ldots, X_{\frac{g-1}{2}})$$

be a random walk in the graph, sampled as follows. Let X_0, X_1 be a random edge, and for $i > 1$, let X_i be a random neighbor of X_{i-1} that is not the same as X_{i-2}.

Given X_1, we see that X_2 and X_0 are identically distributed. Hence, the first two edges are identically distributed, and similarly every edge of the walk is identically distributed. The chain rule gives

$$H(X|X_0) = \sum_{i=1}^{\frac{g-1}{2}} H(X_i|X_{i-1}).$$

Bound each term as follows:

$$H(X_i|X_{i-1}) = \sum_v \frac{d_v}{2m} \cdot \log(d_v - 1)$$

$$= \frac{1}{d} \cdot \sum_v \frac{1}{n} \cdot d_v \log(d_v - 1)$$

$$\geq \frac{1}{d} \cdot d \log(d - 1) = \log(d - 1).$$

because the function $z\log(z-1)$ is convex for $z \geq 2$.

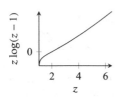

Putting these bounds together, we get:

$$H(X|X_0) \geq \frac{g-1}{2} \cdot \log(d - 1).$$

Because the girth of the graph is g, there can be at most n distinct paths of length $\frac{g-1}{2}$ that begin at X_0. Thus,

$$\log n \geq H(X|X_0) \geq \frac{g-1}{2} \cdot \log(d - 1).$$

□

An Isoperimetric Inequality for the Hypercube Isoperimetric inequalities bound the surface area of a shape given its volume. It is usually interesting to find shapes with the smallest surface area. For example, in three-dimensional Euclidean space, the shape with smallest surface area is a ball. This is the reason soap bubbles tend to be round.

Here we prove a similar fact in a discrete geometric space. The n-dimensional hypercube is the graph whose vertex set is $\{0, 1\}^n$, and whose edge set consists of pairs of vertices that disagree in exactly one coordinate. The hypercube contains 2^n vertices and $\frac{n}{2} \cdot 2^n$ edges.

The volume of a set $S \subseteq \{0, 1\}^n$ of vertices is defined to be $|S|$. The boundary of S is defined to be the set of edges that go from inside S to outside S. We write $\delta(S)$ to denote the size of the boundary of S. An isoperimetric inequality bounds $\delta(S)$ for a given value of $|S|$.

A k-dimensional subcube of the hypercube is a subset of the vertices given by fixing $n - k$ coordinates of the vertices to some fixed value and allowing k of the coordinates to take any value. The volume of such a subcube is exactly 2^k. Each vertex of the subcube has $n - k$ edges that leave the subcube. The boundary of the subcube is of size $(n - k)2^k$.

[7] Harper, 1966; and Samorodnitsky, 2017.

Subcubes minimize boundary size per volume:[7]

Theorem 6.7 *For any subset S of the vertices, $\delta(S) \geq |S|(n - \log|S|)$.*

Proof Let $e(S)$ be the number of edges contained in S. Thus,

$$\delta(S) = n|S| - 2e(S).$$

the degree of each vertex is n.

Instead of minimizing $\delta(S)$ we maximize $e(S)$.

Let X be a uniformly random element of S. For a vertex $x \in \{0,1\}^n$ and $i \in [n]$, denote by $x \oplus e_i \in \{0,1\}^n$ the vertex that disagrees with x only in the ith entry. For every $x \in S$ and $i \in [n]$,

Here X_{-i} denotes
$(X_1, X_2, \ldots, X_{i-1}, X_{i+1}, \ldots, X_n)$.

$$\mathsf{H}(X_i | X_{-i} = x_{-i}) = \begin{cases} 1 & \text{if } \{x, x \oplus e_i\} \subset S, \\ 0 & \text{otherwise.} \end{cases}$$

So,

$$\sum_{i=1}^{n} \mathsf{H}(X_i | X_{-i}) = \sum_{i=1}^{n} \sum_{x \in S} \frac{1}{|S|} \mathsf{H}(X_i | X_{-i})$$

$$= \frac{1}{|S|} \sum_{x \in S} |\{i \in [n] : \{x, x \oplus e_i\} \subset S\}|$$

$$= \frac{2e(S)}{|S|}.$$

Because conditioning does not increase entropy,

$$\log |S| = \mathsf{H}(X) = \sum_{i=1}^{n} \mathsf{H}(X_i | X_{<i}) \geq \sum_{i=1}^{n} \mathsf{H}(X_i | X_{-i}) = \frac{2e(S)}{|S|}.$$

Finally,

$$\delta(S) = n|S| - 2e(S) \geq |S|(n - \log |S|).$$

□

Shearer's Inequality

Shearer's inequality is a generalization of the subadditivity of entropy. Suppose $X = X_1, \ldots, X_k$ is a collection of k jointly distributed random variables, and $S \subseteq [k]$ is a set of coordinates sampled independent of X. Denote by X_S the collection of variables that corresponds to S. One way to interpret subadditivity is that when S is uniformly random subset of size 1,

$$\mathsf{H}(X_S | S) \geq \tfrac{1}{n} \mathsf{H}(X).$$

Shearer's inequality allows to handle general sets S:

Lemma 6.8 *If $p(i \in S) \geq \epsilon$ for every $i \in [n]$, then $\mathsf{H}(X_S | S) \geq \epsilon \cdot \mathsf{H}(X)$.*

Proof For $i \in [k]$, denote by S_i the set of $j \in S$ so that $j < i$. Thus,

$$\mathsf{H}(X_S | S) = \mathop{\mathbb{E}}_{S} \left[\sum_{i \in S} \mathsf{H}(X_i | X_{S_i}) \right]$$

chain rule.

conditioning does not increase entropy.

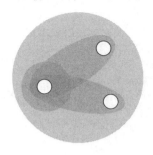

Figure 6.4 Two intersecting families of sets on a universe of size 3.

Can you think of an example of $\mathcal{F}$ satisfying the bound in the claim?

[8] Ellis et al., 2012.

[9] Chung et al., 1986.

Similar ideas can be used to show that any family of graphs that intersects in an r-clique is of size at most $2^{\binom{n}{2}}/2^{r-1}$. See Exercise 6.5.

$$\geq \underset{S}{\mathbb{E}} \left[\sum_{i \in S} \mathsf{H}(X_i | X_{<i}) \right]$$

$$= \sum_{i=1}^{n} p(i \in S) \cdot \mathsf{H}(X_i | X_{<i}) \geq \epsilon \cdot \mathsf{H}(X).$$

$\square$

Shearer's inequality is a useful tool. Here is a simple example from graph theory. We start with an easy question. Suppose $\mathcal{F}$ is a family of subsets of $[n]$ such that any two sets in $\mathcal{F}$ intersect. How large can such a family be? See Figure 6.4 for an illustration.

Claim 6.9 $|\mathcal{F}| \leq 2^{n-1}$.

Proof The complement of any set in $\mathcal{F}$ cannot be in $\mathcal{F}$. So, only half of all the sets can be in $\mathcal{F}$. $\square$

Here is an analogous question for families of graphs. Let $\mathcal{G}$ be a family of graphs on n vertices. The size of $\mathcal{G}$ is at most $2^{\binom{n}{2}}$. We are interested in families $\mathcal{G}$ of graphs such that every two graphs in $\mathcal{G}$ intersect in a *triangle*, namely a cycle of length 3. There is a family of $2^{\binom{n}{2}}/8$ graphs with this property – take all graphs including a fixed triangle. This bound is known to be tight.[8] Shearer's inequality allows us to prove a weaker statement:[9]

Theorem 6.10 $|\mathcal{G}| \leq 2^{\binom{n}{2}}/4$.

Proof Let G be a uniformly random graph from the family $\mathcal{G}$. The graph G can be described by a binary vector of length $\binom{n}{2}$, where each bit indicates whether a particular edge is present or not. Let S be a uniformly random subset of the vertices so that each vertex v is in S with probability $1/2$ independent of all other vertices.

Let G_S denote the graph obtained from G by deleting all edges that go from S to the complement of S. The probability that any particular edge is retained is exactly $1/2$. Shearer's inequality gives

$$\underset{S}{\mathbb{E}} \left[\mathsf{H}(G_S | S) \right] \geq \mathsf{H}(G)/2.$$

The key observation is as follows. Every two graphs g and g' in $\mathcal{G}$ share a triangle. This implies that g_S and g'_S must share an edge, for every S. So, for every S, the number of graphs of the form G_S is at most half of all possible options, by Claim 6.9. The total number of edges possible in the graph G_S is

$$e(S) = \binom{|S|}{2} + \binom{n - |S|}{2}.$$

We see that $H(G_S|S) \leq e(S) - 1$. The expected value $\mathbb{E}\left[e(S)\right]$ is exactly $\binom{n}{2}/2$. Thus, we have

$$\frac{1}{2} \cdot \binom{n}{2} = \mathbb{E}_{S}\left[e(S)\right] \geq H(G_S|S) + 1 \geq \frac{1}{2} \cdot H(G) + 1.$$

So $H(G) \leq \binom{n}{2} - 2$, which implies that $|\mathcal{G}| \leq 2^{\binom{n}{2}}/4$. □

Divergence and Mutual Information

ENTROPY IS A USEFUL CONCEPT when we are working with a single distribution. Mutual information and divergence allow us to compare two distributions. They provide tools that help us understand the flow of information in a variety of situations.

Suppose (X, Y) are random inputs to a communication protocol, sampled from a distribution p_0. Denote by $M = M_1, \ldots, M_T$ the T bits transmitted during the execution of the protocol. Consider the sequence of distributions $p_1, p_2, \ldots, p_T$, where p_t is the distribution of (X, Y) conditioned on the value of $M_1, \ldots, M_t$. If the protocol is carrying out a meaningful computation, we would expect p_T to be far from p_0.

The flow of information in the protocol can be quantified by the evolution of the distance of p_t from p_0, as t grows. Having a good understanding of this flow of information often enables us to prove interesting statements about communication protocols. What notion of distance should we use? At time $t = 0$, the distance ought to be 0, and eventually the distance should be large. The *divergence* gives a natural measure for the distance.

The divergence between two distributions $p(x)$ and $q(x)$ is defined to be

$$D(p(x) \| q(x)) = \sum_x p(x) \log \frac{p(x)}{q(x)} = \mathbb{E}_{p(x)}\left[\log \frac{p(x)}{q(x)}\right].$$

> Formally, p_t is a random variable.

> The divergence is sometimes called Kullback-Leibler divergence or KL-divergence and is often denoted $D(p\|q)$. It is part of a larger family of functions called f-divergences.

Figure 6.5 plots the divergence between two distributions on bits. In line with the intuition that divergence is a measure of distance, we have

Fact 6.11 $D(p(x) \| q(x)) \geq 0$, *and equality holds if and only if p and q are identical.*

> By convention, $0 \log \frac{0}{0} = 0$ and $z \log \frac{z}{0} = \infty$ for $z > 0$.

Proof By convexity of $\log(\cdot)$,

$$D(p(x) \| q(x)) = -\sum_x p(x) \log \frac{q(x)}{p(x)} \geq -\log \sum_x p(x) \frac{q(x)}{p(x)} = \log 1 = 0.$$

Because $\log(\cdot)$ is strictly convex, the inequality is a strict inequality unless $p(x)/q(x)$ is the same for every x. This can happen only when $p(x)$ and $q(x)$ are the same distribution. □

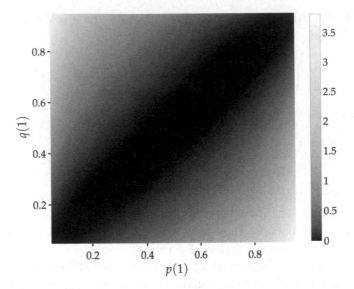

Figure 6.5 The divergence between two distributions on bits p, q.

The divergence is, however, not symmetric – sometimes

$$D(p(x)\|q(x)) \neq D(q(x)\|p(x)).$$

The divergence can also be infinite, for example if p is supported on a point that has 0 probability under q.

As with the entropy, the divergence has a nice interpretation in terms of efficient encodings. Recall that a near optimal encoding for X encodes each x using roughly $\lceil \log(1/p(x)) \rceil$ bits. Such an encoding has an expected length of at most $H(X) + 1$ when X is drawn from p.

Now, the quantity $H_{p,q} = \mathbb{E}_{p(x)} \left[\log(1/q(x)) \right]$ is, up to a $+1$, the expectation with respect to p of the length of the encoding designed for q. The divergence

$$D(p(x)\|q(x)) = \mathop{\mathbb{E}}_{p(x)} \left[\log(1/q(x)) - \log(1/p(x)) \right] = H_{p,q} - H_{p,p}$$

can be thought of as the loss incurred when we encode X using the *wrong* distribution q. We could get an encoding length close to $H_{p,p}$, but we only get $H_{p,q}$.

Entropy corresponds to the divergence from the uniform distribution – if X is an ℓ-bit string, then

$$H(X) = \mathop{\mathbb{E}}_{p(x)} \left[\log(1/p(x)) \right] = \ell - \mathop{\mathbb{E}}_{p(x)} \left[\log \frac{p(x)}{2^{-\ell}} \right] = \ell - D(p(x)\|q(x)),$$

where $q(x)$ is the uniform distribution on ℓ-bit strings.

The divergence allows us to quantify the dependence between two random variables. If $p(a,b)$ is the joint distribution of two random variables A and B, we define the *mutual information* between A and B to be

If divergence is used to measure the flow of information in a communication protocol as per the discussion above, the divergence

$$D(p_t(x,y)\|p_0(x,y))$$

corresponds to the gain that the parties have made in reducing the encoding length of their inputs after t steps of the protocol.

As explained in the conventions chapter, $p(a)$ denotes the marginal distribution of A.

$$I(A : B) = D(p(a,b) \| p(a)p(b)) = \underset{p(a,b)}{\mathbb{E}} \left[\log \frac{p(a,b)}{p(a)p(b)} \right].$$

Roughly speaking, the mutual information between A and B is small if A and B are close to being independent, and it is large when they are far from independent. When $A = B$, we have $I(A : B) = H(B)$. At the other extreme, $I(A : B) = 0$ exactly when A and B are independent.

Here are a few more ways to think about mutual information. By Bayes's rule,

$$I(A : B) = \underset{p(a,b)}{\mathbb{E}} \log \frac{p(b|a)}{p(b)} = \underset{p(a)}{\mathbb{E}} \left[D(p(b|a) \| p(b)) \right] = H(B) - H(B|A).$$

The third expression is the expected divergence between $p(b|a)$ and $p(b)$ – it measures the distance of $p(b|a)$ from $p(b)$, for an average a. The fourth expression says that the information measures the decrease in the entropy of B when conditioning on A. By symmetry, $I(A : B) = H(A) - H(A|B)$ as well.

In general, the mutual information satisfies

$$0 \le I(A : B) = H(A) - H(A|B) \le H(A).$$

The first inequality follows from the fact that divergence is non-negative, and the second from the fact that entropy is nonnegative.

Lower Bound for Indexing

WE HAVE GATHERED ENOUGH tools to begin discussing our first lower bound on communication using information theory. We shall prove a lower bound on the *indexing problem*.

Suppose Alice has a uniformly random n bit string x, and Bob is given an independent uniformly random index $i \in [n]$. The goal of the parties is to compute x_i. But they are only allowed to execute a one-way protocol – the protocol must start with a message from Alice to Bob, after which Bob must output the answer. We prove that $\Omega(n)$ bits of communication are necessary, even in the average-case setting.

If there is a protocol for this problem where Alice sends a message M that is ℓ bits long, then M can only give ℓ bits of information about x. So, we should be able to argue that M carries only ℓ/n bits of information about a typical coordinate x_i. If this is the case and $\ell/n \ll 1$, then M should not be useful to help Bob determine x_i. Let us use information theory to make this a formal proof.

Chain Rules for Divergence and Mutual Information

We have already seen a chain rule for entropy and used it a few times. Divergence and mutual information have similar chain rules that are equally useful. For the indexing problem, the chain rule implies that M can convey only ℓ/n bits of information about X_I.

by Fact 6.11.

The entropy, mutual information, and divergence are all expectations over the universe of various log-ratios.

If Bob could tell Alice i in the first step, that would give a protocol with communication complexity $1 + \lceil \log n \rceil$.

It is easy to prove a deterministic lower bound for this problem. After Alice's message, Bob must know x, so Alice must send n bits.

The chain rule for divergence states that for every two distributions $p(a, b)$ and $q(a, b)$,

$$D(p(a, b) \| q(a, b)) = D(p(a) \| q(a)) + \underset{p(a)}{\mathbb{E}} \left[D(p(b|a) \| q(b|a)) \right].$$

The proof is a straightforward calculation:

$$D(p(a, b) \| q(a, b)) = \underset{p(a,b)}{\mathbb{E}} \left[\log \frac{p(a) \cdot p(b|a)}{q(a) \cdot q(b|a)} \right]$$

$$= \underset{p(a,b)}{\mathbb{E}} \left[\log \frac{p(a)}{q(a)} \right] + \underset{p(a,b)}{\mathbb{E}} \left[\log \frac{p(b|a)}{q(b|a)} \right].$$

In words, the total divergence is the sum of the divergence from the first variable, plus the expected divergence from the second variable.

Before we state the chain rule for information, it is worthwhile to think about a simple example. Suppose $A, B,$ and C are three random bits that are all equal to each other. Then $I(AB : C) = 1 < 2 = I(A : C) + I(B : C)$. On the other hand, if $A, B,$ and C are three random bits satisfying $A + B + C = 0 \mod 2$, we have $I(AB : C) = 1 > 0 = I(A : C) + I(B : C)$.

To state the chain rule, we need the right definitions. For three random variables $A, B,$ and C, define

$$I(B : C|A) = \underset{p(a)}{\mathbb{E}} \left[D(p(b, c|a) \| p(b|a) \cdot p(c|a)) \right].$$

It is the expectation over A, of the mutual information between B and C conditioned on the value of A.

The chain rule for mutual information is

$$I(AB : C) = I(A : C) + I(B : C|A).$$

This chain rule also has an intuitive meaning: the information AB give about C is the information A gives about C plus the information B gives about C when we already know A. The proof is a straightforward application of the chain rule for divergence.

Subadditivity

Unlike entropy, mutual information can increase under conditioning. For example, if $A, B,$ and C are three random bits subject to $A + B + C = 0 \mod 2$, then $0 = I(A : B) < I(A : B|C) = 1$. Nevertheless, subadditivity holds when the variables are independent.

Theorem 6.12 *Let $A_1, \ldots, A_n$ be independent random variables, and B be jointly distributed. Then,*

$$\sum_{i=1}^{n} I(A_i : B) \leq \sum_{i=1}^{n} I(A_i : BA_{<i}) = I(A_1, \ldots, A_n : B).$$

Proof We have

$$I(A_1, \ldots, A_n : B) = H(A_1, \ldots, A_n) - H(A_1, \ldots, A_n | B).$$

The first term is exactly equal to $\sum_{i=1}^{n} H(A_i)$ because $A_1, \ldots, A_n$ are independent. The chain rule gives that

$$H(A_1, \ldots, A_n | B) = \sum_{i=1}^{n} H(A_i | BA_{<i}).$$

So, we get

$$I(A_1, \ldots, A_n : B) = \sum_{i=1}^{n} H(A_i) - H(A_i | BA_{<i}) = \sum_{i=1}^{n} I(A_i : BA_{<i}).$$

Because conditioning does not increase entropy,

$$\sum_{i=1}^{n} H(A_i) - H(A_i | BA_{<i}) \geq \sum_{i=1}^{n} H(A_i) - H(A_i | B) = \sum_{i=1}^{n} I(A_i : B).$$

$\square$

Returning to the indexing problem, Theorem 6.12 applied to $X_1, \ldots, X_n$ and M yields

$$I(X_I : M | I) \leq \frac{1}{n} \sum_{i=1}^{n} I(X_i : MX_{<i}) \leq \frac{H(M)}{n} \leq \frac{\ell}{n}.$$

This inequality captures our intuition that Alice's message does not contain much information about the bit that Bob cares about, when $\ell \ll n$. The proof, however, is not yet complete. We need to prove that if M and X_i have low mutual information then Bob cannot use M to predict the value of X_i. We need one more technical tool to prove this – Pinsker's inequality.

Pinsker's Inequality

Pinsker's inequality bounds the statistical distance between two distributions p and q in terms of the divergence between them. The inequality is illustrated in Figures 6.6 and 6.7.

See the notational remarks in the Probability section of the Conventions chapter.

Lemma 6.13 $|p(x) - q(x)|^2 \leq \frac{\ln 2}{2} \cdot D(p(x) \| q(x)).$

Proof Let T be the event that maximizes $p(T) - q(T)$. Define the indicator random variable

$$y = \begin{cases} 1 & \text{if } x \in T, \\ 0 & \text{otherwise.} \end{cases}$$

Think of x and y as jointly distributed. By the chain rule, because divergence is nonnegative,

$$D(p(x) \| q(x)) \geq D(p(y) \| q(y)).$$

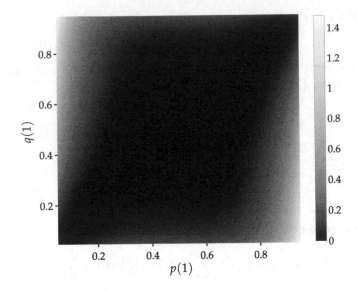

Figure 6.6 Pinsker's inequality for two bits. The difference between the divergence and its lower bound is shown.

Figure 6.7 The solid line plots the divergence of an ϵ-biased bit from a bit with bias $2/3$. The dashed line plots $\frac{2}{\ln 2}(\epsilon - 2/3)^2$.

Because $|p - q| = p(T) - q(T) = p(y = 1) - q(y = 1)$, it remains to prove that

$$D(p(y)\|q(y)) \geq \frac{2}{\ln 2} \cdot (p(y = 1) - q(y = 1))^2.$$

Let $\epsilon = p(y = 1)$ and $\gamma = q(y = 1)$. It is enough to prove that

$$\epsilon \log \frac{\epsilon}{\gamma} + (1 - \epsilon) \log \frac{1 - \epsilon}{1 - \gamma} - \frac{2}{\ln 2} \cdot (\epsilon - \gamma)^2 \qquad (6.4)$$

is always nonnegative. The expression in (6.4) is 0 when $\epsilon = \gamma$, and its derivative with respect to γ is

$$\frac{-\epsilon}{\gamma \ln 2} + \frac{1 - \epsilon}{(1 - \gamma) \ln 2} - \frac{4(\gamma - \epsilon)}{\ln 2} = \frac{(\gamma - \epsilon)}{\ln 2} \left(\frac{1}{\gamma(1 - \gamma)} - 4 \right).$$

Because $\frac{1}{\gamma(1-\gamma)}$ is always at most 4, the derivative is nonpositive when $\gamma \leq \epsilon$, and nonnegative when $\gamma \geq \epsilon$. This proves that (6.4) is indeed always nonnegative. $\square$

Pinsker's inequality implies that two variables that have low mutual information are statistically close to being independent.

Corollary 6.14 *If A, B are random variables then on average over b,*

$$p(a|b) \overset{\epsilon}{\approx} p(a),$$

where $\epsilon = \sqrt{\frac{\ln 2 \cdot I(A:B)}{2}}$.

Another useful corollary is that conditioning on a low entropy random variable cannot change the distribution of many other independent random variables:

Corollary 6.15 *Let $A_1, \ldots, A_n$ be independent random variables, and B be jointly distributed. Let $I \in [n]$ be uniformly random and independent of all other variables. Then on average over $i, b, a_{<i}$,*

$$p(a_i|i, b, a_{<i}) \stackrel{\epsilon}{\approx} p(a_i|i),$$

where $\epsilon \le \sqrt{\frac{H(B)\ln 2}{2n}}$.

Proof By Theorem 6.12, $H(B) \ge \sum_{j=1}^{n} I(A_j : BA_{<j})$. Thus,

$$I(A_I : BA_{<I}|I) \le \frac{H(B)}{n}.$$

The claim follows from Corollary 6.14. □

We are finally ready to prove the lower bound for the indexing problem. By Corollary 6.15, on average over m and i,

$$p(x_i|m) \stackrel{\epsilon}{\approx} p(x_i),$$

with $\epsilon = \sqrt{\frac{\ell \ln 2}{2n}}$. Because $p(x_i)$ is uniform for each i, the probability that Bob makes an error is at least

$$\mathop{\mathbb{E}}_{p(m,i)} \left[\frac{1}{2} - |p(x_i|m) - p(x_i)| \right] \ge \frac{1}{2} - \sqrt{\frac{\ell \ln 2}{2n}}.$$

It follows that at least $\Omega(n)$ bits must be transmitted if the protocol has error at most $\frac{1}{3}$.

The Power of Interaction

ARE INTERACTIVE PROTOCOLS SHORTER than protocols that have less interaction?[10] Yes! For several natural problems, the best protocols are much longer if the number of rounds is bounded.

Because the information about the number of rounds is lost once we move to viewing a protocol as a partition into rectangles, it seems hard to prove a separation between a few rounds and many rounds using the techniques we have seen before this chapter. None of those techniques distinguish protocols with few rounds from protocols with many rounds.

The ideas we used to prove the lower bound on indexing are quite powerful. We showed that Alice's message provides no useful information about the coordinate that Bob cares about. These ideas can be used to prove lower bounds on multiround protocols as well.

Greater-Than

The greater-than function $GT(x, y)$ gets inputs $x, y \in [n]$ and outputs

$$GT(x, y) = \begin{cases} 1 & \text{if } x > y, \\ 0 & \text{otherwise.} \end{cases}$$

In Chapter 1, we saw that every deterministic protocol for GT requires $\log n$ bits of communication. In Chapter 3, we discussed a randomized protocol computing GT with $O(\log \log n)$ bits of communication.

The square-root dependence is tight: If Alice sends the majority of all her bits, that bit is equal to a random coordinate with probability $1/2 + \Omega(1/\sqrt{n})$. See Exercise 6.3.

If Alice has a random set from a family of sets of size $2^{\Omega(n)}$, the lower bound for indexing still holds. The lower bound even extends to the case that Bob knows $x_1, \ldots, x_{i-1}$.

[10] Yao, 1983; Duris et al., 1987; Halstenberg and Reischuk, 1993; and Nisan and Wigderson, 1993.

[11] Sen and Venkatesh, 2008.

Here we show[11] that randomized protocols require much more communication if the protocols involve a small number of rounds of communication.

Theorem 6.16 *Any randomized k-round protocol for computing greater-than requires communication at least*

$$\Omega\left(\frac{(\log n)^{1/k}}{k^2}\right).$$

Proof We define a sequence $\mu_0, \mu_1, \ldots$ of hard input distributions. The distribution μ_k is meant to be hard for k-round protocols where the length of each round is at most c.

Define the first distribution μ_0 as follows. Let m be an odd integer. Let $X \in [m]$ be a uniformly random even integer, and let $Y \in [m]$ be a uniformly random odd integer. The probability that $X > Y$ is exactly $1/2$. Thus, any protocol that computes $\mathsf{GT}(X, Y)$ *without* communicating must make an error with probability at least $1/2$.

Define μ_1 as follows. Set $t = \lceil c/\epsilon^2 \rceil$. Sample t independent variables

$$(X_1, Y_1), (X_2, Y_2), \ldots, (X_t, Y_t)$$

from the distribution μ_0, and sample $I \in [t]$ uniformly at random. Set

$$X = (X_1 - 1) \cdot m^{t-1} + (X_2 - 1) \cdot m^{t-2} + \ldots + (X_t - 1).$$

Intuitively, this is the number whose digits are obtained by concatenating the digits of $X_1, X_2, \ldots, X_t$. Set

$$Y = (X_1 - 1) \cdot m^{t-1} + \ldots + X_{i-1} \cdot n^{t-i+1} + Y_I \cdot m^{t-i}.$$

This is the number whose digits are obtained by concatenating the digits of $X_1, X_2, \ldots, X_{I-1}, Y_i, 0, 0, \ldots, 0$. Because the most significant digits of X, Y are the same, and $X_I \neq Y_I$, we have $\mathsf{GT}(X, Y) = \mathsf{GT}(X_I, Y_I)$.

We claim that a deterministic one-round protocol in which Alice sends c bits to Bob must make an error with probability at least $1/2 - \epsilon$, when the inputs are sampled from μ_1. Indeed, Corollary 6.15 implies that on average over $i, m, x_{<i}$,

$$p(x_i|m, x_{<i}) \overset{\epsilon}{\approx} p(x_i).$$

For fixed $i, m, x_{<i}$, we have

$$|p(x_i, y_i|m, x_{<i}) - p(x_i, y_i)|$$
$$= \frac{1}{2} \sum_{x_i, y_i} |p(x_i|m, x_{<i}) \cdot p(y_i|mx_{\leq i}) - p(x_i) \cdot p(y_i|x_i)|$$
$$= \frac{1}{2} \sum_{x_i, y_i} p(y_i|x_i) \cdot |p(x_i|m, x_{<i}) - p(x_i)|$$
$$= |p(x_i|m, x_{<i}) - p(x_i)|.$$

because
$p(y_i|m, x_{\leq i}) = p(y_i|x_i)$.

As we saw in the analysis of μ_0, the error of the protocol for fixed $i, m, x_{<i}$ is at least $1/2 - |p(x_i, y_i | m, x_{<i}) - p(x_i, y_i)|$. Taking expectation over $i, m, x_{<i}$, we see that the overall error is at least $1/2 - \epsilon$.

The above argument can be repeated for general k. There is a distribution μ_k on inputs so that the error of every k-round protocol with c bits of communication per round is at least $1/2 - \epsilon k$. The construction of μ_k from μ_{k-1} is similar to the construction of μ_1 from μ_0. The size of the inputs increases in each step from m to $m^{\lceil c/\epsilon^2 \rceil}$. In μ_0, choose x, y from the set $[3]$. For the target k, the size of the universe is $3^{\lceil c/\epsilon^2 \rceil^k}$. We set $\epsilon = 1/8k$ and $c = \lfloor \frac{(\log n)^{1/k}}{128k^2} \rfloor$. The final inputs are supported on a set of size at most n. The error of any such protocol is at least $1/2 - 1/8 = 1/4$. $\qquad \square$

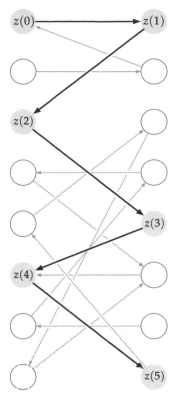

Figure 6.8 An example of an input to pointer-chasing, with $n = 8, k = 5$.

Pointer-Chasing

Pointer-chasing is a natural problem where having many rounds of communication is useful. Alice is given $x \in [n]^n$ and Bob is given $y \in [n]^n$. The vectors x, y define a bipartite directed graph with $2n$ vertices, in which each vertex has exactly one edge coming out of it. The edges emanating from the vertices on the left are specified by x, and the edges from the right are specified by y. There is an edge from i on the left to j on the right if and only if $x_i = j$, and there is an edge from i on the right to j on the left if and only if $y_i = j$. An example is shown in Figure 6.8.

The graph defines a path $z(0), z(1), z(2), \ldots$ by setting $z(0) = 1$, $z(1) = x_{z(0)}, z(2) = y_{z(1)}$, and so on. Namely, $z(i)$ is the vertex obtained by following i edges in the graph starting at the vertex $z(0) = 1$ on the left. Suppose the parties want to compute whether or not $z(k)$ is even.

There is an obvious deterministic protocol that takes k rounds and $k\lceil \log n \rceil$ bits of communication. In round i, the relevant party announces the value of $z(i)$.

There is also a randomized protocol with $k - 1$ rounds and $O((k + n/k) \log n)$ bits of communication.[12] In the first step, Alice and Bob use shared randomness to pick $10n/k$ vertices in the graph and announce the edges that originate at these vertices. Alice and Bob then continue to use the deterministic protocol, but do not communicate if one of the edges they need has already been announced. This protocol has $< k$ rounds with high probability.

We shall prove that any randomized or deterministic protocol with $k - 1$ rounds must have much more communication than the k-round protocol. A lower bound of $\Omega(\frac{n}{k} - k \log n)$ is known.[13] Here, we prove a lower bound of $\Omega(n/k^2) - k \log n$ using information.

Actually, we prove that it is hard to compute *any information* about $z(k)$ in at most $k - 1$ rounds of communication. The key idea is quite similar to the lower bound for the indexing problem. Assume x, y are chosen uniformly at random and independently. We argue, by induction on the number of rounds, that the distribution of $z(k)$ is *close to uniform*

[12] Nisan and Wigderson, 1993.

The probability that none of the announced values help to save a round of communication is exponentially small in k, as long as $\Omega(k)$ of the values z_i are distinct. If the values are not distinct, then less than k rounds of communication are required anyway.

[13] Yehudayoff, 2016.

even after conditioning on the messages in the first $k - 1$ rounds of the protocol.

Theorem 6.17 *Any randomized $(k - 1)$-round protocol for the k-step pointer-chasing problem that is correct with probability $1/2 + \epsilon$ requires $\frac{\epsilon^2 n}{k^2} - k \log n$ bits of communication.*

Proof Let X, Y be distributed uniformly and independently. Let π be a deterministic protocol of length ℓ. Let M_t be the message sent at the tth round of π. Define the random variable

$$R_{k-1} = (M_1, \ldots, M_{k-1}, Z(1), \ldots, Z(k - 1)).$$

We inductively prove that on average over r_{k-1}, the distribution $p(z(k)|r_{k-1})$ is $(k \cdot \delta)$-close to uniform with

$$\delta = \sqrt{\frac{\ell + k \log n}{n}}.$$

This suffices – it must hold that $k\delta \geq \epsilon$, which gives the lower bound.

When $k = 1$, the statement is trivial. Suppose $k \geq 2$ and k is even. The proof is similar when k is odd. We shall repeatedly use the following fact about statistical distance: If U, V are independent and $p(u) \overset{\gamma}{\approx} p(v)$,

Try to prove this basic fact. then $p(g(u)) \overset{\gamma}{\approx} p(g(v))$ for any function g.

The variables R_{k-2}, M_{k-1} contains at most $\ell + k \log n$ bits of information. Corollary 6.15 implies that if I is uniformly random in $[n]$ and independent of all other variables, then on average over i, r_{k-2}, m_{k-1},

$$p(y_i|i, r_{k-2}) \overset{\delta}{\approx} p(y_i) \overset{\delta}{\approx} p(y_i|i, m_{k-1}, r_{k-2}). \tag{6.5}$$

There are two cases to consider:

Alice sends the message m_{k-1}. In this case,

$$p(y_i|r_{k-1}) = p(y_i|z(k - 1), r_{k-2}),$$

because after fixing r_{k-2}, we know that Y_i is independent of M_{k-1}. By induction, on average over r_{k-2},

$$p(z(k - 1)|r_{k-2}) \overset{(k-1)\delta}{\approx} p(i).$$

We can deduce:

$$p(z(k)|r_{k-1}) = p(y_{z(k-1)}|z(k - 1), r_{k-2}) \overset{(k-1)\delta}{\approx} p(y_i|i, r_{k-2}).$$

Combining this with (6.5) gives that $p(z(k)|r_{k-1}) \overset{k\delta}{\approx} p(y_i)$.

Bob sends the message m_{k-1}. In this case, after fixing R_{k-2}, we know that $Z(k - 1)$ is independent of Y, and therefore also of M_{k-1}, which is a function of Y. So,

$$p(z(k - 1)|r_{k-2}) = p(z(k - 1)|m_{k-1}, r_{k-2}).$$

By induction,

$$p(z(k-1)|m_{k-1}, r_{k-2}) \overset{(k-1)\delta}{\approx} p(i).$$

We can deduce:

$$p(z(k)|r_{k-1}) = p(y_{z(k-1)}|z(k-1), m_{k-1}, r_{k-2})$$
$$\overset{(k-1)\delta}{\approx} p(y_i|i, m_{k-1}, r_{k-2}).$$

Combining this with (6.5) gives that $p(z(k)|r_{k-1}) \overset{k\delta}{\approx} p(y_i)$.

$\square$

Similar intuitions can be used to show that the *deterministic* communication of the pointer-chasing problem is $\Omega(n)$ if fewer than k rounds of communication are used:[14]

Theorem 6.18 *Any $k - 1$ round deterministic protocol that computes the k-step pointer-chasing problem requires $\frac{n}{16} - k$ bits of communication.*

Randomized Complexity of Disjointness

ONE OF THE TRIUMPHS of information theory in communication complexity is optimal lower bounds on the randomized communication complexity of disjointness.[15]

Theorem 6.19 *Any randomized protocol that computes disjointness function with error $1/2 - \epsilon$ must have communication $\Omega(\epsilon^2 n)$.*

The most natural way to prove lower bounds on randomized protocols is to find a *hard distribution* on the inputs. If we adopt this approach, we need not worry about the protocol being randomized; we can assume that it is deterministic without loss of generality. Indeed, by Theorem 3.3, any lower bound implies the existence of a hard distribution.

This is the approach we took when we proved lower bounds on the inner-product function, in Theorem 5.6 – the hard distribution was uniform. This is also the approach we used to prove our lower bounds of $\Omega(\sqrt{n})$ on disjointness, where the distribution we used was essentially uniform on sets of size $\approx \sqrt{n}$. The uniform distribution on all sets, however, is not hard for disjointness. Two uniformly random sets X, Y intersect with very high probability, so the protocol can output 0 without communicating and still have very low error. In fact, it can be shown that *any* distribution where X and Y are independent cannot be used to prove a linear lower bound. Therefore, the hard distribution, if one exists, must involve correlations between X and Y.

[14] Nisan and Wigderson, 1993.

[15] Kalyanasundaram and Schnitger, 1992; Razborov, 1992; Bar-Yossef et al., 2004; and Braverman and Moitra, 2013.

This result is very important because many other lower bounds in various models, as we see in Part II, rely on Theorem 6.19.

We do not know how to prove this lower bound without information theory.

See Exercise 6.8.

Given these constraints, we use a natural distribution on correlated sets. The distribution of X, Y is a convex combination of two distributions:

1. Two random disjoint sets.
2. Two sets that intersect in exactly one element.

Once we restrict our attention to such a distribution, we have a second challenge. The pairs of variables X_i, Y_i and X_j, Y_j are not independent for $i \neq j$. This makes arguments involving subadditivity much harder to carry out because subadditivity of information crucially relies on independence. The subtleties in the proof arise from circumventing these obstacles.

Proving Theorem 6.19

Given a randomized protocol with error $1/2 - \epsilon$, one can make the error an arbitrarily small constant by repeating the protocol $O(1/\epsilon^2)$ times and outputting the majority outcome. This means that it suffices to show that any protocol with error $\frac{1}{32}$ must have communication $\Omega(n)$.

We start by defining the hard distribution on inputs. View the sets X, Y as n-bit strings, by setting $X_i = 1$ if and only if $i \in X$. Pick an index $T \in [n]$ uniformly at random. Let X_T, Y_T be uniformly random and independent bits. For $i \neq T$, sample (X_i, Y_i) to be one of $(0,0), (0,1), (1,0)$ with equal probability, and independent of all other pairs (X_j, Y_j). The random sets X and Y intersect in at most 1 element, and they intersect with probability $\frac{1}{4}$.

Here is some intuition for the validity of (6.6). If M computes disjointness, then it is not hard to see that it must have information about the pair X_T, Y_T – the probability of the intersection cannot remain $1/4$ after we condition on M. The subtlety is that we need to prove that the information is large *after* conditioning on $\mathcal{D}$.

Let M denote the messages of a deterministic protocol of length ℓ and error at most $1/32$. We shall prove that the protocol conveys a significant amount of information about X_T or Y_T, when the sets are disjoint. Let $\mathcal{D}$ denote the event that X, Y are disjoint. The key claim is:

$$I(X_T : M | T, X_{<T} Y_{\geq T}, \mathcal{D}) + I(Y_T : M | T, X_{\leq T}, Y_{>T}, \mathcal{D}) \geq \Omega(1). \quad (6.6)$$

Before proving (6.6), we use it together with the subadditivity of mutual information to prove that $\ell \geq \Omega(n)$.

We start by using the chain rule to prove:

Lemma 6.20 *Let $X = (X_1, \ldots, X_n)$ and $Y = (Y_1, \ldots, Y_n)$ be random variables such that the n pairs $(X_1, Y_1), \ldots, (X_n, Y_n)$ are independent. Let M be an arbitrary random variable. Then*

$$\sum_{i=1}^{n} I(X_i : M | X_{<i} Y_{\geq i}) \leq I(X : M | Y),$$

and

$$\sum_{i=1}^{n} I(Y_i : M | X_{\leq i} Y_{>i}) \leq I(Y : M | X).$$

Proof Using the chain rule:

$$\sum_{i=1}^{n} I(X_i : M | X_{<i} Y_{\geq i}) \leq \sum_{i=1}^{n} I(X_i : M Y_{<i} | X_{<i} Y_{\geq i})$$

$$= \sum_{i=1}^{n} I(X_i : Y_{<i} | X_{<i} Y_{\geq i}) + I(X_i : M | X_{<i} Y)$$

$$= \sum_{i=1}^{n} I(X_i : M | X_{<i} Y) = I(X : M | Y). \qquad \text{because}$$
$$I(X_i : Y_{<i} | X_{<i} Y_{\geq i}) = 0.$$

The second bound is proved similarly. □

We see that $X, Y, M | \mathcal{D}$ satisfy the assumptions of Lemma 6.20. Moreover T is uniform in $[n]$ and independent of X, Y, M, conditioned on $\mathcal{D}$. So Lemma 6.20 gives:

$$\frac{2\ell}{n} \geq \frac{I(X : M | Y \mathcal{D}) + I(Y : M | X \mathcal{D})}{n} \qquad \text{because } M \text{ has at most } \ell \text{ bits.}$$

$$\geq I(X_T : M | T X_{<T} Y_{\geq T} \mathcal{D}) + I(Y_T : M | T X_{\leq T} Y_{>T} \mathcal{D}) \qquad \text{by Lemma 6.20.}$$

$$\geq \Omega(1), \qquad \text{by (6.6).}$$

which proves that $\ell \geq \Omega(n)$.

It only remains to prove (6.6). Let $Z = (M, T, X_{<T}, Y_{>T})$. The intuition for the proof is as follows. Suppose toward a contradiction that the information is small. If we sample Z conditioned on $\mathcal{D}$, then with high probability the resulting value z has the property that $p(x_t, y_t | z)$ is close to the distribution of two uniformly random bits. However, this leads to a high probability of errors for the protocol because conditioned on $\mathcal{D}$ the protocol must typically output that the sets are disjoint.

For any z, let α_z be the statistical distance of $p(x_t, y_t | z)$ from uniform. Let

$$I(X_T : M | T, X_{<T} Y_{\geq T}, \mathcal{D}) + I(Y_T : M | T, X_{\leq T}, Y_{>T}, \mathcal{D}) = 2\gamma^4 / 3.$$

Let $\mathcal{G}$ be the set of z such that $\alpha_z \leq 2\gamma$. We shall use Pinsker's inequality to prove:

Claim 6.21 $p(z \in \mathcal{G}) \geq \frac{1-4\gamma}{4}$.

Before proving the claim, we use it to complete the proof. Conditioned on $Z = z$ the output of the protocol is determined. In addition, when $z \in \mathcal{G}$, we know that x_t, y_t are close to uniform. The error for $z \in \mathcal{G}$ is at least $\frac{1}{4} - 2\gamma$. The overall error is at least

$$\frac{1}{32} \geq p(\text{error}) \geq p(z \in \mathcal{G}) \cdot p(\text{error} | z \in \mathcal{G}) \geq \frac{1 - 4\gamma}{4} \cdot \left(\frac{1}{4} - 2\gamma \right).$$

It follows that $\gamma \geq \Omega(1)$.

Proof of Claim 6.21 Because X_T, Y_T are independent and because M defines a rectangle, for all z,

$$p(x_t|z) = p(x_t|z, y_t = 0) = p(x_t|z, y_t = 0, \mathcal{D}).$$

Let $\alpha_{z,x}$ be the statistical distance of $p(x_t|z)$ from uniform. We have

$$\frac{2}{3} \cdot I(X_T : M|T, X_{<T}Y_{>T}, Y_T = 0, \mathcal{D})$$
$$\leq I(X_T : M|T, X_{<T}Y_{\geq T}, \mathcal{D})$$
$$\leq 2\gamma^4/3.$$

By convexity and Pinsker's inequality (Lemma 6.13),

$$\mathop{\mathbb{E}}_{p(z|y_t=0)} [\alpha_{z,x}] \leq \sqrt{\mathop{\mathbb{E}}_{p(z|y_t=0)} [\alpha_{z,x}^2]} \leq \sqrt{\gamma^4} = \gamma^2.$$

In particular,

$$\gamma \geq p(\alpha_{z,x} > \gamma | y_t = 0)$$
$$\geq p(x_t = 0|y_t = 0) \cdot p(\alpha_{z,x} > \gamma | y_t = 0 = x_t)$$
$$= \frac{p(\alpha_{z,x} > \gamma | x_t = 0 = y_t)}{2}.$$

So $p(\alpha_{z,x} > \gamma | x_t = 0 = y_t) \leq 2\gamma$.

Let $\alpha_{z,y}$ be the statistical distance of $p(y_t|z)$ from uniform. A symmetric argument proves that the probability that $\alpha_{z,y} > \gamma$ conditioned on $x_t = 0 = y_t$ is at most 2γ.

We use the following simple lemma, whose proof is left as an exercise:

See Exercise 6.9.

Lemma 6.22 *Let $a(x, y) = a(x) \cdot a(y)$ and $b(x, y) = b(x) \cdot b(y)$ be product distributions. Then,*

$$|a(x, y) - b(x, y)| \leq |a(x) - b(x)| + |a(y) - b(y)|.$$

Because $p(x_t, y_t|z)$ and the uniform distribution are both product distributions,

$$\Pr[\alpha_z > 2\gamma | x_t = 0 = y_t]$$

by Lemma 6.22.

$$\leq \Pr[\alpha_{z,x} + \alpha_{z,y} > 2\gamma | x_t = 0 = y_t]$$

by the union bound.

$$\leq \Pr[\alpha_{z,x} > \gamma | x_t = 0 = y_t] + \Pr[\alpha_{z,x} > \gamma | x_t = 0 = y_t]$$
$$\leq 4\gamma.$$

Hence,

$$p(z \in \mathcal{G}) \geq p(x_t = 0 = y_t)p(z \in \mathcal{G}|x_t = 0 = y_t)$$
$$\geq \frac{1}{4} \cdot (1 - 4\gamma).$$

$\square$

Exercises

Ex 6.1 – Use entropy to prove that a graph with m edges and average degree d must have at least $m(d-1)$ paths of length 2. *Hint: Use a non backtracking walk as in the bound for the girth.*

Ex 6.2 – Show that for any two distributions $p(x,y), q(x,y)$ with the same support, we have

$$\mathop{\mathbb{E}}_{p(y)} \left[D(p(x|y) \| p(x)) \right] \leq \mathop{\mathbb{E}}_{p(y)} \left[D(p(x|y) \| q(x)) \right].$$

Ex 6.3 – Suppose n is odd, and $x \in \{0,1\}^n$ is sampled uniformly at random from the set of strings with $\sum_{i=1}^n x_i \geq n/2$.

1. Use Pinsker's inequality to show that the expected number of 1s in x is at most $n/2 + O(\sqrt{n})$.
2. Use the fact that $\binom{n}{\lfloor n/2 \rfloor} \approx 2^n / \sqrt{n}$ to show that

$$p(x_i = 1) \geq 1/2 + \Omega(1/\sqrt{n}),$$

for every i. Conclude that Pinsker's inequality is tight.

Ex 6.4 – Let X be a random variable supported on $[n]$ and $g : [n] \to [n]$ be a function. Prove that

$$\Pr[X \neq g(X)] \geq \frac{H(X|g(X)) - 1}{\log n}.$$

Use the fact that $\alpha \log \alpha \geq \frac{-\log e}{e} \geq -1$, for $\alpha > 0$.

Use this bound to show that if Alice has a uniformly random vector $Y \in [n]^n$, Bob has an independent uniformly random input $I \in [n]$, and Alice sends Bob an ℓ-bit message M, then the probability that Bob guesses Y_I is at most $\frac{1 + \ell/n}{\log n}$.

Ex 6.5 – Let $\mathcal{G}$ be a family of graphs on n vertices, such that every two graphs in the family share a clique on r vertices. Show that the number of graphs in the family is at most $2^{\binom{n}{2}} / 2^{r-1}$.
Hint: Partition the graph into $r-1$ parts uniformly at random and throw away all edges that do not stay within a part. Analyze the entropy of the resulting distribution on graphs.

Ex 6.6 – Prove the data processing inequality: if $A - B - C$ then $I(A : B) \geq I(A : C)$.

Ex 6.7 – Suppose Alice is given uniformly random n-bit string X, and Bob is given a uniformly random index $I \in [n]$, as well as the values $X_1, X_2, \ldots, X_{I-1}$. Show that if there is a randomized protocol where Alice sends Bob ℓ-bits and Bob outputs X_I with probability $2/3$, then $\ell \geq \Omega(n)$.

Ex 6.8 – In this exercise, we show that disjointness can be computed efficiently if the sets X, Y are independent, no matter what distribution they are sampled from. Suppose $X, Y \subseteq [n]$ are independently distributed. Consider the following protocol. If there is a coordinate $j \in [n]$ such that $H(X_j)$ are $H(Y_j)$ are both at least ϵ, then Alice and Bob communicate X_j, Y_j. They condition on the values that they see and repeat this step until no such coordinate can be found. At this point, Alice and Bob use Shannon's coding theorem to encode X, Y. Show how to set ϵ so that the expected communication can bounded by $n^{2/3} \cdot \log^2 n$. *Hint: Use the fact that* $\mathsf{H}(X_j) \geq \epsilon$ *implies that* $\Pr[X_j = 1] \geq \Omega(\epsilon/(\log(1/\epsilon)))$.

Ex 6.9 – Prove Lemma 6.22.

Ex 6.10 – Give an information theory based proof that the communication complexity of computing the inner product $\langle X, Y \rangle$ over $\mathbb{F}_2$ is $\Omega(n)$ over the uniform distribution by following these steps:

1. Use the chain rule to argue that if the communication complexity of the protocol is small, then for typical values of i, $\mathsf{H}(X_i Y_i | M X_{<i} Y_{>i})$ must be close to 1.
2. Argue that this implies that the protocol makes an error with significant probability.

7

Compressing Communication

WHAT IS the interactive analog of entropy? Shannon's entropy captures the amount of information in a single message. We would like to measure the information in a conversation in a way that captures its interactive nature. In this chapter, we explore how to do this for two-party protocols. As we shall see, these definitions lead to several results in communication complexity that do not concern information at all.

We shall be working in the distributional setting. The inputs X, Y to Alice and Bob are sampled from some known distribution μ. The protocols we consider are still randomized. We start with several examples to illustrate what the information of protocols ought to be.

It remains open to define a similarly useful notion of information for multi-party protocols.

In previous chapters, we could always assume in the distributional setting that the protocols are deterministic. As we shall see later on, in terms of information, randomness is crucial even in the distributional setting.

- Consider a protocol where all the messages of the protocol are 0, no matter what the inputs are. The messages of the protocol are known ahead of time, and Alice and Bob might as well not send them. This protocol does not convey any information.

The *information* is 0.

- Suppose X, Y are independent uniformly random n bit strings. Alice sends X as her first message, and Bob sends Y in response. In this case, the protocol cannot be simulated with less than $2n$ bits.

The *information* is $2n$.

- Suppose X, Y are independent uniformly random n-bit strings. In the protocol, Alice privately samples k uniformly random bits, independent of X, and sends them to Bob. This protocol can be simulated by a randomized communication protocol with no communication. Alice and Bob can use shared randomness to sample the k bit string, so that they do not have to send it.

The *information* is 0, but the entropy of the message is k.

- Suppose X, Y are independent uniformly random n-bit strings. Alice uses private randomness to sample a uniformly random subset $T \subseteq [n]$ of size k with k. Alice sends n bits to Bob, where the ith bit is X_i if $i \notin T$, and $1 - X_i$ otherwise.

One can simulate this protocol with less than n bits of communication. Alice and Bob can use public randomness to sample a set $S \subseteq [n]$ of size k, as well a uniformly random n-bit string R. Alice computes the number of coordinates $i \in S$ such that $R_i \neq X_i$. If there are t such coordinates, she samples a uniformly random subset $T' \subseteq [n] - S$ of

121

size $k - t$. Alice sends the $n - k$ bits of M_i that Bob does not already know in

$$M_i = \begin{cases} R_i & i \in S, \\ 1 - X_i & i \in T', \\ X_i & \text{otherwise.} \end{cases}$$

For any fixed value of X, the string M is identically distributed to how it was in the original protocol. The simulation succeeds with communication $n - k$.

- Suppose X, Y are uniformly random n-bit strings that are always equal. Suppose Alice sends X to Bob in the first message. Then this message can be simulated with 0 communication because Bob already knows X.

We provide two natural ways to define the information of a protocol. Let R denote the public randomness of the protocol, and let M denote the messages that result from executing the protocol. The *external information*[1] of the protocol is defined to be

$$I(XY : M|R).$$

It measures the amount of information about the inputs that an external observer learns from the messages and the public randomness of the protocol. The *internal information*[2] of the protocol is defined to be

$$\underbrace{I(X : M|YR)}_{\text{info learned by Bob}} + \underbrace{I(Y : M|XR)}_{\text{info learned by Alice}}.$$

It measures the amount of information that Alice and Bob learn about each other's inputs from the messages and public randomness of the protocol.

As the intuition suggests, the external information is always at least as large as the internal one – the parties know more, so they must learn less:

Theorem 7.1 *The internal information never exceeds the external information. The two quantities are equal when X, Y are independent.*

Proof Apply the chain rule to express the internal information as:

$$I(X : M|YR) + I(Y : M|XR)$$
$$= \sum_i I(X : M_i|YRM_{<i}) + I(Y : M_i|XRM_{<i}),$$

where $M_1, M_2, \ldots$ are the bits of M. The definition of communication protocols ensures that $M_{<i}$ determines whether Alice or Bob sends the next bit of the protocol. For each fixed value $m_{<i}$, if Alice sends the next bit, then

$$I(Y : M_i|XRm_{<i}) = 0,$$

because M_i is determined by the variables $XRm_{<i}$ and the private randomness of Alice. So, when Alice sends the next bit,

$$I(X : M_i|YRm_{<i}) + I(Y : M_i|XRm_{<i})$$
$$\leq I(X : M_i|YRm_{<i}) + I(Y : M_i|Rm_{<i})$$
$$= I(XY : M_i|Rm_{<i}).$$

The inequality is an equality when X, Y are independent, because in this case Y is independent of M_i after fixing $R, m_{<i}$. A similar bound holds when Bob sends the next bit. Putting it together,

$$I(X : M|YR) + I(Y : M|XR)$$
$$= \sum_i I(X : M_i|YRM_{<i}) + I(Y : M_i|XRM_{<i})$$
$$\leq \sum_i I(XY : M_i|RM_{<i})$$
$$= I(XY : M|R). \qquad \square$$

The same argument proves that $I(X : M|YR)$ is at most the expected number of bits sent by Alice in the protocol, and $I(Y : M|XR)$ is at most the expected number of bits sent by Bob in the protocol.

What we are really after is an analogy of Shannon's coding theorem, Theorem 6.1. The coding theorem is about a particular one-round deterministic protocol – Alice gets X and needs to send X to Bob. The expected communication complexity of this problem is characterized by the entropy of X. In this simple case all three quantities – internal information, external information, and entropy – are equal:

There is no input Y and no randomness R in this case.

$$I(X : M|Y) + I(Y : M|X) = I(XY : M) = H(X).$$

We are after an interactive generalization of Shannon's theorem where the parties also have access to randomness.

Can a protocol with low information be simulated by a protocol with low communication? Is it true that every protocol with external/internal information I can be simulated by a protocol with communication close to I? Answering these questions would be immensely useful because the quantities defining information are much easier to work with than communication complexity.

We shall see that private randomness and public randomness play very different roles in this discussion.

There are several subtleties involved in deciding whether or not one protocol simulates another. We discuss these issues next.

Simulations

A COMPRESSION OF A PROTOCOL is a new protocol of smaller length that simulates the original protocol. Before we describe how to compress communication protocols, we need to define *simulations*. Intuitively, a protocol σ simulates a protocol π if the leaves of the protocol tree of σ can be translated to the leaves of π in a way that induces the correct distribution on the leaves of π.

We start by setting some notation. Let π be a two-party protocol. Suppose $(X, Y) \in \mathcal{X} \times \mathcal{Y}$ are jointly distributed random inputs to Alice and Bob. Let R_π be the public randomness used in the protocol π, and let M_π be the messages of π. Let $\mathcal{M}_\pi$ be the set of the possible messages in π, and $\mathcal{R}_\pi$ be the set of possible values of public randomness in π. Let σ be a protocol with public randomness R_σ and messages of M_σ. Let $\mathcal{M}_\sigma$ be the set of the possible messages M_σ, and $\mathcal{R}_\sigma$ be the set of possible values of R_σ.

We say that σ simulates π with error $\epsilon > 0$ if there are two maps

F_A maps the private data (X, M_σ, R_σ) of Alice in σ to the public data (M_π, R_π) in π.

F_B maps the private data of Bob in σ to the public data in π.

$$F_A : \mathcal{X} \times \mathcal{M}_\sigma \times \mathcal{R}_\sigma \rightarrow \mathcal{M}_\pi \times \mathcal{R}_\pi$$

and

$$F_B : \mathcal{Y} \times \mathcal{M}_\sigma \times \mathcal{R}_\sigma \rightarrow \mathcal{M}_\pi \times \mathcal{R}_\pi$$

so that

$$p(x, y, F_A(x, m_\sigma, r_\sigma), F_B(y, m_\sigma, r_\sigma)) \overset{\epsilon}{\approx} p(x, y, m_\pi, r_\pi, m_\pi, r_\pi).$$

Roughly speaking, this means that (X, M_σ, R_σ) and (Y, M_σ, R_σ), which are known to Alice and Bob after executing σ, can be translated to (M_π, R_π) with the correct distribution.

This version of simulation is *internal* – only the parties are guaranteed to understand how to translate the transcript of σ to that of π. An external observer who only has access to M_σ, R_σ may not understand the outcome of the simulation. We say that σ is an *external simulation* if F_A does not depend on X and F_B does not depend on Y. In this case, the public data (M_σ, R_σ) can be translated to the public data (M_π, R_π).

Compressing Protocols with No Private Randomness

WE START BY GIVING AN INTERACTIVE GENERALIZATION of Shannon's theorem for protocols with no private randomness.[3]

[3] Dietzfelbinger and Wunderlich, 2007.

We shall later see that private randomness completely changes the nature of the question and makes it more interesting and challenging.

Theorem 7.2 *Every protocol with no private randomness and external information I can be simulated by a protocol with expected communication $O(I + 1)$ and no error.*

The ideas that go into proving Theorem 7.2 are very similar to those we used to balance protocols in Chapter 1. We need the following generalization of Lemma 1.8.

Let p be a distribution on the leaves of a protocol tree. For every node v in the protocol tree, let $\mathcal{E}_v$ denote the set of leaves contained in the subtree of the protocol tree rooted at v. Namely, $\mathcal{E}_v$ is the set of leaves that are descendants of v.

The proofs of the Lemma 1.8 and Lemma 7.3 are similar.

Lemma 7.3 *Either there is a leaf w in the tree with $p(\mathcal{E}_w) \geq 2/3$, or there is a vertex v with $1/3 \leq p(\mathcal{E}_v) < 2/3$.*

The lemma suggests a method for compressing protocols. Intuitively, a compression needs to transmit 1 bit of information using $O(1)$ bits of communication. This is exactly what the lemma allows us to do. The lemma finds a node u so that $\mathcal{E}_u$ is worth ≈ 1 bit of information. This 1 bit of information can be gained by communicating just 2 bits.

We use the lemma to prove the following theorem. Recall that $\pi(x, y)$ denotes the leaf that the protocol reaches on input x, y.

Theorem 7.4 *Given any deterministic protocol π and a distribution p on the leaves of π, there is a deterministic protocol σ_p such that on input x, y, the protocol σ_p computes $\pi(x, y)$ after communicating at most $2 \cdot \log_{3/2}(1/p(\pi(x, y))) + 2$ bits.*

Before proving Theorem 7.4, let us show how it implies Theorem 7.2.

Proof of Theorem 7.2 Let π be a protocol with no private randomness. Let X, Y be inputs to the protocol sampled from some known distribution, and let R denote the public randomness of the protocol. Let M denote the messages of the protocol.

The external information of π is

$$I(XY : M|R) = H(M|R) - H(M|RXY) = H(M|R),$$

where the second inequality follows from the fact that M is determined by X, Y, and R.

Our simulating protocol samples $R = r$, sets p to be the distribution of M conditioned on $R = r$, and carries out the simulation promised by Theorem 7.4. For fixed r, the expected number of bits communicated by the simulation is at most

$$\mathop{\mathbb{E}}_{p(xy|r)} \left[2\log_{3/2}(1/p(xy|r)) \right] + 2 \leq \frac{2\log 3}{\log 2} \cdot H(M|R = r) + 2.$$

In expectation, the protocol communicates $O(H(M|R) + 1)$ bits. □

Proof of Theorem 7.4 We give a protocol for computing $\pi(x, y)$. Let u be the node of the protocol tree promised by Lemma 7.3. As we proved in Lemma 1.4, this node corresponds to a rectangle R_u in the set of inputs. Alice and Bob communicate two bits to determine if $(x, y) \in R_u$. If this is the case, they continue to execute the protocol after replacing $p(xy) = p(xy|\mathcal{E}_u)$. Otherwise, they continue, setting $p(xy) = p(xy|\neg\mathcal{E}_u)$. The protocol terminates when $p(\pi(x, y))$ is supported on a single leaf.

Let $c_{x,y}$ denote the number of bits communicated by the protocol when the inputs are x, y. We prove by induction that the communication of the protocol is at most

$$2 \cdot \log_{3/2}(1/p(x, y)) + 2.$$

The base case is when $\log_{3/2}(1/p(x, y)) < 1 \Rightarrow p(x, y) > 2/3$. In this case, the protocol terminates after 2 bits of communication because the vertex found in the application of Lemma 7.3 is a leaf.

In the general case, the protocol replaces the distribution by the distribution q so that either

$$q(x, y) = \frac{p(x, y)}{p(\mathcal{E}_u)} \geq (3/2) \cdot p(x, y)$$

or

$$q(x, y) = \frac{p(x, y)}{p(\neg \mathcal{E}_u)} \geq (3/2) \cdot p(x, y).$$

In either case, we have $\log_{3/2}(1/q(x, y)) \leq \log_{3/2}(1/p(x, y)) - 1$. By induction, the communication of the protocol is at most

$$2 + 2 \log_{3/2}(1/q(x, y)) + 2 \leq 2 \log_{3/2}(1/p(x, y)) + 2.$$

$\square$

Correlated Sampling

WHEN THE INFORMATION OF A PROTOCOL is much less than 1, we can use *correlated sampling*[4] to compress communication. Suppose we are given a protocol with large length but close to zero internal information. In this case, the protocol teaches Alice and Bob almost nothing about each other's inputs, so they should be able to simulate its execution without communicating.

[4] Holenstein, 2009.

Variants of correlated sampling also appear in probability theory in the context of coupling.

Lemma 7.5 *There is a protocol using public randomness and no communication with the following functionality. Suppose Alice is given as input a distribution $p(m)$ on a set $\mathcal{U}$, and Bob is given a distribution $q(m)$ on $\mathcal{U}$. After the protocol terminates,*

- *Alice holds a value M^A, which is distributed according to p.*
- *Bob holds a value M^B, which is distributed according to q.*
- *The probability that $M^A \neq M^B$ is at most $2|p - q|$.*

In other words, Alice samples M^A using the public randomness, Bob samples M^B using the public randomness, and if p, q are close then they sample the same value most of the time. Hence the term *correlated sampling*. This simulation is exact, in the sense that Alice samples from p exactly and Bob samples from q exactly.

Although the protocol uses an infinite number of random bits, one can approximate its behavior using finitely many bits.

Proof We interpret the public randomness as a sequence

$$(M_1, \rho_1), (M_2, \rho_2), \ldots$$

of independent identically distributed samples, where M_i is a uniformly random element from $\mathcal{U}$, and ρ_i is uniformly random from $[0, 1]$. Alice sets $m^A = M_I$ where I is the minimum index for which $\rho_I < p(M_I)$. Similarly, Bob sets $M^B = M_J$ where J is the minimum index such that $\rho_J < p(M_J)$.

It remains to prove that the protocol has the desired properties. First, observe that the probability that Alice and Bob find some acceptable I, J is 1.

Now, we claim that M^A is distributed according to p. A similar argument proves that M^B is distributed according to q. Let $\mathcal{E}$ denote

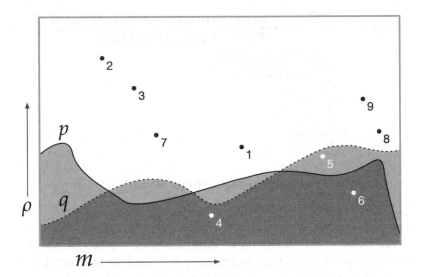

Figure 7.1 An illustration of the sampling procedure. (M_4, ρ_4) is selected in this case, and $M^A = M^B$. Note that $\rho_5 < q(M_5)$ but $\rho_5 > p(M_5)$.

the event that $\rho_1 < p(M_1)$. Think of (M_1, ρ_1) as a point in the plane $\mathcal{U} \times [0, 1]$ distributed uniformly at random. Imagine the graph of p drawn in this plane, as in Figure 7.1. The event $\mathcal{E}$ happens when the point (M_1, ρ_1) is under the graph of p. The total area of the plane is $u|\mathcal{U}|$, and the total area under p is 1. Thus,

$$\Pr[\mathcal{E}] = \frac{1}{u},$$

and

$$\Pr[M^A = m | \mathcal{E}] = \frac{\Pr[M_1 = m, \rho_1 < p(m)]}{\Pr[\mathcal{E}]} = \frac{(1/u) \cdot p(m)}{1/u} = p(m).$$

On the other hand, by the definition of the process, the distribution of M^A conditioned on $\neg \mathcal{E}$ is the same as the distribution of M^A. Thus,

$$\Pr[M^A = m] = \Pr[\mathcal{E}] \Pr[M^A = m | \mathcal{E}] + \Pr[\neg \mathcal{E}] \Pr[M^A = m | \neg \mathcal{E}]$$

$$= \Pr[\mathcal{E}] p(m) + \Pr[\neg \mathcal{E}] \Pr[M^A = m].$$

This implies that $\Pr[M^A = m] = p(m)$.

We now bound the probability that $M^A \neq M^B$. Let $\mathcal{B}$ be the event that $q(M_I) < \rho_I < p(M_I)$ or $p(M_J) < \rho_J < q(m_J)$. The event that $M^A \neq M^B$ implies the event $\mathcal{B}$. So it suffices to bound $\Pr[\mathcal{B}]$ from above. Denote by $\mathcal{F}$ the event that $I = 1$ or $J = 1$. In other words, $\mathcal{F}$ is the event that $\rho_1 < \max\{p(M_1), q(M_1)\}$. As above, $\Pr[\mathcal{B}|\neg\mathcal{F}] = \Pr[\mathcal{B}]$, which implies that $\Pr[\mathcal{B}] = \Pr[\mathcal{B}|\mathcal{F}]$. Finally,

$$\Pr[\mathcal{B}|\mathcal{F}] = \frac{\Pr[\min\{p(M_1), q(M_1)\} \leq \rho_1 < \max\{p(M_1), q(M_1)\}]}{\Pr[\rho_1 < \max\{p(M_1), q(M_1)\}]}$$

$$= \frac{\sum_m |p(m) - q(m)|}{\sum_m \max\{p(m), q(m)\}}$$

$$= \frac{2|p - q|}{1 + |p - q|}$$

$$\leq 2|p - q|.$$

□

Compressing a Single Round

NEXT, LET US CONSIDER COMPRESSION OF ONE-ROUND protocols. As we shall see, even this seemingly simple task is not trivial. Because the definition of information of a protocol involves conditioning on the public randomness, it is no loss of generality to assume that the protocols we consider do not have public randomness.

External Compression

Suppose we would just like to compress the first message in a protocol down to its external information. If the message M is sent by Alice, who holds X, and Bob holds Y, then the external information is

after fixing X, the variables Y and M are independent.

$$I(XY : M) = I(X : M) + I(Y : M|X)$$
$$= I(X : M).$$

[5] Harsha et al., 2007; and Braverman and Garg, 2014.

We prove that there is a way to simulate[5] the sending of the message M using $I(X : M) + O(\log I(X : M))$ bits of communication in expectation. This compression is based on the following sampling procedure.

Compare to Shannon's theorem (Theorem 6.1).

Theorem 7.6 *Suppose Alice knows two distributions p, q over the same set $\mathcal{U}$, and Bob knows q. There is a protocol for Alice and Bob to sample an element according to p using*

The factor 2 before the log in the theorem can be replaced by 1, and 1 is sharp up to the additive constant. See Exercise 7.3.

$$D(p\|q) + 2\log(1 + D(p\|q)) + O(1)$$

bits of communication in expectation. This is a one-round protocol in which Alice sends a single message to Bob.

As a corollary, we get the claimed one-round compression.

This is a perfect simulation – the parties sample exactly from p.

Corollary 7.7 *Alice and Bob can use public randomness to simulate sending M with expected communication $I(X : M) + 2\log(1 + I(X : M)) + O(1)$. The simulation is one round, external, and without error.*

Proof Let $r(x, m)$ denote the joint distribution of X, M. Given x, the parties run the protocol with $p(m) = r(m|x)$ and $q(m) = r(m)$. Recall that

$$I(X : M) = \mathop{\mathbb{E}}_{r(x)}\left[D(r(m|x)\|r(m))\right].$$

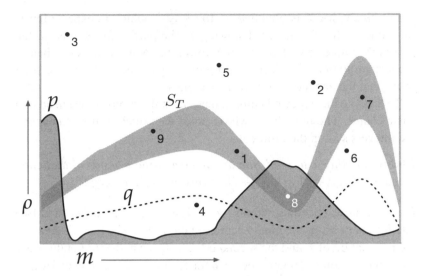

Figure 7.2 The sampling procedure of Theorem 7.6. Here T is 3, and the sampled point is the 3'rd point of S_T.

The expected communication of the resulting protocol is as claimed because log is concave.   □

The compression is based on *rejection sampling*. Rejection sampling is a mechanism for reweighting a distribution q to generate a distribution p. It is most commonly applied when q is the uniform distribution, as we did in correlated sampling. Here is an example that illustrates the high level idea. Assume p and q are so that $p(m) \leq 2q(m)$ for all m. Suppose we are given a sample M from q. Reject M with probability $\frac{p(m)}{2q(m)}$, and resample. Otherwise, use M as the sample. It is easy to verify that the accepted sample is distributed according to p, and each sample is accepted with probability at least $1/2$.

Proof of Theorem 7.6 As in correlated sampling, the public random tape consists of a sequence of independent identically distributed samples $(M_1, \rho_1), (M_2, \rho_2), \ldots$, where each M_i is a uniformly random element from the support of the messages, and ρ_i is a uniformly random number from $[0, 1]$. Alice finds the minimum index R such that $\rho_R < p(m_R)$. See Figure 7.2 for a visualization of the sampling procedure. As we proved when we analyzed correlated sampling, the value M_R has exactly the correct distribution. Unfortunately, communicating R can be too expensive. So, Alice needs to properly encode R.

Alice sends the positive integer

What is the expectation of $\log R$?

$$T = \left\lceil \frac{\rho_R}{q(M_R)} \right\rceil$$

to Bob. Given T, Alice and Bob can both compute the set of integers

$$S_T = \left\{ j : T = \left\lceil \frac{\rho_j}{q(M_j)} \right\rceil \right\}.$$

Alice also sends Bob the number K for which R is the Kth element of S_T.

Intuitively, $\log T$ is bounded by $\log \frac{p(M_R)}{q(M_R)}$, which in expectation is the same as the divergence. Knowing T, the parties focus only on the part of the universe with the given p-to-q ratio. Now, as we show below, a constant number of rejection sampling steps is needed, and we shall prove that the expected value of K is at most 2.

To analyze the expected communication of the protocol, we need two basic claims. The first claim, whose proof we sketch, is used to encode the integers sent in the protocol.

Claim 7.8 *Alice can send Bob any integer using a protocol that communicates* $\log z + 2 \log \log z + O(1)$ *bits to send the integer* z.

Proof A naive encoding would take $2\lceil \log z \rceil$ bits. Alice can send two bits for every bit in the binary representation of z. The first bit encodes the relevant bit of z, and the second bit specifies whether or not there are more bits to come. To get a better bound, first send the integer $\lceil \log z \rceil$ using the naive encoding, and then send $\lceil \log z \rceil$ more bits to encode z. ☐

To argue that the expected encoding length of T is small, we need the following claim:

Claim 7.9 *For any two distribution* $p(m), q(m)$, *the contribution of the terms with* $p(m) < q(m)$ *to the divergence is at least* -1:

$$\sum_{m:p(m)<q(m)} p(m) \log \frac{p(m)}{q(m)} > -1.$$

By Claim 7.8, the expected number of bits required to transmit T is at most

$$\mathbb{E}\left[\log T + 2\log\log T + O(1)\right] \leq \mathbb{E}\left[\log T\right] + 2\log \mathbb{E}\left[\log T\right] + O(1),$$

where the inequality follows from concavity of log. By Claim 7.9, we can bound

$$\mathbb{E}\left[\log T\right] \leq \sum_m p(m) \log \left\lceil \frac{p(m)}{q(m)} \right\rceil$$

$$\leq \sum_{m:p(m)>q(m)} p(m) \left(1 + \log \frac{p(m)}{q(m)}\right)$$

$$\leq 1 + \mathsf{D}(p(m)\|q(m)) - \sum_{m:p(m)<q(m)} p(m) \log \frac{p(m)}{q(m)}$$

$$\leq \mathsf{D}(p(m)\|q(m)) + 2.$$

So the expected number of bits used to transmit T is at most

$$\mathsf{D}(p(m)\|q(m)) + 2 \log \left(2 + \mathsf{D}(p(m)\|q(m))\right) + O(1).$$

Proof of Claim 7.9: Let $\mathcal{E}$ denote the subset of ms for which $p(m) < q(m)$. Bound

$$\sum_{m\in\mathcal{E}} p(m) \log \frac{p(m)}{q(m)}$$

$$\geq -p(\mathcal{E}) \cdot \sum_{m\in\mathcal{E}} p(m|\mathcal{E})$$

$$\times \log \frac{q(m)}{p(m)}$$

$$\geq -p(\mathcal{E}) \cdot \log \sum_{m\in\mathcal{E}} p(m|\mathcal{E})$$

$$\times \frac{q(m)}{p(m)}$$

$$= -p(\mathcal{E}) \cdot \log \frac{q(\mathcal{E})}{p(\mathcal{E})}$$

$$\geq p(\mathcal{E}) \cdot \log p(\mathcal{E}).$$

For $0 \leq x \leq 1$, the map $x \log x$ is minimized when its derivative is zero; $\log e + \log x = 0$. So the minimum is attained at $x = 1/e$, proving that $p(\mathcal{E}) \log p(\mathcal{E}) \geq \frac{-\log e}{e} > -1$.

It only remains to bound the number of bits required to transmit K. We shall prove that $\mathbb{E}[K] \leq 2$. This implies that the expected number of bits required to transmit K is a constant.

Consider the event $\mathcal{A}$ that $\rho_1 \leq p(M_1)$. Define the random variable

$$Z = \begin{cases} 1 & \text{if } 1 \in S_T, \\ 0 & \text{otherwise.} \end{cases}$$

When $\mathcal{A}$ happens, $K = 1$. When $\mathcal{A}$ does not happen, we have $\mathbb{E}[K|\neg\mathcal{A}] = \mathbb{E}[K] + \mathbb{E}[Z|\neg\mathcal{A}]$. Thus,

$$\mathbb{E}[K] = \Pr[\mathcal{A}] + \Pr[\neg\mathcal{A}](\mathbb{E}[K] + \mathbb{E}[Z|\neg\mathcal{A}]),$$

$$\mathbb{E}[K] = \frac{\Pr[\mathcal{A}] + \Pr[\neg\mathcal{A}] \cdot \mathbb{E}[Z|\neg\mathcal{A}]}{1 - \Pr[\neg\mathcal{A}]}$$
$$= \frac{\Pr[\mathcal{A}] + \Pr[\neg\mathcal{A}] \cdot \mathbb{E}[Z|\neg\mathcal{A}]}{\Pr[\mathcal{A}]}$$
$$= 1 + \frac{\Pr[\neg\mathcal{A}] \cdot \mathbb{E}[Z|\neg\mathcal{A}]}{\Pr[\mathcal{A}]}.$$

which implies

$$\mathbb{E}[K] = 1 + \frac{\Pr[\neg\mathcal{A}] \cdot \mathbb{E}[Z|\neg\mathcal{A}]}{\Pr[\mathcal{A}]} = 1 + \frac{\Pr[\neg\mathcal{A}, 1 \in S_T]}{\Pr[\mathcal{A}]}.$$

Now,

$$\Pr[\mathcal{A}] = \frac{1}{|\mathcal{U}|} \sum_m p(m) = \frac{1}{|\mathcal{U}|}$$

This step is similar to the analogous step in the analysis of correlated sampling.

and

$$\Pr[\neg\mathcal{A}, 1 \in S_T] \leq \Pr[1 \in S_T]$$
$$= \Pr[(T-1)q(M_1) < \rho_1 \leq Tq(M_1)]$$
$$= \mathbb{E}\left[\frac{1}{|\mathcal{U}|} \sum_m Tq(m) - (T-1)q(m)\right] = \frac{1}{|\mathcal{U}|}.$$

Finally, $\mathbb{E}[K] \leq 2$. $\qquad\square$

Internal Compression

Now suppose we wish to compress a single message M sent from Alice, who knows X, to Bob, who knows Y. We want to bound the length of the simulation using the internal information

$$I(X : M|Y) + I(Y : M|X) = I(X : M|Y).$$

This is strictly harder than the problem for external information, and when X, Y are independent, the two problems are the same.

Theorem 7.10 *Suppose Alice knows a distribution p over the set $\mathcal{U}$, and Bob knows q. For every $\epsilon > 0$, there is a protocol for Alice to sample an element according to the distribution p while communicating at most*

$$D(p\|q) + O\left(\sqrt{D(p\|q)}\right) + \log(1/\epsilon) + O(1)$$

Figure 7.3 Sampling from p when the sender knows only one distribution. Here Alice chooses M_7, and it likely takes the parties four rounds to compute M_7.

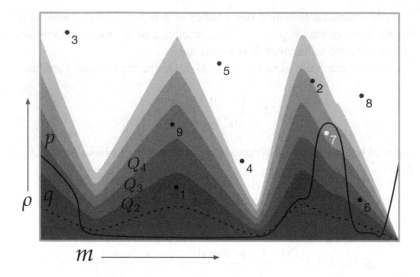

The additive square-root term in this theorem is not sharp. The proof can be altered to yield other bounds.

bits in expectation such that Bob also computes the same sample, except with probability at most ϵ.

As a corollary, we get the one-round internal compression.

Corollary 7.11 *Alice and Bob can use public randomness to simulate sending M with expected communication at most*

$$I(X : M|Y) + O(\sqrt{I(X : M|Y)}) + \log(1/\epsilon) + O(1).$$

This simulation has several rounds, is internal, and has error ϵ.

Proof Let $r(x, y, m)$ denote the joint distribution of X, Y, M. Given x, y, the parties run the protocol from the theorem with $p(m) = r(m|x) = r(m|xy)$ and $q(m) = r(m|y)$. Recall that

$$I(X : M|Y) = \mathop{\mathbb{E}}_{r(x,y)} \left[D(r(m|xy) \| r(m|y)) \right].$$

The expected communication of the resulting protocol is at most $I(X : M|Y) + O(\sqrt{I(X : M|Y)}) + \log(1/\epsilon) + O(1)$ because square-root is concave. □

This compression is based on an interactive version of rejection sampling. It is, however, not perfect – the parties may end up with inconsistent samples.

Proof of Theorem 7.10 Alice and Bob again use public randomness to sample a sequence of independent identically distributed points $(M_1, \rho_1), (M_2, \rho_2), \ldots$, where each M_i is a uniformly random element of the support, and ρ_i is a uniformly random number in $[0, 1]$. Alice picks the smallest index R such that $\rho_R < p(M_R)$; see Figure 7.3. She would like to send Bob enough data for him to be able to recover M_R.

Alice would really like to compute the ratio $\left\lceil \frac{\rho_R}{q(M_R)} \right\rceil$ as in the case of external compression. Unfortunately, Alice does not know q, so she cannot compute it without interacting with Bob. Alice and Bob try to *approximate* this ratio. They gradually increase a threshold until it is larger than this ratio. They are able to locate the correct time to stop using hashing, which eventually yields some probability of error.

Before describing the protocol, we set some notation. For each index i, let $H(i) = (H(i)_1, H(i)_2, \ldots)$ be an infinite sequence of uniformly random bits, sampled publicly. The sequence $H(i)$ is thought of as a hash function evaluated at i. For a positive integer k, let Q_k be the set of indices with ρ-to-q ratio at most 2^{k^2}:

> The choice of 2^{k^2} is not crucial; other choices will work as well while causing some change in parameters.

$$Q_k = \left\{ j : 2^{k^2} \geq \frac{\rho_j}{q(M_j)} \right\}.$$

For positive integers i, j, let

$$g(i, j) = \min\{\ell \in Q_i : H(\ell)_{\leq j} = H(R)_{\leq j}\}.$$

Intuitively, this is Bob's candidate for R in Q_i, with respect to the first j hash values.

As we have shown in the correlated sampling section, M_R is correctly distributed. Alice always outputs M_R. Bob's output is determined after a few rounds of communication. In round k, Alice sends Bob all the bits of $H(R)_{\leq k^2 + \log(1/\epsilon)}$ that she has not already sent. Bob computes $g(i, j)$ for each $i \leq 2^{k^2}$ and $j \leq k^2$. If there is any index $s \leq k$ such that $g(s, k^2 + \log(1/\epsilon)) = g(s, (k-1)^2)$, then Bob stops the protocol and outputs $M_{g(s,(k-1)^2)}$ for the smallest such index s. If there is no such index s, then Bob sends Alice a bit to indicate that the protocol should continue, and the parties go to the next round.

> During the protocol, Alice keeps sending Bob hashes, by revealing $H(R)_j$ for larger and larger values of j. If Bob's estimate $g(i, j)$ is incorrect, then it will soon change as more hashes are revealed. Bob will stop Alice and accept the current value of $g(i, j)$ if it does not change for a while.

Before proving that the protocol achieves its goal, we provide some intuition. If k is too small so that Q_k does not contain R, then the hashes show that $R \notin Q_k$, and $g(s, k^2 + \log(1/\epsilon)) \neq g(s, (k-1)^2)$ for all $s \leq k$. When k becomes large enough so that Q_k contains R then most likely $R = g(s, k^2 + \log(1/\epsilon)) = g(s, (k-1)^2)$, and Bob's choice is correct.

Now, let us analyze the probability that the protocol makes an error. The parties output different samples only if

$$g(s, k^2 + \log(1/\epsilon)) = g(s, (k-1)^2) \neq R$$

for some integers k and $s \leq k$. The probability of this event, for fixed k, s, is at most

$$2^{-(k^2 + \log(1/\epsilon) - 1 - (k-1)^2)} \leq 2^{-2k - \log(1/\epsilon)}.$$

Thus, by the union bound, the probability of an error is at most

$$\sum_{k=1}^{\infty} \sum_{i=1}^{k} 2^{-2k - \log(1/\epsilon)} = \sum_{k=1}^{\infty} k \cdot 2^{-2k - \log(1/\epsilon)} < \epsilon.$$

> because $\sum_{k=1}^{\infty} k 2^{-2k} < \sum_{k=1}^{\infty} 2^{-k} = 1$.

It remains to analyze the expected communication of the protocol. Let T be the smallest positive integer such that $2^{T^2} \geq \frac{\rho_R}{q(M_R)}$. In particular, $R \in Q_T$. Let J be the minimum integer such that $g(T, J) = R$ and $J \geq T^2$. In other words, for every ℓ between T^2 and $J - 1$, the first element in Q_T with ℓ correct hashes is not R, and for every $\ell \geq J$, the first element in Q_T with ℓ correct hashes is R. $\qquad\qquad\square$

Claim 7.12 $\mathbb{E}[J] \leq \mathsf{D}(p(m)\|q(m)) + 3\sqrt{\mathsf{D}(p(m)\|q(m))} + O(1).$

Before proving the claim, we show how it completes the proof. For every k so that $(k-1)^2 \geq J$, the protocol certainly terminates by round k because

$$g(T, k^2 + \log(1/\epsilon)) = R = g(T, (k-1)^2).$$

The smallest value of k satisfying this inequality is at most $\sqrt{J} + 2$. The number of bits communicated up to round k by Alice is at most $k^2 + \log(1/\epsilon)$, and by Bob is at most k. Hence, the expected communication of the protocol is at most

$$\mathbb{E}\left[\left(\sqrt{J} + 2\right)^2 + \sqrt{J} + 2 + \log(1/\epsilon)\right]$$

by convexity.
$$\leq \mathbb{E}[J] + 5\sqrt{\mathbb{E}[J]} + \log(1/\epsilon) + O(1)$$

by Claim 7.12.
$$\leq \mathsf{D}(p(m)\|q(m)) + O\left(\sqrt{\mathsf{D}(p(m)\|q(m))}\right) + \log(1/\epsilon) + O(1).$$

Proof of Claim 7.12 The claim is implied by the following inequalities:

$$\mathbb{E}[J|T, R] \leq 2 + \log\left(1 + \frac{2^{T^2} R}{u - 1}\right) \tag{7.1}$$

$$\mathbb{E}\left[T^2\right] \leq \mathsf{D}(p(m)\|q(m)) + 2\sqrt{\mathsf{D}(p(m)\|q(m))} + 3 \tag{7.2}$$

$$\mathbb{E}\left[\log \frac{u - 1 + R}{u - 1}\right] \leq 3 \tag{7.3}$$

where $u > 1$ is the size of the universe. Because

$$\mathbb{E}\left[\log \frac{u - 1 + 2^{T^2} R}{u - 1}\right] \leq \mathbb{E}\left[\log \frac{2^{T^2}(u - 1 + R)}{u - 1}\right]$$

$$= \mathbb{E}\left[T^2\right] + \mathbb{E}\left[\log \frac{u - 1 + R}{u - 1}\right],$$

these three inequalities imply the claim. We prove the inequalities in turn.

We start by proving (7.1). Let L denote the number of elements of Q_T that precede R. We prove the stronger statement that

$$\mathbb{E}[J|T, R, L] \leq 3 + \log(1 + L). \tag{7.4}$$

To see that (7.4) implies (7.1), use convexity and that

$$\mathbb{E}\left[L|T, R\right] \le R \cdot \Pr[\rho_1 \le 2^{T^2} q(M_1)|\rho_1 \ge p(M_1)]$$
$$= R \cdot \frac{(1/u) \sum_m \Pr[p(m) \le \rho_1 \le 2^{T^2} q(m)]}{(u-1)/u}$$
$$\le \frac{2^{T^2} R}{u-1}.$$

We now prove (7.4). For $L = 0$, we indeed have $\mathbb{E}\left[J|T, R, L\right] = 1 \le 3$. So we can assume that $L > 0$. For every integer $j \ge 1$,

$$\Pr[J \ge j + 1|T, R, L] = 1 - \Pr[J \le j|T, R, L]$$
$$= 1 - \left(1 - 2^{-j}\right)^L$$
$$\le 1 - e^{-L2^{-j+1}}. \qquad \text{because } e^{-2x} \le 1 - x \text{ for } 0 \le x \le 1/2.$$

So for $j > 1 + \log L$ we have $\Pr[J \ge j + 1|T, R, L] \le 1 - e^{-2^{-j}}$. Hence,

$$\mathbb{E}\left[J|T, R, L\right] = 1 + \sum_{j=1}^{\infty} \Pr[J \ge j + 1|T, R, L] \qquad \text{partition the sum to two parts.}$$
$$\le 2 + \log L + \sum_{j>0} 1 - e^{-2^{-j}} \qquad \text{because } 1 - x \le e^{-x} \text{ for all } x.$$
$$\le 2 + \log L + \sum_{j>0} 2^{-j} - 3 + \log L.$$

We now prove (7.2). Let $T' = \max\left\{\log \frac{\rho_R}{q(M_R)}, 0\right\}$ so that

$$T^2 \le \left(\sqrt{T'} + 1\right)^2 = T' + 2\sqrt{T'} + 1.$$

By convexity, we can bound

$$\mathbb{E}\left[T^2\right] \le \mathbb{E}\left[T'\right] + 2\sqrt{\mathbb{E}\left[T'\right]} + 1.$$

Bound $\mathbb{E}\left[T'\right]$ as follows. As in previous sections, $\Pr[R = 1] = \frac{1}{u}$ and the distribution of T' conditioned on the event $R > 1$ is the same as the distribution of T'. Hence,

$$\mathbb{E}\left[T'\right] = \Pr[R = 1]\,\mathbb{E}\left[T'|R > 1\right] + \Pr[R > 1]\,\mathbb{E}\left[T'|R > 1\right]$$
$$= \Pr[R = 1]\,\mathbb{E}\left[T'|R = 1\right] + \Pr[R > 1]\,\mathbb{E}\left[T'\right].$$

Conditioned on the event that $R = 1$ and $M_1 = m$, the variable ρ_1 is uniform in the interval $(q(m), p(m)]$. Therefore,

$$\mathbb{E}\left[T'\right] = \mathbb{E}\left[T'|R=1\right]$$

because
$\Pr[R=1] = \Pr[M_1=m]$ and
log is monotone.

$$= \frac{1}{\Pr[R=1]} \sum_{m:p(m)>q(m)} \Pr[M_1=m] \int_{q(m)}^{p(m)} \log \frac{\rho}{q(m)} d\rho$$

$$\leq \sum_{m:p(m)>q(m)} p(m) \log \frac{p(m)}{q(m)}$$

by Claim 7.9.

$$= D(p(m)\|q(m)) - \sum_{m:p(m)<q(m)} p(m) \log \frac{p(m)}{q(m)}$$

$$\leq D(p(m)\|q(m)) + 1.$$

Finally, we prove (7.3). By convexity,

$$\mathbb{E}\left[\log \frac{u-1+R}{u-1}\right] \leq \log \frac{u-1+\mathbb{E}[R]}{u-1}.$$

Again, $\Pr[R=1] = \frac{1}{u}$, and the distribution of R conditioned on $R > 1$ is the same as the distribution of $R+1$. So,

$$\mathbb{E}[R] = \frac{1}{u} + \left(1 - \frac{1}{u}\right)(\mathbb{E}[R]+1).$$

So $\mathbb{E}[R] = u$ and

$$\mathbb{E}\left[\log \frac{u-1+R}{u-1}\right] \leq 3.$$

$\square$

Internal Compression of Protocols

[6] Barak et al., 2010.

As usual, it is enough to show
how to compress protocols
that only use private
randomness.

HERE WE DESCRIBE HOW TO COMPRESS GENERAL PRO-TOCOLS with low internal information.[6] The generality comes with a cost – the simulating protocol is not as efficient as the simulations we saw earlier, and there is a small probability of making an error.

Suppose we are given inputs X, Y sampled according to some known distribution. The inputs X, Y are fed into a protocol π of length C and internal information

$$I = I(X : M|Y) + I(Y : M|X).$$

We would like to simulate the distribution of the messages M of π by an efficient protocol.

Theorem 7.13 *For every $\epsilon > 0$, one can simulate π with a protocol of length $O\left(\frac{\sqrt{IC}\log(C/\epsilon)}{\epsilon}\right)$. This simulation is internal and has error ϵ.*

An interesting property of the
simulating protocol σ is that
an outside observer cannot
interpret the messages of σ as
messages of π. In other words,
the simulation is not external.

In a nutshell, the idea is that Alice and Bob use correlated sampling to repeatedly guess the bits of the messages in the protocol *without* communicating. Naturally, not all of their guesses are correct. They repeatedly communicate a few bits to *fix* the errors. The protocol is illustrated in Figure 7.4.

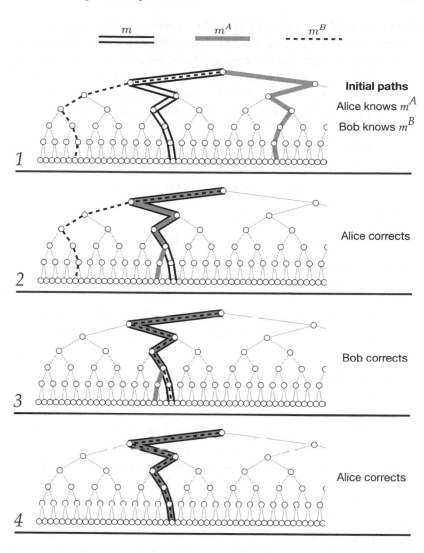

Figure 7.4 Finding the correct path m. In this case, m is found after three mistakes have been fixed.

Proof Without loss of generality we assume that the protocol tree is a full binary tree of depth C. The simulation uses correlated sampling. Because we sample bits and not elements of a large universe, the sampling procedure is particularly simple. For each prefix $m_{<i}$ of messages, define the number

$$\gamma(m_{<i}) = p(M_i = 1 | xym_{<i}).$$

These numbers define the *correct* distribution that our simulation protocol attempts to compute: for all m,

$$\prod_{i=1}^{C} \gamma(m_{<i})^{m_i} (1 - \gamma(m_{<i}))^{1-m_i} = \prod_{i=1}^{C} p(m_i | xym_{<i}) = p(m|xy).$$

Here is a useful way to sample from this distribution. Let $\rho_1, \ldots, \rho_C$ be independent identically distributed random variables from the interval $[0, 1]$, sampled uniformly at random. Now, for each i, set $M_i = 1$ if $\rho_i < \gamma(M_{<i})$, and set $M_i = 0$ otherwise. It follows that $\Pr[M = m] = p(m|xy)$. Namely, M has exactly the correct distribution. Thinking of $\rho_1, \ldots, \rho_C$ as public randomness, the parties attempt to compute $m = m(\rho_1, \ldots, \rho_C)$.

Although Alice and Bob cannot compute $\gamma(m_{<i})$ without communicating, Alice can compute the number

$$\gamma^A(m_{<i}) = p(M_i = 1|x, M_{<i} = m_{<i}),$$

and Bob can compute the number

$$\gamma^B(m_{<i}) = p(M_i = 1|y, M_{<i} = m_{<i}).$$

The key observation is

Claim 7.14 *Either $\gamma(m_{<i}) = \gamma^A(m_{<i})$ or $\gamma(m_{<i}) = \gamma^B(m_{<i})$.*

Proof If it is Alice's turn to speak to send M_i when $M_{<i} = m_{<i}$, then $\gamma^A(m_{<i}) = \gamma(m_{<i})$. If it is Bob's turn to speak, then $\gamma^B(m_{<i}) = \gamma(m_{<i})$.
□

Alice and Bob use γ^A and γ^B as proxies for γ in order to guess m. Alice computes m^A by setting $m_i^A = 1$ if and only if $\rho_i < \gamma^A(m_{<i})$. Bob computes m^B by setting $m_i^B = 1$ if and only if $\rho_i < \gamma^B(m_{<i})$. Of course, m^A and m^B are likely to be quite different. However, by Claim 7.14, if they happen to be the same, then they must both be equal to m.

To compute m, the parties communicate. They start by finding the first index i where $m_i^A \neq m_i^B$. By Exercise 3.1, this takes $O(\log(C/\delta))$ communication, if the probability of making an error is $\delta > 0$. If $m_{<i}^A$ dictates that Alice was supposed to send the ith bit, then Bob sets $m_i^B = m_i^A$ and recomputes the rest of m^B using $\rho_{i+1}, \ldots, \rho_C$. Otherwise Alice sets $m_i^A = m_i^B$ and recomputes m^A. They repeat this procedure until $m^A = m^B = m$.

The protocol is an internal simulation of π. By the union bound, the simulation error is at most $C\delta = \epsilon/2$. The length of the simulation is at most $O(\log(C/\epsilon))$ times the number of times the parties need to correct their guesses. It remains to bound the number of corrections from above.

We say that the protocol made a *mistake* at i if during its execution m_i^A was found to be not equal to m_i^B. This happens exactly when ρ_i lies in between the numbers $\gamma^A(m_{<i})$ and $\gamma^B(m_{<i})$. When this happens, $m_{<i}$ is distributed exactly as in π. So, the probability that there is a mistake at i is at most

$$\underset{p(xym)}{\mathbb{E}} \left[|\gamma^A(m_{<i}) - \gamma^B(m_{<i})| \right]$$

$$= \underset{p(xym)}{\mathbb{E}} \left[|p(m_i = 1|xm_{<i}) - p(m_i = 1|ym_{<i})| \right].$$

For each fixing of $m_{<i}$, if the ith message is supposed to be sent by Alice, then

$$\underset{p(xy|m_{<i})}{\mathbb{E}} \left[|p(m_i = 1|xm_{<i}) - p(m_i = 1|ym_{<i})|\right]$$

$$= \underset{p(xy|m_{<i})}{\mathbb{E}} \left[|p(m_i = 1|xym_{<i}) - p(m_i = 1|ym_{<i})|\right]$$

$$\leq \sqrt{\mathsf{I}(X : M_i|Ym_{<i})}. \qquad \text{by Corollary 6.14.}$$

If the ith bit was to be sent by Bob, then we have

$$\underset{p(xy|m_{<i})}{\mathbb{E}} \left[|p(m_i = 1|xm_{<i}) - p(m_i = 1|ym_{<i})|\right]$$

$$= \underset{p(xy|m_{<i})}{\mathbb{E}} \left[|p(m_i = 1|xm_{<i}) - p(m_i = 1|xym_{<i})|\right]$$

$$\leq \sqrt{\mathsf{I}(Y : M_i|Xm_{<i})}.$$

In either case, by convexity, the expected number of mistakes is at most

$$\sum_{i=1}^{C} \sqrt{\mathsf{I}(X : M_i|YM_{<i}) + \mathsf{I}(Y : M_i|XM_{<i})}$$

$$\leq \sqrt{C} \cdot \sqrt{\sum_{i=1}^{C} \mathsf{I}(X : M_i|YM_{<i}) + \mathsf{I}(Y : M_i|XM_{<i})} \qquad \text{by the Cauchy-Schwartz inequality.}$$

$$= \sqrt{C} \cdot \sqrt{\mathsf{I}(X : M|Y) + \mathsf{I}(Y : M|X)} = \sqrt{IC}. \qquad \text{by the chain rule.}$$

The expected length of the protocol is at most $O(\sqrt{IC}\log(C/\epsilon))$. By Markov's inequality, the probability that the length exceeds $2/\epsilon$ times this number is at most $\epsilon/2$, as claimed. □

Direct Sums in Randomized Communication Complexity

DIRECT SUM IS ABOUT relating the complexity of solving several problems to the complexity of each individual problem. In Chapter 1, we proved a direct sum theorem for deterministic communication complexity (Theorem 1.39). Compression is deeply connected to direct sum results for randomized communication complexity. The results about compression we have seen so far allow us to prove the following direct sum theorem.[7]

[7] Barak et al., 2010; and Braverman et al., 2013.

Theorem 7.15 *If the randomized communication complexity of g is c, then the randomized communication complexity of g^k is at least $\Omega(c\sqrt{k}/\log c)$.*

The idea is that a protocol for g^k of length ℓ can be interpreted as a protocol for g with information $I \leq \ell/k$. The intuition is that the information contained in the ℓ bits of the protocol are distributed over the k copies of g, giving ℓ/k bits of information for an average copy of g. We can now compress it to a protocol for a single copy of g of length $\approx \sqrt{I\ell} = \ell/\sqrt{k}$. This implies that $\ell/\sqrt{k} \gtrsim c$.

Proof Suppose there is a randomized protocol computing g^k in the worst-case, with ℓ bits of communication and success probability at least $3/4$.

By the minimax principle, Theorem 3.3, there is a distribution μ on inputs to g such that every deterministic protocol that computes g with less than c bits of communication has error more than $1/3$ over inputs from μ.

By feeding into the protocol inputs from μ^k and fixing the randomness, we get a deterministic protocol π computing g^k with error less than $1/4$ on inputs from μ^k.

Consider the following protocol for computing g on inputs from the distribution μ. Alice and Bob get inputs (X', Y') sampled from μ. The public randomness R consists of three parts:

1. A uniformly distributed $J \in [k]$.
2. A collection of $J - 1$ independent variables $X_{<J}$ distributed according to μ^{J-1}.
3. A collection of $n - J$ independent variables $Y_{>J}$ distributed according to μ^{n-J}.

Alice privately samples $X_{>J}$ conditioned on $Y_{>J}$, and Bob privately samples $Y_{<J}$ conditioned on $X_{<J}$, according to the conditional marginal distributions of μ. Finally, they set $(X_J, Y_J) = (X', Y')$. The parties now run the protocol π on the inputs $X = (X_1, \ldots, X_k)$ and $Y = (Y_1, \ldots, Y_k)$ they thus generated.

A crucial observation is that the inputs X, Y the parties generated in the above protocol are distributed according to μ^k. Let M denote the messages of this protocol when the inputs are sampled as above. By Lemma 6.20, we have

$$\sum_{i=1}^{k} I(X_i : M | X_{<i} Y_{\geq i}) \leq I(X : M | Y) \leq \ell$$

and

$$\sum_{i=1}^{k} I(Y_i : M | X_{\leq i} Y_{>i}) \leq I(Y : M | X) \leq \ell.$$

This means that the internal information cost of the protocol is

$$
\begin{aligned}
& I(X' : M | Y' R) + I(Y' : M | X' R) \\
&= I(X' : M | Y' J X_{<J} Y_{>J}) + I(Y' : M | X' J X_{<J} Y_{>J}) \\
&= \sum_{j=1}^{k} \frac{1}{k} \left(I(X_j : M | X_{<j} Y_{\geq j}) + I(Y_j : M | X_{\leq j} Y_{>j}) \right) \leq \frac{2\ell}{k}.
\end{aligned}
$$

Recall that we can reduce the error by repetition.

The length of this protocol is ℓ. Hence, by Theorem 7.13, the protocol can be simulated with error $\frac{1}{20}$ and communication

$$L = O(\sqrt{\ell \cdot \ell/k} \log \ell) = O(\ell \sqrt{1/k} \log \ell).$$

We get a protocol for computing a single copy of g with error less than $\frac{1}{4} + \frac{1}{20} < \frac{1}{3}$ and length L. Because $L \geq c$, we get that

$$\ell \geq \Omega(c\sqrt{k}/\log c).$$

□

Other Methods to Compress Protocols

COMPRESSION OF COMMUNICATION PROTOCOLS is a relatively new line of research that is still evolving. For this reason and for the clarity of exposition, we have not included all known compression-related results in this chapter. We conclude this chapter with a survey of these results.

The first result we state is an external compression:[8]

[8] Barak et al., 2010.

Theorem 7.16 *For every $\epsilon > 0$, one can simulate any protocol with external information I and length C by a protocol of length $O\left(\frac{I \log C}{\epsilon^2}\right)$. This simulation is external and has error ϵ.*

For product distributions, the external and internal informations are equal.

Later on, this compression was improved to be independent of the communication length, for the special case of product distributions:[9]

Theorem 7.17 *For every $\epsilon > 0$, one can simulate any protocol with internal information I by a protocol of length $O\left(\frac{I}{\epsilon} \log^2 \frac{I}{\epsilon}\right)$ when the inputs X, Y are independent. This simulation is external and has error ϵ.*

[9] Kol, 2016; and Sherstov, 2016.

For general compression, the following result gives a bound that is independent of the communication of the initial protocol:[10]

[10] Braverman, 2015.

Theorem 7.18 *For every $\epsilon > 0$, one can simulate any protocol with internal information I by a protocol of length $2^{O(I/\epsilon)}$. This simulation is internal and has error ϵ.*

If we measure the information learned by Alice as $I_A = I(Y : M|XR)$, and by Bob as $I_B = I(X : M|YR)$, then one can compress the protocol to take advantage of a large asymmetry between these quantities:

Theorem 7.19 *If Alice learns information I_A and Bob learns information I_B, then the protocol can be simulated by a protocol of communication $I_A \cdot 2^{O(I_B)}$. If the total communication of the original protocol is C, one can carry out the simulation using communication proportional to $I_A + C^{3/4} I_B^{1/4} \log C + \sqrt{C^{1/2} \cdot I_B^{1/2}}$. These simulations are internal and have error $\frac{1}{3}$.*

When the protocols have only public-randomness, we have seen an optimal external compression. In this case, a different internal compression is known:[11]

[11] Bauer et al., 2015.

Theorem 7.20 *For every $\epsilon > 0$, one can simulate any protocol with no private randomness, internal information I, and length C by a protocol of length $O\left(\frac{I^2}{\epsilon^2}\log\frac{\log C}{\epsilon}\right)$. This simulation is internal and has error ϵ.*

[12] Barak et al., 2010; Pankratov, 2012; and Brody et al., 2016.

A simulation of length $O\left(\frac{I}{\epsilon}\log(C/\epsilon)\right)$ is also known in this case.[12]

In the other direction, we also know some impossibility results regarding the compressibility of protocols. The following theorem shows the limitations of internal compression:[13]

[13] Rao and Sinha, 2015; and Ganor et al., 2016.

Theorem 7.21 *For every $k > 0$, there is a protocol π and a distribution on inputs μ such that the internal information of the protocol is $O(k)$, yet every protocol simulating π on the same distribution of inputs with error at most $1/3$ must have communication $2^{\Omega(k)}$.*

[14] Braverman, 2015; and Ganor et al., 2016.

The following theorem shows limitations of external compression:[14]

Theorem 7.22 *For every $k > 0$, there is a protocol π and an input distribution μ such that the external information of the protocol is $O(k)$, yet every simulation of the protocol with error $1/3$ must have communication at least $2^{\Omega(k)}$.*

Exercises

Ex 7.1 – In the correlated sampling, Lemma 7.5, show that $\Pr[M^A \neq M^B]$ must be at least $|p - q|$.

Ex 7.2 – In correlated sampling, Lemma 7.5, show that the expected values of I and J are proportional to the size of the universe.

Ex 7.3 – Let X, Y be jointly distributed in $\{0, 1\}^n$ as follows. Let $I \in [n]$ be uniform, and let (X, Y) be uniform conditioned on $X_{<I} = Y_{<I}$ and $X_I \neq Y_I$.

1. Compute $I(X : Y)$.
2. Show that if the parties have shared randomness, Alice gets X as input, Bob gets Y as input, and Alice sends a message M to Bob in a way that allows Bob to deduce the value of X from M, Y then the expected length of M is at least $n/2 - O(1)$.
3. Deduce Corollary 7.7 does not hold without the logarithmic term.[15]

[15] Braverman and Garg, 2014.

Ex 7.4 – Let X be a random variable taking values in the positive integers. Let $E = \mathbb{E}[\log X]$. Prove that $\mathsf{H}(X) \leq E + \log E + O(1)$. Deduce that the constant 2 in Corollary 7.7 can be replaced by a 1.[16]

[16] Braverman and Garg, 2014.

Ex 7.5 – In the sense of Claim 7.8, show that there is no encoding of the positive integers so that each integer z is encoded with $\log(z) + \log\log(z) + 10$ bits.

Ex 7.6 – In Theorem 7.10, suppose the parties are promised that $D(p\|q) \le 2$. Show that the parties cannot hope to sample from p *without error* while communicating a constant number of bits in expectation. *Hint: Consider the problem where Alice and Bob have inputs $X, Y \in \{0,1\}^n$ that are equal with high probability, and Alice wants to send X to Bob using a randomized protocol.*

Ex 7.7 – Let X, Y be jointly distributed random variables. Show that there is a random variables Z so that

- Z is independent of (X, Y).
- Conditioned on $Z = z$, the variables Y becomes a deterministic function of X.
- $H(Y|Z) \le I(X : Y) + 2 \log I(X : Y) + O(1)$.

Ex 7.8 – Consider the compression in Theorem 7.13. Show that if the protocol π is deterministic then the simulating protocol has length at most $O(I \log C)$ for error $\frac{1}{3}$.

8

Lifting

[1] Raz and McKenzie, 1997.

LIFTING IS A TECHNIQUE THAT GIVES LOWER BOUNDS on general models by reduction to lower bounds on restricted models.[1] This is counterintuitive – general models can simulate restricted models, so lower bounds for general models should imply lower bounds for restricted models, not the other way around. At a high level, lifting transforms an efficient algorithm in the general model into an efficient algorithm in the restricted model.

Lifting has led to some lower bounds that we do not know how to prove in any other way. One of the most prominent examples is the

[2] Göös et al., 2015; and Ambainis et al., 2016.

separation between communication complexity and partition numbers[2] we discussed in Chapter 1.

In this chapter, we describe the most basic lifting theorem.[3] We

[3] Raz and McKenzie, 1997; and Chattopadhyay et al., 2017.

show how to transform communication protocols into algorithms in a simpler model – *decision trees*. This allows to prove lower bounds on communication protocols by appealing to lower bounds on decision trees.

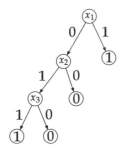

Figure 8.1 A decision tree computing $x_1 \vee (x_2 \wedge x_3)$.

Decision Trees

A DECISION TREE is an extremely simple model of computation. It captures the complexity of an algorithm that reads the input bit by bit. The only cost paid is the number of bits read by the algorithm.

Formally, a decision tree τ is encoded by a rooted binary tree, as in Figure 8.1. The leaves of the tree are labeled by values in $\{0, 1\}$. Every nonleaf vertex v has exactly two children, v_0, v_1, and is labeled by an element of $[n]$. Given an input $z \in \{0, 1\}^n$, the decision tree is executed by starting at the root of the tree. At each nonleaf vertex v labeled i, the algorithm probes z_i. If $z_i = 0$, the algorithm moves to v_0, and otherwise it moves to v_1. The computation halts when the algorithm reaches a leaf, which is labeled by the output of the computation. Each input $z \in \{0, 1\}^n$ defines a path from the root to a leaf. The output $\tau(z)$ is the label of that leaf.

The cost of the tree is its depth. The *decision tree complexity* of a function $f : \{0,1\}^n \to \{0,1\}$ is the minimum depth of a decision tree computing f.

Fact 8.1 *The decision tree complexity of* $f : \{0,1\}^n \to \{0,1\}$ *is at most n.*

Proving lower bounds on decision tree complexity is often easy. Our goal is to deduce communication complexity lower bounds from decision tree lower bounds. In other words, we want to transform an efficient communication protocol into an efficient decision tree. While this cannot be done in general, it does work for functions that have a certain structure.

Suppose $z = (x, y)$. Can you show that a decision tree of depth d for $f(z)$ leads to a two-party communication protocol of length d computing f?

The proof of the fact is left as Exercise 8.1.

See the exercises for examples of functions for which one can easily prove lower bounds.

The Lifting Theorem

A LIFTING THEOREM IN OUR SETTING uses lower bounds for decision trees to obtain lower bounds in communication complexity. We shall show how any function $f : \{0,1\}^n \to \{0,1\}$ with large decision tree complexity can be transformed into a related function F with high communication complexity.

The transformation uses the inner-product function IP of two d-bit vectors, as defined in Chapter 1. Let $x, y \in (\{0,1\}^d)^n$. For $i \in [n]$, let $x_i \in \{0,1\}^d$ be the ith part of the input x. For any $f : \{0,1\}^n \to \{0,1\}$, define

$$F(x, y) = f(\mathsf{IP}(x_1, y_1), \ldots, \mathsf{IP}(x_n, y_n)).$$

The main result of this chapter is:[4]

Theorem 8.2 *Suppose* $n \geq 10$ *and* $d > 7 \log n$. *Then the deterministic communication complexity of* F *is equal, up to constant factors, to* d *times the decision tree complexity of* f.

[4] Raz and McKenzie, 1997; and Chattopadhyay et al., 2017.

The theorem describes an equivalence between the communication complexity of F and the decision tree complexity of f. There are two directions to the equivalence. The easy direction is to show that the communication complexity of F is at most $O(d)$ times the decision tree complexity of f. This is a simple exercise. The hard direction is that the decision tree complexity of f is at most $O(\frac{1}{d})$ times the communication complexity of F. The rest of this chapter is devoted to proving the hard direction.

Here we used IP as a *gadget* to obtain F from f. Many other gadgets can be used, but for concreteness, we focus on IP in this chapter.

Say we are given a deterministic protocol π computing F of length ℓ. We need to use π to come up with a decision tree τ computing f whose depth is $O(\ell/d)$. The computation of F involves a conversation between Alice and Bob, whereas in the computation of f there is a single party, call him Charlie. Charlie needs to be able to use the protocol π to compute f. The solution, in a nutshell, is that on input z, Charlie attempts to simulate a legal conversation for F that is consistent with z.

We start with an informal description of Charlie's algorithm. Initially, Charlie knows nothing about z and sets R to be the space of all possible inputs x, y to F. He chooses the first message of the conversation to be the bit that is more likely to be sent given the current set of inputs R. This choice restricts his options for x, y to a new set R. Now, there are two cases to consider. If for each $j \in [n]$, there are many available options for x_j, y_j, Charlie continues to *simulate* the protocol without making a query. Namely, he chooses the next message in the conversation to be the most likely bit. Otherwise, if for some $j \in [n]$, the number of options for x_j, y_j has become too few, he queries z_j. Charlie now needs to adjust R so that it remains consistent with z_j; he makes sure that $\mathsf{IP}(x_j, y_j) = z_j$ for all potential inputs.

Eventually, Charlie queries some coordinates of z and computes a leaf v of the protocol tree with the following property. For every z that is consistent with the queries that Charlie made, there are inputs x, y to F that are consistent with both z and v – for every $j \in [n]$, we have $z_j = \mathsf{IP}(x_j, y_j)$, and (x, y) belongs to the rectangle defined by v. If these conditions are met, Charlie can safely output the value determined by v in the communication protocol.

Charlie moves down the protocol tree in a way that is consistent with z. To ensure that Charlie has enough freedom to find x, y that are consistent with v and all the possible values for z, he exploits a key property of IP – it admits a family of pseudorandom monochromatic rectangles. We start by discussing this property.

For ease of the exposition, we assume that d is even, though the same ideas hold for odd d. Let M be an invertible $d \times d$ matrix over $\mathbb{F}_2$. Let A_M be the subspace spanned by the first $\frac{d}{2}$ rows of M, and let B_M be the subspace spanned by the last $\frac{d}{2}$ columns of M^{-1}. Let R_M^0 be the rectangle $A_M \times B_M$. It is easy to check that R_M^0 is 0-monochromatic

To see, for example, that R_M^0 is 0-monochromatic, observe that for any (x, y) in R_M^0,

$$\mathsf{IP}(x, y) = a^\top M M^{-1} b$$
$$= a^\top b = 0,$$

where a is nonzero only in the first half of its coordinates, and b is nonzero only in the second half.

for IP. Similarly, if we define A_M to be the affine subspace obtained by adding the first row of M to the span of the next $\frac{d}{2} - 1$ rows of M, and B_M to be the affine subspace obtained by adding the first column of M^{-1} to the span of the last $\frac{d}{2} - 1$ columns, then the rectangle $R_B^1 = A_M \times B_M$ is 1-monochromatic.

Not only are these rectangles monochromatic, but they are also sufficiently pseudorandom that a random rectangle of this form is quite likely to intersect an arbitrary large rectangle. This is captured by the following lemma:

Lemma 8.3 *Let $b \in \{0, 1\}$. For arbitrary sets $U, V \subseteq \{0, 1\}^d$, each of size at least 2,*

$$\Pr_M[R_M^b \cap (U \times V) = \varnothing] \le 2\left(\frac{2^{d/2}}{|U|} + \frac{2^{d/2}}{|V|}\right),$$

where M is chosen uniformly at random from the set of invertible matrices.

Intuitively, a random subspace of dimension $d/2$ behaves like a random set of size $2^{d/2}$. The expected size of $A_M \cap U$ is therefore $\approx |U| 2^{-d/2}$. So if U has much more than $2^{d/2}$ points, then we expect to see many points in the intersection. We defer the proof of this lemma and move on to describing Charlie's algorithm.

The function F was defined by composing f with n copies of the gadget IP. We could, more generally, use some other gadget

$$g : \{0,1\}^d \times \{0,1\}^d \to \{0,1\}$$

and consider the function

$$F(x,y) = f(g(x_1,y_1), \ldots, \\ g(x_n, y_n)).$$

The Algorithm

Throughout the algorithm, Charlie maintains three pieces of information: (i) a vertex v in the protocol tree, (ii) a set of $S \subseteq [n]$ of the coordinates in z that have not yet been queried, and (iii) a rectangle $R = A \times B \subseteq (\{0,1\}^d)^n \times (\{0,1\}^d)^n$. Charlie maintains the invariant that every $(x,y) \in R$ is consistent with the bits of z that have been queried by the algorithm, as well as the vertex v of the protocol tree. Namely, if z_j has been queried, then $\mathsf{IP}(x_j, y_j) = z_j$ for all $(x,y) \in R$.

In what follows, the notation $A\!\downarrow_S$ is the projection of the elements in A to the coordinates in S. We write $R\!\downarrow_S$ to denote $A\!\downarrow_S \times B\!\downarrow_S$. For a vertex u of the protocol tree, recall that R_u is the rectangle that corresponds to u. For ease of notation, we write $S - j$ to denote the set $S \setminus \{j\}$.

Initially, v is the root of the tree, $S = [n]$, and $A = B = (\{0,1\}^d)^n$. The algorithm terminates as soon as S becomes empty, or v becomes a leaf of the protocol tree. Charlie repeats the following steps until the algorithm terminates. It may be helpful to keep Figure 8.2 in mind. For ease of notation, let $D = 2^{d/7}$.

What are the properties of g that make lifting work? The key property we need is analogous to Lemma 8.3. Namely, g should admit a set of monochromatic rectangles that *hit* every large rectangle in the space. The monochromatic rectangles of g should be both large and well-distributed in the space. In other words, g must be simultaneously *structured* and *pseudorandom*. Interestingly, a random function g would not be structured enough to allow us to analyze lifting. In a random function, the sizes of the monochromatic rectangles are too small for the hitting property to hold.

1. If for every $j \in S$,

$$\frac{|A\!\downarrow_S|}{|A\!\downarrow_{S-j}|} \geq D^6 \quad \text{and} \quad \frac{|B\!\downarrow_S|}{|B\!\downarrow_{S-j}|} \geq D^6, \tag{8.1}$$

then Charlie *simulates* the protocol.

Simulate: Let u_0, u_1 be the two children of v in the protocol tree. Charlie picks $b \in \{0,1\}$ to maximize $|(R \cap R_{u_b})\!\downarrow_S|$. He updates $R = R \cap R_{u_b}$ and $v = u_b$.

2. If (8.1) does not hold, then Charlie checks whether for all $j \in S$, all $a \in A\!\downarrow_{S-j}$ and $b \in B\!\downarrow_{S-j}$,

Intuitively, $|A\!\downarrow_S|/|A\!\downarrow_{S-j}|$ is a measure of the number of choices available in the jth coordinate once all other coordinates are fixed.

$$|\{x \in A\!\downarrow_S : x\!\downarrow_{S-j} = a\}| \geq D^4 \tag{8.2}$$

and

$$|\{y \in B\!\downarrow_S : y\!\downarrow_{S-j} = b\}| \geq D^4. \tag{8.3}$$

If one of these two conditions does not hold, then Charlie *prunes* the rectangle.

If the ratios in (8.1) are small, the intuition is that the protocol has learned $\Omega(d)$ bits of information about the coordinate j, so Charlie needs to query z_j before he loses the freedom to set x_j, y_j.

Prune: If (8.2) does not hold because of j, a, then Charlie deletes all the elements $x \in A$ with $x \downharpoonright_{S-j} = a$. If (8.3) does not hold because of j, b, then Charlie deletes all the elements $y \in B$ with $y \downharpoonright_{S-j} = b$. He keeps deleting elements in this way until (8.2) and (8.3) hold. He updates R to be the resulting rectangle.

3. If (8.1) does not hold because of some coordinate $j \in S$, but (8.2) and (8.3) hold, then Charlie makes a *query*.

Query: Charlie queries z_j and updates R as follows. For each invertible matrix M as in Lemma 8.3, define

$$R_M = \{(x, y) \in R : (x_j, y_j) \in R_M^{z_j}\}.$$

Charlie picks M to maximize $|R_M \downharpoonright_{S-j}|$ and updates $R = R_M$ and $S = S - j$.

When the algorithm stops, either every coordinate of z has been queried, in which case Charlie outputs $f(z)$, or v is a leaf of the protocol tree, in which case Charlie outputs the label of v.

The Analysis

We now analyze the number of queries Charlie makes and prove that he outputs the correct value. We start with the following observation:

Observation 8.4 *A prune step can only occur immediately after a simulate step.*

If S, P, Q denote *simulate, prune,* and *query* then a sequence of steps might contain $SSPQQSPQSPSP$, but we can never see QP or PP.

Proof Once Charlie prunes the rectangle, (8.2) and (8.3) hold, so he does not prune in the next step. Moreover, if his next step is to query, then (8.2) and (8.3) hold even after the query step because the query step only fixes some information in a coordinate that is removed from S, and after the pruning step both (8.2) and (8.3) hold for all $j \in S$. □

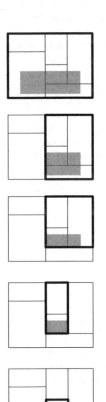

Figure 8.2 The evolution of R_v and R during the algorithm.

To analyze the algorithm, we place a bound on the size of the rectangle after each step. The evolution of the algorithm is shown in Figure 8.2.

Lemma 8.5 *In each of the steps of the algorithm, let R, S denote the rectangle and set of unqueried variables at the beginning of the step, and R', S' denote the rectangle and set of variables at the end of the step. Then, $|R' \downharpoonright_{S'}| \geq |R \downharpoonright_{S'}|/2$.*

Proof Whenever Charlie simulates the protocol, by the choice of b, we have

$$|(R \cap R_{u_b}) \mathord{\downharpoonright}_S| \geq |R \mathord{\downharpoonright}_S|/2.$$

Whenever Charlie prunes the rectangle, he must have done a simulate step just before (in a simulate step, one of $A\mathord{\downharpoonright}_S, B\mathord{\downharpoonright}_S$ does not change). So, in this case we must have

$$\frac{|A\mathord{\downharpoonright}_S|}{|A\mathord{\downharpoonright}_{S-j}|} \geq D^6/2 \quad \text{and} \quad \frac{|B\mathord{\downharpoonright}_S|}{|B\mathord{\downharpoonright}_{S-j}|} \geq D^6/2,$$

because the simulate step can decrease these ratios by at most $1/2$. Thus, the number of elements that were pruned from $A\mathord{\downharpoonright}_S$ is at most

$$\sum_{j \in S} |A\mathord{\downharpoonright}_{S-j}| \cdot D^4 \leq n \cdot |A\mathord{\downharpoonright}_S| \cdot 2/D^2 \leq |A\mathord{\downharpoonright}_S|/8,$$

because $D \geq n$ are large. Similarly, at most $1/8$ fraction of $B\mathord{\downharpoonright}_S$ is pruned. Thus, the density of $R\mathord{\downharpoonright}_S$ decreases by a factor of at most 2 because $(1 - 1/8)^2 \geq 1/2$.

When Charlie decides to query, (8.2) and (8.3) must hold. Fix any $(a, b) \in R\mathord{\downharpoonright}_{S-j}$, and let

$$U = \{x \in A\mathord{\downharpoonright}_S : x\mathord{\downharpoonright}_{S-j} = a\} \quad \text{and} \quad V = \{y \in B\mathord{\downharpoonright}_S : y\mathord{\downharpoonright}_{S-j} = b\}.$$

By Lemma 8.3, the probability that $R_M^{z_j}$ intersects $U \times V$ is at least

$$1 - 2\Big(\frac{2^{d/2}}{|U|} + \frac{2^{d/2}}{|V|}\Big) \geq 1 - 2^{d/2+2}/D^4 \geq 1/2. \qquad \text{because } 2^d = D^7.$$

So, by linearity of expectation, there is a choice for M ensuring that $|R_M\mathord{\downharpoonright}_{S-j}| \geq |R\mathord{\downharpoonright}_{S-j}|/2$. □

Now, let us use Lemma 8.5 to prove that the algorithm makes at most $O(\ell/d)$ queries.

Claim 8.6 *Charlie makes at most $50\ell/d$ queries.*

Proof Consider the following density:

$$\frac{|R\mathord{\downharpoonright}_S|}{2^{2d|S|}}.$$

This is the density of the projection of the rectangle in the underlying space, so it can never be larger than 1. Whenever Charlie queries j, we have

by Lemma 8.5.

because (8.1) does not hold for j, and because, for example, $|A \rfloor_S| \leq 2^d |A \rfloor_{S-j}|$.

$$
\begin{aligned}
\frac{|R_M \rfloor_{S-j}|}{2^{2d(|S|-1)}} &\geq \frac{|R \rfloor_{S-j}|}{2^{2d(|S|-1)+1}} \\
&= \frac{|A \rfloor_{S-j}| \cdot |B \rfloor_{S-j}|}{2^{2d(|S|-1)+1}} \\
&> \frac{|A \rfloor_S| \cdot |B \rfloor_S|}{D^6 \cdot 2^d \cdot 2^{2d(|S|-1)+1}} \\
&= \frac{D}{2} \cdot \frac{|R \rfloor_S|}{2^{2d|S|}}
\end{aligned}
$$

So, the density increases by a factor of at least $D/2$ in a query step. There can be at most 2ℓ nonquery steps before the algorithm terminates – there can be at most ℓ simulate steps and so at most ℓ prune steps by Observation 8.4. Each of these steps decreases the density by at most a factor of 2, by Lemma 8.5. So, if there are q query steps then

$$
2^{q(d/7-1)} \cdot 2^{-2\ell} = (D/2)^q \cdot 2^{-2\ell} \leq 1.
$$

$\square$

Next, we argue that the protocol computes the correct value.

Claim 8.7 *Charlie correctly computes $f(z)$.*

Proof By the choice of R throughout the protocol, all the inputs in R are always consistent with v. Moreover, whenever Charlie queries z_j, he restricts R to ensure that $z_j = \mathsf{IP}(x_j, y_j)$ for all $(x, y) \in R$. So, we only need to worry about the coordinates $j \notin S$ when the protocol terminates.

To reason about these coordinates, let us do a thought experiment. Let π' be the communication protocol where Alice and Bob first run π and then send each other x, y. Imagine that Charlie continues simulating the steps of π' after π has terminated. By the time this second simulation ends, he must query all of the coordinates in z because (8.1) does not hold when R is of size 1. When Charlie stops simulating π', he ends with some nonempty rectangle R' such that $z_j = \mathsf{IP}(x_j, y_j)$ for all choices of $j \in [n]$. This R' is contained in the R that Charlie ended with when simulating π. So, the original rectangle contains inputs x, y that are consistent with both z and v. Because π computes F, Charlie computes f. $\square$

Monochromatic Rectangles for Inner-Product

It only remains to prove the relevant pseudorandom property of IP.

Proof of Lemma 8.3 We focus on the case $b = 0$, a similar argument works when $b = 1$. Let $R_M^0 = A_M \times B_M$. We shall prove that the probability that A_M is disjoint from U is at most $2^{1+d/2}/|U|$. The same argument applies to bound the probability that B_M is disjoint from V. The proof is then completed by the union bound.

We may assume that $0 \notin U$ because otherwise $A_M \cap U$ is always non-empty. When $b = 1$, this case distinction is not important. Let W be the number of elements in $A_M \cap U$. The variable W can be expressed as the sum of $|U|$ indicator random variables, $W = \sum_{u \in U} W_u$, where $W_u = 1$ if and only if A_M contains u. Symmetry implies that for each u in U, we have $\Pr[W_u = 1] = (2^{d/2} - 1)/(2^d - 1)$. Similarly, for $u \neq u'$ in U, we have $\Pr[W_u = W_{u'} = 1] = \binom{2^{d/2}-1}{2}/\binom{2^d-1}{2}$. The covariance of W_u and $W_{u'}$ is, therefore,

The number of nonzero elements in a subspace of dimension $d/2$ is $2^{d/2} - 1$, while the number of nonzero elements in $\{0, 1\}^d$ is $2^d - 1$.

$$\mathbb{E}\left[W_u W_{u'}\right] - \mathbb{E}\left[W_u\right] \mathbb{E}\left[W_{u'}\right] \leq 0.$$

It follows that the variance of W is at most

$$\mathbb{E}\left[W^2\right] - \mathbb{E}\left[W\right]^2 \leq \mathbb{E}\left[\sum_{u \in U} W_u^2 - \mathbb{E}\left[W_u\right]^2\right] \leq \mathbb{E}\left[W\right].$$

By Chebyshev's inequality,

$$\Pr[A_M \cap U = \emptyset] \leq \Pr[|W - \mathbb{E}\left[W\right]| \geq \mathbb{E}\left[W\right]]$$

$$\leq \frac{1}{\mathbb{E}[W]} = \frac{2^d - 1}{2^{d/2} - 1} \frac{1}{|U|} \leq \frac{2^{d/2}}{|U|}. \qquad \square$$

Separating Rank and Communication

EQUIPPED WITH THE LIFTING THEOREM, we can prove lower bounds on the communication complexity of composed functions. As we mentioned earlier, this is the only way we know how to give tight separations between the logarithm of the partition number and communication complexity.

Recall that in Chapter 1, we used the probabilistic method to show that k-disjointness, with $k = O(\log n)$, admits a monochromatic cover of size $2^{O(\log n)}$, even though its communication complexity is $\Omega(\log^2 n)$. However, this cover is not a partition.

Here we describe a function with communication complexity c, yet its 1s admit a partition of size $\approx 2^{\sqrt{c}}$ into monochromatic rectangles. This means that the rank of the function is at most $\approx 2^{\sqrt{c}}$ as well. It follows that Conjecture 2.16 cannot hold with an exponent that is less than 2.

The lower bound on communication complexity is proved by lifting. Lifting allow us to move from communication complexity to decision tree complexity. To understand decision tree complexity, we use the concept of *certificates*. Certificates are to decision trees what monochromatic rectangles are to communication protocols.

Given a Boolean function $f : \{0, 1\}^n \to \{0, 1\}$, a set $S \subseteq [n]$ and $a \in \{0, 1\}^S$, the pair (S, a) is called a *certificate* if $f(x) = f(y)$ for all x, y and S with $x \restriction_S = y \restriction_S = a$. The length of the certificate is $|S|$. A collection of certificates is said to *certify* f if every element of $\{0, 1\}^n$ is consistent with at least one certificate in the collection. The collection is said to be *unambiguous* if each input is consistent with at most one certificate.

Here $x_i, y_i \in \{0,1\}^d$ for all i.

Unambiguous certificates that certify f correspond to a monochromatic partition into rectangles, as Lemma 8.8 shows. To lift f, define:

$$F(x, y) = f(\mathsf{IP}(x_1, y_1), \ldots, \mathsf{IP}(x_n, y_n)).$$

Lemma 8.8 *If f can be certified with k certificates, each of length at most ℓ, then F has a monochromatic cover with $k \cdot 2^{2d\ell}$ rectangles. Moreover, if the certificates are unambiguous, then the rectangles are disjoint.*

Proof For each certificate (S, a), and each $(x, y) \in (\{0,1\}^d)^S \times (\{0,1\}^d)^S$ satisfying $\mathsf{IP}(x_j, y_j) = a_j$ for all $j \in S$, define the rectangle

$$R_{S,a,x,y} = \{(x', y') : x'\lvert_S = x, y'\lvert_S = y\}.$$

By definition, these rectangles are monochromatic, and there are at most $k2^{2d\ell}$ of them. If the certificates are unambiguous, then the rectangles are disjoint. □

Lemma 8.8 establishes an upper bound on the size of the cover, and Theorem 8.2 establishes the lower bound on communication complexity.

We see that separating the cover numbers and communication complexity of F boils down to a similar separation between the certificate complexity and decision tree complexity of f.

Now, let us build a function that exhibits a strong separation between certificate complexity and decision tree complexity. As usual, disjointness has something to say here. Let $X_1, \ldots, X_m \subseteq [m]$ be m sets, and let $X = (X_1, \ldots, X_m)$. Define $\mathsf{Disj}(X)$ to be 1 if and only if the intersection $X_1 \cap \cdots \cap X_m$ is empty.

One can think of the sets X as given by an $m \times m$ Boolean matrix whose rows are the indicator vectors of the sets.

Lemma 8.9 $\mathsf{Disj}(X)$ *can be certified with $m^m + m$ certificates of length m.*

The certificates either reveal an all 1s column of the matrix, or reveal a 0 entry from each of the columns.

Proof To account for all the inputs that intersect, it is enough to have a certificate certifying that there is an element $i \in X_1 \cap \cdots \cap X_m$. This can be done with a certificate of length m, and there are m such certificates. Inputs that are disjoint can be certified by revealing a bit to show that each $i \in [m]$ does not belong to one of the sets. This requires a certificate of length m, and there are m^m such certificates. □

See Exercise 8.5.

On the other hand, $\mathsf{Disj}(X)$ has decision tree depth at least $m^2 - m$. So, if $f(X) = \mathsf{Disj}(X)$, and $d = O(\log m^2)$, we get that F admits a monochromatic cover of size $2^{O(m \log m)}$, yet the communication complexity of F is at least $\Omega(m^2)$. This gives another nearly quadratic separation between the logarithm of the cover numbers, $O(m \log m)$, and communication complexity, $\Omega(m^2)$.

The certificates in the lemma, however, are not unambiguous. Let us try to fix that. We present an example that admits unambiguous certificates just for the inputs evaluating to 1. To this end, it will be helpful to consider non-Boolean functions. Define $I : \{0,1\}^{m \times m} \to [m+1]$ by setting $I(X)$ to be the smallest index $i \in [m]$ that belongs to all sets

$X_1, \ldots, X_m$. If the sets are disjoint, let $I(X) = m + 1$. So, $\text{Disj}(X) = 1$ if and only if $I(X) = m + 1$.

Lemma 8.10 *The function I defined above can be certified with at most m^{m+1} certificates of length at most $2m$.*

Proof To certify that $I = i$, for each $j < i$, the certificate reveals a bit to establish that j does not belong to one of the sets, as well as m bits to establish that i is in all sets. □

Next, we define a function that requires that its inputs themselves specify a certificate! Let $y = (y_1, y_2, \ldots, y_m) \in [m]^m$, and $X = (X_1, \ldots, X_m) \in \{0, 1\}^{m \times m}$. Define a Boolean function $f(X, y)$ as follows. Intuitively, we require that y_i encodes a certificate that $I(X) = i$. Formally, set $f(X, y) = 1$ if and only if $j \notin X_{y_{I(X)},j}$ for all $j < I(X)$. The following two lemmas summarize the key properties of f.

This is the so-called cheat-sheet method.

Lemma 8.11 *The function f can be certified using m^{2m+1} certificates of length $2m + m \log m$. Moreover, all the 1 inputs are certified unambiguously.*

Lemma 8.12 *The decision tree complexity of f is $\Omega(m^2)$.*

We are ready for the final conclusion:

The proofs of the lemmas are left to Exercises 8.6 and 8.7.

Theorem 8.13 *The rank of the communication matrix of F is at most $2^{O(m \log m)}$, while its communication complexity is at least $\Omega(m^2 \log m)$.*

In fact, the nonnegative rank of F is at most $2^{O(m \log m)}$, proving that Theorem 2.14 is nearly tight.

Proof Setting $d = O(\log m)$, Theorem 8.2 and Lemma 8.12 imply the lower bound on the communication complexity. To prove the upper bound on rank, use Lemmas 8.8 and 8.11, together with the observation that the rank is at most the size of the smallest collection of disjoint 1-rectangles covering the inputs evaluating to 1. □

Exercises

Ex 8.1 – Prove Fact 8.1.

Ex 8.2 – Show that the function $z_1 + z_2 + \cdots + z_n \mod 2$ has decision tree complexity n.

Ex 8.3 – Show that there is a decision tree with $O(n)$ vertices that computes a function $f : \{0, 1\}^n \to \{0, 1\}$, so that the decision tree complexity of f is n. Conclude that decision trees cannot be balanced.

Ex 8.4 – This exercise describes the pseudorandom property of the indexing function that is useful for lifting. Let $\text{IND} : [d] \times \{0, 1\}^d$ be the indexing function, defined by $\text{IND}(i, y) = y_i$. Show that there is a constant $1 > \epsilon > 0$ such that for every $b \in \{0, 1\}$, there is a distribution on b-monochromatic rectangles

$R_b \subseteq [d] \times \{0, 1\}^d$, such that for every $U \subseteq [d]$ and $V \subseteq \{0, 1\}^d$ with $|U| \geq d^{1-\epsilon}$ and $|V| \geq 2^d/d^\epsilon$,

$$\Pr[R_b \cap (U \times V) \neq \emptyset] \geq 1/2.$$

Ex 8.5 – Prove that $\mathrm{Disj}(X_1, \ldots, X_n)$ requires decision trees of depth $n^2 - n$.

Ex 8.6 – Prove Lemma 8.11.

Ex 8.7 – Prove Lemma 8.12.

Part II

Applications

9

Circuits and Proofs

ALTHOUGH COMMUNICATION COMPLEXITY ostensibly studies the amount of communication needed between parties that are far apart, it is deeply involved in our understanding of many other concrete computational models and discrete systems. In this chapter, we discuss applications of communication complexity to Boolean circuits and proof systems.

Boolean Circuits

BOOLEAN CIRCUITS ARE THE MOST NATURAL model for computing Boolean functions. A *Boolean circuit* is a directed acyclic graph whose vertices, often called *gates*, are associated with either Boolean operators or input variables. Every gate with in-degree 0 corresponds to an input variable, the negation of an input variable, or a constant bit. All other gates compute either the logical AND (denoted by the symbol ∧) or the OR (denoted by the symbol ∨) of the inputs that feed into them. Usually, the fan-in of the gates is restricted to being 2. We adopt this convention, unless we explicitly state otherwise. See Figure 9.1 for an illustration.

Every gate v in a circuit naturally computes a Boolean function f_v of the inputs to the circuit. We say that a circuit computes a function f if $f = f_v$ for some gate v in it.

Every circuit is associated with two standard complexity measures. The *size* of the circuit is the number of gates. It corresponds to the number of operations the circuit performs. The *depth* of the circuit is the length of the longest directed path in the underlying graph. The depth corresponds to the parallel time it takes the computation to end, using many processors.

We thus get a measure of computational complexity – circuits have costs and functions have complexities. Every Boolean function f can be computed by a Boolean circuit. The circuit complexity of f is the size of the smallest circuit that computes it. Understanding the circuit complexity of interesting functions is a fundamental problem in computer science.

Boolean circuits can efficiently simulate algorithms. Any function that can be computed by an algorithm in $T(n)$ steps can also be

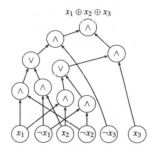

Figure 9.1 A circuit computing the parity $x_1 \oplus x_2 \oplus x_3$. This circuit has size 15 and depth 4.

One may consider circuits where every gate has fan-in 2 and computes an arbitrary function of its inputs. This only changes the size and depth of the circuit by a constant factor.

computed by circuits of size approximately $T(n)$. So, to prove lower bounds on time complexity, it suffices to prove that there are no small circuits that can carry out the computation.

For example, a super-polynomial lower bound on the circuit size of an NP problem would imply that P ≠ NP, resolving the most important open problem in computer science.

Every Boolean function $f : \{0, 1\}^n \rightarrow \{0, 1\}$ can be computed by a circuit[1] of depth n and size at most $O(2^n/n)$. Counting arguments imply that almost every function requires circuits of exponential size.[2] However, we do not know of any emphexplicit function for which we can prove even a super-linear lower bound.

We do not yet understand in circuit complexity is the power of depth:

[1] Lupanov, 1958.

[2] Shannon, 1949.

Open Problem 9.1 *Can every function that is computable using circuits of size polynomial in n be computed by circuits of depth $O(\log n)$?*

The number of circuits of size s is at most $2^{O(s \log s)}$. The number of functions f is 2^{2^n}. So, if $s \ll 2^n/n$, one cannot hope to compute every function with a circuit of size s.

We now describe a general connection between circuit complexity and communication complexity. We focus on two restricted families of circuits. A *formula* is a circuit whose underlying graph is a tree. Equivalently, the fan-out of every gate is 1. Every circuit of depth d can always be turned into a formula whose size is at most 2^d, and depth is at most d. A *monotone* circuit is a circuit that does not use negated variables. A monotone circuit computes a *monotone* function; $f(y) \geq f(x)$ whenever $y_i \geq x_i$ for all i.

Counting arguments imply that there is a constant ϵ such that the set of functions computable by size $s \log s$ circuits is strictly larger than the set of functions computable by size ϵs circuits. Similarly, counting arguments show that circuits of depth d compute a bigger set of functions than those computable in depth ϵd.

Karchmer-Wigderson Games

EVERY BOOLEAN FUNCTION defines a communication problem via its *Karchmer-Wigderson* game.[3] In the game defined by the function $f : \{0, 1\}^n \rightarrow \{0, 1\}$, Alice gets $x \in f^{-1}(0)$, Bob gets $y \in f^{-1}(1)$, and they seek to find $i \in [n]$ such that $x_i \neq y_i$. When f is monotone, we define the *monotone* Karchmer-Wigderson game as follows: Alice and Bob want to find an index i such that $x_i < y_i$.

Several restricted classes of circuits are not discussed in this book. We focus on methods related to communication complexity.

The basic observation is that circuit-depth is equivalent to communication complexity, as the following two lemmas show.

[3] Karchmer and Wigderson, 1990.

Lemma 9.2 *A circuit of depth d computing f yields a length d deterministic protocol for the associated game. If the circuit is monotone, the protocol solves the monotone game.*

In the Karchmer-Wigderson game, Alice and Bob are computing a relation rather than a function – there may be many indices i with the property they seek.

Proof The construction of the protocol is by induction on the depth of the circuit. If the top gate in the circuit is an AND gate ($f = g \wedge h$), then either $g(x) = 0$ or $h(x) = 0$, while $g(y) = h(y) = 1$. Alice can announce whether $g(x)$ or $h(x)$ is 0, and the parties can continue the protocol using g or h. Similarly if $f = g \vee h$, Bob can announce whether $g(y) = 1$ or $h(y) = 1$, and the parties then continue with either g or h. If f is the negation of g, then the parties can continue the protocol using g, without communicating at all. If f is the ith input variable, the parties identify an index i for which $x_i \neq y_i$.

When the circuit is monotone, the same simulation finds an index i such that $x_i = 0$ and $y_i = 1$ because there are no negated variables.

The topology of the circuit determines the topology of the protocol tree. Every AND gate corresponds to a node in the protocol tree where Alice speaks, every OR gate corresponds to a node where Bob speaks, and every input gate corresponds to a leaf in the protocol tree. Thus, a circuit of depth d gives a protocol of length at most d. □

Lemma 9.3 *If the Karchmer-Wigderson game for a function f can be solved with d bits of communication, then there is a circuit of depth d computing f. If f is monotone, and the monotone game can be solved with d bits of communication, then there is a monotone circuit of depth d computing f.*

If the function is constant, the Karchmer-Wigderson game is not well defined. The circuit-size is 1, and the depth is 0.

Proof We shall prove, by induction on d, that for any nonempty sets $A \subseteq f^{-1}(0)$ and $B \subseteq f^{-1}(1)$, the following holds. If there is a protocol such that whenever $x \in A$ is given to Alice and $y \in B$ is given to Bob, they can exchange d bits to find i such that $x_i \neq y_i$, then there is a circuit of depth d computing a Boolean function g with $g(A) = 0$ and $g(B) = 1$. When $A = f^{-1}(0)$ and $B = f^{-1}(1)$, this implies the lemma.

When $d = 0$, the protocol must have a fixed output i, and so we must have that $x_i \neq y_i$ for every $x \in A$ and $y \in B$. Thus, setting g to be the ith variable or its negation works.

Suppose $d > 0$ and Alice speaks first. Her message partitions the set A into two disjoint sets $A = A_0 \cup A_1$, where A_0 is the set of inputs that lead her to send 0 as the first message, and A_1 is the set of inputs that lead her to send 1. If one of A_0 or A_1 is empty, then we can ignore the first message, and the proof is complete. So, both A_0 and A_1 are nonempty. By induction, the two children of the root correspond to Boolean functions g_0 and g_1, with $g_0(A_0) = g_1(A_1) = 0$ and $g_0(B) = g_1(B) = 1$. Consider the circuit that takes the AND of the two gates obtained inductively and denotes the function it computes by g. For all $y \in B$, we have $g(y) = g_0(y) \wedge g_1(y) = 1$. For all $x \in A$, either $x \in A_0$ or $x \in A_1$. In either case $g(x) = g_0(x) \wedge g_1(x) = 0$. If the first bit of the protocol is sent by Bob, the proof is similar, except we take the OR of the gates obtained by induction.

If we are working with the monotone game, the resulting circuit is monotone. □

The Karchmer-Wigderson connection between circuit complexity and communication complexity is a powerful tool for proving lower bounds on circuit complexity.

Monotone Circuit-Depth Lower Bounds

A matching in a graph is a collection of disjoint edges. One of the most studied combinatorial problems is finding the largest matching in a graph. Today, we know of several efficient algorithms for solving this problem.[4]

[4] Kleinberg and Tardos, 2006.

We focus on the following decision problem. Given a graph G on n vertices, define

$$\text{Match}(G) = \begin{cases} 1 & \text{if } G \text{ has a matching of size at least } n/3 + 1, \\ 0 & \text{otherwise.} \end{cases}$$

Because there are polynomial time algorithms for finding matchings, one can obtain polynomial sized circuits that compute Match. However, we do not know of any logarithmic depth circuits that compute Match. Here we show that there are no monotone circuits of depth $o(n)$ computing Match.[5]

[5] Raz and Wigderson, 1992.

Match is a monotone function.

Theorem 9.4 *Every monotone circuit computing* Match *has depth* $\Omega(n)$.

By Lemma 9.3, it is enough to prove a lower bound on the communication complexity of the corresponding monotone Karchmer-Wigderson game. In the monotone matching game, Alice gets a graph G with $\text{Match}(G) = 1$ and Bob gets a graph H with $\text{Match}(H) = 0$. Their goal is to find an edge that is in G, but not in H.

Theorem 9.5 *Any randomized protocol solving the matching game must communicate* $\Omega(n)$ *bits.*

Proof The theorem is proved by reduction to the disjointness lower bound proved in Theorem 6.19. We shall show that if there is a protocol for the monotone matching game with length c, then there is a randomized protocol with length $O(c)$ solving the disjointness problem on a universe of size $m = \Omega(n)$. By Theorem 6.19, this implies that $c \geq \Omega(n)$.

Suppose Alice and Bob get inputs $X \subseteq [m]$ and $Y \subseteq [m]$. They encode X and Y as two graphs G_X and H_Y on the vertex set $[3m + 2]$. They use public randomness to permute the vertices of the graphs and feed them into the protocol for the monotone matching game. Figure 9.2 shows an example for G_X and H_Y. These graphs are constructed as follows:

Alice builds G_X: For each $i \in [m]$, the graph G_X contains the edge $\{3i, 3i - 1\}$ if $i \in X$ and has the edge $\{3i, 3i - 2\}$ if $i \notin X$. In addition, G_X contains the edge $\{3m + 1, 3m + 2\}$.

The construction ensures that G_X contains a matching of size $m + 1$.

Bob builds H_Y: For each $i \in [m]$, if $i \in Y$ then Bob connects $3i - 2$ to *all* the other $3m + 1$ vertices of the graph, and if $i \notin Y$ then Bob connects $3i$ to all the other vertices.

By construction, there are m vertices so that every edge of H_Y touches one of these vertices (the gray vertices in Figure 9.2). So, H_Y does not contain a matching of size $m + 1$.

If X and Y are disjoint, the outcome of the protocol must be the edge corresponding to $\{3m + 1, 3m + 2\}$. On the other hand, if X and Y intersect in $k > 0$ elements, then there are exactly $k + 1$ edges in G_X that are not in H_Y.

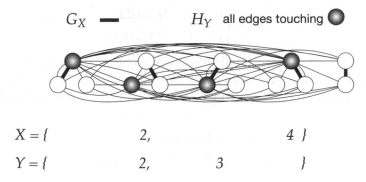

Figure 9.2 A schematic description of G_X and H_Y.

Because the graph is permuted uniformly at random before the protocol is executed, and the protocol for the game does not know the permutation, the outcome of the protocol is equally likely to be one of these $k + 1$ edges. Indeed, let e and e' be two of these $k + 1$ edges, and let σ be a permutation of the vertices such that σ maps the edge e to the edge e'. For every permutation τ, if the protocol outputs the edge $\tau(e)$ when it samples τ, then it outputs $\tau(e')$ when it samples $\tau \circ \sigma$.

When the sets are disjoint, the protocol outputs the edge corresponding to $\{3m + 1, 3m + 2\}$. When the sets are not disjoint, the output corresponds to $\{3m + 1, 3m + 2\}$ with probability at most $1/2$. Repeating this experiment a constant number of times, the parties are able to solve disjointness with probability of error at most $1/3$. $\qquad\square$

Monotone Circuit-Depth Hierarchy

BOOLEAN CIRCUITS CAN BE GRADED by their depth. It is natural to conjecture that for constant k, circuits of depth $k + 1$ are strictly more powerful than circuits of depth k. Communication complexity allows us to prove this in the monotone setting.

Let $F = F_{n,k}$ be the full AND-OR formula with fan-in n and depth k. All noninput gates in F have fan-in exactly n. The gates of odd depth are OR gates, and the gates of even depth are AND gates. Every input gate is labeled by a distinct unnegated variable. The size of F is $O(n^k)$.

We prove that any monotone circuit of smaller depth computing F must have exponential size.

Theorem 9.6 *Any monotone circuit of depth $k - 1$ that computes F must have size at least $2^{\Omega(n/k)}$.*

Proof Assume that there is a monotone circuit of size s and depth $k - 1$ computing F. The circuit yields a protocol for the monotone Karchmer-Wigderson game with $k - 1$ rounds and length at most $O(k \log s)$.

It thus suffices to prove that the monotone game requires communication at least $n/16 - k$. We prove this by reduction to the pointer-chasing problem, that we studied in Chapter 6. In pointer-chasing, Alice and Bob are given $x, y \in [n]^n$ and want to compute $z = z(k)$, where $z(0) = 1$, and $z(1), z(2), \ldots$ are inductively defined using the rule

Throughout this section, we work with circuits of arbitrarily large fan-in.

We do not know how to prove a similar statement for general circuits.

We think of F both as a formula and as a function.

$$z(i) = \begin{cases} x_{z(i-1)} & \text{if } i \text{ is odd,} \\ y_{z(i-1)} & \text{if } i \text{ is even.} \end{cases}$$

Given inputs x, y to the pointer-chasing problem, the inputs x', y' in $\{0, 1\}^{[n]^k}$ to F are constructed as follows. Every variable in the formula can be described by a string in $v \in [n]^k$. We say that v is consistent with x if

$$v_i = \begin{cases} x_1 & \text{when } i = 1, \\ x_{v_{i-1}} & \text{when } i \text{ is odd and not } 1. \end{cases}$$

We say that v is consistent with y if $v_i = y_{v_{i-1}}$ when i is even. Alice sets all the coordinates of x' that are consistent with her input to be 0, and all other coordinates to be 1. Bob sets all the coordinates of y' that are consistent with his input to be 1, and all other coordinates to be 0.

We now prove that $F(x') = 0$ and $F(y') = 1$. We focus on $F(x')$; a similar argument works for $F(y')$. Every a gate of depth d in the formula corresponds to a vector in $[n]^d$. We claim that every gate that corresponds to a vector that is consistent with x evaluates to 0 on x'. This is true for the input gates at depth k because that is how we set the variables in x'. For gates at depth $d < k$, if the gate is an AND gate then one of its children is consistent with x and so evaluate to 0, and if the gate is an OR gate then all of its children are consistent with x and so evaluate to 0.

For every x, y, there is a unique input gate v that is consistent with both x and y. This gate is the output $v = z(k)$ of the pointer-chasing problem. The only place where x' is 0 and y' is 1 is the vth entry.

Any protocol for the monotone Karchmer-Wigderson game, therefore, gives a protocol solving the pointer-chasing problem. By Theorem 6.18, the communication of the game must be at least $n/16 - k$. $\square$

Boolean Formulas

FORMULAS CORRESPOND TO COMPUTATIONS that use each sub-computation exactly once. One immediate consequence of the Karchmer-Wigderson connection is a sharp lower bound on the formula-size of parity. In Chapter 1, we proved that solving the Karchmer-Wigderson games for parity requires at least $2 \log n - O(1)$ bits of communication. This shows that its circuit-depth is at least $2 \log n - O(1)$. The formula complexity of parity is therefore $\Theta(n^2)$.

A similar lower bound holds for the circuit-depth of majority. See Exercise 1.4.

For example, parity has linear-size formulas using $\oplus$ gates, but requires quadratic-size formulas using AND, OR and NOT gates.

When it comes to formulas, the choice of basis can affect the formula size by more than a constant factor. Nevertheless, one can prove super-linear lower bounds even when allowing each gate to compute an arbitrary function of two bits.

Consider the function Distinct : $[2n]^{n+1} \to \{0, 1\}$, defined as

$$\text{Distinct}(x_1, \ldots, x_{n+1}) = \begin{cases} 1 & \text{if } x_1, \ldots, x_{n+1} \text{ are distinct,} \\ 0 & \text{else.} \end{cases}$$

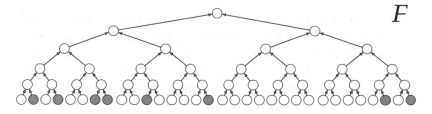

F

Figure 9.3 A formula F and the tree T_i that corresponds to the input gates of x_i. Shaded input gates correspond to x_i.

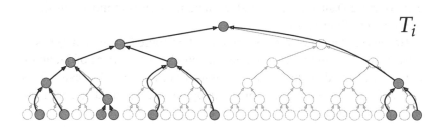

T_i

Distinct is a Boolean function that depends on $O(n \log(n))$ bits. We shall prove:[6]

[6] Neciporuk, 1966; and Klauck, 2007.

Theorem 9.7 *Any formula computing* Distinct *must have at least* $n^2 - O(n \log n)$ *input gates.*

We start by proving a simple communication complexity lower bound. Suppose Alice is given n numbers $y_1, \ldots, y_n \in [2n]$, and Bob is given $z \in [2n]$. They want to compute $\text{Distinct}(y_1, \ldots, y_n, z)$.

Lemma 9.8 *If there is a 1-round protocol where Alice sends Bob t bits and Bob outputs* $\text{Distinct}(y_1, \ldots, y_n, z)$, *then* $t \geq \log \binom{2n}{n} \geq 2n - O(\log n)$.

Proof It is enough to consider the case when $y_1, \ldots, y_n$ are distinct elements. In this case, Alice's message must determine $S = \{y_1, \ldots, y_n\}$, or else Bob will not be able to compute Distinct. This is because if $S \neq S'$ are two sets of size n that are consistent with Alice's message, then there must be $z \in S$ such that $z \notin S'$. The element z is distinct from S', but not from S.

The number of bits transmitted by Alice must, therefore, be at least $\log \binom{2n}{n} \geq 2n - O(\log n)$. ☐

We are ready to prove the formula lower bound:

Proof of Theorem 9.7 Suppose there is a formula F computing Distinct using s gates. Each input gate in the formula reads a bit of one of the numbers x_i. For each $i \in [n+1]$ we define the tree T_i as follows (see Figure 9.3). Every vertex of T_i corresponds to a gate in F. Start by discarding all the gates in F that do not depend on x_i. In the graph that remains, iteratively replace every gate that has only one input feeding into it with an edge connecting its input to its output.

Now, suppose Alice knows all of the input numbers except x_i, Bob knows x_i, and Alice and Bob want to compute $\text{Distinct}(x_1, \ldots, x_{n+1})$.

The middle binomial coefficient is maximal, so $\binom{2n}{n} \geq \frac{2^{2n}}{n+1}$. A more accurate bound using Stirling's approximation gives $\binom{2n}{n} = \Theta(\frac{2^{2n}}{\sqrt{n}})$.

They can use the tree T_i to carry out the computation efficiently. Bob already knows the values at the leaves of T_i. Every gate v in T_i computes a Boolean function f_v, which depends on gates in T_i and some number of Alice's inputs. There are $2^{2^2} = 2^4$ Boolean functions that depend on two variables, so Alice can send 4 bits to Bob to indicate which of these functions he should use to compute $f_v(x_1, \ldots, x_{n+1})$ using the two inputs that correspond to gates of T_i. Using this information, Bob can compute Distinct. The overall communication is at most four times the number of vertices in T_i.

Because F has only s gates, there must be some i for which T_i has at most $\ell = s/n$ leaves. If m denotes the number of vertices of T_i, and e the number of edges in T_i, then we must have $e = m - 1$ because T_i is a tree. Counting the number of edges by adding up the degrees of the vertices, we have

$$2(m - 1) = 2e \geq 3(m - \ell - 1) + \ell.$$

So, $m \leq 2\ell + 1 \leq 2s/n + 1$.

By Lemma 9.8, we get $2s/n + 1 \geq 2n - O(\log n)$, proving the theorem. □

Formulas with Arbitrary Gates

Communication complexity allows us to prove nontrivial lower bounds even when gates are allowed to compute arbitrary functions of a linear number of variables.[7] Suppose we want to express a function $f : \{0, 1\}^n \to \{0, 1\}$ as

$$f = g(g_1, \ldots, g_k),$$

where each of the functions $g_1, \ldots, g_k$ depends on at most $2n/3$ input bits. What is the minimum k required?

We can represent Distinct in this form with $k = O(\log n)$.[8] Nevertheless, the closely related scrambled distinctness function requires $k \geq n^{\Omega(1)}$. Assume n is a power of 2. For a subset S of $[n \log(2n)]$ of size $\log(2n)$, and $b \in \{0, 1\}^{n \log(2n)}$, define SDistinct$(S, b)$ as follows. Use the coordinates of S in b to define a number $z \in [2n]$. Use the remaining bits of b to define $y_1, \ldots, y_{n-1} \subseteq [2n]$. Output Distinct$(y_1, \ldots, y_{n-1}, z)$.

Theorem 9.9 SDistinct(S, b) requires $k \geq n^{\Omega(1)}$.

Proof As in the formula lower bound, we shall appeal to Lemma 9.8. Suppose we can write SDistinct as $g(g_1, \ldots, g_k)$, where each of the gates g_i depends on at most $2/3$rds of the input variables.

We claim that if k is small, there must be some S for which every gate g_i reads at most $\frac{4}{5} \log(2n)$ of inputs that correspond to S. Indeed, suppose we pick the elements of S independently and uniformly at random. For each $i \in [k]$, the expected number of coordinates of S read by g_i is at most $\frac{2}{3} \log(2n)$. By the Chernoff-Hoeffding bound, the probability that more than $\frac{4}{5} \log(2n)$ of the coordinates are read in g_i is at most $e^{-\Omega(\log(2n))} = n^{-\gamma}$, for some constant $\gamma > 0$. The probability that the $\log(2n)$ coordinates sampled are not all distinct is at most $\log^2(2n)/n$.

[7] Hrubes and Rao, 2015.

Counting arguments show that most functions f require $k = \Omega(n)$.

[8] To see this, let $S_1, \ldots, S_k \subset [n]$ be sets of size $n/2$ so that that for every $i, j \in [n]$, there is some set of the sequence that contains both i, j. One can show that a random choice of $O(\log n)$ sets satisfies this property with positive probability. Use these sets to construct a formula. For each i, let g_i be the function that reads the numbers x_ℓ for $\ell \in S_i$, and outputs 1 if and only if these numbers are distinct. Let g be the OR function.

It remains an open problem to find an explicit function for which $k = \Omega(n)$.

The input to SDistinct can be encoded using $n \log(2n) + \log^2 n$ bits.

Overall, if $k < n^\gamma/2$, then $k \cdot n^{-\gamma} + \log^2(2n)/n < 1$, and there is a set S satisfying the properties we want.

Given such a set S, Alice and Bob can use the circuit to obtain a protocol solving the distinctness problem. Bob sets the coordinates of b in S according to his input, and Alice sets the remaining coordinates according to her input. Each gate g_i depends on at most $\frac{4}{5}\log(2n)$ of Bob's bits. There are $2^{O(n^{4/5})}$ Boolean functions that depend on $\frac{4}{5}\log(2n)$ bits, so Alice can send Bob $k \cdot O(n^{4/5})$ bits to describe the function Bob should evaluate to compute each g_i.

Finally, by Lemma 9.8, we must have that

$$k \geq \Omega(\min\{n^\gamma, n^{1/5}\}).$$

$\square$

Boolean Depth Conjecture

CAN WE EFFICIENTLY balance circuits? Can every polynomial sized circuit be simulated by a circuit of logarithmic depth? Recall that we showed how to balance a protocol tree in Chapter 1.

See Exercise 9.3.

This seemingly simple problem remains open, despite much effort to resolve it. Here we discuss an approach[9] for proving a negative answer. The approach is based on direct-sum in communication complexity. Its goal is to prove that there are functions that can be computed using polynomial sized circuits but *cannot* be computed by a circuit of logarithmic depth.

[9] Håstad and Wigderson, 1990; Karchmer et al., 1995; Edmonds et al., 2001; Gavinsky et al., 2014; and Dinur and Meir, 2016.

The idea is to start with a function $f : \{0,1\}^t \to \{0,1\}$ that requires circuits of depth $\Omega(t)$. A random function requires such depth with high probability. The function we are interested in is obtained from f by composition. Given functions $h : \{0,1\}^t \to \{0,1\}$ and $g : \{0,1\}^k \to \{0,1\}$, define their composition $h \circ g : \{0,1\}^{tk} \to \{0,1\}$ by

$$h \circ g(x_1, \ldots, x_t) = h(g(x_1), \ldots, g(x_t)),$$

where each x_i is a k-bit string. Define $f^{\circ t}$ as the t-fold composition of f with itself. The function $f^{\circ t}$ can be computed naively by a circuit of size $O(n^2)$. Indeed, f can be computed using a circuit of size $O(2^t)$. To compute $f^{\circ t}$ we need to evaluate f at most $O(t^t)$ times. We obtain a circuit computing $f^{\circ t}$ with $O(t^t \cdot 2^t) \leq O(n^2)$ gates.

It is natural to conjecture that this naive circuit has essentially smallest possible depth. Namely, that the depth complexity of $f^{\circ t}$ is at least $\Omega(t^2)$. This is much larger than $O(\log n)$.

If there is a function f as above for which for all $k < t$, the circuit-depth of $f \circ f^{\circ k-1}$ must be at least ϵt more than the circuit depth of $f^{\circ k-1}$, then the circuit-depth of $f^{\circ t}$ is at least $\epsilon t^2 \gg t \log t = \log n$. In other words, if there is such an f, then there is a Boolean function depending on n variables that can be computed using $O(n^2)$ gates, but cannot be computed with a circuit of depth $O(\log n)$.

In terms of communication complexity, all that is needed is an example of a function f for which the communication complexity of the

Karchmer-Wigderson game of f^{ok} is at least ϵt larger than the communication complexity of the game of $f^{o(k-1)}$. This looks quite similar to understanding the direct-sum question in communication that we studied in Chapters 1 and 7. The ideas we discussed there, unfortunately, do not seem to apply in this situation.

Proof Systems

PROOF SYSTEMS PROVIDE A FORMAL FRAMEWORK for proving theorems and for studying the complexity of proofs. A proof system is a specific language for expressing proofs. It consists of a set of rules that allow one to logically derive theorems from axioms. The study of proof systems has led to many interesting results, including Gödel's famous incompleteness theorem.[10]

[10] Gödel, 1931.

Resolution Refutations

[11] Robinson, 1965.

Some terminology: A literal is a variable or its negation. A clause is an expression of the form $C = \bigvee_j \ell_j$ where each ℓ_j is a literal. We assume that each variable occurs at most once in a clause. A CNF formula is an expression of the form $F = C_1 \wedge C_2 \wedge \ldots \wedge C_m$ where C_i is a clause.

THE SIMPLEST proof system is *resolution*.[11] It allows us to refute Boolean formulas expressed in conjunctive normal form (CNF). A proof in resolution shows that a CNF formula cannot possibly be satisfied.

Let us start with an example. Consider the formula

$$F = (x_2 \vee x_1) \wedge (\neg x_2 \vee x_1) \wedge (\neg x_1 \vee x_3 \vee \neg x_4)$$

$$\wedge (\neg x_1 \vee x_3 \vee x_4) \wedge (\neg x_1 \vee \neg x_3).$$

The formula F cannot be satisfied by any Boolean assignment. To prove that the formula is unsatisfiable, we repeatedly use the *resolution* rule. The rule derives a clause that must be true if two other clauses are both true:

$$\left. \begin{array}{c} a \vee B \\ \neg a \vee C \end{array} \right\} \Rightarrow B \vee C,$$

where a is a variable, B, C are clauses and $B \vee C$ is the derived clause obtained by including all the literals in B and C. This rule is *sound*. Namely, if both $a \vee B$ and $\neg a \vee C$ are true then at least one of B or C must be true. The resolution refutation shown in Figure 9.4 repeatedly applies this rule to prove that F cannot be satisfied.

A *resolution refutation* is a sequence of clauses. The sequence starts with the clauses of the CNF formula. Each new clause is derived from two previously derived clauses using the resolution rule. The proof ends when the empty clause is derived. The empty clause represents a contradiction.

One can think of a resolution refutation as a directed acyclic graph, like a circuit. The initial clauses correspond to input gates, and the intermediate clauses obtained from the resolution rule correspond to the

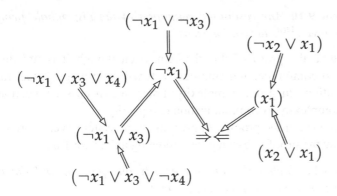

Figure 9.4 A refutation of F. In each step, two clauses are combined to give a new clause that must be true. The final step produces an empty clause, which represents a contradiction.

noninput gates. A refutation is said to be *tree-like* if every derived clause is used only once. Tree-like proofs are the analog of Boolean formulas in proof complexity.

The problem of understanding whether a Boolean formula is satisfiable is a central problem because of its connection[12] to the complexity classes NP and coNP. The best solvers known today try to find satisfying assignments while simultaneously trying to refute formulas obtained after partial assignments. It is important, therefore, to classify the kinds of formulas can be efficiently refuted.

To study the power of a given proof system, like resolution, we need to a family of formulas of growing complexity. A basic example of such a sequence is the pigeonhole principle.

[12] Wikipedia, 2016b.

P = coNP if and only if there is a proof system in which every unsatisfiable Boolean formula can be refuted in a polynomial number of steps.

The Pigeonhole Principle

The pigeonhole principle states that if n pigeons are placed in $n - 1$ holes, then some hole must contain at least two pigeons. One can use the principle to construct a sequence of unsatisfiable Boolean formulas. For $i \in [n]$ and $j \in [n-1]$, we have the variable $x_{i,j}$ which indicates that the ith pigeon is in the jth hole. Define the following $n + 1$ formulas:

$$P_i = \bigvee_{j \in [n-1]} x_{i,j} \qquad \text{for all } i \in [n]$$

Pigeon i must be in some hole.

$$H = \bigwedge_{\substack{i < i' \in [n] \\ j \in [n-1]}} (\neg x_{i,j} \vee \neg x_{i',j}).$$

Each hole contains at most one pigeon.

The pigeonhole principle states that

$$P = H \wedge \bigwedge_i P_i$$

is not satisfiable.

How hard is it to prove that P is unsatisfiable? If one uses resolution, it is very hard.[13]

[13] Haken, 1985; and Beame and Pitassi, 1996.

The proof actually shows that an exponential number of steps are required in any proof system where each step derives a clause using *any* derivation rule from two clauses!

Theorem 9.10 *Any resolution refutation of the pigeonhole principle must involve $2^{\Omega(n)}$ derivation steps.*

We give the proof of this theorem, even though it is not directly related to communication complexity. It will help us get a feel for the basic notions in proof complexity. Later, we discuss connections of proof complexity to communication complexity.

A key idea in the proof is to give the proof system even more power. We allow the proof to assume the following axiom for free.

Axiom 9.11 *Each hole contains exactly one pigeon, and the $n - 1$ pigeons that are in the holes are distinct.*

H is implied by Axiom 9.11.

In other words, we only consider assignments to the variables that satisfy this axiom. Adding an axiom can only make it easier to derive a contradiction. Axiom 9.11 implies that for each i, j,

$$\neg x_{i,j} \Leftrightarrow \bigvee_{i' \neq i} x_{i',j}.$$

This allows us to replace every negated variable in the proof with a disjunction of unnegated variables.

It is no loss of generality to assume that 4 divides n. If this is not the case, replace n with a nearby multiple of 4. Consider any refutation of P that derives s clauses. Let C be one of the clauses derived in the proof. We say that C is *big* if there is a set $S \subset [n]$ of size $|S| \geq n/4$ such that for each $i \in S$ the number of j's so that C contains $x_{i,j}$ is at least $n/4$.

Let us see how a random assignment affects the refutation. Pick $n/4$ of the pigeons uniformly at random, and randomly assign them to $n/4$ different holes. If pigeon i is assigned to hole j in this process, then we set $x_{i,j} = 1$, we set $x_{i',j} = 0$ for all $i' \neq i$, and $x_{i,j'} = 0$ for all $j' \neq j$. This makes sure that the relevant pigeons and holes are not involved with any of the remaining holes and pigeons.

After this assignment to the variables, $n/4$ of the pigeon clauses become true. Moreover, several variables disappear, and the formula becomes equivalent to the corresponding formula for $3n/4$ pigeons and $3n/4 - 1$ holes. The resolution refutation must still derive a contradiction.

Claim 9.12 *One of the big clauses must survive the assignment.*

Proof Consider the refutation of P after the random assignment. Say that a clause has pigeon complexity w if there is a set $S \subset [n]$ of size w such that

The implication is allowed to use Axiom 9.11.

$$\bigwedge_{i \in S} P_i \Rightarrow C,$$

yet no smaller set S has this property.

The contradiction can only be derived from all $3n/4$ pigeon clauses that remain because one can satisfy any strict subset of those clauses with some assignment to the variables. So, the empty clause in the proof has pigeon complexity at least $3n/4$. Because the empty clause is derived from two clauses, one of the clauses used to derive the contradiction must have pigeon complexity at least $3n/8$. Continuing in this way, we obtain a sequence of clauses in the proof, where each clause requires at least half as many pigeon clauses as the previous one. Because the clauses of P have pigeon complexity at most 1, there must be a clause C in this sequence that has pigeon complexity at least $n/4$ and at most $n/2 - 1$.

Because n is a multiple of 4.

Let $S \subset [n]$ be the minimal set of pigeon clauses that imply C, and let $i \in S$. Because S is minimal, there must be an assignment x' to all the variables where $\bigwedge_{i' \in S-\{i\}} P_{i'}$ is true, yet C is false. This assignment places all of the pigeons of S into holes, except for the ith pigeon. Suppose j is a hole that did not receive a pigeon during the random assignment, and does not receive a pigeon from S in x'. We claim that C contains the variable $x_{i,j}$. By Axiom 9.11, every hole gets a pigeon in all the assignments under consideration. So, there is a pigeon $i_0 \notin S$ that gets mapped to hole j in this assignment—$x'_{i_0,j} = 1$. Consider what happens when we change the assignment by setting $x'_{i_0,j} = 0$ and $x'_{i,j} = 1$, and leave the rest of the variables as they are. Doing so *must* make C true because $\bigwedge_{i' \in S} P_{i'} = 1$ in the assignment. Because C is a disjunction of unnegated variables, this can only happen if C contains $x_{i,j}$.

We remove the pigeon i_0 from hole j and put i into hole j.

Thus, for each $i \in S$, there must be at least

$$n - 1 - n/4 - (n/2 - 1) - n/4$$

values of j for which $x_{i,j}$ is in the clause C. So, not only is C big, it is big even after the random assignment. □

Claim 9.13 *If a clause C is big, then the probability that C survives the random assignment is at most $\left(\frac{63}{64}\right)^{n/8}$.*

Proof Consider what happens when the first pigeon is assigned to a hole. The probability that the pigeon is one of the $n/4$ pigeons relevant to C is at least $1/4$. The probability that it is assigned to one of the $n/4$ holes that would imply C is at least $1/4$. So the probability that C becomes true after the first pigeon is assigned to a hole is at least $1/16$. Continuing in this way, we see that for each of the first $n/8$ pigeons that we assign to a hole in the random assignment, there are at least $n/4 - n/8 = n/8$ pigeons, which if assigned to $n/4 - n/8 = n/8$ holes would lead to the clause becoming true. Thus, the probability that C survives the first $n/8$ assignments of pigeons to holes is at most

$$\left(1 - \frac{(n/8) \cdot (n/8)}{n^2}\right)^{n/8} = \left(\frac{63}{64}\right)^{n/8}.$$

□

We are ready to prove the theorem:

Proof of Theorem 9.10 Suppose toward a contradiction that the refutation of P has less than $(64/63)^{n/8}$ clauses. By Claim 9.13, there is a partial assignment of the pigeons to holes such that every big clause does not survive. On the other hand, by Claim 9.12, at least one big clause must survive.   □

Cutting Planes

A STRONGER PROOF SYSTEM than resolution can be obtained by reasoning about linear inequalities. Clauses are converted into linear inequalities, and the rules allow to combine two linear inequalities to get a new one.

The proof system operates on linear inequalities of the form

$$\langle c, x \rangle \leq t$$

> The clause $a \vee \neg b \vee c$ can be viewed as asserting that the Boolean variables a, b, c satisfy the linear inequality
>
> $-a + b - c \leq 0.$

where x is an n-bit vector, c is an n-dimensional vector with integer coefficients, and t is a rational number. Because the variables are Boolean, we allow the proof to use the inequalities $x_i \leq 1$ and $-x_i \leq 0$ for free. There are two type of rules in the proof system. For any nonnegative rationals α, α', we can take a linear combination of two inequalities to derive

$$\left. \begin{array}{l} \langle c, x \rangle \leq t \\ \langle c', x \rangle \leq t' \end{array} \right\} \Rightarrow \langle \alpha c + \alpha' c', x \rangle \leq \alpha t + \alpha' t',$$

as long as $\alpha c + \alpha' c'$ is a vector of integers. We also allow the *rounding rule*:

$$\langle c, x \rangle \leq t \Rightarrow \langle c, x \rangle \leq \lfloor t \rfloor.$$

Namely, we can replace t with the largest integer that is at most t. This rule is sound because the left-hand side is always an integer.

> Cutting planes is complete in the sense that every collection of inequalities that has a solution over $\mathbb{R}^n$ but does not have a solution over $\mathbb{Z}^n$ can be refuted in it.

The proof system allows us to refute a collection of linear inequalities by deducing the contradiction $1 \leq 0$. Cutting planes can efficiently simulate resolution, line-by-line:

Lemma 9.14 *If a formula can be refuted in s steps using resolution, then it can be refuted in $O(ns)$ steps using cutting planes.*

We do not prove the lemma here, but provide an illustrative example. Consider the resolution derivation

$$\left. \begin{array}{l} \neg x \vee y \vee z \\ x \vee y \vee \neg w \end{array} \right\} \Rightarrow y \vee z \vee \neg w.$$

Viewing the clauses as inequalities, this corresponds to

$$\left. \begin{array}{l} x - y - z \leq 0 \\ -x - y + w \leq 0 \end{array} \right\} \Rightarrow -y - z + w \leq 0.$$

This derivation does not directly follow by taking linear combinations. If we add the first two inequalities, we get $-2y - z + w \leq 0$, which is not quite what we want. However, we can derive the inequality we seek using the rounding rule:

$$\left.\begin{array}{r} x - y - z \leq 0 \\ w \leq 1 \end{array}\right\} \Rightarrow x - y - z + w \leq 1,$$

$$\left.\begin{array}{r} -x - y + w \leq 0 \\ -z \leq 0 \end{array}\right\} \Rightarrow -x - y - z + w \leq 0,$$

$$\left.\begin{array}{r} \frac{1}{2} \cdot (x - y - z + w - 1 \leq 1) \\ \frac{1}{2} \cdot (-x - y - z + w \leq 0) \end{array}\right\} \Rightarrow -y - z + w \leq \lfloor 1/2 \rfloor = 0.$$

In fact, cutting planes is strictly stronger than resolution. For example, cutting planes allows us to refute the pigeonhole principle using just $O(n^2)$ steps.[14] Rewriting the clauses of the pigeonhole principle as linear inequalities, we get

[14] Cook et al., 1987; and Jukna, 2012.

$$P_i \equiv -\sum_{j=1}^{n-1} x_{i,j} \leq -1,$$

Pigeon i must be in some hole.

$$H_{i,i',j} \equiv x_{i,j} + x_{i',j} \leq 1.$$

Hole j cannot contain both i, i'.

We claim that for each j, we can derive the inequality

$$L_{k,j} \equiv \sum_{i-1}^{k} x_{i,j} \leq 1$$

in $O(k)$ steps. The inequality $L_{2,j}$ is $H_{1,2,j}$. To derive $L_{k,j}$ from previously derived inequalities, use the derivation rules $O(k)$ times to get

$$(k - 1) \cdot L_{k-1,j} + \sum_{i=1}^{k-1} H_{i,k,j}$$

$$\equiv k(x_{1,j} + x_{2,j} + \cdots + x_{k,j}) \leq 2k - 1.$$

Now, divide by k and round to get $L_{k,j}$. To complete the proof, observe

$$\sum_{j=1}^{n-1} L_{n,j} \equiv \sum_{j=1}^{n-1} \sum_{i=1}^{n} x_{i,j} \leq n - 1,$$

while

$$\sum_{i=1}^{n} P_i \equiv -\sum_{i=1}^{n} \sum_{j=1}^{n-1} x_{i,j} \leq -n.$$

Adding these last two inequalities gives $1 \leq 0$.

To summarize, cutting planes can efficiently prove the pigeonhole principle, although resolution cannot. Can we find a formula that is difficult to refute using cutting planes? Communication complexity provides such an example.

Lower Bounds on Cutting Planes

Here we give an example of an unsatisfiable formula that requires an exponential number of steps to refute in the cutting planes proof system. The formula is based on properties of graphs.

Given a graph, a *vertex cover* is a set of vertices U such that every edge of the graph contains at least one vertex from U. A *matching* is a set of disjoint edges. We design the formula to encode the fact that the size of every vertex cover must be larger than the size of every matching.

> Every edge in the matching must be covered by one vertex from any vertex cover, and the edges are disjoint.

We construct a formula that asserts that the input graph has a vertex cover of size $k - 1$, as well as a matching of size k. This ensures that the formula is unsatisfiable. For each possible edge $e = \{v, u\} \subset [n]$, we have the variable x_e which is 1 if and only if the edge e is present in the graph. For $i \in [k]$ and e, the variable $y_{i,e}$ encodes whether e is the ith edges in the matching. For $j \in [k-1]$ and a vertex $v \in [n]$, the variable $z_{j,v}$ encodes whether v is the jth vertex in a cover. Now, define the following formulas:

> Every edge is covered.

$$C = \bigwedge_{e \in \binom{[n]}{2}} \left(\neg x_e \vee \bigvee_{v \in e, j \in [k-1]} z_{j,v} \right),$$

> The jth vertex in the cover is unique.

$$C_j = \left(\bigvee_{v \in [n]} z_{j,v} \right) \wedge \bigwedge_{v \neq v' \in [n]} (\neg z_{j,v} \vee \neg z_{j,v'}) \quad \text{for all } j \in [k-1],$$

> Edges in matching are disjoint.

$$M = \bigwedge_{e, e' \in \binom{[n]}{2}:|e \cap e'|=1} \bigwedge_{i \neq i' \in [k]} (\neg y_{i,e} \vee \neg y_{i',e'}),$$

> The ith edge of the matching is a unique edge in the graph.

$$M_i = \left(\bigvee_{e \in \binom{[n]}{2}} y_{i,e} \right) \wedge \left(\bigwedge_{e \neq e' \in \binom{[n]}{2}} (\neg y_{i,e} \vee \neg y_{i,e'}) \right) \quad \text{for all } i \in [k],$$

> Edges in the matching are in the graph.

$$K = \bigwedge_{e \in \binom{[n]}{2}, i \in [k]} (x_e \vee \neg y_{i,e}).$$

Finally, define the formula:

$$F = C \wedge \left(\bigwedge_{j=1}^{k-1} C_j \right) \wedge \left(\bigwedge_{i=1}^{k} M_i \right) \wedge M \wedge K.$$

The formula F has at most $O(n^4)$ clauses. However, an exponential number of inequalities are needed to refute it, at least with a tree-like proof.[15]

[15] Impagliazzo et al., 1994; Krajíček, 1997; Pudlák, 1997; and Hrubeš, 2013.

Theorem 9.15 *Any tree-like cutting planes refutation of F with $n/4 \leq k \leq n/2$ must derive $2^{\Omega(n/\log n)}$ inequalities.*

The proof is by reduction to the communication complexity of the matching game, for which we already proved a lower bound in Theorem 9.5. In the matching game, Alice gets a graph G that has a matching of size $k \approx n/3$, and Bob gets a graph H that does not have a matching of size k. Their goal is to find an edge in G that is not in H.

Lemma 9.16 *If there is a tree-like cutting plane proof of size s refuting F, then there is a randomized protocol for the matching game with communication $O(\log(s)(\log(n) + \log\log(s)))$.*

By the lemma and Theorem 9.5,

$$\log(s)(\log(n) + \log\log(s)) \geq \Omega(n),$$

which proves Theorem 9.15.

The proof of the lemma shows how to efficiently convert a cutting planes refutation to a communication protocol. The proof extends to many other formulas that have similar structure. For simplicity, we limit the discussion to this particular formula.

Proof of Lemma 9.16 Alice sets the variables $y_{i,e}$ to be consistent with her matching, and Bob sets the variables $z_{j,v}$ and x_e to be consistent with the graph H. Under this setting of variables, all of the clauses in M_i, M, C_j, C are true, but one of the clauses in K must be false. This false clause specifies an edge that is in Alice's graph G but not in Bob's graph H. Our goal is to find this clause using the refutation of F.

By Lemma 1.8, the proof must derive an inequality L that depends on at most $2s/3$ of the clauses, and on at least $s/3$ of the clauses. Our aim is to check whether L is satisfied under the assignment to the variables described above. The inequality L can be written as

$$\kappa + \sum_{i,e} \alpha_{i,e} \cdot y_{i,e} \leq \sum_{j,v} \beta_{j,v} \cdot z_{j,v} + \sum_e \gamma_e \cdot x_e.$$

All of the variables on the left-hand side are known to Alice, and all the variables on the right-hand side are known to Bob. Because the variables are Boolean, there are at most 2^{n^3} possible values for the left-hand side, and at most 2^{2n^3} possible values for the right-hand side. Alice and Bob know L, so they also know all these $\leq 2^{1+2n^3}$ possible values. The parties can use the randomized protocol for solving the greater-than problem to compute whether or not this inequality is satisfied by their variables, as in Exercise 3.1. They expend $O(\log(n/\epsilon))$ bits of communication in order to make sure that output of their computation is correct with error ϵ.

If the inequality L is not satisfied, Alice and Bob can safely discard the clauses that are not used to derive L and continue to find a false clause. Otherwise, all of the clauses used to derive L can safely be discarded, and Alice and Bob can start their search again after discarding all the inequalities used to derive L. In either case, they discard at least $s/3$ clauses.

This process can repeat at most $O(\log s)$ times, so the probability that they make an error is at most $O(\epsilon \log s)$ by the union bound. Setting ϵ to be small enough so that this number is at most $1/3$, we obtain a protocol whose length is at most $O(\log(s)(\log n + \log \log s))$.   □

Exercises

Ex 9.1 – Prove that every circuit of size s can be simulated by a formula of size 2^s.

Ex 9.2 – We know that every function can be computed by a circuit of depth n, and that most functions require depth $\Omega(n)$. Show that there is a function that can be computed in depth $O(\sqrt{n})$, but cannot be computed in depth $O(n^{1/4})$.

Ex 9.3 – Show that any Boolean formula can be *balanced*. Prove that if a Boolean function can be computed by a formula of size s, then it can be computed using a formula of depth $O(\log s)$. *Hint: This is similar to how we balanced protocol trees in Chapter 1.*

Ex 9.4 – We showed that any formula that computes whether or not $x \in [2n]^n$ corresponds to n distinct numbers requires a formula of size $\Omega(n^2)$. This gives a Boolean function that depends on m bits but requires $\Omega(m^2 / \log^2 m)$ size formulas. Show how you can improve the lower bound to get a Boolean function depending on m bits that requires formulas of size $\Omega(m^2 / \log m)$. *Hint: Consider the element distinctness function with $x \in [n]^k$ for the appropriate n and k.*

Ex 9.5 – Suppose $\phi(x_1, \ldots, x_n, y_1, \ldots, y_n)$ is a Boolean formula in conjunctive normal form that is unsatisfiable. Suppose Alice and Bob are given $x, y \in \{0, 1\}^n$, respectively, and want to find a specific clause in ϕ that is not satisfied.

1. Show that if the formula has a resolution refutation of depth d, then Alice and Bob can find this clause with d bits of communication using a deterministic protocol.
2. Show that if the formula has a cutting-planes refutation of depth d, then Alice and Bob can find this clause with $d \log d$ bits of communication using a randomized protocol.

Ex 9.6 – In this exercise we give another lower bound for the cutting planes proof system. Consider the game where Alice is given a permutation $\pi : [n] \to [n]$, and Bob is given a subset $Y \subseteq [n]$, with the promise that $\pi(1) \in Y, \pi(n) \notin Y$. Their goal is to compute i such that $\pi(i) \in Y, \pi(i+1) \notin Y$. One can show that $\Omega(\log^2 n)$ communication is required.[16]

[16] Karchmer et al., 1995.

1. Give a protocol that solves the game with $O(\log^2 n)$ communication.
2. Consider the monotone function that takes a graph G as input, and outputs whether or not the vertex 1 is connected to 2. Use the lower bound described above to prove that any monotone formula for this function must be of size at least $n^{\Omega(\log n)}$.

10

Memory Size

MEMORY IS AN IMPORTANT RESOURCE. In this chapter, we present two models that measure the amount of memory used by algorithms. Our focus is on proving lower bounds on memory complexity. As usual, our main tool is communication complexity.

The standard way to model algorithms with bounded memory is via branching programs. A *branching program* of length ℓ and width w is a layered directed graph whose set of vertices is a subset of $[\ell + 1] \times [w]$. For $u \in [\ell + 1]$, layer u consists of all vertices of the form $\{(u, i) : i \in [w]\}$. Each layer is associated with a variable in $x_1, \ldots, x_n$. Every vertex of the first ℓ layers has two outgoing edges, each labeled by a distinct symbol from $[d]$. Edges go from layer u to layer $u + 1$ for $u \leq \ell$. The vertices in layer $\ell + 1$ are labeled with an output of the program. See Figure 10.1 for an illustration.

Branching programs compute functions in the natural way. On input $x \in [d]^n$, the program is executed by starting at the vertex $(1, 1)$, and reading the variables associated with each layer in turn. The input x defines a path through the program. The program outputs the label of the last vertex on this path.

Intuitively, if an algorithm uses only s bits of memory, then it can be modeled as a branching program of width at most 2^s. Each point in time corresponds to a layer, and at any time, the algorithm can be in one of at most 2^s states.

Every function $f : [d]^n \rightarrow \{0, 1\}$ can be computed by a branching program of width d^n and length n. Counting arguments show that most functions require exponential width.

Perhaps one of the most surprising results about branching programs is that programs of width 5 can efficiently simulate Boolean formulas:[1]

Theorem 10.1 *If f can be computed by a Boolean circuit of depth D, then it can be computed by a branching program of width 5 and length $2^{O(D)}$.*

Barrington's theorem implies that if a function requires a super-polynomial length when the width is restricted to being 5, then it requires circuits of super-logarithmic depth. As we discussed in

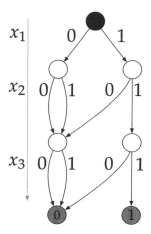

Figure 10.1 A branching program computing $x_1 \wedge x_2 \wedge x_3$.

In the literature, the programs we define here are referred to as *oblivious* branching programs. General branching programs are not layered, and every vertex is associated with some variable.

Carry out the counting argument yourself. How many branching programs of width w and length ℓ are there?

[1] Barrington, 1986.

We do not prove Barrington's theorem here. The reason the width of the simulation is 5 is that 5 is the least integer so that the permutation group over 5 elements is not solvable.

175

Streaming algorithms are
sometimes called *oblivious
read-once branching
programs* in the literature.

One can also study the model
where a small number of
passes (not just one) are
allowed.

Chapter 9, finding an explicit function that requires super-logarithmic depth is a major open problem.

A *streaming algorithm* is a specific type of branching program. The inputs, often called the *data stream*, are read once in order: $x_1, x_2, \ldots, x_n$. Streaming algorithms are motivated by applications where massive amounts of data need to be processed quickly. We cannot afford to store all the data that is coming in. We need to process it on the fly and yet be able to achieve some computational goal.

The parameter $\log w$ is called the *space* of the streaming algorithm. This is because after reading $x_1, \ldots, x_i$, the state of the program can be described with $\lceil \log w \rceil$ bits. We start by describing a couple of clever streaming algorithms.

Maximum Matching Suppose the data stream consists of a sequence of edges $e_1, \ldots, e_m$ in a graph with vertex set $[n]$. The goal is to find a matching of largest size in the graph whose edges are $e_1, \ldots, e_m$.

There is a simple algorithm for finding a matching that is within a factor of 2 of the largest one, using space at most $n \log n$. Store each new edge as long as it does not intersect any of the previously stored edges. At most $n/2$ edges are stored at the end, and these edges must form a matching. The space of the algorithm is at most $\frac{n}{2} \cdot \log n^2 \leq n \log n$.

This algorithm finds a matching that is at least half as big as the largest matching in the graph. Indeed, let M_{out} be the output of the algorithm, and let M_{max} be a matching in the graph of maximum size. Every edge in M_{out} can intersect at most two edges of M_{max} because the edges of M_{max} are disjoint. Every edge e in M_{max} must intersect at least one of the edge of M_{out}, or else e would have been included in M_{out}. Thus, $2|M_{out}| \geq |M_{max}|$.

Frequency Moments Suppose the data stream consists of a sequence of numbers $x_1, \ldots, x_m \in [n]$. For $i \in [n]$, let $f(i)$ denote the number of times that i occurs in the data stream. The tth moment is defined to be $\sum_{i=1}^{n} f(i)^t$.

We can efficiently compute the 1st moment $\sum_{i=1}^{n} f(i)$. This is just m, which can be computed using space $O(\log m)$.

The 0th moment is the number of distinct elements in the sequence. Although computing the 0th moment requires space n in general, one can estimate it with less space using randomness. The randomized algorithm is based on sampling.

It uses similar ideas to the
protocol for the
Gap-Hamming problem we
described in Chapter 3.

Let $S \subset [n]$ be a random subset obtained by sampling k uniformly random independent elements of $[n]$. In Chapter 3, we showed that counting the number of distinct elements in S is enough to approximate the number of distinct elements in the sequence, up to an additive error of $O(n/\sqrt{k})$, with probability at least $2/3$. The number of distinct elements within the set S can be computed using space $O(k)$. Better algorithms are known,[2] if we wish to estimate the number of distinct elements up to a small multiplicative factor.

[2] Alon et al., 1999.

Let us see a clever algorithm for computing the 2'nd moment $\sum_{i=1}^{n} f(i)^2$ of the stream[3] efficiently.

The second moment can be used to estimate the number of *heavy hitters* – elements that occur much more often than others.

Theorem 10.2 *For every $\epsilon, \delta > 0$, we can estimate the 2'nd moment up to a multiplicative factor of $1 - \epsilon$, with probability of error δ, using memory $O\left(\frac{\log m}{\epsilon^2 \delta}\right)$.*

[3] Alon et al., 1999.

The proof is based on the following idea. If we are interested in estimating some quantity q, it is often useful to find an *unbiased estimator* of q. Namely, a random variable with expectation q. If the random variable has small variance, then taking a few samples of it provides a good estimate for the value of q.

Proof To prove the theorem, we find an *unbiased estimator* Y for the 2nd moment $M_2 = \sum_{i=1}^{n} f(i)^2$ that can be computed with small memory. Let $E_1, \ldots, E_n$ be n independent identically distributed variables, each uniform in $\{\pm 1\}$. Let

An unbiased estimator is a random variable whose expectation is the desired quantity.

$$Y = \sum_{i \in [n]} E_i f(i).$$

First, observe that Y^2 is an unbiased estimator:

$$\mathbb{E}\left[Y^2\right] = \mathbb{E}\left[\left(\sum_{i=1}^{n} E_i f(i)\right)^2\right]$$

$$= \mathbb{E}\left[\sum_{i=1}^{n} E_i^2 \cdot f(i)^2\right] + \mathbb{E}\left[\sum_{i \neq i'} E_i \cdot E_{i'} \cdot f(i) f(i')\right] = M_2.$$

because $\mathbb{E}\left[E_i^2\right] = 1$ and $\mathbb{E}\left[E_i E_{i'}\right] = 0$ for $i \neq i'$.

Second, the variance of Y^2 is small:

$$\mathbb{E}\left[Y^4\right] = \mathbb{E}\left[\left(\sum_{i=1}^{n} E_i f(i)\right)^4\right]$$

$$= \mathbb{E}\left[\sum_{i=1}^{n} E_i^4 \cdot f(i)^4\right] + \mathbb{E}\left[\sum_{i \neq i'} \binom{4}{2} \cdot E_i^2 \cdot E_{i'}^2 \cdot f(i)^2 f(j)^2\right]$$

as above, the odd degree terms vanish.

$$= \sum_{i=1}^{n} f(i)^4 + 6 \sum_{i \neq i'} f(i)^2 f(i')^2,$$

so the variance of Y^2 is

$$\mathbb{E}\left[Y^4\right] - \mathbb{E}\left[Y^2\right]^2 = 4 \sum_{i \neq i'} f(i)^2 f(i')^2 \leq 4M_2^2.$$

To estimate M_2, we maintain the average Z of k independent unbiased estimators $Y_1^2, \ldots, Y_k^2$ for large enough k. The variance of Z can be bounded:

In general, the variance of the average of k independent identically distributed random variables is always smaller by a factor of k than the variance of each one.

$$\mathbb{E}\left[Z^2\right] - \mathbb{E}\left[Z\right]^2 = \mathbb{E}\left[\left(\frac{1}{k} \cdot \sum_{j=1}^{k} Y_j^2\right)^2\right] - \mathbb{E}\left[\frac{1}{k} \cdot \sum_{j=1}^{k} Y_j^2\right]^2$$

because $Y_1, \ldots, Y_k$ are independent.

$$= \frac{1}{k^2} \cdot \sum_{i=1}^{j} \mathbb{E}\left[Y_j^4\right] - \mathbb{E}\left[Y_j^2\right]^2 \leq \frac{4}{k} M_2^2.$$

Finally, Chebyshev's inequality implies

$$\Pr\left[|Z - M_2| \geq \epsilon M_2\right] \leq \frac{4}{\epsilon^2 k} < \delta,$$

for $k = O\left(\frac{1}{\epsilon^2 \delta}\right)$. We can compute Z with memory at most k times $O(\log m)$. □

Lower Bounds for Streaming Algorithms

THE DOMINANT METHOD for proving lower bounds on the memory required in streaming applications is by appealing to lower bounds in communication complexity.

[4] Alon et al., 1999.

One approach is to break the data stream into two parts.[4] Alice simulates the execution of the algorithm on the first part of the stream. She then sends Bob the contents of the memory, allowing him to continue the simulation over the second half of the data stream. Perhaps surprisingly, this simple approach often gives tight lower bounds.

To illustrate this basic idea, let us start with computing the frequency moments.

Lower Bounds for Estimating Moments

The input is a stream of numbers $x_1, \ldots, x_m \in [n]$, and $f(i)$ denotes the number of times that $i \in [n]$ occurs in the stream.

First, consider the problem of computing the 0th moment, which is the number of distinct elements in the stream. The following lower bound[5] follows by reduction to the lower bound on the communication complexity of the Gap-Hamming problem.

[5] Indyk and Woodruff, 2003; and Chakrabarti and Regev, 2012.

Theorem 10.3 *Any randomized streaming algorithm estimating the number of distinct elements in a stream of length $m = n$ of integers in $[n]$ up to an additive error of $\sqrt{n}$ requires memory of size at least $\Omega(n)$.*

Proof Suppose Alice has a string $x \in \{0, 1\}^n$, and Bob has a string $y \in \{0, 1\}^n$. They wish to estimate the Hamming distance between x, y. Viewing x as the indicator vector for a set $S = \{i_1, i_2, \ldots, i_s\} \subseteq [n]$, Alice simulates the execution of the given algorithm on the stream $i_1, \ldots, i_s$, and computes the contents of the memory after the algorithm made a pass on this stream. Alice sends Bob the contents of the memory, as well as $|S|$. Bob continues executing the algorithm on the elements of the set T, obtained by viewing y as the indicator vector of T.

After the algorithm has finished executing, Bob recovers a number k, which is equal to $|S \cup T|$ with probability $2/3$, and outputs $2k - |S| - |T|$. The Hamming distance between x and y is exactly

$$|S \cup T| - |S \cap T| = 2 \cdot |S \cup T| - |S| - |T|.$$

The parties just solved the Gap-Hamming problem. By Theorem 5.17, the memory must take $\Omega(n)$ bits to encode. $\qquad\square$

Next, suppose we are interested in computing the maximum frequency: $\max_i f(i)$. A simple reduction to the communication complexity of disjointness[6] gives the following lower bound.

[6] Alon et al., 1999.

Theorem 10.4 *Any randomized algorithm that can estimate* $\max_i f(i)$ *within a multiplicative factor of* 1.9 *must use memory* $\Omega(n)$.

The maximum frequency is the ∞-moment:

$$\lim_{t \to \infty} \left(\sum_{i=1}^{n} f(i)^t \right)^{1/t}.$$

Proof Suppose Alice and Bob have sets $x, y \subseteq [n]$ and want to know whether the sets are disjoint or not. Alice simulates an execution of the streaming algorithm whose input stream consists of the elements of x, and then sends the contents of the memory to Bob. Bob continues the simulation using the elements of y. If x and y are disjoint, the maximum frequency is at most 1. If they are not disjoint, then the maximum frequency is 2. So, the output of the algorithm allows Alice and Bob to distinguish the two cases. By Theorem 6.19, the memory must contain $\Omega(n)$ bits. $\qquad\square$

Lower Bounds for Maximum Matching

The streaming algorithm described above has nearly linear memory size, but produces only a $1/2$ approximation of the maximum matching. The following theorem[7] shows that a $2/3$ approximation requires much larger memory size.

[7] Goel et al., 2012.

Theorem 10.5 *For any constant* $\gamma > 0$, *there is a constant* $c > 0$ *such that any randomized streaming algorithm that computes a matching whose size is at least* $2/3 + \gamma$ *fraction of the size of the maximum matching, with probability* $2/3$, *must have memory* $\ell \geq \Omega(\gamma^2 n^{2-c/\log\log n})$.

Memory size $O(n^2)$ easily suffices for exactly solving the maximum matching problem. The theorem implies that any randomized streaming algorithm with a 0.67 approximation ratio for the maximum matching problem must have memory size at least $\Omega(n^{1.99})$. A similar lower bound is known to hold[8] even when the approximation factor is $1 - 1/e$. We prove the easier result here.

[8] Kapralov, 2013.

A key combinatorial construction that is useful to prove the lower bound is a dense graph that can be covered by a few induced matchings. A matching is *induced* if no two edges in the matching are connected by an edge of the graph.

Many interesting upper bounds are also known for algorithms that make multiple passes on the data stream.

Let us see how one can construct such a graph. Theorem 4.2 asserts that there is a subset $T \subseteq [n]$ of size at least $n/2^{-\Omega(\sqrt{\log n})}$ that does not contain any nontrivial arithmetic progressions of length 3. One can use the set T to construct[9] a graph. Let A, B be two disjoint sets of vertices, each of size $3n$. Identify each of these sets with $[3n]$. Put an edge between two vertices $x \in A$ and $y \in B$, if $x = v + t$ and $y = v - t$ for some $n \leq v < 2n$ and $t \in T$. We get n matchings, one for every choice of v. Moreover, these matchings are induced. Indeed, consider two edges of the form $(v + t, v - t)$ and $(v + t', v - t')$ for $t \neq t'$ in T. We need to show that the edge $(v + t', v - t)$ is not present in the graph. If the edge is present, then $t + t' = (v + t) - (v - t') = 2t''$ for some $t' \in T$, so t, t'', t' is an arithmetic progression of length 3. This is impossible.

The graph described above does not have the parameters we need to prove the strongest lower bound. A better construction is known.[10]

Theorem 10.6 *For every $\delta > 0$, there is a constant $c > 0$ such that for every n there is a bipartite graph with n vertices on each side that is the disjoint union of $n^{1-c/\log\log n}$ induced matchings, and each matching has at least $(1/2 - \delta)n$ edges.*

Given Theorem 10.6, and ideas from the communication complexity lower bound for indexing, we can prove the lower bound on streaming algorithms.

Proof of Theorem 10.5 Consider the following communication game. Alice gets a set of edges H, and Bob gets a set of edges J. Their goal is to output a large matching that is contained in the union of their edges. In the game, Alice must send a message to Bob, and Bob must output the final matching.

Alice and Bob can always use the streaming algorithm to get a protocol for the game. Alice simulates the execution of the algorithm on her edges and then sends the contents of the memory to Bob, who completes the execution on his edges and outputs the edges found by the algorithm.

To prove the lower bound, we find a hard distribution on the inputs H, J. As usual, it is no loss of generality to assume that the protocol of the parties is deterministic because we can always fix their randomness in the best possible way.

Let $\gamma > 0$ be as in the theorem statement. Choose $\delta > 0$ to be a small enough constant that we shall set later. Let G be the graph on $2n$ vertices promised by Theorem 10.6, which consists of

$$k \geq n^{1-c/\log\log n}$$

induced matchings $G_1, \ldots, G_k$, each of size $t = (1/2 - \delta)n$. Let S be a new set of $2n$ vertices. For each $i \in [k]$, let H_i be the random graph obtained by picking exactly $(1 - \delta)t$ of the edges in G_i uniformly and independently. The graph H is defined to be the union of $H_1, \ldots, H_k$. Let $I \in [k]$ be uniformly random. The graph J is a random matching of

---

[9] Ruzsa and Szemerédi, 1978.

[10] Goel et al., 2012.

We do not describe the graph proving Theorem 10.6 here.

We shall choose $\delta = \Omega(\gamma)$.

We assume t and $(1 - \delta)t$ are integers.

A graph used to generate inputs

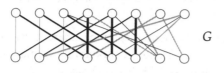

G

Figure 10.2 An example of the hard inputs H, J for the matching problem. The graph G has many large induced matchings. Alice gets a random subgraph H of G. Bob gets a graph J, which matches all the vertices not included in some matching of G. The maximum matching includes the edges touching S and all the edges contained in a random induced matching.

Inputs

1. Alice gets a random subgraph of G

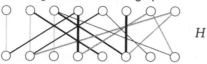

H

2. Bob gets the dashed edges

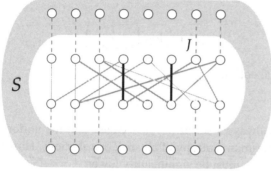

all the edges that *do not* touch the vertices in G_I to vertices in S. For an example, see Figure 10.2.

The largest matching in the graph $H \cup J$ is $H_I \cup J$. Indeed, if any matching in $H \cup J$ includes an edge of G that is not in G_I, then we can remove that edge and replace it with two edges touching S to obtain a larger matching. The size of this matching is

$$\begin{aligned} \sigma &= 2(n - t) + (1 - \delta)t \\ &= 2(n - (1/2 - \delta)n) + (1 - \delta)(1/2 - \delta)n \\ &= 3n/2 + (\delta/2)n + \delta^2/n \geq 3n/2. \end{aligned}$$

When the algorithm does not make an error, the number of edges from H_I that Bob outputs must be at least

$$\begin{aligned} r &= (2/3 + \gamma)\,\sigma - 2(n - t) \\ &\geq 3\gamma n/2 + n - 2t \geq \gamma n, \end{aligned} \tag{10.1}$$

if δ is small enough.

The intuition is that a short message from Alice cannot describe so many edges from H_I. Let M denote the ℓ-bit message that Alice sends to Bob. By Theorem 6.12, because $H_1, \ldots, H_k$ are independent,

$$\sum_{i=1}^{k} I(H_i : M) \le I(H_1, \ldots, H_k : M) \le \ell.$$

By applying Markov's inequality twice, there must be an $i \in [k]$ for which $I(H_i : M) \le 2\ell/k$ and the probability of making an error conditioned on $I = i$ is at most $2/3$. Fix such an index i.

Let E be the indicator random variable for the event that the algorithm makes an error. Namely, $E = 1$ if the algorithm outputs a matching of size at most $(2/3 + \gamma)\sigma$, and $E = 0$ otherwise. Thus,

$$I(H_i : ME) \le \tfrac{2\ell}{k} + 1.$$

It remains to give a lower bound on

$$I(H_i : ME) = H(H_i) - H(H_i|ME).$$

Because H_i is a uniformly random set of $(1 - \delta)t$ edges chosen from t edges, we have

$$H(H_i) = \log \binom{t}{(1-\delta)t}.$$

The conditional entropy

$$H(H_i|M, E = 1) \le H(H_i),$$

because H_i is always a set of $(1 - \delta)t$ edges, and the uniform distribution has the maximum entropy of all such distributions. However, when $E = 0$, the entropy must be significantly lower:

See (10.1).

$$H(H_i|M, E = 0) \le \log \binom{t - r}{(1-\delta)t - r}.$$

Because $\Pr[E = 0] \ge 1/3$, we get

$$H(H_i|ME) \le \frac{1}{3} \log \binom{t - r}{(1-\delta)t - r} + \frac{2}{3} H(H_i).$$

Overall,

$$I(H_i : ME)$$
$$\ge \log \binom{t}{(1-\delta)t} - \frac{1}{3} \cdot \log \binom{t - r}{(1-\delta)t - r} - \frac{2}{3} \cdot \log \binom{t}{(1-\delta)t}$$
$$= \frac{1}{3} \log \frac{\binom{t}{(1-\delta)t}}{\binom{t-r}{(1-\delta)t-r}}.$$

Because

$$\frac{\binom{a}{b}}{\binom{a-r}{b-r}} = \prod_{j=0}^{r-1} \frac{a - j}{b - j} \ge \left(\frac{a}{b}\right)^r,$$

we get

$$I(H_i : ME) \geq \frac{r}{3} \log \frac{1}{1-\delta} \geq \Omega(\gamma^2 n).$$

because $r \geq \gamma n$ and $\log \frac{1}{1-\delta} \geq \delta \geq \Omega(\gamma)$.

Finally,

$$\ell \geq \Omega\left(\gamma^2 k n\right) \geq \Omega(\gamma^2 n^{2-c/\log\log n}).$$

□

Lower Bounds for Branching Programs

BRANCHING PROGRAMS ARE MORE POWERFUL than streaming algorithms. A branching program may read the variables multiple times and in arbitrary order. Communication complexity can be used to prove lower bounds on branching programs as well. We present explicit functions that cannot be computed by branching programs that are simultaneously short and narrow.

To prove the lower bound, we first show that any branching program can be efficiently simulated, at least in some sense, by a communication protocol in the number-on-forehead model, discussed in Chapter 4.

Let $g : (\{0,1\}^r)^k \to \{0,1\}$ be a function that k-parties wish to compute in the number-on-forehead model. Define the function g' by

$$g'(x, S_1, \ldots, S_k) = g(x|_{S_1}, \ldots, x|_{S_k}),$$

where $x \in \{0,1\}^n$, $S_1, \ldots, S_k$ are subsets of $[n]$ of size r, and $x|_{S_i} \in \{0,1\}^r$ is the projection of x to the coordinates in S_i. The input to g' can be described using at most $n + O(kr \log n)$ bits.

The key claim[11] is that any branching program computing g' can be used to obtain an efficient protocol computing g in the number-on-forehead model.

[11] Babai et al., 1989; and Hrubes and Rao, 2015.

We set γ_0 to be small enough so that $\sqrt{\gamma} \leq 1/(16\log(4e))$.

Theorem 10.7 *There is a constant $\gamma_0 > 0$ such that for every $0 < \gamma < \gamma_0$ and for every g, g' as above with $k > 10\sqrt{\gamma}\log n$ and $r \leq \sqrt{n}$ the following holds. If g' can be computed by a branching program of length $\gamma n \log^2 n$ and width w, then g can be computed by k parties with communication at most $O(\gamma \log(w) \log^2(n))$ in the number-on-forehead model.*

The simulation in Theorem 10.7 gives a deterministic communication protocol. The lower bound from Theorem 5.8 is for randomized protocols.

Setting g to be the generalized inner-product function, Theorem 10.7 and the lower bound from Theorem 5.8 imply that any branching program with length at most $\gamma n \log^2 n$ that computes g' must have width at least $2^{n^{\Omega(1)}}$. No better trade-off between the length and width of branching programs is known.

Let us first sketch the proof of a weaker lower bound – either the width of the program is $2^{n^{\Omega(1)}}$, or the length of the program is at least $\Omega(n \log n)$. Given inputs $y_1, \ldots, y_k$ to generalized inner-product $g(y_1, \ldots, y_k)$, we show that the parties can use a program for g' to compute g. There are a couple of challenges to overcome. First, generalized inner-product can easily be computed by a branching program of width 3 and length n. This can be circumvented by *scrambling* the input using the sets $S_1, \ldots, S_k$. The key idea is to have each party in the communication protocol simulate many steps of the execution of the branching program by herself.

The scrambling is similar to the approach used in Theorem 9.9, and in many other proofs.

The challenge is that the variables in the program can appear multiple times and in arbitrary order, while the parties in the number-on-forehead model are only allowed to see a certain structured part of the input. How can we ensure that each party sees enough of the input to be able to simulate the execution of the program?

Suppose for the sake of finding a contradiction that the program computing g' has length $(n \log n)/20$, and width $w = 2^{n^{0.01}}$. Partition the program into disjoint intervals of time, each of length $n/2$. In order to decide where to place the inputs of the parties, namely $S_1, \ldots, S_k$, define the following bipartite graph. The graph has $k = (\log n)/10$ vertices on the left and n vertices on the right. Every vertex on the left corresponds to one of the k parts of the program. Every vertex on the right corresponds to one of the n variables $x_1, \ldots, x_n$. Connect a part to a variable by an edge if that part does not contain the variable in the program. By the choice of parameters, each vertex on the left is connected to at least $n/2$ vertices on the right. This property is enough to ensure that one can find k disjoint sets $S_1, \ldots, S_k$ on the right, each of size $r = \sqrt{n}$, such that the ith vertex on the left is connected to every vertex of S_i. One can find these sets greedily – let S_1 be r neighbors of 1, then delete these neighbors and repeat to find $S_2, \ldots, S_k$. Fixing the choice of $S_1, \ldots, S_k$, the parties let $x|_{S_1} = y_1, \ldots, x|_{S_k} = y_k$. Any variable not determined by this step is fixed to 0. We have $g'(x, S_1, \ldots, S_k) = g(y_1, \ldots, y_k)$, and the parties can simulate the execution of the program to compute g'. The ith party sees enough information to simulate the execution of the ith part of the program, which is of length $n/2$. In each step of the simulation, one of the parties sends $\log w = n^{0.01}$ bits to tell the next party how to continue the simulation. Overall, we get a protocol computing g with communication at most $n^{0.01} \log n$. However, the lower bound for generalized inner-product says that the communication must be at least $\Omega(r/4^k) = \Omega(\sqrt{n}/n^{0.2}) \geq \Omega(n^{0.33})$. This is a contradiction.

To give tighter parameters, we need to give a more efficient simulation of the branching program by communication protocols.

Proof of Theorem 10.7 Consider a branching program of length $\gamma n \log^2 n$ and width w computing g'. Partition the layers of the program into consecutive parts in such a way that each part reads at most $n/3$ variables, and there at most $3\gamma \log^2 n$ parts.

We assume $\sqrt{n}$ is an integer.

Consider the bipartite graph where every vertex on the left corresponds to a part of the partition, and every vertex on the right corresponds to one of the n variables $x_1, \ldots, x_n$ of g'. Connect two vertices if the variable does not occur in the corresponding part in the partition.

The following claim describes a useful partition of this graph. See Figure 10.3.

Claim 10.8 *One can partition the vertices on the left to k sets $Q_1, \ldots, Q_k$ and find k pairwise disjoint sets of vertices on the right $R_1, \ldots, R_k$, each of size $r = \sqrt{n}$, such that for each $i \in [k]$, every vertex of Q_i is connected to every vertex of R_i by an edge.*

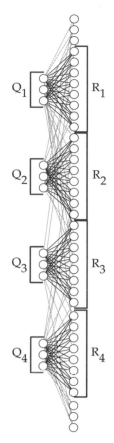

Before proving the claim, let us see how to use it. Given an input $(x_1, \ldots, x_k)$ to g, use the branching program for g' with inputs $(x, R_1, \ldots, R_k)$ where $x|_{R_i} = x_i$ and x is zero outside $\bigcup_i R_i$. Thus, $g(x_1, \ldots, x_k) = g'(x, R_1, \ldots, R_k)$.

The protocol for computing g proceeds as follows. The first vertex on the left corresponds to at least $n/3$ steps of the branching program. This vertex belongs to some Q_i. Party i runs the steps of the program corresponding to the first part by herself because she knows all the relevant variables in x. She then uses $\lceil \log w \rceil$ bits to announce the result of this simulation. Now the party that corresponds to the steps in the next part simulates the program and announces the outcome, and so on. The overall communication is at most $3\gamma \log^2 n \cdot \lceil \log w \rceil$. The protocol indeed computes g. It only remains to prove the claim. □

Proof of Claim 10.8 We prove the claim by repeatedly using Lemma 5.4. Initially, the degree of each vertex on the left is at least $2n/3$, so the edge density is at least $2/3$. Because the initial edge density of the graph is more than $1/2 \geq 2 \cdot \frac{2\sqrt{\gamma} \log n}{8\sqrt{\gamma} \log n}$, we can apply Lemma 5.4 to find a set Q_1 on the left and R_1 on the right of sizes $|Q_1| \geq 2\sqrt{\gamma} \log n$ and $|R_1| = \sqrt{n}$ such that every vertex of Q_1 is connected to every vertex of R_1.

Removing Q_1, R_1 from the graph, we can repeat the process to find pairs of disjoint sets

$$(Q_2, R_2), (Q_3, R_3), \ldots, (Q_t, R_t)$$

with the same property, as long as the edge density remains at least $1/2$ and the number of vertices on the left remains at least $8\sqrt{\gamma} \log n$.

The number of times t we can apply this process is

$$t \leq t_0 = \frac{3\gamma \log^2(n)}{2\sqrt{\gamma} \log n} \leq 2\sqrt{\gamma} \log n.$$

The number of vertices on the right that are removed is at most $t_0 \cdot r \leq n/6$, for large n. This means that the edge density always remains at least $1/2$, so the process ends when we reach a state where the number of vertices on the left is $k' < 8\sqrt{\gamma} \log n$.

Figure 10.3 The bipartite graph defined by the branching program can be partitioned into cliques. The Q_is and R_is in the claim are not necessarily consecutive blocks, and some of the Q_is may be of size 1.

At this point, we set Q_{t+1} to be a singleton set $\{q_{t+1}\}$ and R_{t+1} to be a set of $r \leq n/2$ of the neighbors of q_{t+1}. We remove Q_{t+1}, R_{t+1} and similarly keep building (Q_{t+2}, R_{t+2}) as long as there are vertices on the left. During this process, the total number of vertices that are removed from the right side is at most $(t_0 + k') \cdot r \leq n/6$. So the edge density always remains at least $1/2$. $\qquad\qquad$ □

Exercises

Ex 10.1 – Show that any randomized algorithm that estimates the ∞-moment $\max_i f(i)$ within an additive factor of 1 must use memory $\Omega(n)$.

Ex 10.2 – Consider the connectivity problem for streaming algorithms. The input stream consists of edges in a graph with vertex set $[n]$. The algorithm should decide if the vertices 1 and n are connected by a path.

1. Show that this problem can be solved with $O(n \log n)$ memory.
2. Show that the memory size of such an algorithm is at least $\Omega(n)$.

   Hint: Use such an algorithm to solve disjointness.

Ex 10.3 – In this exercise, we prove Barrington's theorem.

1. Show that there are two permutations $\pi, \sigma : [5] \to [5]$ with the property that $\pi\sigma \neq \sigma\pi$. Here $\pi\sigma$ denotes the map obtained by composing π and σ.

For any fixed input, an interval in a width 5 program can be thought of as computing a map from [5] to [5].

2. Prove by induction on d that if there is a Boolean circuit computing $f(x_1, \ldots, x_n)$ with depth d, then there are three width 5 programs, each of length $O(4^d)$, computing each of the maps $\pi^{f(x_1,\ldots,x_n)}, \pi^{-f(x_1,\ldots,x_n)}, \sigma^{f(x_1,\ldots,x_n)}$. Here $\pi^1 = \pi$, and π^0 is the identity.
3. Given a Boolean circuit of depth d, show that there is a branching program of width 5 and length $O(4^d)$ that computes the same function.

Ex 10.4 – Consider the *perfect matching* problem for streaming algorithm. The input stream consists of edges in a graph with $2n$ vertices, and the algorithm needs to decide if the graph contains a matching of size n. Using a reduction similar to the one for approximating matchings, show that $\Omega(n)$ space is required.

11

Data Structures

DATA STRUCTURES PROVIDE EFFICIENT ACCESS TO DATA.
Many fundamental algorithms rely on data structures. For example,
data structures play a crucial role in Dijkstra's algorithm for finding
the shortest path in directed graphs and in Kruskal's algorithm for
computing minimum spanning trees. Lower bounds on the performance
of data structures are often obtained by appealing to communication
complexity.

There are several ways to measure the cost of data structures. We
focus on the space of the data structure and on the time that it takes to
perform operations. Space is defined to be the total number of memory
cells used, and time is defined to be the number of memory cells that are
accessed during an operation. There is, typically, a trade-off between
these costs.

We begin with several examples of useful and clever data structures.
Later, we explain how to prove complexity trade-offs for data structures
using ideas from communication complexity.

Dictionaries

A DICTIONARY IS A DATA STRUCTURE that maintains a set
$S \subseteq [n]$. It supports the operations of adding and deleting elements from
the set. It also supports membership queries of the form *is $i \in S$?*

The most straightforward implementation of a dictionary is to maintain a string $x \in \{0, 1\}^n$ that is the indicator vector of S. This allows
us to add and delete elements, as well as answer membership queries in
time 1. The space, however, is n.

A more efficient randomized alternative is to use hashing. Suppose
we only perform m operations, and we permit the data structure to make
an error with small probability. Then, for a parameter $\epsilon > 0$, we can pick
a random function $h : [n] \to [n']$ with $n' = \lceil m^2 / \epsilon \rceil$. Now, we encode
S using a string $x \in \{0, 1\}^{n'}$, by setting $x_j = 1$ if and only if there is
an $i \in S$ such that $h(i) = j$. To add i, set $x_{h(i)} = 1$, and to delete i, set
$x_{h(i)} = 0$. This data structure uses only n' cells of memory. If at most m
operations are involved, the probability that this data structure makes an
error is at most ϵ.

Figure 11.1 A heap. Here the minimum (3) is deleted from the heap, and a new number (2) is added.

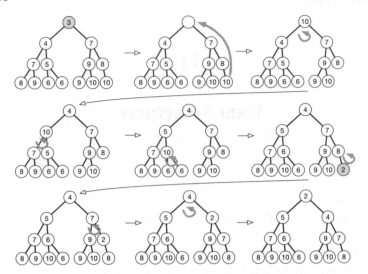

It is a tantalizing open problem to prove that there is no deterministic data structure using space that is linear in the size of the set stored:

Open Problem 11.1 *Find a deterministic dictionary for $S \subset [n]$ where each memory cell has $O(\log n)$ bits, all operations can be carried out in time $O(1)$, and the total space used is $O(s)$ for sets of size s. Alternatively, show that there is no such data structure.*

Ordered Sets

EFFICIENT ALGORITHMS FOR ACCESSING SORTED LISTS are key primitives in algorithm design, with countless applications. In many cases, we do not need to completely sort the inputs. It is enough to be able to recover some information about the sorted list, such as its minimum element.

Sort Statistics

Suppose we want to maintain a set $S \subseteq [n]$ of k numbers. As before, we want to quickly add and delete elements from the set. Now, we also want to compute the minimum of the set.

These operations are useful, for example, for computing the shortest path in weighted graphs.

A trivial solution is to store the k numbers in a list. Adding a number is fast, but finding the minimum might take k steps. A better solution is to maintain a *heap*, as in Figure 11.1. The numbers are stored on the nodes of a balanced binary tree, with the property that every node is at most the value of its children. Heaps allow us to add a number and to query or delete the minimum element. One can add a number by adding it at a new leaf and bubbling it up the tree. One can delete the minimum by deleting the number at the root, inserting the number at the last leaf into the root, and bubbling down that number. Each operation takes only $O(\log k)$ time steps.

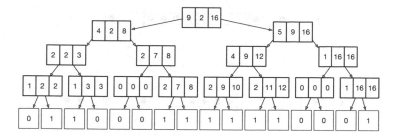

Figure 11.2 Maintaining numbers in a binary search tree with $S = \{2, 3, 7, 8, 9, 10, 11, 12, 16\}$.

Another solution is to maintain the numbers in a *binary search tree*, as in Figure 11.2. Each memory location corresponds to a node in a binary tree with n leaves. Each leaf corresponds to an element of $x \in [n]$ and stores a Boolean value indicating if $x \in S$ or not. Each inner node maintains three numbers: (i) the number of elements of S in the corresponding subtree, (ii) the minimum of S in that subtree, and (3) the maximum of S in that subtree. An element can be added or deleted in $O(\log n)$ time steps, by updating all the memory cells that correspond to the ancestors of the element in the tree. One can also compute the ith smallest element of S in $O(\log n)$ steps, by starting at the root and moving to the appropriate subtree.

If the subtree is empty, the minimum and maximum are set to 0.

The update time can be improved at the expense of increasing the query time by changing the arity of the tree.

Predecessor Search

Suppose we want to maintain a set of numbers $S \subseteq [n]$. We wish to support addition and deletion of elements from the set. We also want to quickly determine the predecessor of $x \in [n]$ defined as

The maximum of the empty set is zero.

$$P(x) = P_S(x) = \max\{y \in S : y < x\}.$$

If we maintain the numbers using a binary search tree, as in Figure 11.2, we can handle updates in $O(\log n)$ time. Queries can be answered even faster, in time $O(\log \log n)$.

The update time can be improved using van Emde Boas trees.[1] We sketch the solution. Let $I_1, I_2, \ldots, I_{\sqrt{n}}$ be $\sqrt{n}$ consecutive intervals of integers, each of size $\sqrt{n}$. We store the maximum and the minimum elements of the set S in two memory cells. We recursively store the set $T_S = \{i : S \cap I_i \neq \emptyset\}$ using a van Emde Boas tree on a universe of size $\sqrt{n}$. Finally, for each i, we recursively store the set $S \cap I_i$ using a van Emde Boas tree on a universe of size $\sqrt{n}$. See Figure 11.3 for an illustration.

To compute $P(x)$ in a binary search tree, let $a_0, a_1, \ldots, a_d$ be the nodes on the path from the root to x. A binary search over $a_0, a_1, \ldots, a_d$ can be used to compute $P(x)$ with $O(\log d)$ accesses.

For simplicity of the description, assume $\sqrt{n}$ is an integer.

[1] van Emde Boas, 1975.

To compute $P(x)$ from the van Emde Boas tree, let i be such that $x \in I_i$. If x is less than the minimum of $S \cap I_i$, then $P(x)$ is the maximum of $S \cap I_j$, where $j < i$ is the largest index for which $S \cap I_j$ is nonempty. To find $P(x)$, find the predecessor of the relevant interval in T_S, and output its maximum element. Otherwise, $P(x)$ is in $S \cap I_i$, and we can compute it recursively using the recursive structure that stores $S \cap I_i$.

Figure 11.3 An example of a van Emde Boas tree.

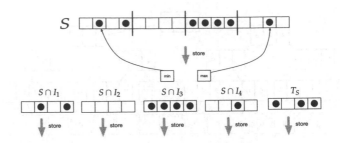

We made just one recursive call. Because the universe shrinks from n to $\sqrt{n}$, there can be at most $O(\log \log n)$ recursive calls before $P(x)$ is found. Similarly, one can add and delete numbers in time $O(\log \log n)$.

Later in this chapter, we shall prove that van Emde Boas trees are essentially optimal when it comes to the predecessor search problem. The tree can also be used to query the minimum, median and maximum of a set in time $O(\log \log n)$. Surprisingly, we still do not know whether this is the optimal data structure. Some lower bounds for restricted types of data structures are known.[2]

Open Problem 11.2 *Find a data structure that can maintain a set $S \subseteq [n]$, support the addition and deletion of elements, and support querying the minimum or median of the set in time $\ll \frac{\log \log n}{\log \log \log n}$. Alternatively, prove that there is no data structure that can carry out all operations in time $O(1)$.*

Union-Find

THE UNION-FIND DATA STRUCTURE[3] allows us to efficiently keep track of a partition $S_1, \ldots, S_k$ of $[n]$. The initial partition is the partition to n sets of size 1. The data structure supports the union operation, which forms a new partition by replacing two sets, S_i, S_j, in the partition by their union, $S_i \cup S_j$. It also supports queries that *find* $x \in [n]$, which return an identifier for the unique set S_i containing x.

This data structure has numerous applications. For example, it plays a key role in the fastest algorithms for computing the minimum spanning tree of a graph.

Here is the high-level scheme for an implementation of a union-find data structure, with operations that take time $O(\log n)$. See Figure 11.4 for an illustration. The data structure associates each element of $[n]$ with a memory cell storing $O(\log n)$ bits. The idea is to represent each set S_i in the partition by a rooted tree T_i with $|S_i|$ nodes. The nodes of T_i are labeled by the elements of S_i. The edges of the tree T_i are directed toward the root. The cell corresponding to $x \in [n]$ stores the name of its parent, as well as the depth of the subtree rooted at x. This takes $O(\log n)$ bits. If x is the root of the whole tree, then x points to itself. The find operation with input $x \in [n]$ follows the pointers from

[2] Brodal et al., 1996; and Ramamoorthy and Rao, 2017.

[3] Galler and Fisher, 1964.

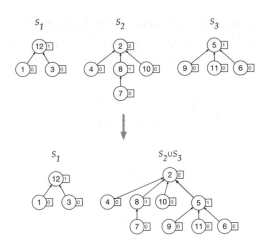

Figure 11.4 Maintaining a partition of the universe into sets using the union-find data structure. Each cell is associated with an element of the universe, and stores a pointer to the cell corresponding to its parent, as well as the height of the subtree rooted at the element. The result of merging two sets is shown.

x to the root of the tree it belongs to and outputs the name of the root. The union operation for S_i, S_j merges the corresponding trees T_i, T_j by ensuring that the root of the shallower tree becomes a child of the root of taller tree T_j, and adjusting the depths of the two roots appropriately. This ensures that no tree ever has depth more than $O(\log n)$, and so all operations take at most $O(\log n)$ time.

Later, we shall show that this union-find solution is essentially optimal.

Prove that any tree of depth d that occurs in the data structure always has at least 2^d elements in it. Conclude that depth of every tree has depth at most $O(\log n)$.

Approximate Nearest Neighbor Search

IN THE NEAREST NEIGHBOR SEARCH PROBLEM, we wish to store a set $S \subseteq \{0,1\}^d$ of size n so that one can quickly compute a nearest neighbor $N(x)$ of a query $x \in \{0,1\}^d$. A nearest neighbor of x is an element $y \in S$ minimizing the Hamming distance

$$\Delta(x, y) = |\{i \in [d] : x_i \neq y_i\}|.$$

Typically $n \gg d$.

We can always store the set using nd bits and answer queries in time nd. We could also store a table with 2^d cells, each with d bits, recording the response for every possible query. This implementation yields a constant query time, but exponential space.

Here we sketch a $1 + \epsilon$ approximation for nearest neighbor.[4] Namely, we can use the data structure to find some $y \in S$ so that

$$\Delta(x, y) \leq (1 + \epsilon) \cdot \Delta(x, S).$$

[4] Kushilevitz et al., 2000.

We use the notation

$\Delta(x, S) = \min\{\Delta(x, w) : w \in S\}.$

Theorem 11.3 *For every $\epsilon > 0$, there is a data structure that allows us to find the $1 + \epsilon$-approximate nearest neighbor such that*

- *The number of cells is at most $d \log(d)(n \log(\log(d / \epsilon)))^{O(1/\epsilon^2)}$.*
- *Each cell contains $d + 1$ bits.*
- *The query time is $O(d \log(\log(d)/\epsilon))$.*

The query time can be
improved if the data structure
is allowed to be randomized.

The key idea is to use *locality sensitive hashing* – hashing that helps to determine the Hamming weight of a string. For a parameter $1 > \delta > 0$, let Z be a random $r \times d$ matrix with independent identically distributed entries distributed as

$$Z_{i,j} = \begin{cases} 1 & \text{with probability } \delta, \\ 0 & \text{with probability } 1 - \delta. \end{cases}$$

For a binary vector w, let $|w|$
denote the number ones in w.
For an integer vector x, denote
by x mod 2 the binary vector
obtained by reducing each
coordinate modulo 2.

Think of w as a column vector.

Lemma 11.4 *For every $\gamma, \epsilon > 0$, there is $r = O(\log(1/\gamma)/\epsilon^2)$ so that for all $k \in [d]$ there is a bias $\delta > 0$ for the entries of Z and an interval $T \subset \mathbb{R}$, so that for every $d \times 1$ binary vector w:*

- *If $|w| \le k$ then $\Pr\left[|Zw \mod 2| \in T\right] \ge 1 - \gamma.$*
- *If $|w| \ge k(1 + \epsilon)$ then $\Pr\left[|Zw \mod 2| \in T\right] \le \gamma.$*

Before proving the lemma, let us see how to use it. We describe a random construction that yields the required data structure with high probability. Let $S \subset \{0, 1\}^d$ be the given set of n vectors. Let $\epsilon > 0$ be the approximation parameter. Set γ to be $\frac{1}{n \log(\log(d)/\epsilon))}$ times a small constant to be determined.

Apply Lemma 11.4 several times with

$$k = 1, (1 + \epsilon), (1 + \epsilon)^2, \dots$$

as long as $k \le d$. The total number of times we apply the lemma is $O(\log(d)/\epsilon)$. For each value of k, independently sample m matrices $Z^{(k,1)}, \dots, Z^{(k,m)}$, and choose the interval $T^{(k)}$ as in the lemma, for some $m = O(d)$ to be determined below.

For each $r \times 1$ binary vector q, and $j \in [m]$, the data structure stores a cell with $d + 1$ bits that contains $y \in S$ if

$$|q - Z^{(k,j)}y \mod 2| \in T^{(k)}.$$

If there are several such ys, the cell stores just one of them. If there are no such ys, the cell is left empty. The total number of cells and the number of bits in each cell is as promised.

The number of cells is

$O(m \log(d)2^r / \epsilon)$

$= d \log(d)(n \log$

$(\log(d/\epsilon)))^{O(1/\epsilon^2)}.$

We now sketch how the data structure answers queries. Fix a query $x \in \{0, 1\}^d$. For each $j \in [m]$, choose $y_j \in S$ using binary search as follows. For $k_0 \approx d/2$ check if there is $y \in S$ so that

$$|Z^{(k_0,j)}(x - y) \mod 2| \in T^{(k_0)},$$

by looking at the cell corresponding to $q = Z^{(k_0,j)}(x) \mod 2$. If the answer is yes, continue the search among the ks that are smaller than k_0. If the answer is no, search among the ks that are larger. The element $y_j \in S$ is the last element obtained in this binary search.

Claim 11.5 *For fixed x and j,*

$$\Pr[y_j \in S, \ \Delta(y_j, x) \le (1 + \epsilon)\Delta(x, S)] \ge 2/3.$$

Proof Sketch There are n elements in S and $O(\log(\log(d)/\epsilon))$ values of k in the binary search. By the union bound and Lemma 11.4, the probability in question is at least $1 - O(\gamma n \log(\log(d)/\epsilon)) \geq 2/3$ by the choice of γ. □

The claim and the Chernoff-Hoeffding bound imply that for fixed x, the probability that for at least $m/2$ of the js we have $y_j \in S$ and $\Delta(y_j, x) \leq (1 + \epsilon)\Delta(x, S)$ is at least $1 - 1/2^{d+1}$. The union bound over all x now implies that there is a choice of matrices and intervals so that at least half of the y_js are proper solutions to the problem. For this choice, the data structure can properly answer all queries. The query time is m times the length of the binary search, as claimed.

It only remains to prove the hashing lemma.

Proof of Lemma 11.4 We first claim that for a single row z of Z,

$$\Pr_z \left[\langle z, w \rangle = 0 \quad \bmod 2 \right] = \frac{1 + (1 - 2\delta)^{|w|}}{2}.$$

Indeed, if we set $p = \Pr_z \left[\langle z, w \rangle = 0 \quad \bmod 2 \right]$, then

$$2p - 1 = \mathbb{E}_z \left[(-1)^{\langle w, z \rangle} \right] = \mathbb{E}_z \left[\prod_{i=1}^d (-1)^{w_i z_i} \right]$$

$$= \prod_{i=1}^d \mathbb{E}_{z_i} \left[(-1)^{w_i z_i} \right]$$

$$= (1 - 2\delta)^{|w|}.$$

Now set δ so we have

$$b(\delta, k) = \frac{1 + (1 - 2\delta)^k}{2} = 2/3.$$

Observe that

$$b(\delta, k) - b(\delta, k(1 + \epsilon)) = 1/3 - (1/3)^{1+\epsilon}$$
$$= (1/3) \cdot (1 - 2^{-\epsilon \cdot \log 3})$$
$$\geq (1/3) \cdot (1 - (1 - \epsilon \cdot (\log 3)/2)) \qquad \text{because } 2^{-2x} \leq 1 - x \text{ for}$$
$$\geq \Omega(\epsilon). \qquad\qquad\qquad 0 \leq x \leq 1/2.$$

Let T be the interval

$$T = \left[\left(\frac{2}{3} - \frac{b(\delta, k) - b(\delta, k(1 + \epsilon))}{2} \right) r, \ 1 \right].$$

By the Chernoff-Hoeffding bound, if $|w| \leq k$ then

$$\Pr \left[|Zw \quad \bmod 2| \in T \right] \geq 1 - e^{-\Omega(\epsilon^2 r)}.$$

Similarly, if $|w| \geq k(1 + \epsilon)$

$$\Pr \left[|Zw \quad \bmod 2| \in T \right] \leq e^{-\Omega(\epsilon^2 r)}.$$

Choosing $r = O(\log(1/\gamma)/\epsilon^2)$ completes the proof. □

Lower Bounds on Static Data Structures

A STATIC DATA STRUCTURE specifies a way to store data in memory, and to answer queries about the data, without the ability to update the data. There are three main parameters that we seek to optimize:

In the next section, we consider dynamic data structures that permit updates to the data as well.

Space *s*: The space is the total number of memory cells used to store the data.

Word size *w*: The number of bits in each memory cell.

Query time *t*: The number of cells that need to be accessed to answer a query.

Ideally, we would like to minimize all three parameters.

The primary method for proving lower bounds on the parameters of static data structures is via communication complexity. In a nutshell, efficient data structures lead to efficient communication protocols. Say we are given a data structure for a particular problem. We define the corresponding data structure game as follows: Alice is given a query to the data structure, and Bob is given the data that is stored in the data structure. The goal is for Alice to compute the result of evaluating her query on the data.

There are also randomized and distributional versions of this lemma.

Lemma 11.6 *If there is a data structure of size s, word size w, and query time t for solving a particular problem, then there is a deterministic protocol solving the related communication game with 2t rounds. In each pair of subsequent rounds, Alice sends* log *s bits, and Bob responds with w bits.*

Proof Alice and Bob simulate the execution of the data structure algorithm. Alice sends $\log s$ bits to indicate the name of the memory cell she wishes to read, and Bob responds with w bits encoding the contents of the appropriate cell. After t such steps, Alice and Bob know the result of the computation.   □

Lower bounds in communication complexity therefore give us lower bounds on the parameters of data structures. Here are some examples.

Set Intersection

Suppose we wish to store an arbitrary subset $Y \subseteq [n]$ so that on input $X \subseteq [n]$ one can quickly compute whether or not $X \cap Y$ is empty.[5] Here are a few potential solutions:

[5] Miltersen et al., 1998.

1. We could store Y as string of n bits broken up into words of size w. This would give the parameters $s = t = \lceil n/w \rceil$.

2. We could store whether or not Y intersects every potential set X. This would give $s = 2^n$ and $w = t = 1$.

3. For every subset $V \subseteq [n]$ of size at most p, we could store whether or not Y intersects V. Because X is always the union of at most $\lceil n/p \rceil$ sets of size at most p, this gives $s = \sum_{i=0}^{p} \binom{n}{i}$, $w = 1$, and $t = \lceil n/p \rceil$.

The communication game that corresponds to this data structure is exactly the same as computing disjointness. So, every data structure leads to a communication protocol for computing set disjointness. Because the communication complexity of set disjointness is $n + 1$, we get the following lower bound on data structures.

Theorem 11.7 *Any data structure that solves the set intersection problem must have $t \cdot (\lceil \log s \rceil + w) \geq n + 1$.*

Lopsided Set Intersection

In practice, the bit complexity of the queries is often much smaller than the amount of data being stored.

In the k-lopsided set intersection problem, the data structure is required to store a set $Y \subseteq [n]$. A query to the problem is a set $X \subseteq [n]$ of size $k \ll n$. The data structure must compute whether or not X intersects Y.

When $k = 1$, we can get $s = \lceil n/w \rceil$ and $t = 1$. No better parameters are possible. The problem becomes more interesting when $k > 1$. We can get a solution with $s = \lceil \binom{n}{k}/w \rceil \leq (1/w)(en/k)^k$ and $t = 1$ by storing whether or not Y intersects each set of size k.   See Exercise 11.4.

Theorem 1.29 yields the following lower bound:

Theorem 11.8 *For any data structure solving the k-lopsided set intersection problem, $t(\log s + w) \geq n/(s^{t/k} + 1)$.*

For example, the theorem proves that if $w = 1$ and $n^{1/3} > k > t$, then for large n, we have $s \geq \binom{n}{k}^{1/(2t)}$. This is because if s is smaller, then we have

Here we use the bounds $(n/k)^k \leq \binom{n}{k} \leq (en/k)^k$.

$$k \log(n/k) + t \geq t(\log s + w) \geq \frac{n}{s^{t/k} + 1} \geq \frac{n}{\sqrt{en/k} + 1} \geq \frac{\sqrt{nk}}{2\sqrt{e}},$$

which cannot hold for large n.

The Span Problem

In the span problem,[6] the goal is to store $n/2$ vectors $y_1, \ldots, y_{n/2} \in \mathbb{F}_2^n$,   [6] Miltersen et al., 1998. with n even. A query is a vector $x \in \mathbb{F}_2^n$. The data structure must quickly compute whether or not x is a linear combination of $y_1, \ldots, y_{n/2}$.

Theorem 1.32 yields the lower bound:

Theorem 11.9 *In any static data structure solving the span problem,*

$$tw \geq n^2/4 - t \log s \cdot (n + 1) - n \log n.$$

For example, if $s < 2^{n/8t}$, then $tw = \Omega(n^2)$.

Predecessor Search

In the predecessor search problem, the data structure is required to encode a subset $S \subseteq [n]$ of size at most k. The data structure should compute the predecessor $P_S(x)$ of any element $x \in [n]$.

Recall that the predecessor of x is the largest element of S that is at most x.

There is a simple static data structure with space $s = n$ and time $t = 1$ for this problem. The data structure stores the value of $P_S(x)$ for every x. To compute $P_S(x)$, we simply need to read the relevant cell where this value has been stored. When $s \ll n$, we prove lower bounds.[7]

[7] *Ajtai, 1988; Beame and Fich, 2002; Pătraşcu and Thorup, 2006; and Sen and Venkatesh, 2008.*

Theorem 11.10 *Suppose that there is a static data structure for predecessor search for sets of size ℓ in a universe of size n with word size $w = \lceil \log n \rceil$ that solves the predecessor search problem in time t and space s. Then,*

$$t \geq \Omega \left(\min\{ \frac{\log \log n}{\log \log(s \log n)}, \frac{\log \ell}{\log \log(\ell n)} \} \right). \qquad (11.1)$$

The theorem is essentially tight. We have seen that there is a data structure that can allow for additions, deletions, and predecessor queries, all in time $t \leq O(\log \log n)$. This dynamic data structure leads to an efficient static data structure.[8] Here is a sketch of the construction. Suppose the set S is promised to be of size at most ℓ. One can use the dynamic data structure to add each element of the set S, which takes total time $t\ell$. Every predecessor query can be handled in time t using the dynamic data structure. To make this intuition formal, hashing is used to reduce the space of the data structure. This gives a static data structure with space at most polynomial in ℓ and time at most $O\left(\frac{\log \log n}{\log \log \log n} \right)$.

[8] *Beame and Fich, 2002.*

Proof of Theorem 11.10 We prove the lower bound using the round-elimination method introduced in Chapter 6. The data structure yields a communication protocol for the following problem. Alice gets $x \in [n]$, and Bob gets the set $S \subseteq [n]$ of size at most ℓ. Their goal is to compute $P(x)$.

We iteratively construct hard distributions on inputs as follows. Let us start with the base case. Suppose the communication protocol has 0 rounds. Define the distribution μ_0 on x, S by choosing $x \in \{2, 4\}$ uniformly at random and setting $S = \{1, 3\}$. The predecessor $P(x)$ is a uniformly random element of S. So, any 0-round protocol makes an error with probability at least $1/2$ under this distribution.

The size of the universe increases from μ_k to μ_{k+1}. Initially, the size of the universe is 4.

Now, suppose we have already constructed the hard distribution μ_k for k-round protocols over a universe of size $n = n_k$. The construction of μ_{k+1} depends on who sends the first message in the protocol.

This corresponds to writing X in base m with the digits $X_0, X_1, X_2, \ldots, X_{r-1}$, and setting the yth element of S to be $X_0, X_1, \ldots, X_{i-1}, y, 0, \ldots, 0$ for $y \in S_I$.

When Alice sends the first message, define μ_{k+1} as follows. Set $r = \lceil ((8t)^2 \log s) \rceil$. Sample $(X_1, S_1), \ldots, (X_r, S_r)$ independently according to the distribution μ_k. Let $I \in [r]$ be uniformly random. Set

$$X = \sum_{j=0}^{r-1} X_j \cdot n^{r-j-1},$$

and

$$S = \left\{ \sum_{j=0}^{I-1} X_j \cdot n^{r-j-1} + y \cdot n^{r-I-1} : y \in S_I \right\}.$$

The crucial point is that every element of S has exactly the same most significant bits as X, so $P_S(X)$ determines $P_{S_I}(X_I)$.

When Bob sends the first message, the construction is different. Set $r = \lceil (8t)^2 w \rceil$. Again, choose $(X_1, S_1), (X_2, S_2), \ldots, (X_r, S_r)$ independently from μ_k and $I \in [r]$ uniformly at random. Set

$$X = (I - 1) \cdot n + X_I,$$

and

$$S = \bigcup_{j=0}^{r-1} \{ j \cdot n + y : y \in S_j \}.$$

The predecessor of X in S determines the predecessor of X_I in S_I.

As in the lower bound for the greater-than function, we apply round elimination. A protocol with $k + 1$ rounds and error ϵ over μ_{k+1} yields a protocol with k rounds and error $\epsilon + 1/(8t)$ over μ_k. For example, when Alice sends the first message, her message M has entropy at most $\lceil \log s \rceil$. By Corollary 6.15, on average over $i, m, x_{<i}$,

$$p(x_i | i, m, x_{<i}) \overset{\frac{1}{8t}}{\approx} p(x_i).$$

Fix some value of $i, m, x_{<i}$ for which this error is achieved. We argue that

$$p(x_i, s_i | i, m, x_{<i}) \overset{\frac{1}{8t}}{\approx} p(x_i, s_i).$$

Indeed,

$$|p(x_i, s_i | i, m, x_{<i}) - p(x_i, s_i)|$$
$$= \sum_{x_i, s_i} |p(x_i | i, m, x_{<i}) \cdot p(s_i | i, m, x_{\leq i}) - p(x_i) \cdot p(s_i | x_i)|$$
$$= \sum_{x_i, s_i} p(s_i | x_i) \cdot |p(x_i | i, m, x_{<i}) - p(x_i)| \qquad \text{because}$$
$$\qquad\qquad\qquad\qquad\qquad\qquad\qquad\qquad\qquad p(s_i | i, m, x_{\leq i}) = p(s_i | x_i).$$
$$= \sum_{x_i} |p(x_i | i, m, x_{<i}) - p(x_i)|.$$

We get a k-round protocol for computing the predecessor over a smaller universe. The parties run the $k + 1$-round protocol but with the first message fixed and with the input inserted in the ith position.

Suppose, for the sake of finding a contradiction, that t does not satisfy (11.1), and that there is a $2t$-round protocol for the predecessor with error $1/4$ in which Alice sends messages of length $\lceil \log s \rceil$ and Bob sends messages of length w.

The initial set is of size 2. The size of the set does not increase when Alice speaks and is increased by a factor of $(8t)^2 w$ when Bob speaks.

This is because
$$t \ll \frac{\log \ell}{\log \log(\ell n)}.$$

The size of the eventual set is thus at most $2 \cdot ((8t)^2 w)^t \leq \ell$. The initial universe is of size 4. The size of the universe is raised to the power $\lceil (8t)^2 \log s \rceil$ when Alice speaks and is multiplied by a factor of $(8t)^2 w$ when Bob speaks. The size of the eventual universe is at most $(4 \cdot (8t)^2 w)^{\lceil (8t)^2 \log s \rceil^{2t}} \leq n$.

This is because
$$t \ll \frac{\log \log n}{\log \log(s \log(n))}.$$

Finally, performing $2t$ round eliminations, we get a protocol with no communication that finds the predecessor over μ_0 with error less than $1/2$. This is impossible.   □

Approximate Nearest Neighbor Search

[9] Andoni et al., 2006.

We now prove a lower bound for the nearest neighbor search problem.[9] The lower bound nearly matches the upper that we discussed earlier in Theorem 11.3.

Theorem 11.11 *For every $\beta > 0$ and $0 < \gamma < 1$, the following holds. If there is a static data structure that allows to $1 + \epsilon$ approximate nearest neighbor on n points in dimension at most $O(\log(n)/\epsilon^2)$ with $\epsilon > n^{-\gamma}$, then either*

$$s \geq n^{\Omega(\frac{1}{t\epsilon})} \quad or \quad t \geq \Omega(n^{1-\beta}/w).$$

The constants in the Ω notation depend on β and γ and on the constant in the O notation.

The lower bound is proved by appealing to the lower bound on the communication complexity of lopsided disjointness. In this problem, Alice is given a set $X \subseteq [d]$ of size ℓ, and Bob is given a set $Y \subseteq [d]$ of size n with $\ell \ll n$. Their goal is to decide if X and Y are disjoint or not.

In Chapter 1, we proved a lower bound for the deterministic communication complexity of lopsided disjointness, stated in Theorem 1.29. Here we need to use a randomized lower bound.

We do not prove Theorem 11.12 here. The proof uses a randomized analog of richness, analogous to Definition 1.25.

Theorem 11.12 *For every $\beta > 0$ and $0 < \gamma < 1$, if there is a randomized protocol solving lopsided disjointness as above for the case $\ell < n^\gamma$ and $d \geq 2\ell n$, then either Alice must send at least $\Omega(\ell \log n)$ bits or Bob must send at least $\Omega(n^{1-\beta})$ bits.*

We assume for simplicity that $1/\epsilon$ is an integer.

There is a straightforward reduction from the communication problem to the data structure problem. Suppose Alice and Bob have sets $x, y \subseteq [d]$ with $|x| = \ell = 1 + \frac{2}{\epsilon}$ and $|y| = n$, and they want to know if x and y are disjoint or not. Alice thinks of x as its indicator vector in $\{0, 1\}^d$. Bob encodes y by the set $S = \{e_i : i \in y\}$, where $e_i \in \{0, 1\}^d$ is the vector that has 1 in the ith entry and 0 elsewhere. Now, if the sets x, y are disjoint then $\Delta(x, S) = \ell + 1$, and otherwise $\Delta(x, S) \leq \ell - 1$. Because $(1 + \epsilon)(\ell - 1) = \frac{2}{\epsilon} + 2 = \ell + 1$, a $1 + \epsilon$ approximation for nearest neighbor allows to solve lopsided disjointness.

This approach, however, does not suffice to prove the strong lower bound in the theorem. To get the stronger bound, we store S using locality sensitive hashing, as in the proof of the *upper bound* for nearest neighbor search.

Proof of Theorem 11.11 Alice and Bob wish to solve lopsided disjointness on inputs x and y. Alice thinks of x as an element of $\{0, 1\}^d$. Bob encodes y as $S = \{e_i : i \in y\}$. Let $k = \ell - 1$.

Use Lemma 11.4 with $k = \ell - 1$ and $\gamma = \frac{1}{3n}$. Let the matrix Z, the interval T, and the parameter $r = O(\log(3n)/\epsilon^2)$ be as in the lemma. By the proof of Lemma 11.4, there is $\epsilon' = \Omega(\epsilon)$ so that for all $e \in S$ with $\Delta(x, e) = k$ we have

$$\Pr\left[r - |Z(x - e) \mod 2| > \left(\frac{1}{3} + \epsilon'\right)r\right] \le \frac{1}{3n},$$

and for all $y \in S$ with $\Delta(x, e) \ge (1 + \epsilon)k$ we have

$$\Pr\left[r - |Z(x - e) \mod 2| < \left(\frac{1}{3} + 2\epsilon'\right)r\right] \le \frac{1}{3n}.$$

The parties choose Z using public randomness. Alice encodes x as

$$x' = (J + Zx) \mod 2$$

where J is the all-ones vector. Bob uses the data structure to store the random set

$$S' = \{Ze \mod 2 : e \in S\}.$$

Note that

$$\Delta(x', S') = \min\{|x' + y' \mod 2| : y' \in S'\}$$
$$= \min\{r - |Z(x - e) \mod 2| : e \in S\}.$$

By the union bound over the n elements of S, with probability at least $2/3$, if $\Delta(x, S) \le k$ then $\Delta(x', S') \le (\frac{1}{3} + \epsilon')r$, and otherwise $\Delta(x', S') \ge (\frac{1}{3} + 2\epsilon')r$.

> Either $\Delta(x, S) \le k$ or $\Delta(x, S) = (1 + \epsilon)k$.
>
> $\frac{(1/3)+2\epsilon'}{(1/3)+\epsilon'} \ge 1 + \epsilon'.$

Suppose, for the sake of finding a contradiction, that there is a data structure with parameters s, t, w that computes a $1 + \epsilon'$ approximate nearest neighbor. By Lemma 11.6, we obtain a protocol computing lopsided disjointness where Alice sends at most $O(t \log s)$ bits and Bob sends at most $O(tw)$ bits, with success probability at least $2/3$. The lower bound in Theorem 11.12 completes the proof. □

Lower Bounds on Dynamic Data Structures

DYNAMIC DATA STRUCTURES allow to query the data as well as updating it. The union-find data structure, the van Emde Boas tree, heaps, and binary search trees are all examples of dynamic data structures. In this section, we develop methods for proving lower bounds on such data structures.

> Unlike for static data structures, not all of methods for proving lower bounds on dynamic data structures involve reductions to communication complexity. Nevertheless, intuitions from understanding the role of information play a role here as well.

Dynamic data structures have three main parameters:

Word size w: The number of bits in each memory cell.

Query time t_q: The number of cells that are accessed to answer a query.

Some data structures do not provide good guarantees on the worst-case update and query times, but provide good *amortized* update and query times. For example, a common scheme is to use hashing to maintain a small subset $S \subseteq [n]$ of a large universe. After many operations, the size of the set S may exceed the capacity of the hash function to effectively avoid collisions. In this case the data structure *rehashes* the entire space using a less efficient hash function that avoids collisions for larger sets. The rehashing operation can be very expensive, but it needs to be performed infrequently, and the time complexity of the data structure per update/query remains small. The techniques developed in this section actually allow to prove lower bounds even on the amortized time complexity of data structures. But we do not discuss this here.

[10] Fredman and Saks, 1989; and Patrascu and Thorup, 2014.

[11] Fredman and Saks, 1989.

This result applies even if the data structure is only required to compute $q(i) \mod 2$.

Update time t_u: The number of cells that are accessed to update the data.

We allow data structures to be randomized, and this may induce errors. The *error* of the data structure is $\epsilon > 0$ if for every sequence of updates followed by a single query, the probability that the query is computed correctly is at least $1 - \epsilon$.

Sorted Lists of Numbers

Suppose we want to maintain a set $S \subseteq [n]$ so that we can add and delete elements from the set, as well as compute the ith element of the set in the sorted order.

We prove the following lower bound.[10] The proof does not explicitly involve communication complexity. It does, however, use the concepts from information theory that we developed in Chapter 6.

Theorem 11.13 *Any data structure maintaining a sorted list of numbers with error at most $1/3$ for $m \geq 3n^2$ operations satisfies $t_q \cdot \log(t_u w) \geq \Omega(\log n)$.*

For example, if t_u, w are polylogarithmic in n, then

$$t_q \geq \Omega(\log n / \log \log n).$$

The lower bound is proved by considering a different task called *prefix sum*.[11] In prefix sum we want to maintain a binary string $x \in \{0, 1\}^n$. Initially x is 0. We want to allow updating the value of x_i to be $1 - x_i$ for any $i \in [n]$. We also want to allow to query $q(i) = \sum_{j=1}^{i} x_j$.

Theorem 11.14 *Any data structure correctly computing prefix sum of an n bit string with error at most $1/3$ for $m \geq n \log n$ operations satisfies $t_q \cdot \log(t_u w) \geq \Omega(\log n)$.*

Before proving Theorem 11.14, we show how to use it to prove a lower bound for maintaining a sorted list of numbers. We show how to solve the prefix sum problem using a data structure for maintaining a sorted list of numbers.

Proof of Theorem 11.13 Initialize the set of numbers to be

$$T = \{j \in [n^2] : j \neq 1 \mod n\}.$$

This takes at most n^2 update operations, starting from the empty set. We also explicitly maintain the indicator vector of the set T using n^2 bits. This allows us to add and delete elements and check whether $j \in T$ in constant time and word size.

Associate every bit x_i with the element $(i - 1)n + 1 \in [n^2]$. Initially, x is zero, and all elements of $[n^2]$ that correspond to entries in x are not in T. Whenever we wish to flip the value of x_i, we check if

Figure 11.5 An example of the sets S_j when $k = 2$ and $r = 6$. The indicator vector of S_j is the $j + 1$st row of the matrix.

$(i - 1)n + 1 \in T$ using the indicator vector. If $(i - 1)n + 1 \in T$, we delete it from T. If $(i - 1)n + 1 \notin T$, we add it to T.

We add or delete from both the data structure and the indicator vector.

Let y_j denote the jth element of T in the sorted order. We claim that

$$y_{(i-1)n+1} = i - q(i) + ((i - 1)n + 1).$$

To see why this is true, note that the element $y_{(i-1)n+1}$ is one of the numbers in the interval in $[(i - 1)n + 1, in]$. The term $i - q(i)$ is the size of $[(i - 1)n + 1] - T$. The set T contains all elements in $[(i - 1)n + 2, in]$.

In particular, i and $y_{(i-1)n+1}$ determine $q(i)$. So, we can compute $q(i)$ by making a single query.

This allows us to simulate $n \log n$ operations of the prefix sum data structure using at most $2n^2 + n \log n \leq 3n^2$ operations of the given sorted set data structure. Theorem 11.14 completes the proof. □

Proof of Theorem 11.14 To prove the lower bound, we use a particular distribution on operations and query. We can thus assume that the data structure is deterministic and makes an error on at most an ϵ fraction of the random sequences of updates and query.

We set $n = k^r$ with $k \leq O(t_u w)$ a parameter to be determined. For $j = 0, 1, 2, \ldots, r$, define

$$S_j = \{a \cdot k^j + 1 : a \in \{0, 1, \ldots, k^{r-j} - 1\}\}.$$

The set S_j consists of k^{r-j} evenly spaced numbers in $[n]$. See Figure 11.5 for an illustration.

Consider the following sequence of random updates. There are $r + 1$ rounds. In the jth round we pick a uniformly random subset $T_j \subseteq S_j$, independent of other choices. For each $i \in T_j$, we flip the value of x_i using the data structure. At the end of these $r + 1$ rounds of updates, we pick a uniformly random coordinate $L \in [n]$ and query $q(L)$ using the data structure.

We shall bound from below the expected number of queries the data structure needs to make to correctly compute $q(L)$. Say that a cell of the data structure *belongs to round j* if it was last touched during the updates of round j. We shall prove that for *every* round j, the probability that a cell belonging to round j is queried during the final query operation is at least $\Omega(1)$. By linearity of expectation, this completes the proof:

$$\mathbb{E}[t_q] \geq \Omega(r) \geq \Omega\left(\frac{\log n}{\log(t_u w)}\right).$$

$r = \log_k n = \frac{\log n}{\log k}$.

First, some intuition. For fixed j, the algorithm must learn information about T_j if it correctly answers the query. All the information about T_j is encoded by cells belonging to rounds $\geq j$. The number of cells belonging to rounds $> j$ is much smaller than the entropy of T_j. So, even accounting for the cells belonging to rounds $> j$, the algorithm must read a cell belonging to round j if it wishes to learn information about T_j.

Now, let us make this intuition more formal. For the rest of the proof, fix a specific round j. Let $A \in \{0,1\}^{k^{r-j}}$ be the indicator vector of T_j inside S_j. Let I be the maximum element in S_j that is at most L. The integer I is uniformly distributed in S_j, and we interpret it as the name of a coordinate of A. For ease of notation, let D be a random variable encoding $L, A_{<I}, T_1, \ldots, T_{j-1}, T_{j+1}, \ldots, T_r$ and the contents and locations of all the cells that belong to rounds $> j$.

The key claim is that the data structure does not learn much information about A_I even knowing all of D. Because $H(A_I) = 1$, this is equivalent to the following.

Claim 11.15 $H(A_I|D) \geq 1 - \frac{2t_u w}{k}$.

Before proving Claim 11.15, let us use it to prove that a cell belonging to round j must be accessed with probability $\Omega(1)$. Define

$$Q = \begin{cases} 1 & \text{if the data structure queries a cell that belongs to round } j, \\ 0 & \text{otherwise,} \end{cases}$$

and

$$E = \begin{cases} 1 & \text{if the data structure makes an error,} \\ 0 & \text{otherwise.} \end{cases}$$

Denote by γ the probability that $Q = 1$.

When $Q = 0$, the output of the algorithm is determined by D because all the cells that are read in order to compute $q(L)$ are determined by D. In addition, when $Q = 0$ and D is known, the value of $q(L)$ is A_I plus a known constant. In other words, when $Q = 0$, the value of A_I is determined by E and D.

Now, by Claim 11.15, we have:

$$1 - \frac{2t_u w}{k} \leq H(A_I|D) \leq H(QA_I|D)$$

by the chain rule.
$$= H(Q|D) + H(A_I|DQ)$$

by subadditivity.
$$\leq H(Q) + H(A_I|DQ).$$

Here $h(\gamma)$ is the binary entropy function $h(\gamma) = \gamma \cdot \log(1/\gamma) + (1-\gamma) \cdot \log(1/(1-\gamma))$.

Thus,

$$1 - \frac{2t_u w}{k} \leq H(Q) + H(A_I|DQ)$$

$$\leq h(\gamma) + \gamma \cdot 1 + (1-\gamma) \cdot H(A_I|D, Q=0)$$

$$\leq h(\gamma) + \gamma + H(E|D, Q=0)$$

$$\leq h(\gamma) + \gamma + H(E|Q=0)$$

The probability of error conditioned on $Q = 0$ is at most $\epsilon/(1-\gamma) \leq 1/2$.
$$\leq h(\gamma) + \gamma + h(\epsilon/(1-\gamma)).$$

If k is set to be a large multiple of $t_u w$, the left-hand side is close to 1. If ϵ, γ are small, the right-hand side is close to 0. Thus we must have $\gamma = \Omega(1)$.

It remains to prove the claim. □

Proof of Claim 11.15 Partition D into two parts. Let B be L, $A_{<I}$, $T_1, T_2, \ldots, T_{j-1}, T_{j+1}, \ldots, T_r$. Let C denote the locations and contents of all the cells that belong to rounds $> j$.

The number of cells that are touched during rounds $> j$ is at most

$$t_u \cdot \sum_{j'=j+1}^{r} k^{r-j'} = t_u \cdot \frac{k^{r-j} - 1}{k - 1} \le 2 t_u k^{r-j-1}.$$

Given B, the variable C can be described by the contents of all cells that are touched during the updates in round $> j$. So, The data structure is deterministic.

$$\mathsf{H}(C|B) \le 2 t_u k^{r-j-1} \cdot w.$$

Therefore,

$$\mathsf{H}(A|BC) \ge \mathsf{H}(A|B) - \mathsf{H}(C|B)$$
$$\ge k^{r-j} - 2k^{r-j-1} t_u w$$
$$\ge k^{r-j} \left(1 - \frac{2 t_u w}{k}\right).$$

By the chain rule, we get

$$\mathsf{H}(A_I|D) = \frac{1}{k^{r-j}} \sum_{i=1}^{k^{r-j}} \mathsf{H}(A_i|A_{<i} BC) \ge 1 - \frac{2 t_u w}{k}.$$

□

Graph Connectivity

EFFICIENT ALGORITHMS THAT MAINTAIN and operate on graphs are widely used in computer science. These provide another source of basic data structure questions.

Suppose we want to implement a static data structure that stores the connectivity relations in a graph on n vertices. Namely, we would like to query if two vertices are connected by a path in the graph or not.

A trivial solution is to store the adjacency matrix of the graph. To answer a query, we can perform *breadth first search*. It takes $\binom{n}{2}$ bits to encode the matrix, but might involve making $\approx n^2$ probes to answer a query as well. The adjacency matrix is the $n \times n$ Boolean matrix encoding whether u, v are connected for every pair of vertices u, v.

A better solution is to store, for each vertex, the *name* of the connected component that the vertex belongs to. This can be stored with n words, each of size $O(\log n)$. Queries can be answered by probing two locations in the data structure.

If we want to maintain the graph using a dynamic data structure that supports the addition of edges and querying whether or not two vertices are connected, we can use the union-find data structure, as in Figure 11.4. At each point in time, the partition of the vertices represents the current connected components. When a new edge is added, if the two vertices of the edge are contained in the same connected component, nothing needs to be done. Otherwise, the two connected components are merged with the union operation.

Static Connectivity in Sparse Directed Graphs

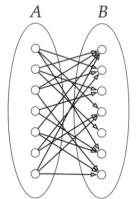

A   B

Connectivity in directed graphs is more complex than in directed graph. We seek a data structure that allows us to answer whether or not there is a directed path from a vertex u to a vertex v. A trivial data structure stores this data for every two vertices u and v. This gives, for n-vertex graphs, time $t = 1$, space $s = n(n - 1)$ and word size $w = 1$.

It is fairly simple to see that one cannot do much better. Let A and B be two disjoint sets of vertices, each of size $n/2$. Consider the graphs where all edges go from A to B. There are $2^{n^2/4}$ such graphs. The data structure must distinguish all of them because the queries allow to reconstruct the underlying graph. So, we must have $sw \geq n^2/4$.

The problem becomes more interesting when we consider sparse graphs. What if we are guaranteed that every vertex only has $O(\log n)$ edges coming out of it? Is there a data structure solving this version of graph connectivity with $s \leq O(n \log n)$, $w \leq O(\log n)$ and $t \leq O(1)$?

Communication complexity can be used to prove that such data structures do not exist:[12]

[12] Pătraşcu, 2011.

Theorem 11.16 *In any static data structure solving the directed graph connectivity problem on graphs with at most nw edges and word size w, we must have*

$$t \geq \Omega\left(\frac{\log n}{\log \frac{sw \log n}{n \log w}}\right).$$

In particular, if $t = O(1)$ and $w = O(\log n)$ then $s = n^{1+\Omega(1)}$.

Proof The proof relies on a special family of sparse directed graphs: subgraphs of the *butterfly* graph. A (d, σ) butterfly graph is a layered directed graph where each vertex corresponds to a pair $(i, u) \in [d + 1] \times [\sigma]^d$. The vertices are partitioned to $d + 1$ layers, according to the value of i. Each layer i has exactly one vertex for each string of length d from the alphabet $[\sigma]$. Each vertex in the ith layer is connected to exactly w vertices from the $i + 1$st layer that agree in all but the ith coordinate. See Figure 11.6 for an illustration.

This graph has the following routing property. There is a unique path connecting each vertex in the first layer to each vertex in the last layer. To go from $(\sigma_1, \ldots, \sigma_d)$ to $(\sigma'_1, \ldots, \sigma'_d)$, the only path is

$$(\sigma_1, \ldots, \sigma_d) \rightarrow (\sigma'_1, \sigma_2, \ldots, \sigma_d)$$
$$\rightarrow (\sigma'_1, \sigma'_2, \sigma_3, \ldots, \sigma_d) \rightarrow \cdots \rightarrow (\sigma'_1, \sigma'_2, \ldots, \sigma'_d).$$

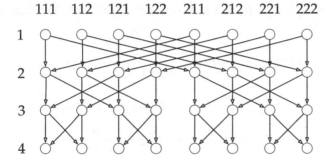

111   112   121   122   211   212   221   222

1

2

3

4

Figure 11.6 The butterfly graph with $d = 3$ and $\sigma = 2$.

The following notation is useful. For $u \in [\sigma]^d$, let $u_{-i} \in [\sigma]^{d-1}$ denote u after deleting the ith coordinate: $u_{-i} = (u_1, u_2, \ldots, u_{i-1}, u_{i+1}, \ldots, u_d)$. There is an edge from (i, u) to (j, v) if and only if $j = i + 1$ and $u_{-i} = v_{-i}$.

The proof also relies on the following lower bound for a version of lopsided disjointness, see Exercise 1.8.

Theorem 11.17 *Suppose Alice is given a string $x \in [\sigma]^k$, and Bob is given a sequence Y of sets $Y_1, \ldots, Y_k \subseteq [\sigma]$. If there is a protocol that determines whether or not there is an i such that $x_i \in Y_i$, with Alice sending a bits and Bob sending b bits, then $a + b \geq \frac{\sigma k}{2^{a/k}+1}$.*

Alice and Bob can use the data structure to solve the lopsided disjointness problem with inputs x, Y as in Theorem 11.17. They encode x, Y using subgraphs of the butterfly graph.

Set σ to be the word size w of the data structure. We set $k = dw^{d-1}$. The size of the graph is $n \leq 2wk$. So,

$$d = \Theta\left(\frac{\log n}{\log w}\right) \quad \text{and} \quad w^{d-1} \geq \Omega\left(\frac{n \log w}{w \log n}\right).$$

Alice uses $x \in [w]^k$ to construct a subgraph G of the butterfly graph. Each coordinate of x is associated with a tuple (i, u_{-i}), and so $x_{(i, u_{-i})} \in [w]$. The edge from (i, u) to $(i + 1, v)$ is included in G if and only if $v_i + u_i = x_{(i, u_{-i})} \mod w$. The graph G consists of w^d vertex disjoint paths from the first layer of the graph to the last layer.

The map $\xi \mapsto \xi + x_{(i, u_i)}$ mod w on $\xi \in [w]$ is one-to-one.

Bob uses $Y_1, \ldots, Y_k$ to construct a subgraph H of the butterfly graph. The edge from (i, u) to $(i + 1, v)$ is included in H if and only if $v_i + u_i \notin Y_{(i, u_{-i})} \mod w$.

If $x_j \notin Y_j$ for all $j \in [k]$, then G is contained in H. If there is a j for which $x_j \in Y_j$, we get w edges that are present in G, but not in H. Alice and Bob can determine if such a j exists by answering w^{d-1} connectivity queries; for every vertex u, Alice only needs to know whether the w^{d-1} paths that start at vertices of the form $(1, (1, u_{-1}))$ in G are included in H or not.

All paths are included in H if and only if $x_j \notin Y_j$ for all j.

Alice and Bob can simulate the execution of these w^{d-1} queries on the data structure in parallel. In each round, Alice sends Bob $\left\lceil \log \binom{s}{w^{d-1}} \right\rceil$ bits to indicate the cells that she needs to look up for each of her queries. Bob responds with $w \cdot w^{d-1} = w^d$ bits to describe the contents of those cells. This simulation gives a protocol where Alice sends

$a = t \left\lceil \log \binom{s}{w^{d-1}} \right\rceil$ bits, and Bob sends $b = tw^d$ bits. Theorem 11.17 implies that

$$2t \log \binom{s}{w^{d-1}} + tw^d \geq \frac{dw^d}{2^t \log \left(\binom{s}{w^{d-1}}\right)/(dw^{d-1}) + 1}.$$

Because $\binom{s}{w^{d-1}} \leq \left(\frac{es}{w^{d-1}}\right)^{w^{d-1}}$, we can simplify the inequality to:

$$2tw^{d-1} \log \left(\frac{es}{w^{d-1}}\right) + tw^d \geq \frac{dw^d}{\left(\frac{es}{w^{d-1}}\right)^{t/d} + 1}$$

or

$$t \left(\log \left(\frac{es}{w^{d-1}}\right) + 1\right) \geq \frac{d}{\left(\frac{es}{w^{d-1}}\right)^{t/d} + 1}.$$

Now, if $t \ll \frac{d}{\log \frac{es}{w^{d-1}}}$, then $\left(\frac{es}{w^{d-1}}\right)^{t/d} \leq 3$, so the right-hand side is at least $\Omega(d)$, but on the other hand the left-hand side is $\ll d$. Thus, we must have

$$t = \Omega\left(\frac{d}{\log \frac{es}{w^{d-1}}}\right) \geq \Omega\left(\frac{\log n}{\log \frac{sw \log n}{n \log w}}\right).$$

□

Lower Bound for Dynamic Graph Connectivity

The union-find data structure solves this problem with parameters $s = O(n)$ and $w = t_u = t_q = O(\log n)$.

[13] Fredman and Saks, 1989.

In the dynamic graph connectivity problem, the data structure is required to maintain a graph on the vertex set $[n]$, supporting addition of edges, as well as connectivity queries. This dynamic problem requires the following amount of resources.[13]

Theorem 11.18 *Any data structure solving the graph connectivity problem with error at most $1/3$ for $m \geq n + 1$ operations satisfies*

$$t_q \cdot \log t_u w \geq \Omega(\log n).$$

Setting $w = O(\log n)$ and $t_u = \text{polylog}(n)$, we get that $t_q \geq \Omega(\log n / \log \log n)$.

The proof shares many ideas with the proof of the lower bound for the prefix-sum problem given in Theorem 11.14.

Proof Assume we have a data structure for solving the dynamic graph connectivity problem. We perform a random sequence of edge additions and then ask a single random connectivity query. We prove that the data structure must probe many locations in expectation. As usual, we can assume that the data structure is deterministic.

Let $k \leq O(t_u w)$ be a parameter to be determined. Assume without loss of generality that $n = 2(k^{r+1} - 1)/(k - 1)$ for some integer r. We sample a random graph as follows. The graph consists of two disconnected k-ary trees, T_0 and T_1, each of depth r. The number of vertices is indeed n. We uniformly permute the names of the vertices in the graph.

We add the edges of this graph to the data structure in r rounds, labeled $j = 1, 2, \ldots, r$. In the first round, we add all $2k^r$ edges that touch the leaves of the trees. In the jth round, we add the edges from depth $r - j$ to $r - j + 1$. After all the edges of the trees have been added, we pick two random leaves and query whether or not they are connected in the graph. The leaves are connected if and only if they belong to the same tree.

Say that a cell of the data structure *belongs to round* j if it was last touched in round j of the updates. We prove that for each j, the probability that a cell that belongs to round j was accessed to answer the query is at least $\Omega(1)$. This completes the proof. The expected number of queries is

$$\mathbb{E}\left[t_q\right] \geq \Omega(r) \geq \Omega\left(\frac{\log n}{\log(t_u w)}\right).$$

For the rest of the proof, fix a particular round j. The number of vertices v of depth $r - j + 1$ in the two trees is $2k^{r-j+1}$. Let $A \in \{0, 1\}^{2k^{r-j+1}}$ be the random variable that describes for each vertex v at depth $r - j + 1$ the tree v belongs to. Formally,

$$A_v = \begin{cases} 1 & \text{if } v \in T_1, \\ 0 & \text{if } v \in T_0. \end{cases}$$

Let U, V be two uniformly random and independent vertices at depth $r - j + 1$ in the graph. Set $R = A_U + A_V \mod 2$. The value of R encodes whether U, V are connected in the graph. Let D be the random variable that contains the following data: U, V, the edges of the graph *not* added in the jth round, and the locations and contents of all cells that belong to rounds $> j$.

The final query to the data structure yields the same distribution on U, V of this form.

Intuitively, D does not provide a lot of information about R. The following key claim makes this precise.

Claim 11.19 $\mathsf{H}(R|D) \geq 1 - \frac{7 t_u w}{k}$.

Claim 11.19 completes the proof, exactly as Claim 11.15 completes the proof of Theorem 11.14. We leave the details to Exercise 11.5. □

Proof of Claim 11.19 Let B be the random variable encoding all the edges *not* added to the graph in the jth round. After fixing the value of B, the roots of the two trees have been fixed, the identities of the leaves have also been determined, but the graph still consists of many disjoint and full k-ary trees, as in Figure 11.7.

After fixing B, we know the identity of the $2k^{r-j+1}$ vertices at depth $r - j + 1$. Exactly half of them get $A_v = 0$, and exactly half get $A_v = 1$. Thus,

$$\begin{aligned} \mathsf{H}(A|B) &= \log \binom{2k^{r-j+1}}{k^{r-j+1}} \\ &\geq 2k^{r-j+1} - 1 - \log k^{(r-j+1)/2} \\ &\geq 2k^{r-j+1} - 2k^{r-j}. \end{aligned}$$

because $\binom{2m}{m} \geq 2^{2m-1}/\sqrt{m}$.

because $\log k^{(r-j+1)/2} \leq k^{(r-j+1)/2} \leq k^{r-j}$.

Figure 11.7 The edges of B
when $k = 3, r = 5$, and $j = 2$.

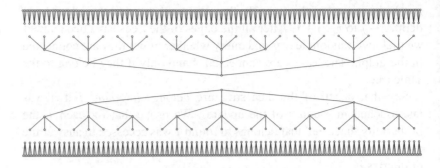

Let C denote the locations and contents of all cells that belong to rounds $> j$. The number of edges added after the jth round is

$$\sum_{i=j+1}^{r} 2k^{r-i+1} = 2k \cdot \frac{k^{r-j} - 1}{k - 1} \le 4k^{r-j}.$$

Given B, each of these edges can contribute at most $t_u w$ to the entropy of C. This is because C can be described by specifying the contents of each of the cells accessed when the algorithm adds these edges. Hence,

$$\begin{aligned}
H(A|BC) &\ge H(A|B) - H(C|B) \\
&\ge 2k^{r-j+1} - 2k^{r-j} - 1 - 4k^{r-j} t_u w \\
&\ge 2k^{r-j+1} - 6k^{r-j} t_u w.
\end{aligned}$$

For any fixed vertex q at the same depth as U, V, we have

$$\Pr[q \in \{U, V\}] = 1 - \left(1 - \frac{1}{2k^{r-j+1}}\right)^2 = \frac{1}{k^{r-j+1}} - \left(\frac{1}{2k^{r-j+1}}\right)^2.$$

Applying Shearer's lemma (Lemma 6.8), we conclude that

$$\begin{aligned}
H(A_U, A_V | UVBC) \\
&\ge \left(\frac{1}{k^{r-j+1}} - \left(\frac{1}{2k^{r-j+1}}\right)^2\right) \cdot \left(2k^{r-j+1} - 6k^{r-j} t_u w\right) \\
&\ge 2 - \frac{1}{2k^{r-j+1}} - \frac{6t_u w}{k} \\
&\ge 2 - \frac{7t_u w}{k}.
\end{aligned}$$

Now, A_U, A_V are determined by R, A_U. So, we have

$$\begin{aligned}
H(R|D) &\ge H(A_U, A_V | D) - H(A_U | D) \\
&\ge 2 - \frac{7t_u w}{k} - 1 \\
&= 1 - \frac{7t_u w}{k}.
\end{aligned}$$

because $H(A_U | D) \le 1$.

$\square$

Exercises

Ex 11.1 – Modify the van Emde Boas tree data structure so that it can maintain the median of n numbers, with time $O(\log \log n)$ for adding, deleting, and querying the median.

Ex 11.2 – We showed that every static data structure problem leads to a communication game and used lower bounds on the total number of bits communicated in the game to prove data structure lower bounds. Show that if the number of possible queries to the data structure is Q, then we will never be able to prove that $s > (2Q)^{1/t}/2^w$ using such an approach. Conclude that any lower bound showing that $t \gg \log Q$ must use a different approach.

Ex 11.3 – For $\delta > 0$, show that n operations of a dynamic data structure with parameters s, t_u, t_q, w and error $\epsilon > 0$ can always be simulated by another data structure with space $n^2(t_u + t_q)/\delta$, update time t_u, query time t_q, word size w, and error $\epsilon + \delta$.

Ex 11.4 – For the k-lopsided set intersection data structure problem, prove that one cannot improve on the trivial solution for $k = 1$.

Ex 11.5 – Show how Claim 11.19 completes the proof of Theorem 11.18.

12

Extension Complexity of Polytopes

POLYTOPE ARE SUBSETS OF EUCLIDEAN SPACE that can be defined by a finite number of linear inequalities. They are fundamental geometric objects that have been studied by mathematicians for centuries. Any $n \times d$ matrix A, and $n \times 1$ vector b defines a polytope P:

Here $a \le b$ means $a_i \le b_i$ for all i.

$$P = \{x \in \mathbb{R}^d : Ax \le b\}.$$

A simple example of a polytope is a three-dimensional cube, shown in Figure 12.1. In this chapter, we explore some questions about the *complexity* of representing polytopes. When can a *complex* polytope be expressed as the shadow of a *simple* polytope? Besides being mathematically interesting, these questions are relevant to understanding the complexity of algorithms based on linear programming, as we explain in detail later in this chapter.

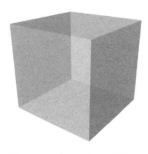

Figure 12.1 A cube in $\mathbb{R}^3$ can be defined by the six inequalities $-1 \le x \le 1, -1 \le y \le 1, -1 \le z \le 1$.

In other texts, polytopes are sometimes assumed to be bounded – it is assumed that there is a finite ball that contains the polytope. Throughout this textbook, polytopes may have infinite volume.

Indeed, if $\gamma \in [0, 1]$, then

$A(\gamma x + (1 - \gamma)y)$

$\le \gamma Ax + (1 - \gamma)Ay$

$\le \gamma b + (1 - \gamma)b = b.$

Polytopes have many nice properties that makes them easy to manipulate and understand. A polytope P is always *convex* – if $x, y \in P$, the line segment connecting x and y is also in P. The definition of a polytope seems to involve only inequalities. However, sets defined using equalities are also polytopes. For example, the set of points $(x, y, z) \in \mathbb{R}^3$ so that

$$x = y + z + 1,$$

$$z \ge 0,$$

is a polytope because the constraints can be rewritten as:

$$x - y - z \le 1,$$

$$-x + y + z \le -1,$$

$$-z \le 0.$$

A *halfspace* H is a polytope defined by a single inequality $H = \{x \in \mathbb{R}^d : hx \le c\}$. Every polytope is an intersection of halfspaces, and every finite intersection of halfspaces is a polytope. In particular, the intersection of two polytopes is also a polytope.

An important fact is that every linear inequality that the points of the polytope satisfy can be derived from the inequalities that define the polytope:

Fact 12.1 *If a nonempty polytope $\{x \in \mathbb{R}^d : Ax \leq b\}$ is contained in a halfspace $\{x \in \mathbb{R}^d : hx \leq c\}$, then there is a $1 \times n$ row vector $u \geq 0$ such that $uA = h$ and $ub \leq c$.*

> This fact is a consequence of Farkas's lemma. See Exercise 12.1.

The vector u promised by Fact 12.1 shows how to derive the inequality of the halfspace from the inequalities defining the polytope. It *proves* that the points of the polytope belong to the halfspace. For every $x \in P$, we have $hx = uAx \leq ub \leq c$.

> Note that $u \geq 0$ is crucial here.

The *dimension* of a polytope P is the dimension of the minimal affine subspace A such that $P \subseteq A$. A point v is on the *boundary* of P if $v \in P$, and for every $\epsilon > 0$, there is a point $u \in A - P$ at distance at most ϵ from v. A *face* of the polytope P is a set of the form $F = P \cap H$, where H is a halfspace that intersects P only on its boundary. There may be multiple halfspaces that generate the same face.

> An affine subspace of dimension k is a set of the form $A = \{v_0 + v : v \in V\}$ where $v_0 \in \mathbb{R}^d$ and $V \subseteq \mathbb{R}^d$ is a k-dimensional vector space.

The faces of a polytope are also polytopes. The dimension of a face is smaller than that of P. When the dimension of the face is exactly one less than the dimension of the polytope itself, we call it a *facet*. A *vertex* of the polytope is a nonempty face of dimension 0 – it consists of a single point.

The boundary of the polytope is the union of all of its facets. Every point on the boundary belongs to some facet, and every point on a facet belongs to the boundary. The inequalities defining the polytope may not correspond to the facets of the polytope. They can be redundant. Nevertheless, by Fact 12.1, a halfspace defining a facet can be derived by combining the inequalities defining the polytope. Figure 12.2 shows the different parts of a polytope.

The number of inequalities needed to express a polytope is at least the number of facets:

> For example, if the polytope is defined by the $3 \times d$ matrix A by $Ax \leq b$, and $A_1 + A_2 = A_3, b_1 + b_2 = b_3$, then the third inequality is implied by the first two. The polytope has at most two facets.

Fact 12.2 *If a polytope is defined by r inequalities, then it has at most r facets.*

Fact 12.3 *If a k-dimensional polytope $P \subseteq \mathbb{R}^d$ has r facets, it can be expressed with r inequalities as $P = \{x : Ax \leq b, Cx = e\}$, where A is an $r \times d$ matrix, b is an $r \times 1$ column vector, C is a $k \times d$ matrix, and e is a $k \times 1$ vector.*

The facets can be used to generate all the other faces of the polytope:

Fact 12.4 *Every face of P can be expressed as the intersection of some of the facets of P.*

One important consequence of Fact 12.4 is that a polytope with k facets can have at most 2^k faces.

> There are 2^k subsets of a set of size k.

Figure 12.2 The anatomy of a polytope. The polytope has dimension 2. The six one-dimensional faces are called facets. The six zero-dimensional faces are called vertices. The intersection between every two facets is a face – it is either a vertex or empty.

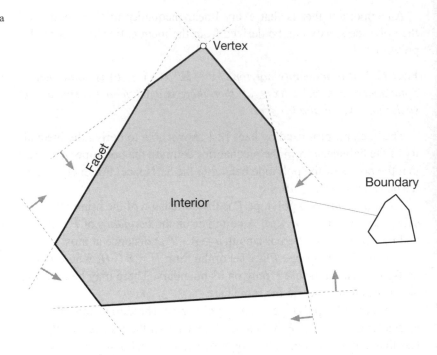

Transformations of Polytopes

POLYTOPES BEHAVE NICELY UNDER some natural transformations. Translating a polytope gives another polytope. If $P = \{x \in \mathbb{R}^d : Ax \leq b\}$ is a polytope, and $z \in \mathbb{R}^d$ is any vector, then the set

$$P + z = \{x + z : x \in P\}$$

is also polytope. This is because

$$P + z = \{y \in \mathbb{R}^d : Ay \leq b + Az\}.$$

Applying an arbitrary linear transformation to a polytope gives another polytope, as in Figure 12.3.

Theorem 12.5 *If L is a linear map from $\mathbb{R}^d$ to $\mathbb{R}^k$, and $P \subseteq \mathbb{R}^d$ is a polytope, then*

$$L(P) = \{L(x) : x \in P\} \subseteq \mathbb{R}^k$$

is also a polytope. Moreover, every face of $L(P)$ is equal to $L(F)$, for some face $F \subseteq P$.

Before proving the theorem, we discuss an application. It is often more convenient to describe a polytope by applying a linear transformation to another polytope. To illustrate this, let us explore a generic way to generate a polytope from a finite set of points. See Figure 12.3 for an example.

Figure 12.1 shows the convex hull of 8 points. Figure 12.2 shows the convex hull of 6 points.

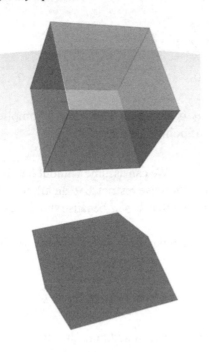

Figure 12.3 A projection of the cube.

Given a set of points $V = \{v_1, \ldots, v_k\} \in \mathbb{R}^d$, the *convex hull* of these points is the minimal convex set containing V. It is the intersection of all convex sets containing V. Equivalently, it is the set of points $x \in \mathbb{R}^d$ satisfying

$$x = \sum_{j=1}^{k} \mu_i \cdot v$$

$$\mu_j \geq 0 \qquad \qquad \text{for } j = 1, 2, \ldots, k$$

$$\sum_{j=1}^{k} \mu_j = 1,$$

for some $\mu_1, \ldots, \mu_k \in \mathbb{R}$. The equations above describe a polytope whose points are of the form $(x_1, \ldots, x_d, \mu_1, \ldots, \mu_k)$. Projecting this polytope onto the variables $x_1, \ldots, x_d$ is a linear transformation, so the convex hull is also a polytope.

For example, a halfspace is not the convex hull of finitely many points.

Not every polytope is the convex hull of a finite set of points. However, every *bounded* polytope is the convex hull of a finite set of points.

Fact 12.6 *A bounded polytope is the convex hull of its vertices.*

A bounded polytope is contained in some ball of finite radius.

The *conical hull* of the finite set $V \subseteq \mathbb{R}^d$ is the set of points that can be obtained by nonnegative linear combinations of the points in V. It is the set of points $x \in \mathbb{R}^d$ satisfying

$$x = \sum_{j=1}^{k} \mu_i \cdot v$$

$$\mu_j \geq 0 \qquad\qquad\qquad \text{for } j = 1, 2, \ldots, k,$$

for some $\mu_1, \ldots, \mu_k \in \mathbb{R}$. Again, Theorem 12.5 implies that the conical hull of a finite set of points is a polytope.

Proof of Theorem 12.5 We can assume without loss of generality that P has full dimension; otherwise restrict L to an affine subspace containing P. We can also assume that $k \leq d$ because the dimension of the image of L is at most k.

Think of L as a $k \times d$ matrix.

If L is invertible, then the proof is straightforward. If $P = \{x : Ax \leq b\}$, then

$$L(P) = \{y : AL^{-1}y \leq b\},$$

so $L(P)$ is also a polytope. In addition, the structure of the polytope is preserved. There is a one-to-one correspondence between the faces of P and the faces of $L(P)$. Every face of F of P corresponds to the face $L(F)$ of $L(P)$.

When L is not invertible, the theorem is more involved to prove. Every matrix L has a singular value decomposition of the form $L = U \cdot \Lambda \cdot V$, where U is an invertible $k \times k$ matrix with $UU^\top = I$, where V is an invertible $d \times d$ matrix with $VV^\top = I$, and where Λ is a $k \times d$ diagonal matrix.

We used singular value decomposition to prove a lower bound for the Gap-Hamming problem in Chapter 5.

Express Λ as $\Lambda = DS$, where D is a $k \times d$ diagonal matrix where all nonzero entries are 1, and S is a $d \times d$ diagonal matrix where all entries on the diagonal are nonzero. The matrix D defines a *projection*. Thus, $L = UDSV$, where U, V, and S are invertible.

In words, Lx can be computed by first applying an invertible linear transformation SV, then *projecting* using D, and then applying another invertible linear transformation U.

The projection of a polytope can actually have a different number of faces and facets than the original polytope. Quantifying how much the number of facets of a polytope can increase under linear transformations is one of the main goals of this chapter.

Lemma 12.7 *If D is a $k \times d$ projection matrix and $P \subseteq \mathbb{R}^d$ is a polytope, then the projection $D(P)$ is also a polytope. Moreover, every face of $D(P)$ is equal to $D(F)$, for some face $F \subseteq P$.*

The lemma suffices to complete the proof.   □

Proof of Lemma 12.7 We prove the lemma by induction. The lemma follows from repeating a process called Fourier-Motzkin elimination. It is enough to prove that the lemma holds when $k = d - 1$.

Suppose D projects a point $(x_1, \ldots, x_k, z)$ in P to $x = (x_1, \ldots, x_k)$. The inequalities defining P can be scaled so that they are of three types, according to the coefficient of z:

$$A_i \cdot x \leq b_i, \qquad \text{type 0.}$$
$$A_i \cdot x + z \leq b_i, \qquad \text{type 1.}$$
$$A_i \cdot x - z \leq b_i. \qquad \text{type } -1.$$

We now define new inequalities that capture the projection $D(P)$. An inequality of type 0 induces the same inequality on $x \in \mathbb{R}^k$. Every two inequalities

$$A_i \cdot x + z \leq b_i$$

and

$$A_j \cdot x - z \leq b_j$$

of type 1 and -1 can be combined to give a single inequality by addition:

$$(A_i + A_j) \cdot x \leq b_i + b_j.$$

If P was defined by n inequalities, we obtain at most n^2 inequalities in this way. Denote by Q the polytope defined by these inequalities. We claim that $D(P) = Q$.

One direction is straightforward. Every inequality we have derived is satisfied by the elements of P. So, $D(P) \subseteq Q$. The other direction is more challenging. Assume $x \in Q$. We need to show that there is a choice of z such that $(x, z) \in P$. Let ℓ be an index maximizing $A_\ell \cdot x - b_\ell$ over all inequalities of type -1. Set $z = A_\ell \cdot x - b_\ell$. This choice of z ensures that (x, z) satisfies all inequalities of type -1:

$$A_j \cdot x - b_j \leq z \Rightarrow A_j \cdot x - z \leq b_j.$$

The point (x, z) also satisfies all inequalities of type 0 because these do not involve z. Every inequality $A_i \cdot x + z \leq b_i$ of type 1 is also satisfied, because

$$(A_i + A_\ell) \cdot x \leq b_i + b_\ell$$
$$\Rightarrow A_\ell \cdot x - b_\ell + A_i \cdot x \leq b_i$$
$$\Rightarrow z + A_i \cdot x \leq b_i.$$

It remains to argue about the faces of $D(P)$. Suppose $H \subseteq R^k$ is a halfspace such that $H \cap D(P)$ is a face of $D(P)$. Express H as the set of points satisfying $h \cdot x \leq c$ for some $h \in \mathbb{R}^k$ and $c \in \mathbb{R}$. Let $H' \subseteq R^{k+1}$ be the set of points (x, z) such that $h \cdot x \leq c$. The set H' is a halfspace, and $D(H') = H$.

We need to verify that $H' \cap P$ is a face of P. That is, to verify that $H' \cap P$ is contained in the boundary of P. Let $v = (x, z) \in H' \cap P$, and let $\epsilon > 0$. This means that $x = D(v)$ belongs to the face $H \cap D(P)$. So, there is a point $u \notin D(P)$ at distance at most ϵ from x. The point (u, z) is not in P, and its distance from v is at most ϵ as well. $\qquad \square$ Recall that P has full dimension.

Algorithms from Polytopes

[1] Wikipedia, 2016a.

POLYTOPES ARE ALSO USEFUL from the perspective of algorithm design. Many interesting computational problems can be reduced
to the problem of optimizing a linear function over some polytope.[1]

Below we provide two examples. Suppose we wish to solve some
optimization problem, like finding the distance between two vertices
in a graph. To do so, we construct a polytope P and a linear function
L so that the maximum of L over P is precisely the quantity we are
interested in.

Shortest Paths

Finding the shortest path between two locations is a central algorithmic
problem with many applications. Say we want to compute the length of
the shortest path between the two vertices 1 and n in an undirected graph
with vertex set $[n]$. We show how to encode this algorithmic problem as
a question about optimizing a linear function over a polytope. For every
pair of distinct vertices $u, v \in [n]$, define the variable $x_{u,v}$, and define
the graph polytope P by

Think of the variable $x_{u,v}$ as the flow from u to v.

flow is nonnegative.

$$x_{u,v} \geq 0 \qquad\qquad \text{for every } u \neq v$$

flow out of 1 is 1.

$$\sum_{w \neq 1} x_{1,w} = 1$$

flow into n is 1.

$$\sum_{w \neq n} x_{w,n} = 1$$

flow into an intermediate vertex is equal to the flow coming out.

$$\sum_{w \neq u} x_{u,w} = \sum_{w \neq u} x_{w,u} \qquad\qquad \text{for every } u \notin \{1, n\}.$$

These equations define a polytope in $P \subseteq \mathbb{R}^d$, with $d = n(n-1)$. It has
at most d facets because it is defined by d inequalities.

Now, given a connected graph G with edge set E, consider the problem of finding the point in the graph polytope P that minimizes the linear
function

$$L(x) = \sum_{\{u,v\} \notin E} n \cdot (x_{u,v} + x_{v,u}) + \sum_{\{u,v\} \in E} (x_{u,v} + x_{v,u}).$$

Claim 12.8 $\min_{x \in P} L(x)$ *is the distance from 1 to n in G.*

Proof Denote by $e_1, e_2, \ldots, e_\ell$ the edges of a shortest path in the graph.
If we give the pairs along this path weight 1 and all other pairs weight
0, we get a point x in the polytope with $L(x) = \ell$.

It remains to show that for each $x \in P$, we have $L(x) \geq \ell$. Suppose
$x \in P$ is such that $x_{u,v} > 0$ for some pair (u, v) that is not on a shortest
path. If $v \notin \{1, n\}$, because the flow into v is equal to the flow out of v,
there must be a vertex w so that $x_{v,w} > 0$. If $w \notin \{1, n\}$, we can now
deduce that there is a vertex z so that $x_{w,z} > 0$, and so on.

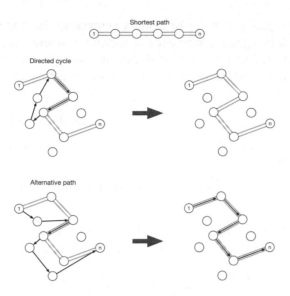

Figure 12.4 One can move the flow from a point x to a chosen shortest path without increasing L.

We conclude that either

1. there is a directed path $e'_1, \ldots, e'_k$ from n to 1 where all edges get positive flow,

2. there is a directed path $e'_1, \ldots, e'_k$ from 1 to n where all edges get positive flow, or

3. there is a directed cycle $e'_1, \ldots, e'_k$ with positive flow as in Figure 12.4.

In the first case, the point x is not a minimizer of L. We can reduce the flow along the path by a small amount, stay inside the polytope, and reduce L.

In the second case, we can reduce the flow along $e'_1, \ldots, e'_k$ and increase the flow along $e_1, \ldots, e_\ell$ by the same amount. This gives a new point in the polytope, and the value of L does not increase because $k \geq \ell$.

In the third case, we can reduce the flow along the cycle and get a new point in the polytope. This reduces the value of L.

These operations do not increase the value of L. They eventually gives a point in P that only places weight on the edges $e_1, \ldots, e_\ell$. The value of L on such a point is ℓ. □

Matchings

Finding a maximum matching in a graph is another important problem with many applications. We show that finding the maximum matching can also be encoded as the problem of optimizing a linear function over some polytope.

For every pair $u, v \in [n]$ of distinct vertices we have the variable $x_{\{u,v\}}$. Each matching corresponds to a point x where $x_{\{u,v\}} = 1$ if u, v are matched and $x_{\{u,v\}} = 0$ if they are not. The convex hull M of these points is called the *matching polytope*. It can be defined by the inequalities:[2]

[2] Edmonds, 1965.

$$x_{\{u,v\}} \geq 0 \qquad\qquad \text{for all distinct } u, v$$

The number of edges touching u is at most 1.

$$\sum_{v \neq u} x_{\{u,v\}} \leq 1 \qquad\qquad \text{for all } u$$

A set of odd size k can contain at most $\lfloor \frac{k}{2} \rfloor$ edges.

$$\sum_{u < v \in A} x_{\{u,v\}} \leq \frac{|A| - 1}{2} \qquad \text{for all } A \subseteq [n] \text{ with } |A| \text{ odd.}$$

This polytope has at most $\binom{n}{2} + n + 2^{n-1}$ facets and is contained in $\mathbb{R}^{\binom{n}{2}}$.

Given a graph with n vertices defined by the set of edges E, let

$$L(x) = \sum_{\{u,v\} \in E} x_{\{u,v\}} - \sum_{\{u,v\} \notin E} x_{\{u,v\}}.$$

Claim 12.9 $\max_{x \in M} L(x)$ *is the size of the largest matching in the graph.*

Proof Let Z denote the set of binary vectors $z \in \mathbb{R}^{\binom{n}{2}}$ that correspond to matchings. Because M is the convex hull Z, we can write every $x \in M$ as $x = \sum_{z \in T} \alpha_z \cdot z$, where $\alpha_z \geq 0$ for all z and $\sum_{z \in Z} \alpha_z = 1$. Thus, if $x \in M$ maximizes $L(x)$, then we have

$$L(x) = L\left(\sum_{z \in T} \alpha_z \cdot z\right) = \sum_{z \in T} \alpha_z \cdot L(z).$$

So some $z \in Z$ must also achieve the maximum $L(z) = L(x)$.

Now, z must correspond to a valid matching of the graph because by the definition of L, if z contains an edge e that is not in the graph, setting $z_e = 0$ gives another point in the polytope whose value under L is even larger. $\qquad\square$

There is a single polytope – the matching polytope – such that every n-vertex graph defines a linear function whose maximum value on the polytope is precisely the maximum size of a matching in the graph.

Unfortunately, the matching polytope has an exponential number of facets, so we cannot use linear programming to efficiently find the size of the largest matching in polynomial time this way.

Exercise 12.8 shows that the *bipartite* matching polytope has $O(n^2)$ facets.

Extension Complexity

THE COMPLEXITY OF SOLVING optimization problems on polytopes is related to the number of facets of the polytope. Therefore, it is important to find polytopes that encode computational problems and have a small number of facets.

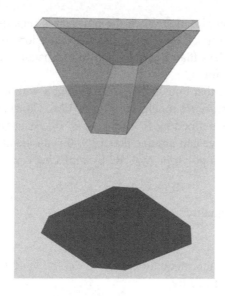

Figure 12.5 A polytope with eight facets that has an extension with six facets. Watch an animation.

A generic way to reduce the number of facets is via *extensions*. A polytope $Q \subseteq \mathbb{R}^k$ is an extension of a polytope $P \subseteq \mathbb{R}^d$ if there is a linear map $L : \mathbb{R}^k \to \mathbb{R}^d$ such that $L(Q) = P$. The *extension complexity* of P is the minimum number of facets achieved by any extension of P.

One can interpret this in terms of computational complexity as follows. The cost of a polytope is the number of facets. A polytope Q allows us to optimize over a polytope P if Q is an extension of P. The complexity of P is the least cost of an extension Q of P.

There are many polytopes that admit nontrivial extensions – extensions with fewer facets. See Figure 12.5 for an example. In terms of proving impossibility results, the following lower bound always holds:

Claim 12.10 *The extension complexity of a polytope with n faces is at least* $\log n$.

Proof Suppose Q is an extension of P. By Theorem 12.5, each face of P corresponds to a face of Q. Each face of Q is the intersection of a subset of the facets of Q. So if Q has k facets, P can have at most 2^k faces. $\qquad\square$

This lower bound is often too weak to be useful. Later on, we develop tools for proving stronger lower bounds for specific cases. First, we explore some natural examples of polytopes with small extension complexity.

Regular Polygons

A polygon is a polytope in the plane $\mathbb{R}^2$. Consider polygons with n facets. There are such polygons whose extension complexity is at least $\Omega(\sqrt{n})$.[3] However, if the polygon is sufficiently symmetric, then it has

[3] Fiorini et al., 2012.

We focus on the case that n is a power of two.

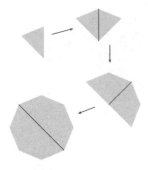

Figure 12.6 An octagon can be built with three reflections.

low extension complexity.[4] When the polygon is *regular*, its extension complexity is $O(\log n)$. By Fact 12.10, the extension complexity of an n-gon cannot be less than $\log n$. So, up to a constant factor, this is the best we can hope for.

The key idea is that one can *mirror* a polygon without increasing its extension complexity by much; see Figure 12.6. Consider any polygon $P \subseteq \mathbb{R}^2$, which is defined by $P = \{x : Ax \leq b\}$. By applying a rotation and a translation, we can assume that $x_1 \leq 0$ is an inequality defining a facet of P. Define a polytope $Q \subseteq \mathbb{R}^3$ by replacing each inequality

$$A_{i,1} \cdot x_1 + A_{i,2} \cdot x_2 \leq b_i$$

of P with the inequality

$$A_{i,1} \cdot x_3 + A_{i,2} \cdot x_2 \leq b_i,$$

for Q, and add in the inequalities $-x_3 \leq x_1 \leq x_3$ to Q. Let π be the projection map defined by

$$\pi(x_1, x_2, x_3) = (x_1, x_2).$$

The polygon $\pi(Q)$ is the union of P and its reflection with respect to the line $x_1 = 0$.

The number of inequalities defining Q is only two more than the number of inequalities defining P, but the number of facets of $\pi(Q)$ may be a *factor* of two larger than the number of facets of P!

We can now construct a regular polygon with $n = 2^k$ facets using $k = \log n$ mirror operations. We start with an isosceles triangle P_0 with one angle of $2\pi/n$. Triangles have three facets. Mirror P_0 to get a kite P_1. Mirror the kite P_1 to get a hexagon P_2. Keep going until the full n-gon is constructed.

Permutahedron

For every permutation $\sigma : [n] \to [n]$, define the point $p^\sigma = (\sigma(1), \sigma(2), \ldots, \sigma(n)) \in \mathbb{R}^n$. The *permutahedron* is the convex hull of these $n!$ points. See Figure 12.7.

Claim 12.11 *The dimension of the permutahedron is $n - 1$.*

Proof First, observe that the permutahedron lies in the hyperplane $\sum_{i=1}^n x_i = \binom{n}{2}$. So its dimension is at most $n - 1$. To see that the dimension is at least $n - 1$, let *id* denote the identity permutation, and let $\sigma_2, \ldots, \sigma_n$ be the $n - 1$ permutations obtained by swapping 1 with $2, \ldots, n$:

$$\sigma_i(k) = \begin{cases} 1 & \text{if } k = i, \\ i & \text{if } k = 1, \\ k & \text{otherwise.} \end{cases}$$

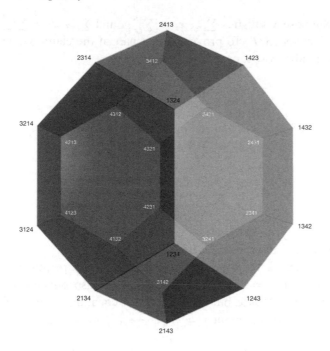

Figure 12.7 The permutahedron with $n = 4$, projected into 3-space. Watch an animation.

The $n - 1$ points of the form $p^{id} - p^{\sigma_i}$ are linearly independent because $p^{id} - p^{\sigma_i}$ is the only such vector with a nonzero entry in the ith coordinate. $\qquad \square$

Although the permutahedron has $n!$ vertices, it has much fewer facets.[5]

[5] Rado, 1952.

Lemma 12.12 *The permutahedron is the set of points satisfying the conditions.*

$$\sum_{i=1}^{n} x_i = \sum_{i=1}^{n} i = \binom{n}{2}, \tag{12.1}$$

$$\sum_{i \in S} x_i \geq \sum_{i=1}^{|S|} i \qquad \text{for all sets } S \subseteq [n] \text{ with } 0 < |S| < n. \tag{12.2}$$

The facets of the permutahedron correspond to these $2^n - 2$ inequalities.

Proof Let Q denote the polytope defined by the constraints. Every permutation satisfies the constraints, so the permutahedron is contained in Q. Here is the key claim for proving Q is contained in the permutahedron.

Claim 12.13 *Let x be a point in Q. The sets that correspond to constraints in (12.2) that x satisfies with equality can be arranged as a chain: $S_1 \subset S_2 \subset \ldots \subset S_k$. Moreover, if $k < n - 1$, then there is a permutation σ and $0 < \epsilon < 1$ such that the point $y = \frac{1}{1-\epsilon}(x - \epsilon \cdot p^{\sigma})$ is in Q and satisfies one more equality in (12.2) than x.*

The chain may be empty.

Proof Suppose x satisfies $\sum_{i \in S} x_i = \sum_{i=1}^{|S|} i$ and $\sum_{i \in T} x_i = \sum_{i=1}^{|T|} i$, for two distinct sets S, T. To prove the first part of the claim, we need to show that either $S \subseteq T$ or $T \subseteq S$. Otherwise,

$$\sum_{i \in S \cup T} x_i = \sum_{i \in S} x_i + \sum_{i \in T} x_i - \sum_{i \in T \cap S} x_i$$

using the inequality for $T \cap S$.

$$\leq \sum_{i=1}^{|S|} i + \sum_{i=1}^{|T|} i - \sum_{i=1}^{|T \cap S|} i$$

because $|T \cap S| < |T|$ and $|S| < |S \cup T|$.

$$= \sum_{i=1}^{|S|} i + \sum_{i=|T \cap S|+1}^{|T|} i < \sum_{i=1}^{|S \cup T|} i.$$

This contradicts the constraint for $S \cup T$.

Now, assume $k < n - 1$. Let σ be an arbitrary permutation with $\sigma(S_j) = S_j$ for $j = 1, 2, \ldots, k$. The point p^σ also satisfies the same equations in (12.2) as x, but it satisfies $n - 1$ equations with equality, so $x \neq p^\sigma$. Consider the point $y = \frac{1}{1-\epsilon}(x - \epsilon p^\sigma)$ for a small $\epsilon > 0$ to be determined.

Choose ϵ to be the largest number so that y satisfies all inequalities in (12.2). This is well defined because y is in Q when $\epsilon = 0$, and y will certainly leave Q before $\epsilon = 1$. We claim that y must satisfy one more equation with equality. For the inequalities in the chain, we have

$$\sum_{i \in S_j} y_i = \frac{1}{1-\epsilon}(1 - \epsilon) \sum_{i \in |S_j|} i.$$

By the choice of ϵ, some other equation must have become tight. So, the point y satisfies one more equation with equality than x. $\square$

We now show that each $x \in Q$ is in the permutahedron. After we have applied the claim n times, we get a point of the form $y = c\left(x - \sum_\sigma \alpha_\sigma p^\sigma\right)$ that is in Q and satisfies $n - 1$ equalities that correspond to the chain $S_1 \subset \cdots \subset S_{n-1}$, where c and the α_σs are positive numbers. The point y must be of the form $y = p^\pi$ for some permutation π – the permutation π is the unique permutation so that $\pi(S_j) = S_j$ for all $j \in [n]$. We see that $x = \frac{1}{c}p^\pi + \sum_\sigma \alpha_\sigma p^\sigma$. Finally, because x and all points of the form p^σ satisfy (12.1), we see that $\frac{1}{c} + \sum_\sigma \alpha_\sigma = 1$. This means that x is in the permutahedron.

To see that each of the inequalities gives a facet, fix a set $S \subset [n]$ with $0 < |S| < n$. For simplicity, suppose $S = [t]$. Denote by Q_S the set of points in Q that satisfies $\sum_{i \in S} x_i = \sum_{i=1}^{|S|} i$. Let $p^{id} = (1, 2, \ldots, n)$ be the identity permutation. For $i = 2, 3, \ldots, t, t + 2, t + 3, \ldots, n$, define σ_i to be the permutation that swaps i with 1 if $i \leq t$, or swaps i with $t + 1$ if $i > t$. That is,

$$\sigma_i(k) = \begin{cases} 1 & \text{if } i \le t, k = i, \\ i & \text{if } i \le t, k = 1, \\ t+1 & \text{if } i > t, k = i, \\ i & \text{if } i > t, k = t+1, \\ k & \text{otherwise.} \end{cases}$$

The $n-2$ points $p^{\sigma_i} - p^{id}$ are linearly independent. Each of these points belongs to the face. Thus, the face Q_S has dimension $n-2$, and so must be a facet.

It remains to prove that all of these facets are different. Let S and T be distinct sets. It suffices to show that the dimension of $Q_S \cap Q_T$ is less than $n-2$. The difference between every two points in $Q_S \cap Q_T$ is orthogonal to the three characteristic vectors χ_S, χ_T and $\chi_{[n]}$ of the three sets S, T and $[n]$. If the three vectors are linearly independent, then $Q_S \cap Q_T$ indeed has dimension at most $n-3$. Otherwise, it must be the case that T is the complement of S. This implies that $Q_S \cap Q_T = \emptyset$ because $\sum_{i=1}^{|S|} i + \sum_{i=1}^{|T|} i \ne \sum_{i=1}^{n} i$. $\square$

Although the permutahedron has $2^n - 2$ facets, it is known[6] that its extension complexity is $O(n \log n)$. This bound is tight. The polytope has $n! = 2^{\Omega(n \log n)}$ vertices. So, its extension complexity is at least $\Omega(n \log n)$ by Fact 12.10.

[6] Goemans, 2015.

Here we show that its extension complexity is at most n^2. Let Q be the polytope of all $n \times n$ *doubly stochastic matrices*. Namely, Q is the set of all $n \times n$ matrices with nonnegative entries so that the sum of the entries in each row is 1 and the sum of the entries in each column is 1.

The polytope Q is sometimes called the Birkhoff polytope or the bipartite perfect matching polytope.

Claim 12.14 *The polytope Q is an extension of the permutahedron.*

The polytope Q is defined by $n^2 + 2n$ inequalities. The claim implies that the extension complexity of the permutahedron is at most $O(n^2)$.

Proof Let v be the $n \times 1$ vector $(1, 2, \ldots, n)$. Define the linear map $L(Y) = Yv$ where Y is an $n \times n$ matrix. We claim that $L(Q)$ is the permutahedron.

Each permutation σ corresponds to a Boolean permutation matrix $Y^\sigma \in Q$. Because $p^\sigma = Y^\sigma v$, every element of the permutahedron can be realized as Yv for some $Y \in Q$. This proves that the permutahedron is contained in $L(Q)$.

$Y_{i,j}^\sigma = 1$ if and only if $\sigma(i) = j$.

To prove that $L(Q)$ is contained in the permutahedron, use Lemma 12.12. For each $Y \in Q$,

$$\sum_{i=1}^{n} (Yv)_i = \sum_{i=1}^{n} \sum_{j=1}^{n} Y_{i,j} \cdot j = \sum_{j=1}^{n} j.$$

So, points in $L(Q)$ satisfy (12.1). In addition, for each set $S \subseteq [n]$ with $0 < |S| = k < n$,

$$\sum_{i \in S} (Yv)_i = \sum_{j=1}^{n} \alpha_j \cdot j,$$

with $\alpha_j = \sum_{i \in S} Y_{i,j}$. For all $j \in [n]$,

$$0 \le \alpha_j \le \sum_{i=1}^{n} Y_{i,j} \le 1,$$

and

$$\sum_{j=1}^{n} \alpha_j = \sum_{i \in S} \sum_{j=1}^{n} Y_{i,j} = k.$$

Under these constraints, the vector $(\alpha_1, \ldots, \alpha_n)$ that minimizes $\sum_{j=1}^{n} \alpha_j \cdot j$ has $\alpha_1 = \cdots = \alpha_k = 1$ and $\alpha_{k+1} = \cdots = \alpha_n = 0$. So, points in $L(Q)$ satisfy (12.2) as well. □

Polytopes from Boolean Circuits

The connection between polytopes and algorithms goes both ways. Efficient algorithms also lead to efficient ways to represent polytopes. To explain this connection, we need the concept of a *separating* polytope; see Figures 12.8 and 12.9

Given a Boolean function $f : \{0, 1\}^n \to \{0, 1\}$, a polytope $P \subseteq \mathbb{R}^n$ is *separating* for f if $f(x) = 1$ if and only if $x \in P$.

Lemma 12.15 *If f can be computed by a circuit with s gates, then there is a separating polytope for f with extension complexity at most $O(s)$.*

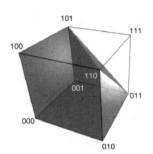

Figure 12.8 A separating polytope for the AND function.

Proof Consider the polytope P defined from the circuit by the following constraints. Let $v_1, \ldots, v_n$ be variables that correspond to the n inputs to f. For every intermediate gate g in the circuit, let v_g be a variable. All variables take values in $[0, 1]$. If $g = \neg h$, add the constraint

$$v_g = 1 - v_h.$$

If $g = h \vee r$, add the constraints

$$v_g \ge v_h,$$
$$v_g \ge v_r,$$
$$v_g \le v_h + v_r.$$

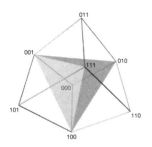

Figure 12.9 A separating polytope for the parity function: $x_1 + x_2 + x_3$ mod 2.

If $g = h \wedge r$, add the constraints

$$v_g \le v_h,$$
$$v_g \le v_r,$$
$$v_g \ge v_h + v_r - 1.$$

Finally, add the constraint $v_r = 1$, where r is the output gate computing f.

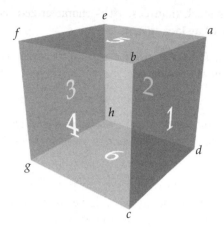

Figure 12.10 A numbering of the facets and vertices of the $1 \times 1 \times 1$ cube.

The constraints, except the final one, ensure that whenever $v_1, \ldots, v_n \in \{0,1\}$, the value of v_g is Boolean and is equal to the value of the corresponding gate in the circuit on input $(v_1, \ldots, v_n)$.

When this polytope is projected onto the inputs, we obtain a polytope P that we claim separates f. Indeed, let $x \in \{0,1\}^n$. If $f(x) = 1$, then $x \in P$ because we can assign all of the variables the values computed in the circuit, and these values satisfy the constraints. On the other hand, if $f(x) = 0$, then there is no way to satisfy all the constraints, so x is not in the polytope. □

Slack Matrices

THE MAIN TOOL FOR UNDERSTANDING extension complexity is the concept of a *slack matrix* A slack matrix of a polytope $P \subset \mathbb{R}^d$ is a matrix that captures key geometric properties of the polytope. It is defined with respect to an $n \times d$ matrix A and an $n \times 1$ vector b such that P is contained in the polytope $\{x : Ax \leq b\}$, and with respect to a finite set of points $V = \{v_1, \ldots, v_k\} \subseteq P$.

Definition 12.16 The *slack matrix* of the polytope with respect to A, b, V is the $n \times k$ matrix S with

$$S_{i,j} = b_i - A_i \cdot v_j$$

where A_i is the ith row of A.

The slack matrix is a nonnegative matrix. All of its entries are nonnegative because by assumptions on A, b, V, we always have $A_i v_j \leq b_i$. If all the rows of A are normalized to have length 1, then $S_{i,j}$ is the distance of v_j from the hyperplane defined by A_i, b_i. It is the slack of the jth point from the ith inequality. See Figure 12.10 and the associated slack matrix in the margin.

A single polytope can have many different slack matrices, depending on the choice of A, b, V. The extension complexity of a polytope P is

The slack matrix corresponding to Figure 12.10:

$$
\begin{array}{c}
\begin{array}{cccccccc}
a & b & c & d & e & f & g & h
\end{array} \\
\begin{array}{c}
1 \\ 2 \\ 3 \\ 4 \\ 5 \\ 6
\end{array}
\left[
\begin{array}{cccccccc}
0 & 0 & 0 & 0 & 1 & 1 & 1 & 1 \\
0 & 1 & 1 & 0 & 0 & 1 & 1 & 0 \\
1 & 1 & 1 & 1 & 0 & 0 & 0 & 0 \\
1 & 0 & 0 & 1 & 1 & 0 & 0 & 1 \\
0 & 0 & 1 & 1 & 0 & 0 & 1 & 1 \\
1 & 1 & 0 & 0 & 1 & 1 & 0 & 0
\end{array}
\right]
\end{array}
$$

determined by its slack matrices.[7] It is characterized by the maximum nonnegative rank of a slack matrix.

Theorem 12.17 *If P has extension complexity r, then every slack matrix of P has nonnegative rank at most r + 1. Conversely, suppose*

$$P = \{x : Ax \le b\}$$

is the convex hull of a finite set V. Suppose the slack matrix of P corresponding to A, b, V has nonnegative rank r, then P has extension complexity at most r.

The theorem gives a powerful way to prove both upper and lower bounds on extension complexity. The lower bounds are usually proved using ideas inspired by communication complexity.

Proof First, suppose the extension complexity of $P \subset \mathbb{R}^d$ is r. There is a polytope $Q \subseteq \mathbb{R}^\ell$ with r facets, and a linear transformation L such that $P = L(Q)$. Without loss of generality, possibly by modifying L, we can assume that Q has full dimension.

Represent L as a $d \times \ell$ matrix.

By Fact 12.3, the polytope Q can be expressed as

$$Q = \{x : Cx \le e\},$$

where C is an $r \times \ell$ matrix, and e is an $r \times 1$ vector. Thus

$$P = \{Lx : Cx \le e\}.$$

Now, let S be the $n \times k$ slack matrix of P with respect to some A, b and $V = \{v_1, \ldots, v_k\}$. For $j \in [k]$, let $w_j \in Q$ be such that $Lw_j = v_j$.

For each $i \in [n]$, because A_i, b_i give a valid inequality for P, we have $A_i Lx \le b_i$ for $x \in Q$. By Fact 12.1, this inequality can be proved by the inequalities defining Q – there is a nonnegative $1 \times r$ vector u_i such that

$$u_i C = A_i L$$

and

$$b_i = u_i e + \alpha_i,$$

with $\alpha_i \ge 0$. Then we have

$$S_{i,j} = b_i - A_i v_j = u_i e + \alpha_i - u_i Cw_j = u_i(e - Cw_j) + \alpha_i.$$

This representation of the entries of S allows us to give an upper bound on the nonnegative rank of S. Let U be the $n \times (r + 1)$ nonnegative matrix whose ith row is

$$\begin{bmatrix} u_i & \alpha_i \end{bmatrix}.$$

Let W be the $(r + 1) \times k$ nonnegative matrix whose jth column is

$Cw_j \le e$ because $w_j \in Q$.

$$\begin{bmatrix} e - Cw_j \\ 1 \end{bmatrix}.$$

Because $S = UW$, the nonnegative rank of S is at most $r + 1$.

Conversely, let P be the convex hull of $V = \{v_1, \ldots, v_k\}$. Suppose the slack matrix corresponding to A, b, V can be expressed as $S = UW$, where U has r columns and W has r rows, both with non-negative entries. Consider the polytope

$$Q = \{(x, y) : Ax + Uy = b, y \geq 0\} \subset \mathbb{R}^{d+r}.$$

It has at most r facets.

We claim that P is equal to the projection of Q to the first d coordinates, proving that it has extension complexity at most r. The projection of Q is contained in P because $b = Ax + Uy \geq Ax$ for all $(x, y) \in Q$. It remains to show that P is contained in the projection of Q. It is enough to prove that V is contained in the projection. Each $v_j \in V$ corresponds to the column W_j of W. The column of S that corresponds to v_j is $UW_j = b - Av_j$. So,

$$Av_j + UW_j = b.$$

This means that v_j is in the projection of Q because $UW_j \geq 0$. We conclude that P is equal to the projection of Q. □

An Upper Bound on Extension Complexity

The characterization of extension complexity by nonnegative rank gives a way to bound the extension complexity of some interesting polytopes from above. Here is an example.

The spanning tree polytope is the convex hull of all trees over the vertex set $[n]$. There is a variable x_e for every potential edge $e = \{u, v\}$. Every tree gives a point x in $\mathbb{R}^{\binom{n}{2}}$ by setting $x_e = 1$ if e is an edge of the tree, and 0 otherwise. The spanning tree polytope is the convex hull of all of these points.

A tree is a connected acyclic graph.

The facets of the spanning tree polytope correspond[8] to the inequalities:

[8] Edmonds, 1971.

$$\sum_e x_e = n - 1,$$

$$\sum_{e \subseteq S} x_e \leq |S| - 1 \qquad \text{for every nonempty } S \subseteq [n].$$

The number of edges in any set of vertices is at most its size minus 1.

Each vertex corresponds to a spanning tree T. Each facet of the polytope corresponds to a subset $S \subseteq [n]$. The slack of the pair S, T is exactly $|S| - 1 - k$, where k is the number of edges of T that are contained in S. If we direct all edges in T toward some fixed $a \in S$, the slack is the number of children in S whose parents are not in S. See Figure 12.11 for an example.

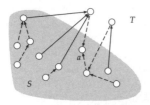

Figure 12.11 The slack of the pair S, T is the number of edges leaving S. In this case, the slack is 4.

Motivated by this observation, we show that the slack matrix has small nonnegative rank. For every tree T, define the vector $w = w(T)$ in $\mathbb{R}^{\binom{n}{3}}$ as follows. For distinct $a, b, c \in [n]$, set

$$w_{a,b,c} = \begin{cases} 1 & b \text{ is the parent of } c \text{ when } T \text{ is rooted at } a, \\ 0 & \text{otherwise.} \end{cases}$$

For every set S, define the vector u by

$$u_{a,b,c} = \begin{cases} 1 & a = \min S, \text{ and } b \notin S, \text{ and } c \in S, \\ 0 & \text{otherwise.} \end{cases}$$

The number $\sum_{a,b,c} u_{a,b,c} w_{a,b,c}$ is exactly the slack of the vertex of T from the facet of S.

This means that we can express the slack matrix as a product of a matrix with $\binom{n}{3}$ columns and a matrix with $\binom{n}{3}$ rows. In other words, the nonnegative rank of the slack matrix is at most $\binom{n}{3}$. By Theorem 12.17, the extension complexity of the spanning tree polytope is at most $\binom{n}{3}$.

Circuit Complexity

We conclude this section with an application to circuit complexity. Recall the connection between circuit complexity and extension complexity described in Lemma 12.15. Here we show how this connection translates lower bounds on nonnegative rank to circuit lower bounds.[9]

[9] Hrubeš, 2016.

For $f : \{0, 1\}^n \to \{0, 1\}$, consider the $|f^{-1}(0)| \times |f^{-1}(1)|$ matrix M^ϵ whose entries are indexed by inputs $x \in f^{-1}(0)$ and $y \in f^{-1}(1)$, and whose (x, y)th entry is

$$M^\epsilon_{x,y} = \Delta(x, y) - \epsilon,$$

where $\Delta(x, y)$ is the Hamming distance between x, y. If $\epsilon \leq 1$, the entries of M^ϵ are nonnegative.

Theorem 12.18 *For every $f : \{0, 1\}^n \to \{0, 1\}$, there is $\epsilon = \epsilon_f > 0$ so that the extension complexity of every separating polytope for f is at least* $\mathsf{rank}_+(M^\epsilon) - 1 - 2n$.

A $-n$ correction term is necessary – see Exercise 12.6.

The extension complexity of a separating polytope for f is at most linear in the circuit complexity of f. So, the number $\min\{\mathsf{rank}_+(M^\epsilon) : 0 < \epsilon \leq 1\}$ is a lower bound on the circuit complexity of f.

Proof Let P_0 be a separating polytope for f with minimum extension complexity. That is, $f^{-1}(1) \subseteq P_0$ and $f^{-1}(0) \cap P_0 = \emptyset$. Let P be the intersection of P_0 with the cube $[0, 1]^n$. Because the cube can be defined with $2n$ inequalities, the extension complexity of P is at most $2n$ plus that of P_0.

Consider some $x \in f^{-1}(0)$. Extend the Hamming distance from x to all of the cube $[0, 1]^n$ by

$$h_x(v) = \sum_{i=1}^{n} (1 - x_i)v_i + x_i(1 - v_i),$$

for $v \in [0, 1]^n$. This is an affine function in v, and $h_x(v) = 0$ for $v \in [0, 1]^n$ if and only if $x = v$. Because $x \notin P$, there is $\epsilon_x > 0$ so that for all $v \in P$ we have $h_x(v) > \epsilon_x$.

Let

$$\epsilon = \min\{\epsilon_x : x \in f^{-1}(0)\}.$$

For each $x \in f^{-1}(0)$ and $v \in P$ we have $h_x(v) > \epsilon$. We have obtained $|f^{-1}(0)|$ inequalities that all points in P satisfy. The matrix M^ϵ is the slack matrix of P with respect to these inequalities and the set of points $f^{-1}(1)$. Theorem 12.17 implies that $\text{rank}_+(M^\epsilon)$ is at most 1 plus the extension complexity of P. □

Lower Bounds on Extension Complexity

THE HIGHLIGHT OF THIS CHAPTER is proving lower bounds on extension complexity. We present a couple of examples. Our main tools are the information theoretic techniques discussed in Chapter 6.

The Correlation Polytope

The *correlation* polytope $\mathcal{C}_n$ is the convex hull of cliques. There are $n + \binom{n}{2} = \binom{n+1}{2}$ variables of the form x_T for $T \subset [n]$ of size 1 or 2. For every $A \subseteq [n]$, define the point

$$x_T^A = \begin{cases} 1 & \text{if } T \subseteq A, \\ 0 & \text{otherwise.} \end{cases}$$

The correlation polytope is the convex hull of these 2^n points. Each point of the correlation polytope can be thought of as a lower triangular matrix whose rows and columns are labeled by elements of $[n]$.

The name correlation polytope stems from its connection to probability theory.

Claim 12.19 *The polytope $\mathcal{C} = \mathcal{C}_n$ has full dimension $\binom{n+1}{2}$.*

Proof Let $A = \{v_0 + v : v \in V\}$ be an affine subspace of minimum dimension containing $\mathcal{C}$. The origin is in $\mathcal{C}$. For every $i \in [n]$, the linear space V contains the vector $x^{\{i\}}$. For every two distinct $i, j \in [n]$, the linear space V contains the vector $x^{\{i,j\}} + x^{\{i\}} - x^{\{j\}}$. These $\binom{n+1}{2}$ vectors are linearly independent. □

A vertex of the correlation polytope with $n = 5$ and $A = \{1, 3, 5\}$:

$$\begin{array}{ccc} & \in A & \in A & \in A \end{array}$$

$$\begin{array}{c} \in A \\ \\ \in A \\ \\ \in A \end{array} \begin{bmatrix} 1 & & & & \\ 0 & 0 & & & \\ 1 & 0 & 1 & & \\ 0 & 0 & 0 & 0 & \\ 1 & 0 & 1 & 0 & 1 \end{bmatrix}$$

The facets of C are hard to determine. No explicit expression is known to capture them.

Ideas from communication complexity can be used to prove a strong lower bound on the extension complexity of the correlation polytope.

Theorem 12.20 *The extension complexity of C_n is at least $2^{\Omega(n)}$.*

The proof harnesses the characterization of extension complexity by nonnegative rank. It exploits a specific slack matrix of C. Consider the inequalities:

$$\sum_{i \in B} x^{\{i\}} \leq 1 + \sum_{T \in \binom{B}{2}} x^T \qquad \text{for all nonempty } B \subseteq [n].$$

For each x^A, the inequalities hold – for a specific B, the left-hand side is exactly $|A \cap B|$, and the right-hand side is exactly $1 + \binom{|A \cap B|}{2}$. So, it is a valid inequality for all the points of C_n.

Consider the slack matrix S for C_n that corresponds to these inequalities and the points of the form x^A. The matrix S, in some locations, is the disjointness matrix. We see that $S_{A,B} = 0$ when A and B intersect in one element, and $S_{A,B}$ is 1 when A and B are disjoint.

To prove Theorem 12.20, it suffices to show that the non-negative rank of S is high. The lower bound is proved, actually, for all $2^n \times 2^n$ nonnegative matrices A so that

$$A_{x,y} \begin{cases} = 1 & \text{if } x, y \text{ are disjoint,} \\ \leq 1 - \delta & \text{if } |x \cap y| = 1, \end{cases} \qquad (12.3)$$

If the entries corresponding to intersecting sets are allowed to be larger than the entries corresponding to disjoint sets, the matrix may have small nonnegative rank. For example, the matrix defined by $S_{x,y} = |x \cap y| + 1$ has nonnegative rank at most $n + 1$. This shows that for $\delta \leq 0$, the nonnegative rank of S can be quite small.

When $\delta < 1$, Theorem 12.21 corresponds to proving a lower bound on the extension complexity of any polytope *approximating* the correlation polytope.

[10] Göös and Watson, 2014.

$q(xy|m)$ is a product distribution because A_m has nonnegative rank 1.

for some $0 \leq \delta \leq 1$. This a rich collection of matrices that contains S as a special case.

Theorem 12.21 *If A is a nonnegative matrix satisfying (12.3) then* $\text{rank}_+(A) \geq 2^{\Omega(\delta^4 n)}$.

The proof of the theorem is an adaptation of the lower bound for the randomized communication complexity of disjointness. A slight modification of the proof[10] allows to improve the lower bound to $2^{\Omega(\delta n)}$.

Proof Consider the distribution on x, y given by

$$q(xy) = \frac{A_{x,y}}{\sum_{a,b} A_{a,b}}.$$

If A has nonnegative rank r, then $M = \sum_{m=1}^{r} A_m$, where each A_m is a nonnegative rank 1 matrix. In other words, $q(xy)$ can be expressed as a convex combination of r product distributions, by setting

$$q(xy|m) = \frac{(M_m)_{x,y}}{\sum_{a,b}(A_m)_{a,b}},$$

and

$$q(m) = \frac{\sum_{a,b}(A_m)_{a,b}}{\sum_{a,b} A_{a,b}}.$$

Let X, Y, M be jointly sampled according to q. Let $\mathcal{D}$ denote the event that the sets X, Y are disjoint. The key step is to prove that for every $i \in [n]$,

$$I(X_i : M | X_{<i}, Y_{\geq i}, \mathcal{D}) + I(Y_i : M | X_{\leq i}, Y_{>i}\mathcal{D}) \geq \Omega(\delta^4). \qquad (12.4)$$

Before proving (12.4), we show how to use it. Because $M_{x,y} = 1$ for disjoint sets x, y, we know that $q(xy|\mathcal{D})$ is the uniform distribution on all pairs of disjoint sets. In particular, conditioned on $\mathcal{D}$, the coordinates $(X_1, Y_1), \ldots, (X_n, Y_n)$ are independent. By Lemma 6.20, we get that

$$2 \log r \geq \sum_{i=1}^{n} I(X_i : M | X_{<i}, Y_{\geq i}, \mathcal{D}) + I(Y_i : M | X_{\leq i}, Y_{>i}, \mathcal{D})$$
$$\geq \Omega(\delta^4 n).$$

This completes the proof.

It remains to prove (12.4). Fix $i \in [n]$. Denote by γ the number that satisfies

$$I(X_i : M | X_{<i}, Y_{\geq i}, \mathcal{D}) + I(Y_i : M | X_{\leq i}, Y_{>i}\mathcal{D}) = \tfrac{2}{3} \cdot \gamma^4.$$

Let $Z = (M, X_{<i}, Y_{>i})$. Let $\mathcal{U}$ denote the event that $X \cap Y \subseteq \{i\}$. Let $p(xym) = q(xym|\mathcal{U})$. For every value z that Z may obtain, let α_z denote the statistical distance of $p(x_i y_i | z)$ from the uniform on $\{0, 1\}^2$. Let $\mathcal{G}$ denote the event that $\alpha_z \leq 2\gamma$. Let $\mathcal{Q}$ denote the event $i \notin X, i \notin Y$.

The main claim is that the probability of $\mathcal{G}$ conditioned on $\mathcal{Q}$ is high.

Claim 12.22 $p(\mathcal{G}|\mathcal{Q}) \geq 1 - 4\gamma$.

Before proving the claim, we use it to complete the proof. Let $\mathcal{I}$ denote the event that $i \in X, i \in Y$. Whenever $\alpha_z \leq 2\gamma$,

$$\frac{p(\mathcal{I}, Z = z)}{p(\mathcal{Q}, Z = z)} \geq \frac{1/4 - 2\gamma}{1/4 + 2\gamma} = \frac{1 - 8\gamma}{1 + 8\gamma}.$$

So, we have

$$p(\mathcal{I}) \geq p(\mathcal{I}, \mathcal{G}) \geq \frac{1 - 8\gamma}{1 + 8\gamma} \cdot p(\mathcal{Q}, \mathcal{G}).$$

Using Claim 12.22, we can conclude

$$p(\mathcal{I}) \geq \frac{1 - 8\gamma}{1 + 8\gamma} \cdot (1 - 4\gamma) \cdot p(\mathcal{Q}) = (1 - O(\gamma)) \cdot p(\mathcal{Q}).$$

Equation (12.3) implies that $p(\mathcal{I}) \leq (1 - \delta) \cdot p(\mathcal{Q})$. So, we must have $\gamma \geq \Omega(\delta)$. $\qquad \Box$

Proof of Claim 12.22 Let β_z denote the statistical distance of $p(x_i | z)$ from the uniform distribution on $\{0, 1\}$. We collect some data that allows to upper bound the expected value of β_z. By definition of γ, because conditioning on $\mathcal{D}$ induces the uniform distribution on disjoint sets,

$$\tfrac{2}{3} \cdot I(X_i : M | X_{<i}, Y_{>i}, Y_i = 0, \mathcal{D}) \leq I(X_i : M | X_{<i}, Y_{\geq i}, \mathcal{D}) \leq \tfrac{2}{3} \cdot \gamma^4.$$

The distribution of X_i conditioned on the value of $X_{<i}, Y_{>i}$ and on $Y_i = 0, \mathcal{D}$ is uniform in $\{0, 1\}$. The distribution $p(z|y_i = 0)$ is identical to $q(z|y_i = 0, \mathcal{D})$. Convexity and Pinsker's inequality (Lemma 6.13) thus imply

$$\mathop{\mathbb{E}}_{p(z|y_i=0)} [\beta_z] \leq \sqrt{\mathop{\mathbb{E}}_{p(z|y_i=0)} [\beta_z^2]} \leq \sqrt{\gamma^4} = \gamma^2.$$

Now, Markov's inequality implies

$$\gamma > p(\beta_z > \gamma | y_i = 0)$$
$$\geq p(x_i = 0 | y_i = 0) \cdot p(\beta_z > \gamma | x_i = 0 = y_i)$$
$$= \frac{p(\beta_z > \gamma | x_i = 0 = y_i)}{2}.$$

So,

$$p(\beta_z > \gamma | x_i = 0 = y_i) \leq 2\gamma.$$

A symmetric argument proves that the probability that the statistical distance of $p(y_i|z)$ from uniform exceeds γ is less than 2γ. Finally, as in the final step of the proof of Claim 6.21, we can apply Lemma 6.22 and the union bound to complete the proof.   □

The Matching Polytope

The *matching* polytope M_n is the convex hull of all matchings in a graph on n vertices. Its $\binom{n}{2}$ coordinates are labeled by subsets e of $[n]$ of size two. Here we prove that its extension complexity is high.[11]

[11] Rothvoß, 2014.

Theorem 12.23 *The extension complexity of M_n is at least $2^{\Omega(n)}$.*

The proof of the theorem is similar, at a high level, to the proof for the correlation polytope we saw earlier. The matching polytope, however, introduces some new difficulties.

We start by identifying the relevant slack matrix. For a point $z \in \mathbb{R}^{\binom{n}{2}}$, consider the set of inequalities:

We use this notation here because it is more convenient later on.

$$\sum_{e \in \binom{x}{2}} z_e \leq \frac{|x| - 1}{2} \qquad \text{for all } x \subseteq [n] \text{ with } |x| \text{ odd.}$$

These inequalities hold for every matching z because the number of edges from z contained in a set x is an integer and at most $|X|/2$.

Now, suppose n is even. Let S be the slack matrix that corresponds to the inequalities defined above and the set of points in M_n that correspond to *perfect* matchings, namely matchings of size $n/2$. Theorem 12.17 tells us that in order to prove Theorem 12.23, it suffices to bound the nonnegative rank of S from below.

Lemma 12.24 $\text{rank}_+(S) \geq 2^{\Omega(n)}$.

Once again, the proof of the lemma closely follows the ideas from the lower bound on the randomized communication complexity of disjointness.

Proof The rows of S correspond to sets x of odd size, and the column to perfect matchings y. Consider the distribution on (x, y) given by

$$q(xy) = \frac{S_{x,y}}{\sum_{i,j} S_{i,j}}.$$

If S has nonnegative rank r, then $q(xy)$ can be expressed as a convex combination of r product distributions. There is a distribution $q(m)$ on $[r]$, and for each $m \in [r]$, there is a product distribution $q(xy|m)$ on (x, y), so that

$$q(xy) = \sum_{m=1}^{r} q(m) \cdot q(xy|m).$$

It is convenient to work with $4n + 6$ vertices. Let $\mathcal{W}$ be a fixed subset of half the vertices. Let $\mathcal{A}$ be a fixed perfect matching that matches $\mathcal{W}$ to its complement. Let $F = (C, B_1, \ldots, B_n)$ be a uniformly random partition of $\mathcal{W}$ such that $|C| = 3$, and $|B_i| = 2$ for each i. Let A_i denote the set of two edges of $\mathcal{A}$ that touch B_i.

We say that a set x is *consistent* with F if $C \subseteq x \subseteq \mathcal{W}$, and $x_i = x \cap B_i$ is not of size 1 for each i. We say that a perfect matching y is *consistent* with F if y contains the three edges of $\mathcal{A}$ cut by C, and for each i, either $A_i \subseteq y$, or y matches B_i to itself and matches the neighbors of B_i under A_i to themselves. We denote by y_i the edges of y contained in A_i. The set of edge y_i may be empty.

Let X, Y, M be sampled according to the distribution q, independently of F. Let $\mathcal{D}$ denote the event that (X, Y) are consistent with F, and for every i, the set X_i docs not cut the edges of Y_i. See Figure 12.12 for an illustration.

We show below that for each i,

$$I(X_i : M|X_{<i}Y_{\geq i}F\mathcal{D}) + I(Y_i : M|X_{\leq i}Y_{>i}F\mathcal{D}) \geq \Omega(1). \qquad (12.5)$$

This completes the proof. Conditioned on $\mathcal{D}$, for each fixing of F, the pairs

$$(X_1, Y_1), \ldots, (X_n, Y_n)$$

are independent. Lemma 6.20 implies

$$2\log r \geq \sum_{i=1}^{n} I(X_i : M|X_{<i}Y_{\geq i}F\mathcal{D}) + I(Y_i : M|X_{\leq i}Y_{>i}F\mathcal{D}) \qquad \text{M is supported on r elements.}$$

$$\geq \Omega(n). \qquad \text{by (12.5).}$$

Thus, $r \geq 2^{\Omega(n)}$ as required.

Figure 12.12 An example of
$\mathcal{A}, \mathcal{W}, F$ when $n = 6$, and
X, Y conditioned on $\mathcal{D}$.

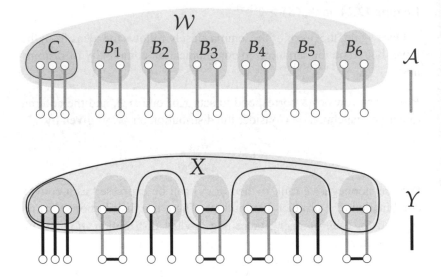

It remains to prove (12.5). Fix i for the rest of the proof. Let $\mathcal{U}$ denote the event that X, Y are consistent with F, and for each $j \neq i$, the edges of Y_j are not cut by X_j. So $\mathcal{D}$ implies $\mathcal{U}$, but under $\mathcal{U}$ the edges of Y_i may be cut by X_i. Let Z denote the random variable $Z = (X_{<i}, Y_{>i}, B_{<i}, B_{>i})$.

Conditioned on the value of Z, In fact, we prove the stronger statement that for *each* fixing $Z = z$, we to define F we need to have $\gamma \geq \Omega(1)$ where
partition 5 vertices to two
sets – C of size 3 and B_i of

$$\gamma^4/2 = \mathsf{I}(X_i : M|Y_i Cz\mathcal{D}) + \mathsf{I}(Y_i : M|X_i Cz\mathcal{D}).$$

size 2.

Fix z for the rest of the proof. Let $q(xycm)$ be the distribution of X, Y, C, M described above. Let

$$p(xycm) = q(xycm|z\mathcal{U}).$$

Given c, m, the distribution $p(x_i y_i|cm)$ is supported on four possible values. Let α_{cm} denote the distance of this distribution from the uniform distribution on these four values. Call a pair (c, m) good if $\alpha_{cm} \leq \gamma$. Denote by $\mathcal{G}$ the set of good pairs. Let $\mathcal{Q}$ denote the event that $X_i = \emptyset, Y_i \neq A_i$. Let $\mathcal{I}$ denote the event that $X_i \neq \emptyset, Y_i = A_i$.

The following two claims are enough to complete the proof. The first is analogous to Claim 12.22 in the proof of Theorem 12.21. The second claim uses the combinatorial structure of matchings to deduce a property of good pairs.

Claim 12.25 $p((C, M) \in \mathcal{G}|\mathcal{Q}) \geq 1 - 4\gamma$.

Claim 12.26 *For any value of m, we have $|\{c : (c, m) \in \mathcal{G}\}| \leq 4$.*

Every vertex in x touches   Let us see how to use the claims to complete the proof. First, we need either one of the k edges   to understand the distribution $p(x_i y_i)$. If x is a set of odd size, and y is leaving x or one of the edges   a perfect matching with k edges that go from x to its complement, then staying within x.

$$|x| = k + 2 \cdot \sum_{e \in \binom{x}{2}} y_e.$$

The slack $S_{x,y}$ is exactly

$$S_{x,y} = \frac{|x| - 1}{2} - \sum_{e \in \binom{x}{2}} y_e = \frac{k - 1}{2}. \qquad (12.6)$$

Let $L = (C, X_{<i}, X_{>i}, Y_{<i}, Y_{>i})$. For every fixing of L, the distribution of X, Y under p is determined by a 2×2 submatrix of S of the form

If $Y_i \neq A_i$ then $Y_i = \emptyset$. If $X_i \neq \emptyset$ then $X_i = B_i$.

$$\begin{array}{c} \\ X_i = \emptyset \\ X_i \neq \emptyset \end{array} \begin{array}{cc} Y_i \neq A_i & Y_i = A_i \\ \left[\begin{array}{cc} 1 & 1 \\ 1 & 2 \end{array} \right]. \end{array} \qquad (12.7)$$

The slack is either $1 = (3 - 1)/2$ or $2 = (5 - 1)/2$. It is 1 if only the 3 edges that go out of C are cut by X. It is 2 if the 3 edges from C and the 2 edges from B_i are cut by X.

Here lies a crucial difficulty in the proof. In the disjointness matrix, used in the proof of Theorem 12.21, the corresponding submatrix is of the form

$$\begin{array}{c} \\ X_i = 0 \\ X_i = 1 \end{array} \begin{array}{cc} Y_i = 0 & Y_i = 1 \\ \left[\begin{array}{cc} 1 & 1 \\ 1 & 1 - \delta \end{array} \right]. \end{array}$$

In that case, we showed that there are many Ms where the entry corresponding to $X_i = 1 = Y_i$ gets as much weight as the entry corresponding to $X_i = 0 = Y_i$. This leads to a contradiction. For the matching polytope, the entry corresponding to intersections is *larger* than the entries corresponding to disjoint sets. It is not clear how to derive a contradiction.

In fact, it seems that there is a counterexample to our efforts. Consider the matrix T, whose entries are indexed by $u, v \in \{0, 1\}^n$ defined by $T_{u,v} = \langle u, v \rangle + 1$. The matrix T has nonnegative rank at most $n + 1$. Nevertheless, it has the same local structure as in (12.7). The freedom to choose C, and Claim 12.26 allow us to avoid this counterexample. In a nutshell, we partition the weight of the 2 entry into many parts. This effectively replaces the 2 by a number smaller than 1.

Whenever $(c, m) \in \mathcal{G}$, we have that $p(x_i y_i | cm)$ is γ-close to uniform. So,

$$\frac{p(\mathcal{I}, c, m)}{p(\mathcal{Q}, c, m)} \geq \frac{1/4 - 2\gamma}{1/4 + 2\gamma} = \frac{1 - 8\gamma}{1 + 8\gamma}. \qquad (12.8)$$

Figure 12.13 Two values of c that intersect in only one element. The set x is consistent with c, and the matching y is consistent with c'.

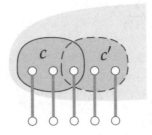 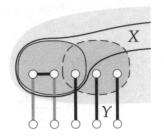

Therefore,

by Claim 12.26.

$$p(\mathcal{I}) = \sum_m p(\mathcal{I}, m) \geq \frac{1}{4} \cdot \sum_{(c,m) \in \mathcal{G}} p(\mathcal{I}, m)$$

because given $X_i \neq \varnothing, Y_i = A_i, m$, the conditional distribution on c is uniform.

$$= \frac{\binom{5}{3}}{4} \cdot \sum_{(c,m) \in \mathcal{G}} p(\mathcal{I}, m) \cdot p(c | \mathcal{I}, m)$$

by (12.8).

$$\geq \frac{5}{2} \cdot \frac{1 - 8\gamma}{1 + 8\gamma} \cdot \sum_{(c,m) \in \mathcal{G}} p(\mathcal{Q}, c, m)$$

by Claim 12.25.

$$\geq \frac{5}{2} \cdot \frac{1 - 8\gamma}{1 + 8\gamma} \cdot (1 - 4\gamma) \cdot p(\mathcal{Q}).$$

By (12.7), we have $p(\mathcal{I}) \leq 2 \cdot p(\mathcal{Q})$. Because $5/2 > 2$, we must have $\gamma \geq \Omega(1)$. $\qquad\square$

Finally, we turn to proving each of the two claims.

Proof of Claim 12.26 Fix m. The set c is a subset of size 3 in a universe of size 5. We claim that if c_1 and c_2 are two sets with $|c_1 \cap c_2| \leq 1$, then we cannot have $(c_1, m) \in \mathcal{G}$ and $(c_2, m) \in \mathcal{G}$. Indeed, assume toward a contradiction that $(c_1, m), (c_2, m) \in \mathcal{G}$, as in Figure 12.13. Because $\alpha_{cm} \leq \gamma < 1/2$, we know that $p(X_i = \varnothing | cm) > 0$. The x shown in Figure 12.13 has positive probability conditioned on m. Similarly, the edges y shown in Figure 12.13 have positive probability conditioned on m. However, because X_i, Y_i are independent conditioned on m, both have positive probability conditioned on m. But this cannot happen because this configuration corresponds to an entry of S that is 0. So it has 0 probability in p.

This means that all of the sets c, c' that are in $\mathcal{G}$ must intersect in at least two elements. We claim that there can be at most four such sets. Indeed, take any two sets $c_1 \neq c_2$ in such a family. Assume without loss of generality that $c_1 = \{1, 2, 3\}$ and $c_2 = \{1, 2, 4\}$. If every other subset c_3 is contained in $[4]$, then indeed there are at most $\binom{4}{3} = 4$ sets. Otherwise, there is a set c_3 such that $5 \in c_3$. Then $\{1, 2\} \subset c_3$, otherwise c_3 cannot share two elements with each of c_1, c_2. Now, if there is a fourth set c_4 in the family then c_4 cannot include both $1, 2$ because then it will be equal to c_1, c_2 or c_3. But if c_4 includes only one of the elements of $\{1, 2\}$, it will intersect one of c_1, c_2, c_3 in just one element, a contradiction. See Figure 12.14. □

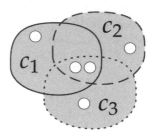

Figure 12.14 If c_1, c_2, c_3 are three sets whose union is of size 5, and pairwise intersections are of size 2, there is no other set that can be added to the collection while keeping the pairwise intersection of size 2.

Proof of Claim 12.25 Because both $q(Y_i \neq A_i | zD)$ and $q(X_i = \emptyset | zD)$ are at least $\frac{1}{2}$, we get

$$I(X_i : M | CzD, Y_i \neq A_i) + I(Y_i : M | CzD, X_i = \emptyset) \leq \gamma^4.$$

Because the events $X_i = \emptyset$ and $\mathcal{U}$ together imply $\mathcal{D}$,

$$p(xycm | X_i = \emptyset) = q(xycm | zD, X_i = \emptyset).$$

The distribution $p(x_i | czD, Y_i \neq A_i)$ is uniform on a universe of size 2 – see (12.7). Let β_{cm} denote the statistical distance of $p(x_i | cm)$ from uniform. By convexity and Pinsker's inequality (Corollary 6.14),

$$\mathop{\mathbb{E}}_{p(cm | X_i = \emptyset)} [\beta_{cm}] \leq \sqrt{\mathop{\mathbb{E}}_{p(cm | X_i = \emptyset)} [\beta_{cm}^2]} \leq \sqrt{\gamma^4} \leq \gamma^2.$$

By Markov's inequality, $p(\beta_{cm} > \gamma | X_i = \emptyset) < \gamma$. So

$$p(\beta_{cm} > \gamma | X_i = \emptyset, Y_i \neq A_i) \leq \frac{p(\beta_{cm} > \gamma | X_i = \emptyset)}{p(Y_i \neq A_i | X_i = \emptyset)} \leq 2\gamma.$$

A symmetric argument proves that the statistical distance of $p(y_i | cm)$ from uniform is at most γ except with probability 2γ. The distribution $p(x_i y_i | cm)$ is a product distribution. Lemma 6.22 and the union bound complete the proof. □

Recall

$$\gamma^4 / 2 = I(X_i : M | Y_i CzD)$$
$$+ I(Y_i : M | X_i CzD)$$

and that $\mathcal{D}$ is the event that (X, Y) are consistent with the partition F, and for each i, the set X_i does not cut the edges of Y_i.

Exercises

Ex 12.1 – Let $P = \{x : Ax \leq 0\}$ be a nonempty polytope that is contained in the halfspace $H = \{x : hx \leq c\}$.

1. Prove that if K is the conical hull of finitely many points, and x is a point outside K, then there is a hyperplane separating x and K. Namely, x lies on one side of the hyperplane, and K on the other side (except the origin).
2. Let $A_1, \ldots, A_n$ be the rows of A. Prove that h is in the conical hull of the n points $A_1, \ldots, A_n$.
3. Conclude that Fact 12.1 is true in this case—there is $u \geq 0$ such that $uA = h$ and $ub \leq c$.

Ex 12.2 – Farkas's Lemma states for every convex set $S \subseteq \mathbb{R}^d$, and every point $x \notin S$, there is a halfspace containing S but not containing x. Use the lemma to prove Fact 12.1. *Hint: Consider the $(n+1) \times (d+1)$ matrix A' obtained by adding b as a column of A and adding one more row: $(0, \ldots, 0, -1)$. Apply Farkas's Lemma to the conical hull of the rows of A' and a point that depends on the given halfspace.*

Ex 12.3 – Show that the nonnegative rank of the slack matrix of a regular 2^k sided polygon in the plane is at most $O(k)$ by giving an explicit factorization of the matrix into nonnegative matrices.

Ex 12.4 – Show that the extension complexity of any regular polygon in the plane with n facets is $O(\log n)$. *Hint: What is the extension complexity of a union of two polygons?*

Ex 12.5 – Show that the nonnegative rank of the slack matrix of the permutahedron with respect to the $2^n - 2$ inequalities from Lemma 12.12 and its $n!$ vertices is $O(n^2)$.

Ex 12.6 – Show that Theorem 12.18 is false if we remove the $-2n$ term from the lower bound. *Hint: The* **AND** *function.*

Ex 12.7 – The cube in n dimensions is the convex hull of the set $\{0, 1\}^n$. Identify the facets of the cube. Is it possible that the extension complexity of the cube is $O(\sqrt{n})$?

Ex 12.8 – Given two disjoint sets A, B, each of size n, define the bipartite matching polytope to be the convex hull of all bipartite matchings—matchings where every edge goes from A to B. Show that the extension complexity of the bipartite matching polytope is at most $O(n^2)$.

Ex 12.9 – Show that there is a k for which the convex hull of cliques of size k has extension complexity $2^{\Omega(n)}$.

Ex 12.10 – The *cut* polytope $\mathcal{K}_n$ is the convex hull of all cuts in a graph. Here the number of variables in $\binom{n}{2}$, one variable for each potential edge $e \subset [n]$ of size 2. For every set $A \subseteq [n]$ define the vertex

$$y_e^A = \begin{cases} 1 & \text{if } |e \cap A| = 1, \\ 0 & \text{otherwise.} \end{cases}$$

The cut polytope is the convex hull of all these points.

1. How many vertices does $\mathcal{K}_n$ have?
2. Prove that the extension complexity of the cut polytope is $2^{\Omega(n)}$. *Hint: Find an invertible linear map that maps the cut polytope to the correlation polytope.*

13

Distributed Computing

DISTRIBUTED COMPUTING is the study of algorithms and protocols for computers operating in a distributed environment. In such an
environment, there are n parties that are connected by a communication
network, yet no single party knows what the whole network looks like.
Nevertheless, the parties wish to solve computational problems together.

The network is defined by an undirected graph on n vertices. Each
vertex represents one of the parties. The parties communicate according
to a protocol in order to achieve some common goal. Each protocol
begins with each party knowing its own name, and perhaps some part of
the input. The protocol proceeds in rounds. In each round, each of the
parties can send a message to all of her neighbors in the graph.

The setup is often interesting even when the goal is to learn something
about the structure of the network itself, and there are no inputs besides
the names.

The distributed setting
presents many algorithmic
challenges. Networks may be
asynchronous. Parties may not
necessarily follow the
protocol. The protocol can be
disrupted by adversarial
actions, etc. We stick to the
model of synchronous
networks. We assume that all
parties execute the protocol
correctly, and there are no
errors in the communication.

Some Protocols

WE START WITH A COUPLE OF PROTOCOLS that help to
understand the model and demonstrate some of the subtitles one needs
to address when studying distributed systems.

Proper Coloring

Suppose the parties in a distributed environment want to properly color
the underlying graph. Each party needs to choose its own color so that
no two neighboring parties have the same color.

Suppose n parties are connected, and every party has at most two
neighbors. Here is a protocol that finds a proper coloring with a constant
number of colors in $O(\log^* n)$ rounds of communication.[1] Initially, each
party colors itself with its name. This is a proper coloring. The goal now
is to iteratively reduce the number of colors.

[1] Cole and Vishkin, 1986.

In each round, the parties send all of their neighbors their current
color. If $a \in \{0, 1\}^t$ denotes the color of one of the parties in a round,
and $b, c \in \{0, 1\}^t$ denote the colors assigned to its neighbors, then the
party sets i to be a number such that $a_i \neq b_i$, and j to be a number such
that $a_j \neq c_j$. Its new color is set to be (i, j, a_i, a_j). The new coloring is
still proper.

In this way, the number of colors has been reduced from t to $O(\log^2 t)$. After $O(\log^* n)$ rounds, the number of colors is constant.

This coloring protocol can be generalized to handle arbitrary graphs of constant degree d. Any graph of degree d can be colored using $d + 1$ colors. Here we give a protocol[2] that uses $O(\log^* n)$ rounds to find a proper coloring with $O(d^2 \log d)$ colors. The protocol relies on the following combinatorial lemma.

The constant in the $O(\log^* n)$ term depends on d.

[2] Linial, 1992.

Lemma 13.1 *For every $t > 0$, there are t sets $T_1, \ldots, T_t \subseteq [m]$ with $m = 5d^2 \lceil \log t \rceil$ such that for any distinct $i_1, i_2, \ldots, i_{d+1} \in [t]$, the set T_{i_1} is not contained in the union of $T_{i_2}, \ldots, T_{i_{d+1}}$.*

Proof The existence of the sets is proved using the probabilistic method. Pick the t sets $T_1, \ldots, T_t$ at random from $[m]$, where each element is included in each set independently with probability $\frac{1}{d}$.

Let us upper bound the probability that T_1 is contained in the union of $T_2, \ldots, T_{d+1}$. For each $j \in [m]$, the probability that $j \in T_1$ and $j \notin \bigcup_{i>1} T_i$ is

because $1 - x \leq 2^{-2x}$ for $x \leq 1/2$.

$$\frac{1}{d} \left(1 - \frac{1}{d}\right)^d \geq \frac{d}{4}.$$

The probability we are interested in is, thus, at most

because $1 - x \leq e^{-x}$ for $x \geq 0$.

$$\left(1 - \frac{d}{4}\right)^m < e^{-d \log t}.$$

By symmetry, a similar bound holds for all $d + 1$ distinct indices. The number of choices for $d + 1$ indices is at most $t^{d+1} \leq 2^{d \log t}$. By the union bound, the probability that the family does not have the property we need is at most $e^{-d \log t} \cdot 2^{d \log t} < 1$.   □

The protocol for coloring networks with degrees at most d proceeds in rounds as before. The initial number of colors is n. Each round reduces the number of colors from some t to $5d^2 \lceil \log t \rceil$. The parties know t, and they also know a family of t sets as promised by Lemma 13.1. Each party sends its current color to all its neighbors. Each party associates each of the $\leq d$ colors she received with a set from the family. Her new color is an element that belongs to her own set but not to any of the others.

Continuing in this way, the number of colors is reduced to $O(d^2 \log d)$ in $O(\log^* n)$ rounds.

Lower Bounds

WE MOVE TO PROVING LOWER BOUNDS in the distributed setting. Communication complexity naturally fits the distributed world. However, the most powerful lower bounds we know how to prove in communication complexity hold when the number of parties is two or relatively small.

The solution is simple and general. Partition the n vertices of the network into a few parts. Think of each part as a party in a standard communication complexity problem. The messages between the parts can be viewed as communication between the parties.

Below, we explain two lower bounds that are proved in this way. Both lower bounds are proved by reduction to the communication complexity of the disjointness problem – one uses two-party communication complexity, and the other uses three-party communication complexity in the number-on-forehead model.

Computing the Diameter

Suppose the parties want to compute the *diameter* of the network – namely, the largest distance between two vertices in the underlying graph. Intuitively, the diameter corresponds to the maximum time it takes to pass a message between two points in the network. To compute the diameter, the network must communicate many bits:[3]

[3] Frischknecht et al., 2012; and Holzer and Wattenhofer, 2012.

Theorem 13.2 *Given any distributed protocol for computing the diameter of an n-vertex graph, there is an input for which $\Omega(n^2)$ bits are transmitted in total.*

The lower bound holds even if the goal is to distinguish whether the diameter of the graph is at most 2 or at least 3, and when the protocol is allowed to be randomized. The proof is by reduction to the randomized two-party communication complexity of disjointness.

Proof Let $X, Y \subseteq [n] \times [n]$ be two subsets of a universe of size n^2. For every such pair of sets, we shall define a graph $G_{X,Y}$. We show that if there is an efficient distributed algorithm for computing the diameter of $G_{X,Y}$, then there is an efficient communication protocol for deciding whether or not X and Y are disjoint.

The graph $G_{X,Y}$ has $4n + 2$ vertices (see Figure 13.1). Let $A = \{a_1, \ldots, a_n\}, B = \{b_1, \ldots, b_n\}, C = \{c_1, \ldots, c_n\}$, and $D = \{d_1, \ldots, d_n\}$ be disjoint cliques, each of size n. Let v be a vertex that is connected to all the vertices in $A \cup B$ and w be a vertex that is connected to all the vertices in $C \cup D$. Connect v and w with an edge as well. For each i, connect a_i to c_i, and b_i to d_i. Finally, connect a_i to b_j if and only if $(i, j) \notin X$, and c_i to d_j if and only if $(i, j) \notin Y$.

Claim 13.3 *The diameter of $G_{X,Y}$ is 2 if X, Y are disjoint, and 3 if X, Y are not disjoint.*

Proof The interesting parts of the claim are the distances between A and D, and between B and C. The distances between all other pairs of vertices are at most 2. Here we focus on the distances between A and D. The case of B and C is similar.

When $(i, j) \notin X$ or $(i, j) \notin Y$, the distance of a_i from d_j is at most 2. For example, if $(i, j) \notin X$, we have the path $a_i \rightarrow b_j \rightarrow d_j$. Otherwise, $(i, j) \in X \cap Y$, and in this case the distance from a_i to d_j is at least 3. $\quad\square$

Figure 13.1 $G_{X,Y}$ for $n = 4$.

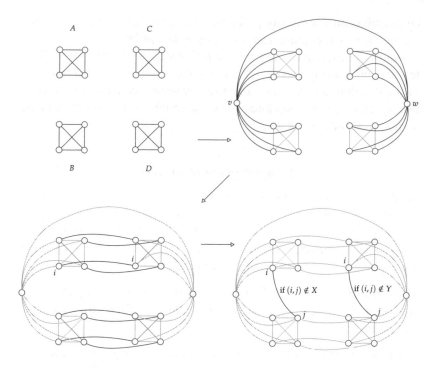

Consider the protocol obtained when Alice simulates all the vertices in A, B, and v, and Bob simulates all the vertices in C, D, and w. This protocol solves the disjointness problem. By Theorem 6.19, the total communication is at least $\Omega(n^2)$. This proves that the $O(n)$ edges that cross from Alice's part to Bob's part must carry at least $\Omega(n^2)$ bits of communication to compute the diameter of the graph.   □

Computing the Girth

ANOTHER BASIC MEASURE ASSOCIATED with a graph is its *girth* – the length of the shortest cycle in the graph. The girth is a fundamental parameter of graphs. Computing the girth in a distributed setting is a nontrivial task:[4]

[4] Drucker et al., 2014.

Theorem 13.4 *Any distributed protocol for computing the girth of an n-vertex graph must involve at least $n^2 2^{-O(\sqrt{\log n})}$) bits of communication.*

The lower bound holds even if the goal is to detect if the girth is at least 3. It is even hard to determine if there is a single triangle in the graph.

This lower bound holds only for deterministic protocols.

Proof The proof is by reduction to disjointness in the number-on-forehead model with three parties. The reduction together with the lower bound from Theorem 5.12 completes the proof.

Suppose Alice, Bob, and Charlie have three sets X, Y, and $Z \subseteq U$ written on their foreheads, where U is a universe we shall soon specify. We define a graph $G_{X,Y,Z}$ that has a triangle if and only if $X \cap Y \cap Z$ is nonempty.

The definition of the graph is based on the coloring promised by Theorem 4.2. This coloring implies that there is a subset $Q \subseteq [n]$ of size at least $n2^{-O(\sqrt{\log n})}$ that does not contain any nontrivial three-term arithmetic progressions.

First define[5] an auxiliary graph G. Its vertex set is the union of three disjoint sets A, B, and C, each of size $2n$. We identify each of these sets with the integers in $[2n]$. The edges are defined as follows: for each $a \in A, b \in B, c \in C$,

[5] Ruzsa and Szemerédi, 1978.

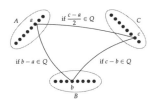

$$\{a, b\} \in E(G) \Leftrightarrow b - a \in Q,$$
$$\{b, c\} \in E(G) \Leftrightarrow c - b \in Q,$$
$$\{a, c\} \in E(G) \Leftrightarrow \frac{c - a}{2} \in Q.$$

See Figure 13.2.

Figure 13.2 The graph G.

Claim 13.5 *The graph G has at least $n|Q|$ triangles, and no two distinct triangles in G share an edge.*

The proof of Claim 13.5 is left to Exercise 13.1.

The universe U is the set of triangles in G. The graph $G_{X,Y,Z}$ is the subgraph of G defined by

$$\{a, b\} \in E(G_{X,Y,Z}) \Leftrightarrow \text{a triangle of } G \text{ containing } \{a, b\} \text{ is in } Z,$$
$$\{b, c\} \in E(G_{X,Y,Z}) \Leftrightarrow \text{a triangle of } G \text{ containing } \{b, c\} \text{ is in } X,$$
$$\{a, c\} \in E(G_{X,Y,Z}) \Leftrightarrow \text{a triangle of } G \text{ containing } \{a, b\} \text{ is in } Y.$$

See Figure 13.3 for an illustration.

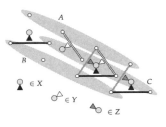

Claim 13.6 *The graph $G_{X,Y,Z}$ contains a triangle if and only if $X \cap Y \cap Z \neq \emptyset$.*

Figure 13.3 The graph $G_{X,Y,Z}$.

Proof If a, b, c are the vertices of a triangle in $X \cap Y \cap Z$, then they form a triangle in $G_{X,Y,Z}$. Conversely, if $G_{X,Y,Z}$ contains a triangle, then each edge of the triangle is contained in a single triangle of G, by Claim 13.5. This implies that the three edges define a triangle in $X \cap Y \cap Z$. $\square$

Given sets X, Y, and Z as input, Alice, Bob, and Charlie execute the protocol for detecting triangles in the network $G_{X,Y,Z}$. Alice simulates the behavior of vertices in A, Bob simulates the behavior B, and Charlie of C. Each of the parties knows enough information to simulate the behavior of these nodes. For example, Alice knows the neighbors of A because she knows Y, Z. Finally, by Theorem 5.12, the total communication of the protocol must be at least

$$\Omega(|U|) = \Omega(n|Q|) = n^2 2^{-O(\sqrt{\log n})}.$$

$\square$

Exercises

Ex 13.1 – Prove Claim 13.5.

Bibliography

The following publications are referred to in their abbreviated title form in these bibliographic entries:

CCC = *Computational Complexity Conference*
ECCC = *Electronic Colloquium on Computational Complexity*
FOCS = *IEEE Symposium on Foundations of Computer Science*
ICALP = *International Colloquium on Automata, Languages and Programming*
LICS = *Logic in Computer Science*
PODC = *Symposium on Principles of Distributed Computing*
SODA = *ACM-SIAM Symposium on Discrete Algorithms*
STOC = *Symposium on the Theory of Computing*
SWAT = *Scandinavian Symposium and Workshops on Algorithm Theory*

A. Aho, J. Ullman, and M. Yannakakis. On notations of information transfer in VLSI circuits. In *STOC*, pages 133–139, 1983.

Miklós Ajtai. A lower bound for finding predecessors in Yao's call probe model. *Combinatorica*, 8(3):235–247, 1988.

Noga Alon, Shlomo Hoory, and Nathan Linial. The Moore bound for irregular graphs. *Graph Combinator*, 18(1):53–57, 2002.

Noga Alon, Yossi Matias, and Mario Szegedy. The space complexity of approximating the frequency moments. *J. Comput. Syst. Sci.*, 58(1):137–147, 1999.

Noga Alon and Alon Orlitsky. Repeated communication and Ramsey graphs. *IEEE Trans. Inf. Theory*, 41(5):1276–1289, 1995.

Andris Ambainis, Martins Kokainis, and Robin Kothari. Nearly optimal separations between communication (or query) complexity and partitions. In *CCC*, pages 1–14, 2016.

Alexandr Andoni, Piotr Indyk, and Mihai Patrascu. On the optimality of the dimensionality reduction method. In *FOCS*, pages 449–458, 2006.

László Babai, Peter Frankl, and Janos Simon. Complexity classes in communication complexity theory (preliminary version). In *FOCS*, pages 337–347, 1986.

László Babai, Anna Gál, Peter G. Kimmel, and Satyanarayana V. Lokam. Communication complexity of simultaneous messages. *SIAM J. Comput.*, 33(1):137–166, 2003.

László Babai, Noam Nisan, and Mario Szegedy. Multiparty protocols and logspace-hard pseudorandom sequences. In *STOC*, pages 1–11, 1989.

Ajesh Babu and Jaikumar Radhakrishnan. An entropy based proof of the Moore bound for irregular graphs. *arXiv:1011.1058*, 2010.

Ziv Bar-Yossef, T. S. Jayram, Ravi Kumar, and D. Sivakumar. An information statistics approach to data stream and communication complexity. *J. Comput. Syst. Sci.*, 68(4):702–732, 2004.

Boaz Barak, Mark Braverman, Xi Chen, and Anup Rao. How to compress interactive communication. In *STOC*, pages 67–76, 2010.

David A. Barrington. Bounded-width polynomial-size branching programs recognize exactly those languages in NC^1. In *STOC*, pages 1–5, 1986.

Balthazar Bauer, Shay Moran, and Amir Yehudayoff. Internal compression of protocols to entropy. In *LIPIcs-Leibniz International Proceedings in Informatics*, volume 40. Schloss Dagstuhl-Leibniz-Zentrum fuer Informatik, 2015.

Paul Beame and Faith E. Fich. Optimal bounds for the predecessor problem and related problems. *J. Comput. Syst. Sci.*, 65(1):38–72, 2002.

Paul Beame and Toniann Pitassi. Simplified and improved resolution lower bounds. In *FOCS*, pages 274–282, 1996.

Felix A. Behrend. On the sets of integers which contain no three in arithmetic progression. *Proc. Nat. Acad. Sci.*, 28(12):561–563, 1946.

Mark Braverman. Interactive information complexity. *SIAM J. Comput.*, 44(6):1698–1739, 2015.

Mark Braverman and Ankit Garg. Public vs private coin in bounded-round information. In *ICALP*, volume 8572, pages 502–513, 2014.

Mark Braverman and Ankur Moitra. An information complexity approach to extended formulations. In *STOC*, pages 161–170, 2013.

Mark Braverman, Anup Rao, Omri Weinstein, and Amir Yehudayoff. Direct products in communication complexity. In *FOCS*, pages 746–755, 2013.

Gerth Stølting Brodal, Shiva Chaudhuri, and Jaikumar Radhakrishnan. The randomized complexity of maintaining the minimum. In *SWAT*, volume 1097, pages 4–15, 1996.

Joshua Brody, Harry Buhrman, Michal Koucký, Bruno Loff, Florian Speelman, and Nikolay Vereshchagin. Towards a reverse Newman's theorem in interactive information complexity. *Algorithmica*, 76(3):749–781, 2016.

Amit Chakrabarti and Oded Regev. An optimal lower bound on the communication complexity of Gap-Hamming-distance. *SIAM J. Comput.*, 41(5):1299–1317, 2012.

Amit Chakrabarti, Yaoyun Shi, Anthony Wirth, and Andrew Yao. Informational complexity and the direct sum problem for simultaneous message complexity. In *FOCS*, pages 270–278, 2001.

Ashok K. Chandra, Merrick L. Furst, and Richard J. Lipton. Multi-party protocols. In *STOC*, pages 94–99, 1983.

Arkadev Chattopadhyay, Michal Koucký, Bruno Loff, and Sagnik Mukhopadhyay. Simulation theorems via pseudorandom properties. *arXiv:1704.06807*, 2017.

Fan R. K. Chung, Ronald L. Graham, Peter Frankl, and James B. Shearer. Some intersection theorems for ordered sets and graphs. *J. Comb. Theory Ser. A*, 43(1):23–37, 1986.

Richard Cole and Uzi Vishkin. Deterministic coin tossing and accelerating cascades: Micro and macro techniques for designing parallel algorithms. In *STOC*, pages 206–219, 1986.

William Cook, Collette R. Coullard, and Gy Turán. On the complexity of cutting-plane proofs. *Discrete Appl. Math.*, 18(1):25–38, 1987.

Martin Dietzfelbinger and Henning Wunderlich. A characterization of average case communication complexity. *Inf. Process. Lett.*, 101(6):245–249, 2007.

Irit Dinur and Or Meir. Toward the KRW composition conjecture: Cubic formula lower bounds via communication complexity. In *LIPIcs-Leibniz International Proceedings in Informatics*, volume 50. Schloss Dagstuhl-Leibniz-Zentrum fuer Informatik, 2016.

Andrew Drucker, Fabian Kuhn, and Rotem Oshman. On the power of the congested clique model. In *PODC*, pages 367–376, 2014.

Pavol Duris, Zvi Galil, and Georg Schnitger. Lower bounds on communication complexity. *Inform. Comput.*, 73(1):1–22, 1987.

Jack Edmonds. Paths, trees, and flowers. *Can. J. Math.*, 17:449–467, 1965.

Jack Edmonds. Matroids and the greedy algorithm. *Math. Program*, 1(1):127–136, 1971.

Jeff Edmonds, Russell Impagliazzo, Steven Rudich, and Jiri Sgall. Communication complexity towards lower bounds on circuit depth. *Comput. Complex.*, 10(3):210–246, 2001.

David Ellis, Yuval Filmus, and Ehud Friedgut. Triangle-intersecting families of graphs. *J. Eur. Math. Soc.*, 14(3):841–885, 2012.

Tomàs Feder, Eyal Kushilevitz, Moni Naor, and Noam Nisan. Amortized communication complexity. *SIAM J. Comput.*, 24(4):736–750, 1995.

Uriel Feige, David Peleg, Prabhakar Raghavan, and Eli Upfal. Computing with noisy information. *SIAM J. Comput.*, 23(5):1001–1018, 1994.

Samuel Fiorini, Thomas Rothvoß, and Hans Raj Tiwary. Extended formulations for polygons. *Discrete Comput. Geom.*, 48(3):658–668, 2012.

Michael L. Fredman and Michael E. Saks. The cell probe complexity of dynamic data structures. In *STOC*, pages 345–354, 1989.

Silvio Frischknecht, Stephan Holzer, and Roger Wattenhofer. Networks cannot compute their diameter in sublinear time. In *SODA*, pages 1150–1162, 2012.

Bernard A. Galler and Michael J. Fisher. An improved equivalence algorithm. *Commun. ACM*, 7(5):301–303, 1964.

Anat Ganor, Gillat Kol, and Ran Raz. Exponential separation of information and communication for Boolean functions. *JACM*, 63(5):46, 2016.

Dmitry Gavinsky and Shachar Lovett. En route to the log-rank conjecture: New reductions and equivalent formulations. In *ICALP*, pages 514–524, 2014.

Dmitry Gavinsky, Or Meir, Omri Weinstein, and Avi Wigderson. Toward better formula lower bounds: An information complexity approach to the KRW composition conjecture. In *STOC*, pages 213–222, 2014.

Kurt Gödel. Über formal unentscheidbare sätze der principia mathematica und verwandter systeme I. *Monatshefte für mathematik und physik*, 38(1):173–198, 1931.

Ashish Goel, Michael Kapralov, and Sanjeev Khanna. On the communication and streaming complexity of maximum bipartite matching. In *SODA*, pages 468–485, 2012.

Michel X. Goemans. Smallest compact formulation for the permutahedron. *Math. Program*, 153(1):5–11, 2015.

Mika Göös, Toniann Pitassi, and Thomas Watson. Deterministic communication vs. partition number. In *FOCS*, pages 1077–1088, 2015.

Mika Göös and Thomas Watson. Communication complexity of set-disjointness for all probabilities. In *LIPIcs-Leibniz International Proceedings in Informatics*, volume 28. Schloss Dagstuhl-Leibniz-Zentrum fuer Informatik, 2014.

Ronald L. Graham. *Rudiments of Ramsey Theory*. Number 45 in Regional Conference series in mathematics. American Mathematical Society, 1980.

Ronald L. Graham, Bruce L. Rothschild, and Joel H. Spencer. *Ramsey theory*. Wiley-Interscience Series in Discrete Mathematics. John Wiley & Sons, New York, 1980.

D. Gregoryev. Lower bounds in algebraic computational complexity. *Theorems in Comput. Complex. 1*, (118):25–82, 1982.

Vince Grolmusz. Circuits and multi-party protocols. *Comput. Complex.*, 7(1):1–18, 1998.

Misha Gromov. In a search for a structure, part 1: On entropy. 2012.

Armin Haken. The intractability of resolution. *Theor. Comput. Sci.*, 39(2–3):297–308, August 1985.

Alfred W. Hales and Robert I. Jewett. On regularity and positional games. *Tr. Amer. Math. Soc.*, 106:222–229, 1963.

Bernd Halstenberg and Rüdiger Reischuk. Different modes of communication. *SIAM J. Comput.*, 22(5):913–934, 1993.

Lawrence H. Harper. Optimal numberings and isoperimetric problems on graphs. *J. Comb. Theory*, 1(3):385–393, 1966.

Prahladh Harsha, Rahul Jain, David A. McAllester, and Jaikumar Radhakrishnan. The communication complexity of correlation. In *CCC*, pages 10–23, 2007.

Juris Hartmanis and Richard E. Stearns. On the computational complexity of algorithms. *T. Amn. Math. Soc.*, 117:285–306, 1965.

Johan Håstad and Avi Wigderson. Composition of the universal relation. In *Advances in Comput. Complex. Theory*, American Mathematical Society, pages 119–134, 1990.

Johan Håstad and Avi Wigderson. The randomized communication complexity of set disjointness. *Theory of Computing*, 3(1):211–219, 2007.

Fred C. Hennie. One-tape, off-line Turing machine computations. *Inform. Control*, 8(6):553–578, 1965.

Thomas Holenstein. Parallel repetition: Simplification and the no-signaling case. *Theory of Computing*, 5(1):141–172, 2009.

Stephan Holzer and Roger Wattenhofer. Optimal distributed all pairs shortest paths and applications. In *PODC*, pages 355–364, 2012.

Pavel Hrubeš. A note on semantic cutting planes. In *ECCC*, 20:128, 2013.

Pavel Hrubeš and Anup Rao. Circuits with medium fan-in. In *CCC*, volume 33, pages 381–391, 2015.

Pavel Hrubeš. *Personal communication*, 2016.

Russell Impagliazzo, Toniann Pitassi, and Alasdair Urquhart. Upper and lower bounds for tree-like cutting planes proofs. In *LICS*, pages 220–228, 1994.

Piotr Indyk and David P. Woodruff. Tight lower bounds for the distinct elements problem. In *FOCS*, pages 283–288, 2003.

Fritz John. Extremum problems with inequalities as subsidiary conditions. In *Traces and Emergence of Nonlinear Programming*, Springer, pages 187–204, 1948.

Stasys Jukna. *Boolean Function Complexity: Advances and Frontiers*, volume 27. Springer Science and Business Media, 2012.

Volker Kaibel and Kanstantsin Pashkovich. Constructing extended formulations from reflection relations. In *Facets of Combinatorial Optimization*, Springer Science and Business Media, pages 77–100, 2013.

Bala Kalyanasundaram and Georg Schnitger. The probabilistic communication complexity of set intersection. *SIAM J. Discrete Math.*, 5(4):545–557, 1992.

Michael Kapralov. Better bounds for matchings in the streaming model. In *SODA*, pages 1679–1697, 2013.

Mauricio Karchmer, Ran Raz, and Avi Wigderson. Super-logarithmic depth lower bounds via the direct sum in communication complexity. *Comput. Complex.*, 5(3/4):191–204, 1995. DOI: 10.1007/BF01206317.

Mauricio Karchmer and Avi Wigderson. Monotone circuits for connectivity require super-logarithmic depth. *SIAM J. Discrete Math.*, 3(2):255–265, 1990.

Hartmut Klauck. One-way communication complexity and the Nečiporuk lower bound on formula size. *SIAM J. Comput.*, 37(2):552–583, 2007.

Jon M. Kleinberg and Éva Tardos. *Algorithm Design*. Addison-Wesley, 2006.

Gillat Kol. Interactive compression for product distributions. In *STOC*, pages 987–998, 2016.

Jan Krajíček. Interpolation theorems, lower bounds for proof systems, and independence results for bounded arithmetic. *J. Symbolic Logic*, 62(02):457–486, 1997.

V. Krapchenko. A method of determining lower bounds for the complexity of π schemes. *Math. Notes Acad. Sci. USSR*, 11:474–479, 1971.

Eyal Kushilevitz, Rafail Ostrovsky, and Yuval Rabani. Efficient search for approximate nearest neighbor in high dimensional spaces. *SIAM J. Comput.*, 30(2): 457–474, 2000.

Nathan Linial. Locality in distributed graph algorithms. *SIAM J. Comput.*, 21(1):193–201, 1992.

László Lovász. Communication complexity: A survey. Technical report, 1990.

László Lovász and Michael E. Saks. Lattices, Möbius functions and communication complexity. In *FOCS*, pages 81–90, 1988.

Shachar Lovett. Communication is bounded by root of rank. In *STOC*, pages 842–846, 2014.

Oleg Lupanov. A method for synthesizing circuits. *Izv. vysshykh uchebnykh zavedenii, Radiofizika*, 1:120–140, 1958.

Peter Miltersen, Noam Nisan, Shmuel Safra, and Avi Wigderson. On data structures and asymmetric communication complexity. *J. Comput. Sys. Sci.*, 57:37–49, 1 1998.

E. I. Neciporuk. On a Boolean function. *Dokl. Akad. Nauk SSSR*, 7:765–766, 1966.

Ilan Newman. Private vs. common random bits in communication complexity. *Inform. Process. Lett.*, 39(2):67–71, 31 July 1991.

Noam Nisan and Avi Wigderson. Rounds in communication complexity revisited. *SIAM J. Comput.*, 22(1):211–219, 1993.

Noam Nisan and Avi Wigderson. On rank vs. communication complexity. *Combinatorica*, 15(4):557–565, 1995.

Denis Pankratov. Direct sum questions in classical communication complexity. *Master's thesis, University of Chicago*, 2012.

Mihai Pătraşcu. Unifying the landscape of cell-probe lower bounds. *SIAM J. Comput.*, 40(3):827–847, 2011.

Mihai Pătraşcu and Mikkel Thorup. Time-space trade-offs for predecessor search. In *STOC*, pages 232–240, 2006.

Mihai Pătraşcu and Mikkel Thorup. Dynamic integer sets with optimal rank, select, and predecessor search. In *FOCS*, pages 166–175, 2014.

Pavel Pudlák. Lower bounds for resolution and cutting plane proofs and monotone computations. *J. Symbolic Logic*, 62(03):981–998, 1997.

Richard Rado. An inequality. *London Journal of Mathematics Society*, 27:1–6, 1952.

Sivaramakrishnan Natarajan Ramamoorthy and Anup Rao. Non-adaptive data structure lower bounds for median and predecessor search from sunflowers. In *ECCC*, 24:40, 2017.

Anup Rao and Makrand Sinha. Simplified separation of information and communication. In *ECCC*, 22:57, 2015.

Anup Rao and Amir Yehudayoff. Simplified lower bounds on the multiparty communication complexity of disjointness. In *CCC*, volume 33, pages 88–101, 2015.

Anup Rao and Amir Yehudayoff. Anti-concentration in most directions. *CoRR*, 2019. URL https://arxiv.org/abs/1811.06510.

Ran Raz and Pierre McKenzie. Separation of the monotone NC hierarchy. In *STOC*, pages 234–243. IEEE, 1997.

Ran Raz and Avi Wigderson. Monotone circuits for matching require linear depth. *JACM*, 39(3):736–744, 1992.

Alexander Razborov. On the distributed complexity of disjointness. *Theoret. Comput. Sci.*, 106:385–390, 1992.

John Alan Robinson. A machine-oriented logic based on the resolution principle. *JACM*, 12(1):23–41, 1965.

Thomas Rothvoß. The matching polytope has exponential extension complexity. In *STOC*, pages 263–272, 2014.

Imre Z. Ruzsa and Endre Szemerédi. Triple systems with no six points carrying three triangles. *Combinatorics (Keszthely, 1976), Coll. Math. Soc. J. Bolyai*, 18: 939–945, 1978.

Alex Samorodnitsky. An inequality for functions on the Hamming cube. *Comb., Probab. Comput.*, 26(3):468–480, 2017.

Pranab Sen and Srinivasan Venkatesh. Lower bounds for predecessor searching in the cell probe model. *J. Comput. Syst. Sci.*, 74(3):364–385, 2008.

Claude E. Shannon. A mathematical theory of communication. *AT&T Tech. J.*, 27, 1948. Monograph B-1598.

Claude E. Shannon. The synthesis of two-terminal switching circuits. *Bell Labs Tech. Jour.*, 28(1):59–98, 1949.

Alexander A. Sherstov. The communication complexity of Gap-Hamming distance. *Theory of Computing*, 8(1):197–208, 2012.

Alexander A. Sherstov. Communication lower bounds using directional derivatives. *J. ACM*, 61(6):34:1–34:71, 2014.

Alexander A. Sherstov. Compressing interactive communication under product distributions. In *FOCS*, pages 535–544, 2016.

Balazs Szegedy. An information theoretic approach to Sidorenko's conjecture. *arXiv:1406.6738*, 2014.

Clark D. Thompson. Area-time complexity for VLSI. In *STOC*, pages 81–88, 1979.

P. van Emde Boas. Preserving order in a forest in less than logarithmic time. In *FOCS*, pages 75–84, 1975.

Thomas Vidick. A concentration inequality for the overlap of a vector on a large set, with application to the communication complexity of the Gap-Hamming-distance problem. *Chicago J. Theor. Comput. Sci*, 2012, 2012.

Emanuele Viola. The communication complexity of addition. *Combinatorica*, 35(6):703–747, 2015. DOI: 10.1007/s00493-014-3078-3.

John von Neumann. Zur Theorie der Gesellschaftsspiele. *Math. Ann.*, 100:295–320, 1928.

Wikipedia. Linear programming – Wikipedia, the free encyclopedia, 2016a. URL https://en.wikipedia.org/wiki/Linear_programming. [Online; accessed August 30, 2016]

Wikipedia. Boolean satisfiability problem – Wikipedia, the free encyclopedia, 2016b. URL https://en.wikipedia.org/wiki/Boolean_satisfiability_problem. [Online; accessed August 30, 2016].

Mihalis Yannakakis. Expressing combinatorial optimization problems by linear programs. *J. Comput. Syst. Sci.*, 43(3):441–466, 1991.

Andrew Chi-Chih Yao. Some complexity questions related to distributive computing. In *STOC*, pages 209–213, 1979.

Andrew Chi-Chih Yao. Lower bounds by probabilistic arguments. In *FOCS*, pages 420–428, 1983.

Amir Yehudayoff. Pointer chasing via triangular discrimination. In *ECCC*, 23, 2016.

Index